The Russian Economy and Foreign Direct Investment

Before the recent Ukrainian crisis, Russia was one of the main sources of foreign direct investment (FDI) outflow and one of the main targets of FDI inflow in the world. However, the events in the Ukraine, the formation of the Eurasian Economic Union, and China's growing interest in the Russian market and its natural resources have changed the picture completely.

This new book brings together an international group of contributors to present a timely and comprehensive analysis of FDI to and from Russia. The book assesses the impact of the changed international political situation on foreign firms operating in Russia, and explores how the new world context has affected Russian investments abroad. The book also considers the future relationship between Russian corporations and the EU and the USA in light of recent events. This book answers an array of key questions including: how have investments from and to Russia developed in the last 100 years; how are Russian businesses spreading to foreign countries through their indirect investments; and how is the Russian Government influencing the investments of Russian businesses abroad?

This volume is of great interest to those who study international economics, modern world economy, and FDI, as well as those interested in international investment movements and the changing role of Russia in international business and the global economy.

Kari Liuhto is Professor of International Business at the Turku School of Economics, the University of Turku, Finland.

Sergei Sutyrin is Professor and Head of the World Economy Department, Saint Petersburg State University, and the WTO chair holder since 2010.

Jean-Marc F. Blanchard is Distinguished Professor at the School of Advanced International and Area Studies, East China Normal University, China, and Executive Director at the Mr. & Mrs. S.H. Wong Center for the Study of Multinational Corporations, USA.

Routledge Studies in the Modern World Economy

The Russian Economy and Foreign Direct Investment

Edited by Kari Liuhto, Sergei Sutyrin, and Jean-Marc F. Blanchard

Routledge
Taylor & Francis Group

LONDON AND NEW YORK

First published 2017
by Routledge
2 Park Square, Milton Park, Abingdon, Oxon OX14 4RN

and by Routledge
52 Vanderbilt Avenue, New York, NY 10017

First issued in paperback 2020

Routledge is an imprint of the Taylor & Francis Group, an informa business

British Library Cataloguing in Publication Data
A catalogue record for this book is available from the British Library

Library of Congress Cataloging in Publication Data
Names: Liuhto, Kari, editor. | Sutyrin, S. F., editor. | Blanchard, Jean-Marc F.,
1962- editor.
Title: The Russian economy and foreign direct investment / edited by Kari
Liuhto, Sergei Sutyrin and Jean-Marc F. Blanchard.
Description: Abingdon, Oxon ; New York, NY : Routledge, 2017. |
Includes index.
Identifiers: LCCN 2016023184| ISBN 9781138121263 (hardback) |
ISBN 9781315651101 (ebook)
Subjects: LCSH: Investments, Foreign–Russia (Federation) | Investments,
Russian. | International business enterprises–Russia (Federation) |
Corporations, Foreign–Russia (Federation) | Russia (Federation–Foreign
economic relations. | Russia (Federation–Economic conditions.
Classification: LCC HG5580.2.A3 R86 2017 | DDC 332.67/30947–
dc23LC record available at https://lccn.loc.gov/2016023184

ISBN 13: 978-0-367-66804-4 (pbk)
ISBN 13: 978-1-138-12126-3 (hbk)

Typeset in Times New Roman
by Cenveo Publisher Services

Contents

Figures

viii *Figures*

Tables

Contributors

Nuran Acur is Associate Professor of Innovation Strategy at the University of Strathclyde, UK, and Ozyegin University, Turkey. Her research and consulting projects include designing technological innovation processes, facilitating global strategy development and open innovation. She has received Scientific and Technological Research Council of Turkey and UK Research Council funding to support several projects related to the fields of technology and open innovation. Dr. Acur is a member of the board of *Journal of Product Innovation Management* and *Creativity and Innovation Management*. Her work has appeared in leading journals including *Journal of Product Innovation M*anagement and *International Journal of Operations and Production Management*.

Wladimir Andreff, Professor Emeritus at the University Paris 1 Panthéon Sorbonne, Honorary Member of the European Association for Comparative Economic Studies, former President of the French Economic Association, Honorary President of the International Association of Sports Economists and the European Sports Economics Association, President of the Scientific Council at the Observatory of the Sports Economy, French Ministry for Sports, has published 400 articles in economic journals and 12 economics books, and has edited 17 economics books.

Elisa Aro, Master of Arts and Master of Science (Economics), has worked at the Pan-European Institute (PEI), University of Turku, since 2015. She has supported various research projects and engaged in data collection and analysis. Her main research interests focus on international marketing, foreign direct investments and born global enterprises. Prior to her current position at the PEI, she worked with projects related to international marketing and the internationalization of Finnish companies in various organizations.

Caner Bakır is Associate Professor of Political Science, with a special focus on political economy and public policy at the Koc University, Istanbul, Turkey. He is Associate Editor of *Policy Sciences* and Co-Director of Center for Globalization, Peace, and Democratic Governance. His research interests include varieties of national financial systems, the political economy of central banking, financial regulation and governance, Turkish multinationals, and economic bureaucracies.

He received the Scientific and Technological Research Council of Turkey 2010 Incentive Award. His work has appeared in leading journals, including *Governance*, *Public Administration*, *Development and Change*, and *New Political Economy*.

Torbjörn Becker has been Director of the Stockholm Institute of Transition Economics (SITE) at the Stockholm School of Economics in Sweden since 2006 and a board member of several economics research institutes in Eastern Europe. Prior to his current position, he worked for nine years at the International Monetary Fund (IMF), where his work focused on international macroeconomics, economic crises, and issues related to the international financial system. He holds a Ph.D. from the Stockholm School of Economics, Sweden. Becker has been published in top academic journals and has contributed to several books and policy reports focusing on Russia and Eastern Europe.

Jean-Marc F. Blanchard, Ph.D., is Distinguished Professor at the School of Advanced International and Area Studies, East China Normal University, and Executive Director at the Mr. & Mrs. S.H. Wong Center for the Study of Multinational Corporations. He has co-authored one book, sole or co-edited eight books and special journal issues, and authored or co-authored nearly 50 articles and book chapters. His research interests include foreign investment in China, Chinese outward investment, and the political economy of national security.

Elena Efimova, Doctor of Economic Science, is Professor at the World Economy Department, Saint Petersburg State University. She is the author of two monographs, has co-authored nine books and handbooks, and authored or co-authored nearly 60 articles and book chapters. Her research interests include regional economics, small and ultra-small economies, international business, and international transport infrastructure.

Liubov Ermolaeva is a Doctoral Student at the Graduate School of Management, Saint Petersburg State University. She is co-author of several articles, case studies, and book chapters. Her research interests include Russian multinational enterprises, cross-border M&As of Russian MNEs, Chinese–Russian investment relations, and absorptive capacity of Russian MNEs.

Eini Haaja, Master of Science (Economics), is University Lecturer at the Pan-European Institute (PEI) in the Turku School of Economics at the University of Turku, Finland. She has specialized in international project business, business networks, and cluster dynamics in energy and maritime sectors, particularly in the Baltic Sea and Barents Sea regions. She has been involved in several research projects and has published articles concerning, for instance, business prospects and risks in the Arctic region.

Irina A. Korgun, Ph.D., is currently Assistant Professor at the Hankuk University of Foreign Studies in Seoul, the Republic of Korea. She graduated from a Ph.D. course at the Saint Petersburg State University in 2010. She works on issues of trade and development and trade policy focused on Korean experience.

Irina A. Korgun is an active member of the international academic community. In 2014, she spent seven months at the University of Leeds (UK) and Hitotsubashi University (Tokyo, Japan), as a visiting scholar. In Korea, she has a rich experience of participation in government-supported projects that involve consultancy on Korean–Russian economic cooperation. Her recent research works include articles on various aspects of Korea's cooperation with WTO, Korea's trade policy, and Korea's cooperation with Russia.

Alexandra Koval, Ph.D., is Associate Professor at the World Economy Department, Saint Petersburg State University. She has authored or co-authored nearly 60 articles and book chapters. Her research interests include Russian–Latin American economic relations, international business, and trade and investment policy in Latin America. She has been a visiting researcher at the UNCTAD, the State University of Rio de Janeiro, the University of Barcelona, and the German Institute of Global and Area Studies. She has participated in the WTO Chair program and now coordinates the EU Marie Curie program "Power and Region in a Multipolar Order" at Saint Petersburg State University.

Alexey Kuznetsov is the youngest corresponding member of the Russian Academy of Sciences (since 2011), Deputy Director of the Primakov National Research Institute of World Economy and International Relations (IMEMO) and Head of its Center for European Studies. He is Professor at the Moscow State Institute of International Relations (MGIMO) as well. Professor Kuznetsov has specialized in FDI and transnational corporations, Russian foreign economic relations, and the EU economy. He is the author of several books, about 150 articles in the Russian language, and 30 articles and chapters in the English language. His book dealing with the investment dimension of Russia's economic internationalization won the medal of the Russian Academy of Sciences in 2007. He graduated with the grade "summa cum laude" from the Lomonosov Moscow State University. He received his Ph.D. from IMEMO in 2003 and his Doctor of Science (Economics) in 2008. Professor Kuznetsov has been the team leader of research projects funded by the Russian Science Foundation, the Russian Foundation for Humanities, the Eurasian Development Bank, the Korea Institute for International Economic Policy, and the Finnish Trade Center (Finpro). Professor Kuznetsov is a member of the Academic Council of the Russian Geographical Society.

Kari Liuhto received his Ph.D. (Social Sciences) from the University of Glasgow, UK, and his Doctor of Science (Economics) from the Turku School of Economics, University of Turku, Finland. Liuhto was appointed as Professor at the Department of Industrial Engineering and Management, Lappeenranta University of Technology, Finland, in 1997. In 2003, Liuhto was invited to hold a tenure professorship in International Business at the Turku School of Economics. In addition to the professorship, Liuhto is Director of the Pan-European Institute (PEI) and Director of the Centrum Balticum Foundation. Liuhto's research interests include foreign direct investment, international energy business, the Russian economy, and regional development in the Baltic Sea region. He has published more than

300 reports and articles in over 20 countries. Professor Liuhto has been involved in several projects funded by the European Commission, the European Parliament, the United Nations, and various Finnish ministries.

Hanna Mäkinen, Master of Arts, is Project Researcher at the Pan-European Institute (PEI) in the Turku School of Economics at the University of Turku, Finland. Her main research interests focus on business networks in the energy and maritime sectors and the role of foreign companies in the development of the Russian energy and maritime industries. She has published numerous articles and has several years of experience in research projects related to, for instance, energy and maritime sectors.

Andrei Panibratov is Professor of Strategic and International Management and Deputy Director of the Center for the Study of Emerging Market and Russian Multinational Enterprises at the Graduate School of Management, Saint Petersburg State University. He has participated in consulting and research projects in a number of international and Russian organizations, universities, and companies. Professor Panibratov is the author/co-author of several books, series of case studies, and many articles published in Russia and abroad. His research interests and lecturing area include internationalization of emerging market firms, Russian multinational enterprises, outward FDI from Russia, and Western MNEs' strategy in Russia.

Alari Purju, Ph.D., is Acting Professor of Supply Chain Management at Tallinn University of Technology. He has been Dean of the Faculty of Economics and Business at Tallinn University of Technology and Advisor to Minister of Economic Affairs of Estonia. His research interests include foreign trade and investment, economic policy issues of transport and logistics sector, and supply chain management and analysis problems.

Vladimir Sherov-Ignatev is Associate Professor at the World Economy Department, Saint Petersburg State University. Sherov-Ignatev is the author of one monograph, and he has authored or co-authored about 50 articles, textbooks, and book chapters. He has been invited as a visiting lecturer to several universities in Belarus, China, and Germany, and participated in a number of international projects. His research interests concentrate on regional integration with the special emphasis on the customs unions.

Sergei Sutyrin is Professor and Head of the World Economy Department, Saint Petersburg State University, and the WTO chair holder since 2010. In addition to his professorship, Sutyrin has delivered lectures in several universities in Finland, Germany, and Japan. His research interests include Russian foreign economic relations, international trading systems, and global governance. He is the author of more than 200 books, pamphlets, and articles in different fields of economic theory. Sutyrin has been involved in many research and educational projects funded, in particular, by the CIDA, the DAAD, the EU, and the International Trading Center.

Olga Trofimenko, Candidate of Economic Science (Ph.D.), is Associate Professor at the World Economy Department, Saint Petersburg State University. She is author or co-author of more than 40 articles and book chapters. She has also been a co-editor of some monographs and conference proceedings. She has been invited as a visiting lecturer to several universities. She has participated in the WTO Chairs program and coordinates the EU Jean Monnet European Module project at the Saint Petersburg State University. Her research interest concentrates on global governance, international trade rules, and foreign direct investments.

Abbreviations and Acronyms

ACWI	All Country World Index
ADR	American depositary receipt
AE	Anadolu Efes
AEB	Association of European Business
aka	also known as
ARMZ	Atomredmetzoloto
ASEA	Allmänna Svenska Elektriska Aktiebolaget (General Swedish Electric Company)
BAM	Baikal-Amur Mainline
bbl	barrel
bcm	billion cubic meter
BEA	US Bureau of Economic Analysis
BIT	bilateral investment treaty
bln, bn	billion
BP	British Petroleum
BRIC	Brazil, Russia, India, and China
BRICS	Brazil, Russia, India, China, and South-Africa
BVI	British Virgin Islands
CBR	Central Bank of Russia (Bank of Russia)
CDIS	Coordinated Direct Investment Survey
CEE	Central and Eastern Europe
CEEC	Central and Eastern European country
CEO	Chief Executive Officer
CIDA	Canadian International Development Agency
CIS	Commonwealth of Independent States
CMEA	Council for Mutual Economic Assistance
CN CEPLA	Russian National Committee for Economic Cooperation with Latin American countries
CNPC	China National Petroleum Corporation
CPI	consumer price index
CSA	country specific advantage
DAAD	Deutscher Akademischer Austauschdienst (German Academic Exchange Service)

DTT	Double Tax Treaty
EAEU	Eurasian Economic Union
EDB	Eurasian Development Bank
EEC	Eurasian Economic Commission
EFTA	European Free Trade Association
e.g.	*exepli gratia* (for example)
EU	European Union
FDI	foreign direct investment
FSA	firm specific advantage
GAAP	Generally Accepted Accounting Principles
GATS	General Agreement on Trade in Services
GATT	General Agreement on Tariffs and Trade
GDP	gross domestic product
GDR	global depositary receipt
GFC	global financial crisis
GFCF	gross fixed capital formation
GfK	Growth from Knowledge
H–O	Heckscher–Ohlin theory
IB	international business
ibid.	*ibidem* (in the same place)
IBV	institution-based view
ICT	Information and Communications Technology
IDP	Investment Development Path (theory)
i.e.	*id est* (that is)
IFDI	inward foreign direct investment
IFRS	International Financial Reporting Standards
IIA	international investment agreement
IMEMO	Institute of World Economy and International Relations
IMF	International Monetary Fund
IPO	initial public offering
IT	Information Technology
JV	joint venture
LNG	liquefied natural gas
M&A	merger and acquisition
MGIMO	Moscow State Institute of International Relations
MIGA	Multilateral Investment Guarantee Agency
mln, mn	million
MMK	Magnitogorskiy Metallurgicheskiy Kombinat (Magnitogorsk Iron and Steel Works)
MNC	multinational company
MNE	multinational enterprise
n.a.	not available
NAFTA	North American Free Trade Agreement
NATO	North Atlantic Treaty Organization

NK	Nordiska Kompaniet (a Swedish department store)
NLMK	Novolipetski Metallurgicheskiy Kombinat (Novolipetsk Steel Company)
NNK	Norilsk Nickel Harjavalta
NOC	National Oil Consortium
OBOR	One Belt, One Road (a Chinese development strategy)
OECD	Organisation for Economic Co-operation and Development
OFDI	outward foreign direct investment
OLI	Ownership, Location, and Internationalization (paradigm)
OLS	ordinary least squares
OPEC	Organization of the Petroleum Exporting Countries
PE	private equity
PEI	Pan-European Institute
Q	Quarter of the Year
QoQ	quarter on quarter
RBV	resource-based view (theory)
R&D	research and development
RF	Russian Federation
RSFSR	Russian Soviet Federative Socialist Republic
RTA	regional free trade agreement
RTS	Russian Trading System
RUB	Russian Ruble
RZD	Rossiyskie Zheleznye Dorogi (Russian Railways)
SCB	Statistics Sweden
SEK	Swedish Krona
SFC	Sovcomflot
SITE	Stockholm Institute of Transition Economics
SKF	Svenska Kullager Fabriken (a Swedish ball bearing factory)
SME	small and medium-sized enterprise
SOE	state-owned enterprise
SPbSU	Saint Petersburg State University
SPE	special purpose entity
sqm	square meter
SRF	Silk Road Fund
SWF	sovereign wealth fund
TCA	Transaction Cost Analysis (theory)
TMK	Trubnaya Metallurgicheskaya Kompaniya (Pipe Metallurgical Company)
TNC	transnational company
TNK	Tyumenskaya Neftyanaya Kompaniya (Tyumen Oil Company)
TPP	Trans-Pacific Partnership
TRIMs	Trade-Related Investment Measures
TRIPs	Agreement on Trade-Related Aspects of Intellectual Property Rights
UK	United Kingdom

UNCTAD	United Nations Conference on Trade and Development
US, USA	United States of America
USC	United Shipbuilding Corporation
USSR	Union of Soviet Socialist Republics
VSMPO	Verkhnesaldinskoye metallurgicheskoye proizvodstvennoye ob'yedineniye (metal company of Verkhnyaya Salda)
WIR	*World Investment Report*
WTO	World Trade Organization
YoY	year on year

Symbols

€	Euro, EUR
£	British pound, GBP
₽	Russian ruble, RUB
$	United States dollar, USD

1   Introduction

Kari Liuhto

Russia is among the top five countries with foreign investments in the world. Russian businesses have invested especially in the neighboring countries. Russia is also an important target for foreign direct investment (FDI). American, Belgian, British, French, and German investments make up more than 90 percent of all FDI in Russia. Foreign investments contribute substantially to Russia's total capital. In some years, foreign investments have accounted for as much as a third of the country's total investments. Foreign banks finance businesses operating in Russia, and foreign businesses are building railways across the country, drilling oil, mining metals, and producing textiles and pharmaceuticals. The public's dissatisfaction with the head of state and social movements have nevertheless increased, which raises the political risk for foreign businesses continuing their operations in Russia considerably.

The previous paragraph could have easily been from a report sent by an embassy operating in Russia to its home country concerning Russia's economic situation a little over 100 years ago. The October Revolution in 1917, the founding of the Soviet Union five years later, and the country's transition to a centrally planned economy at the beginning of the 1930s nevertheless interrupted normal economic development in Russia. With the transition to a centrally planned economy, Russia fell into a half-century of slumber from the perspective of foreign investment. The country was awoken by Mikhail Gorbachev's reform program, Perestroika (reconstruction), towards the end of the 1980s.

Inspired by Perestroika, the Soviet Union passed a Joint Venture Act in 1987, which allowed foreign businesses to set up companies that were co-owned together with a Soviet organization. The growth of foreign investment in the Soviet Union was slow, as joint ventures had to operate in an economic system that was not designed for them. Joint ventures had no trouble finding demand for their products in the Soviet Union's consumer market, but they struggled hard to source raw materials, as joint ventures had not been factored into the design of the country's centralized materials distribution system, Gosplan. Legislation governing businesses and business support services were also practically non-existent.

The promising era of joint ventures ended with the sudden disintegration of the Soviet Union into 15 nations at the end of 1991. With the splintering of the country, the Soviet-era production system was also smashed to smithereens, as a result of which Russia lost approximately 40 percent of its gross domestic product (GDP) over the following five years. In order to prevent the total collapse of the country, Russian leaders were forced to build the foundations of the country's market economy in great haste, which inevitably led to some major structural errors.

The FDI inflow to Russia remained at below $5 billion per year throughout the 1990s. However, a significant change took place in the investment inflow at the beginning of the new millennium, when the country's extremely rapid economic growth began to tempt foreign investors to Russia. In 2000, the Russian economy grew by a staggering 10 percent.

The economic growth sparked an increase in the FDI inflow to Russia. As early as 2004, the country had an FDI inflow of more than $15 billion, and the rate of growth only kept increasing. The growth continued right up to the autumn of 2008, when the global financial crisis shook not just the global economy but also Russia. Despite the crisis, Russia still managed to attract $75 billion in FDI in 2008. As a result of the crisis, Russian GDP shrank by 8 percent in 2009, and the FDI inflow to Russia decreased slightly. However, as soon as 2013 Russia had, from the perspective of FDI, recovered from the global economic shock. The recovery was evidenced by the fact that, in 2013, Russia managed to attract almost $70 billion in FDI.

In 2014, the Ukrainian crisis boiled over, when Russia annexed the Crimean Peninsula, which had belonged to Ukraine since the 1950s, to its territory. After this, the West imposed sanctions on Russia, and Russia responded with its counter-sanctions. As a result of the sanctions, economic growth in Russia slowed even further and, finally, in 2015, Russian GDP shrank by almost 4 percent. Although the majority of the sanctions is not directly targeted at enterprise investments from the West to Russia or vice versa, they have impacted on Russia's economic growth projections and general atmosphere of the investment climate. Foreign investors have become more cautious, and Russian capitalists no longer repatriate their capital from abroad to Russia as eagerly as they did before the overheating of the Ukrainian crisis. Clear evidence of this development is the fact that the net inflow of FDI to Russia had dropped to approximately $5 billion in 2015, when it had been more than ten times that a couple of years previously.

Similarly, in order to understand the development of Russian investment abroad, we should remind ourselves that the October Revolution in 1917 essentially cut off all investment by Russian businesses in foreign countries. Although a few dozen Soviet businesses operated outside the socialist bloc, when the Soviet Union broke up, Russian businesses' total investments abroad amounted to less than $1 billion. In the chaos that followed the disintegration of the country, capital – including some assets of the Communist party – fled Russia through illegal channels to other countries. Russian businesses' legitimate investments abroad nevertheless gradually began to override illegal capital flight.

More and more Western newspapers began to report on the new phenomenon: the flow of Russian capital to the West. I can vaguely remember one article from almost two decades ago. The gist of the article was more or less as follows: Five decades ago the Russians aimed to conquer the West with soldiers and tanks – now they are invading our markets with enterprises and banks.

The aforementioned article was way ahead of its time, as the 1990s were only a first taste of what was to come, as – until the beginning of the new millennium – Russia's total foreign investments were relatively minor. In fact, Russia's outward foreign direct investment (OFDI) stock was as low as approximately $20 billion in 2000. With increases in the prices of oil and other raw materials, Russian investments in other countries nevertheless skyrocketed, as a result of which Russia's OFDI stock grew almost 20-fold during the first decade of this millennium. In 2013 alone, Russian businesses invested more than $90 billion in foreign countries. The figure put Russia in the top five countries with foreign investments in the world after a break of 100 years.

However, in this context, it is important to remember that a considerable share – approximately half – of Russian businesses' foreign investments are sooner or later repatriated to Russia. Circulating capital via foreign countries back to Russia is less to do with criminal activity and more about legal tax sheltering by Russian businesses and securing capital with the help of foreign "corporate citizenship". With the capital boomerang, Cyprus, in particular, has become a second financial home for wealthy Russians, which is why some analysts have even begun to hyphenate the country's name in a new way as Cyp-Rus.

The majority of Russian OFDI has ended up in the European Union. According to the Central Bank of Russia, in mid-2015, two-thirds of Russia's total OFDI is registered in one or other of the EU countries. Similarly, three-quarters of investments in Russia originate from the European Union. Even with Cyprus excluded from the analysis, the EU would still be easily the most important target for Russian investments and by far the most notable source of foreign investment for Russia. In this context, it should be mentioned that the USA only accounts officially for 2 percent of Russian investments abroad and less than 1 percent of Russia's total inward FDI (IFDI) stock. The figures for China were at less than 1 percent, even with Hong Kong included. In addition to the EU, the USA, and China, Russian investments are also to be found elsewhere – especially in the world's tax havens. As official statistics are only able to show development trends, a firm-level analysis is indispensable for getting a realistic picture of the movements of investments to and from Russia.

To recapitulate, Russia has, in practice, made an impressive comeback to the world's investment arena in a quarter of a century. Russia is once more one of the most active foreign investors in the world and one of the most notable target countries for foreign investment. Its comeback is evidenced, for example, by the fact that Russia accounted for more than 5 percent of the global FDI inflow and outflow in 2013.

With the intensification of the Ukrainian crisis, dark clouds have nevertheless begun to gather on Russia's investment horizon. The inflow of FDI to Russia has plummeted, and many Russian businesses are frantically trying to find safe places for their investments outside their home country's borders, where they would not encounter sanctions imposed by the West. The rapid rise of China to become the leader of the global economy in a couple of decades and the founding of the Eurasian Economic Union in 2015 are, together with Western sanctions, transforming Russian's investment projections.

The main objective of this book is, at a time of major upheaval, to increase understanding of the position that Russia will have in the global investment atlas in the future. This goal can be met by looking for answers to the following ten questions:

(1) How have investments from and to Russia developed in the last 100 years?
(2) What is Russia's current role as a target and source of global investment movements?
(3) How is Russian investment cooperation organized at the level of individual businesses with China, the EU, the Eurasian Economic Union, Latin America, South Korea, Turkey, and the USA?
(4) How are Russian businesses spreading to foreign countries through their indirect investments?
(5) How have Russian businesses managed to use their foreign investments to gain access to Western cutting-edge know-how in the age of sanctions?
(6) How have sanctions shaped Russia's political risk to Western oil companies?
(7) Can Russian businesses' foreign investments be explained by means of existing FDI theories or are there special characteristics that should definitely be taken into consideration?
(8) What needs to be taken into account when analyzing FDI statistics relating to Russia?
(9) What is the role of a firm's ownership structure when Russian businesses invest in foreign countries?
(10) How is the Russian Government influencing the investments of Russian businesses abroad?

By answering these questions, a team of almost 20 researchers strives to give readers an understanding of the direction in which Russia's role in the global investment atlas is developing. The research team comprised experts from China, Estonia, Finland, France, Russia, Sweden, and Turkey. Each of the authors of the book has studied Russian FDI for several years. Some authors have been following this phenomenon and its varied stages since the Soviet era. It would be no exaggeration to say that, together, the research team has several centuries of experience of foreign investment relating to Russia.

In their contributions, the researchers have made use of a range of different theories in order to provide as diverse a picture of the phenomenon as possible. In addition to John Dunning's Ownership, Location, and Internationalization (OLI) paradigm and the Investment Development Path (IDP) model, the researchers have, among others, used the following models: the equilibrium model of multinational enterprises, economic gravity model, hierarchical-wave model of spatial FDI diffusion, institutional theories, and political risk model related to FDI. The researchers have based their analyses and conclusions on materials such as statistics, press releases, and interviews with business executives.

The book is structured as follows: In Chapter 2, Jean-Marc F. Blanchard reviews global FDI trends and delves into the global factors that shape global FDI patterns. The chapter speculates about the world's future FDI trends in general and Russia's FDI situation in particular. In Chapter 3, Wladimir Andreff presents four historical stages related to Russian FDI. He also analyzes the role of the Russian Government in Russian OFDI.

Alexey Kuznetsov focuses on investment relations between Russia and the USA in Chapter 4. He pays special attention to FDI motives, industrial structure, and geographical division in Russia and the USA. Moreover, Kuznetsov analyzes the impact of sanctions on Russia–USA FDI flows. In Chapter 5, Sergei Sutyrin and Olga Trofimenko describe the main trends of EU investments to Russia. They aim to identify key institutional amendments in Russia and analyze whether these institutional transformations have led to changes in FDI inflows to Russia.

In Chapter 6, Torbjörn Becker investigates the investment flows between Russia and Sweden. He builds several hypotheses regarding bilateral capital flows and compares them to the actual data before concluding his contribution with some policy-relevant comments. After describing the historical development of Russian investments in Finland, Kari Liuhto and Elisa Aro analyze a knowledge-driven investment of one Russian shipbuilding company in Finland in Chapter 7. In a similar manner, Alari Purju investigates an indirect investment of a Russian ICT company in Estonia in Chapter 8. Both the contributions of Liuhto and Aro and Purju deal with motives, location, mode, characteristics, and timing behind these investments.

Given the political situation caused by the crisis in Ukraine and the related sanctions, Hanna Mäkinen and Eini Haaja study the impact of the Ukrainian crisis on the political risk faced by foreign investors in Russia in Chapter 9. More precisely, the aforementioned authors examine political risk in ExxonMobil's investment in the Kara Sea and Total's investment in Yamal. Chapter 10 is devoted to analyzing trends, motives, and peculiarities of Russian FDI in the Eurasian Economic Union. In this chapter, Elena Efimova and Vladimir Sherov-Ignatev investigate how well these investments fit to the explanations of classical FDI theories.

In Chapter 11, Andrei Panibratov and Liubov Ermolaeva concentrate on studying the Chinese–Russian investment relationship. These authors aim to discover drivers and special features behind this emerging investment partnership. In Chapter 12, Irina A. Korgun investigates investment cooperation between Russia and another Asian country, namely the Republic of Korea. She explains the factors behind the investment flow from Korea to Russia. In addition to statistical analysis, Korgun describes Hyundai's investment project in Russia.

In Chapter 13, Caner Bakır and Nuran Acur identify major Turkish multinationals' greenfield investments and acquisitions in Russia. Their chapter also offers a description of the activities of the two largest Turkish investors, namely Enka and Anadolu Efes, in Russia. In Chapter 14, Alexandra Koval deals with Russian investments in Latin America. With the help of three case studies, the chapter presents motives, barriers, and determinants of Russian OFDI in Latin America. In Chapter 15, Kari Liuhto analyzes the linkage between the ownership structure and outbound investments of ten non-financial Russian corporations with the largest assets abroad. The analysis of these corporations has major strategic significance since these ten companies cover a third of the total value of Russian FDI abroad. Sergei Sutyrin summarizes the main findings of the book and discusses the future development of the phenomenon in Chapter 16.

The chapters are written from each author's own perspective. The researchers' views are not always fully compatible, which is completely natural, as the temporal and geographical scopes of the pieces differ from each other. These differences in views are more of a strength than a weakness of the book, as they show that the phenomenon is extremely dynamic and not independent of time, location or the person interpreting it.

The editors have done an enormous job in standardizing the appearance of the chapters. Despite the substantial editing task, all credit for the chapters and any potential oversights in them belong to the authors. On behalf of the editors, I would like to thank all the authors, as this literary expedition, which has taken more than a year, has finally arrived at its destination. Although this writing project has come to an end, I hope that this book will also inspire other researchers to continue to study this phenomenon. After all, the study of Russian investments is by no means simply a study of capital movements but also a reflection on the state of international politics and Russia's ever-changing role in the global economy. As Russia's future role in international politics and the global economy is in flux, I want to end the introduction of this book with a quote from an American inventor Charles F. Kettering. He is believed to have said the following in 1949: "We should all be concerned about the future because we will have to spend the rest of our lives there."

2 Global FDI Trends

Jean-Marc F. Blanchard

Introduction

The end of the Cold War and the economic liberalization of Eastern Europe in the late 1980s and the 1990s, the birth of the World Trade Organization (WTO) in 1995, continuing improvements in information, communication, and transportation technologies, the economic rise of China, and an increasing view that hosting more foreign direct investment (FDI) was beneficial augured a period of dramatic growth in inward FDI (IFDI), albeit with notable, periodic fluctuations. Whereas annual global FDI flows were only $202 billion in 1990, they reached $331.1 billion by 1995, hit $1.27 trillion in 2000, and ran about $958.7 billion by 2005 (UNCTAD 2000, p. 6; UNCTAD 2001, pp. 2–3; UNCTAD 2008, p. 2).[1] Whatever the year, the statistics make clear the vast majority of FDI flowed from developed to other developed countries.[2] In tandem with FDI's upsurge, the world's leading multinational corporations (MNCs) became ever more massive. To illustrate, as of the end of 1998, the world's top 25 MNCs held over $752 billion in foreign assets, sold $1 trillion abroad, and employed over 2.36 million people overseas (UNCTAD 2000, p. 2). By the end of 2005, they held $2.6 trillion in assets, made over $1.8 trillion in foreign sales, and employed over 4.23 million workers overseas (UNCTAD 2007a, p. 7).

The outbreak of the 2008 global financial crisis (GFC) and a mixture of related as well as distinct economic and political factors broke the pattern of FDI growth highlighted above. More specifically, although global FDI stocks have continued to increase, annual FDI flows have not yet returned to levels witnessed before the 2008 GFC shock. The United Nations Conference on Trade and Development (UNCTAD) 2009 *World Investment Report* (*WIR*) published the year after the outbreak of the GFC starkly put it, "global FDI flows have been severely affected worldwide by the economic and financial crisis" (UNCTAD 2009a, p. 1).[3] As will be shown, after rebounding for several years following the start of the GFC, FDI flows have dropped to levels much lower than that witnessed at the beginning of the GFC and the few years preceding it (UNCTAD 2014a, pp. 3, 10). Still, the reality is that FDI is here to stay and in a big way. FDI stocks are ten times what they were in 1990, the assets of foreign affiliates almost 30 times larger, and the employment and export ramifications of MNCs magnitudes greater than what

existed 20 years ago or so. Indeed, even after the GFC, the sales of foreign affiliates, their assets, and their employment showed growth over the pre-GFC period
(ibid., p. 10).

The variables influencing FDI trends – e.g., amounts, home countries, and
geographic and sectoral orientation – are multidimensional, involving diverse
economic, legal, and political factors. They are multilevel, too, which means they
include drivers at the global, regional, sub-regional, country, industry, and firm
level. Global-level factors include the nature of international economic institutions (a good example is the WTO), prevailing economic ideologies, and technological change. Salient regional-level variables are regional free trade agreements
(RTAs), the existence of regional supply chains, and the quality of transportation
networks. Country-level factors encompass tariff policies, regulatory regimes for
foreign companies, and government corruption. Pertinent firm-level factors
include the quest for markets, higher rates of return, control, diversification,
government incentive, and access to assets like brands, resources, and intellectual
property (UNCTAD 1999, pp. 42–5; Moosa 2002, pp. 23–67; Moody 2007, esp.
chaps. 2–6). Later, this chapter identifies a number of macro-level factors illuminating past global FDI trends. Of course, in-depth assessments of regional, sub-
regional, and sub-regional FDI trends and the investment behavior of individual
firms require analysts to incorporate variables below the global level.

Regardless of the variation in FDI patterns or their economic and political drivers, the growing visibility of FDI has triggered vigorous debates. Some focus on the
costs and benefits of FDI in regards to economic growth rates, development
patterns, employment and labor conditions, the environment, and national independence. The general consensus is that greater FDI is desirable because it supplies
capital and tax revenues, is relatively permanent in contrast to other forms of capital, contributes to host-country technological and knowledge upgrading, fuels
competition, allows for the acquisition of assets that cannot be indigenously
obtained, and provides market access. Many, however, counter that FDI fosters
negative externalities such as job loss, deindustrialization, decreased autonomy,
increased pollution, greater wage inequality, commodity or sectoral lock-in, and
capital outflows (Moran 1978; UNCTAD 1999, pp. 31–5; Chen 2000; Bora 2002;
Moosa 2002; Moran 2006; Petras & Veltmeyer 2007; Blaine 2009). Other analysts
focus on identifying the policies countries can adopt to attract greater amounts of
FDI or FDI in targeted sectors and maximize the gains/minimize the costs of FDI
(UNCTAD 2001, pp. 26–38; UNCTAD 2005, pp. 31–4; Moran 2006; UNCTAD
2007a, pp. 26–31). Yet others debate the variables shaping FDI entry forms – e.g.,
merger and acquisition (M&A) versus greenfield investment – and FDI entry structures –e.g., wholly owned enterprise *versus* joint venture (Kalotay 2010; Shaver
2013; Hernandez & Nieto 2015). There also is an extensive discourse about the
institutions – e.g., bilateral investment treaties (BITs) and international investment
agreements (IIAs) – molding the milieu in which FDI occurs (UNCTAD 2014b,
pp. 126–32; Gordon & Pohl 2015; UNCTAD 2015b, pp. 164–73).

This chapter, which is meant to provide general background as well as a foundation that enables readers to better appreciate the analyses of other contributors

to the edited volume, consists of five sections. The second examines global FDI trends from 2003–12, looking at specific trends regarding, for example, the origins of FDI, and its geographic and sectoral destination.[4] It also offers thoughts about the drivers of those trends. The third section is similar to the second, but focuses on the most recent period of time for which we have complete data. The fourth section focuses on recent FDI trends with respect to three specific countries: the USA, China, and Russia. All three merit attention because of their prominence as both recipients and senders of FDI during the period under study while Russia further deserves attention because it is the focus of this book. The fifth and final section of this chapter reflects briefly about some ongoing developments that likely will shape future global FDI trends and speculates about their implications for Russian IFDI and outward FDI (OFDI).

FDI Developments, 2003-12: A Look at the Data and Drivers

Even before the outbreak of the 2008 GFC, there were years where annual FDI flows and growth rates showed unimpressive results, though the trend clearly was upward. Table 2.1 provides data from 2003–12.

Prior to the outbreak of the GFC, annual IFDI flows increased dramatically from $560 billion in 2003 to $946 billion in 2005 to $1.979 trillion by 2007. The annual growth rate of IFDI flows was quite impressive, registering a "low" 26.96 percent year-on-year (YoY) increase from 2003–4 to as high as 49.15 percent from 2005–6. In the year following the outbreak of the GFC, however, IFDI flows plummeted, dropping 32.05 percent from 2008–9. Nevertheless, for the next two years, they recovered, rising from $1.185 trillion in 2009 to $1.7 trillion in 2011. While the YoY growth percentage increases were hardly as healthy as in the period leading up to the 2008 GFC, they always topped 18 percent annually until 2011. By 2012, the situation again turned bleak with IFDI falling to $1.3 trillion. Overall, the story of annual IFDI flows from 2003–12 was one of significant growth with flows at the end of this period 150.54 percent greater than what they were at the beginning. Moreover, annual average growth rates almost reached 17 percent.

Table 2.2 provides data about FDI home or sender countries both in terms of geography and development status (developed, developing, and transition) from 2003–12.

Table 2.1 Global Inward and Outward FDI, 2003–12 ($ billions)

	2003	2004	2005	2006	2007	2008	2009	2010	2011	2012
IFDI	560	711	946	1,411	1,979	1,744	1,185	1,409	1,700	1,330
OFDI	612	813	837	1,323	2,147	1,911	1,171	1,505	1,712	1,347

Sources: UNCTAD 2004, p. 2; UNCTAD 2006a, p. 7; UNCTAD 2007a, p. 5; UNCTAD 2008, p. 4; UNCTAD 2009a, p. 9; UNCTAD 2010, p. 5; UNCTAD 2011a, p. 5; UNCTAD 2013a, p. 7; UNCTAD 2014a, p. 10

Table 2.2 FDI Senders by Geography and Development Status, 2003–12 ($ billions and percent)

	2003	2004	2005	2006	2007	2008	2009	2010	2011	2012
Amounts in $ billions										
EU	285.0	377.3	606.7	691.7	1,257.9	982.0	381.9	497.8	536.5	323.1
USA	129.4	294.9	15.4	224.2	393.5	308.3	266.9	304.4	396.7	328.9
Japan	28.8	31.0	45.8	50.3	73.5	128.0	74.7	56.3	107.6	122.6
China*	2.9	5.5	12.3	21.2	26.5	55.9	56.5	68.8	74.7	84.2
CIS	10.6	13.8	14.0	23.3	50.1	58.5	47.4	61.5	72.5	55.2
Percentage										
Developed	90.0	85.5	84.4	82.9	84.8	80.7	72.7	68.4	71.0	63.3
Developing	8.1	13.0	14.0	15.4	12.9	16.2	23.1	34.2	24.7	32.7
Transition	1.9	1.5	1.6	1.7	2.4	3.2	4.2	4.1	4.3	4.0
Rank out of top 20										
USA	1	1	0	1	1	1	1	1	1	1
China	0	0	17	18	19	12	6	6	6	3
Russia	15	15	15	17	13	13	7	8	7	8

Sources: UNCTAD 2005, pp. 2–3; UNCTAD 2006a, pp. 2, 4; UNCTAD 2007a, pp. 2–3; UNCTAD 2008, pp. 2–3; UNCTAD 2008b, pp. 6, 14; UNCTAD 2010, pp. 6, 8; UNCTAD 2011a, pp. 3–4; UNCTAD 2011b, pp. 9, 187–90; UNCTAD 2012b, pp. 169–72; UNCTAD 2013a, pp. 3, 5; UNCTAD 2013b, pp. 213–16; UNCTAD 2014a, pp. 3, 5

Note:*It is important to note that UNCTAD figures for China do not include capital that may go through Hong Kong, Macao, or Taiwan

An analysis of Table 2.2 indicates the primary senders of FDI consistently were the USA, the European Union (EU), and Japan – the so-called Triad. This said, there were interesting developments in terms of the geographic origins of OFDI with China becoming increasingly prominent as an OFDI source, especially after 2007 when its total annual OFDI jumped from $26.5 to $55.9 billion. If we look at the home countries in terms of their development status, it is quite clear that the developed world was dominant throughout the entire 2003–12 period while transition economies, in contrast, had trivial relevance. Table 2.2 reveals an interesting change, though. Specifically, after the start of the 2008 GFC, the developing world's importance as an outward investor almost doubled over the first half of the period. Indeed, in both 2010 and 2012, the developing world was a source of more than 30 percent of global OFDI, whereas in 2003 it did not even represent 10 percent.

One interesting empirical and analytical issue is "who" is making FDI. For a long time, it seemed large, private MNCs were the only game in town. By 2008, however, UNCTAD saw fit to highlight sovereign wealth funds (SWFs) as a "new feature of global FDI" (UNCTAD 2008, p. 4). Whereas SWF investments in the form of FDI were miniscule prior to 2004, never topping $2 billion annually, between 2005 and 2007 they exceeded $10 billion every year (ibid., p. 7). In 2012, annual SWF FDI hit close to $20 billion, a doubling YoY (UNCTAD

2013a, p. 5). A second non-traditional investor worth highlighting is private equity (PE) investors, which the *WIR* 2006 specifically singled out. According to UNCTAD studies, PE investors struck 17.7 to 20.3 percent of all cross-border M&A transactions between 2003 and 2005, when their M&A deals hit $134.6 billion (UNCTAD 2006a, pp. 4–5). For various reasons, the 2008 GFC led to a major decline in PE deals over the next two years, but this does not obviate the fact that PE investors concluded M&A deals worth an astounding $1.6 trillion between 2003 and 2010 (UNCTAD 2010b, pp. 12–13). A third, non-traditional source of FDI is state-owned enterprises (SOEs), whose rising role was stressed in *WIR* 2011, where it was pointed out that although SOEs were relatively small in number, they were major sources of OFDI, constituting "11 percent of global FDI flows in 2010" and making up nearly 20 of the world's 100 largest MNCs (UNCTAD 2011a, p. 4). By 2012, SOE FDI jumped 11 percent to reach $145 billion (UNCTAD 2013a, pp. 4–5). This represented more than 11 percent of all global FDI that year.

Turning to FDI hosts, the greatest amounts of IFDI between 2003 and 2012 went to five "regions" (see Table 2.3).

The EU was the largest regional recipient of FDI throughout the entire period. The USA (which essentially received all of North America's IFDI) was the second largest recipient from 2003 until 2008, but switched places with East Asia (excluding Japan) from 2009 onward and received less IFDI than Latin America in 2012. Latin America consistently ranked fourth in terms of IFDI from 2003–11, but was the third largest FDI host region in 2012. Southeast Asia was an important FDI recipient region, dramatically rising in importance after 2009 while the Commonwealth of Independent States (CIS) remained much less important albeit still consequential post the 2008 GFC. Turning to the world's top ten FDI recipient countries (shown in Table 2.4), we see frequent fluctuations over the course of 2003–12 which makes it difficult to generalize. Nevertheless, it can be said that China, the UK, and the USA frequently ranked among the top three FDI recipient countries prior to 2009 with Belgium, Canada, Germany, and Hong Kong also making numerous appearances in the list of top five FDI hosts.[5] Russia, the focus of this book, appeared in the top ten from 2006 onward, breaking into the ranks of the top five FDI hosts in 2008, but falling into the bottom five after 2008.

Table 2.3 Major FDI Recipients by Region, 2003–12 ($ billions)

Regions	2003	2004	2005	2006	2007	2008	2009	2010	2011	2012
EU	243.4	197.1	449.9	535.5	797.7	307.8	391.3	358.6	444.8	364.8
USA	53.1	135.8	104.8	237.1	215.9	306.4	143.6	198.0	229.8	169.7
East Asia	79.5	105.8	123.2	132.9	161.3	186.7	163.8	201.3	233.8	212.4
Latin America	46.1	68.0	75.3	73.5	116.6	137.5	83.5	131.7	163.9	178.0
Southeast Asia	31.4	40.2	43.1	64.6	85.9	50.3	46.1	105.2	93.5	108.1
CIS	15.8	26.4	28.4	51.4	77.3	106.6	63.6	69.6	88.3	80.6

Source: Author's compilation using UNCTAD *WIR* Annex Tables downloaded at http://unctad.org/en/Pages/DIAE/World%20Investment%20Report/Annex-Tables.aspx

Table 2.4 Top Ten FDI Recipient Economies, Excluding Tax Havens, 2003–12

Rank	2003	2004	2005	2006	2007	2008	2009	2010	2011	2012
1	China	USA	UK	USA	USA	USA	USA	USA	USA	USA
2	USA	UK	USA	UK	UK	China	China	China	China	China
3	Belgium	China	China	China	Canada	UK	UK	Hong Kong	Hong Kong	Hong Kong
4	Germany	Belgium	Germany	Canada	Belgium	Spain	Belgium	Germany	Belgium	Brazil
5	Spain	Australia	Belgium	Belgium	China	Russia	Hong Kong	Belgium	Germany	UK
6	Ireland	Hong Kong	Hong Kong	Germany	Germany	Canada	Russia	UK	Brazil	Singapore
7	Italy	Spain	France	Switzerland	Spain	Hong Kong	Australia	Singapore	Australia	Australia
8	Hong Kong	Singapore	Canada	Italy	France	Australia	France	Brazil	Russia	Russia
9	Singapore	Italy	Spain	Hong Kong	Hong Kong	Brazil	Switzerland	Russia	Singapore	Ireland
10	UK	Brazil	Italy	Russia	Russia	France	Brazil	Ireland	UK	Canada

Source: Author's compilation using UNCTAD *WIR* Annex Tables downloaded at http://unctad.org/en/Pages/DIAE/World%20Investment%20Report/Annex-Tables.aspx

For 2003–8, the bulk of FDI poured into the services sector, especially the finance, business activities, and trade subsectors. The dominance of service sector FDI was quite stark. Indeed, for the early part of the 2003–12 period, it routinely ran 2.5 times greater than manufacturing FDI. After the 2008 GFC, however, it plunged from $1.13 trillion (2008) to $570 billion (2011) because of the GFC's severe impact on the financial services sector. In fact, the 2008 GFC led to a stark reversal in the ratio of service to manufacturing investment. To illustrate, whereas service sector FDI was 1.15 times larger than manufacturing FDI in 2008, by 2011 manufacturing investment was 1.15 times larger than service sector FDI. Between 2003 and 2012, manufacturing FDI went largely into the chemicals and chemical products, food, beverages, and tobacco, and metals and metal products subsectors. Two other, notable manufacturing-related FDI subsectors included machinery and equipment, and electrical and electronic equipment (UNCTAD 2006b, p. 268; UNCTAD 2007b, p. 227; UNCTAD 2009b, p. 220). Throughout the 2003–12 period, primary sector FDI was relatively inconsequential. However, rising commodity prices spurred a large increase in primary sector FDI. To illustrate, mining, quarrying, and petroleum FDI nearly doubled from $88.6 billion between 2003 and 2005 to $167.5 billion between 2005 and 2007 (UNCTAD 2007b, p. 227; UNCTAD 2009b, p. 220; UNCTAD 2012b, p. 9).

While there is not space for extensive discussion, three noteworthy FDI trends emerged or strengthened between 2003 and 2012. First, South–South or developing country–developing country FDI flows became an increasingly large component of global FDI flows. This pattern started in the early 1990s, but really took off after 2001 as developing countries went abroad to seek new markets, reduce costs, and access strategic assets as well as to grapple with increasing competition from domestic and foreign firms (UNCTAD 2006a, pp. 18–27; UNCTAD 2006b, pp. 117–21; UNCTAD 2007a, pp. 7, 9). Second, service sector FDI continued to dominate as it had since the 1980s, though surges in commodity prices between 2003 and 2012 occasionally decreased its importance relative to primary sector FDI (UNCTAD 2007b, p. 22). Third, countries generally worked to foster an environment conducive to FDI inflows. Relevant measures included cuts in corporate tax rates, increases in investment incentives, reductions of regulatory burdens, the signing of greater numbers of BITs and double taxation treaties, and the conclusion of sub-regional, regional, and global IIAs or RTAs/economic agreements with implicit or explicit investment provisions.[6]

To isolate the economic drivers of FDI trends between 2003 and 2008, it is helpful to divide the period into two parts, one from 2003 to the outbreak of the 2008 GFC and the other the balance of the period. Key FDI drivers during the first period included a widespread thirst for natural resources and the globalization-fueled quest to access new markets and lower costs. FDI drew further sustenance from low borrowing costs, good asset prices (especially high stock prices which provide the currency to consummate deals), and good economic growth which directly encouraged FDI, but also bolstered profits that generated retained earnings which bolstered FDI (UNCTAD 2005, p. 2; UNCTAD 2006a, pp. 1, 3, 9–11; UNCTAD 2007a, pp. 1, 3; UNCTAD 2008, pp. 1, 3). Over the second period, there were several macro factors influencing FDI trends. A critical one was the fallout of the 2008 GFC which produced lower economic growth and boosted economic risks, severely dented manufacturing-related FDI, reduced profits/ retained earnings, lowered stock prices (which affected the purchasing power of MNCs, SWF, and PE investors), and fueled asset divestments. These factors were somewhat offset by the decline in target asset prices flowing from the 2008 GFC which created attractive investment bargains. Furthermore, globalization continued to push developing countries to expand their OFDI to access markets and resources and gain efficiencies (UNCTAD 2009a, pp. 1–8; UNCTAD 2010, pp. 1–4; UNCTAD 2011a, pp. 1–2). The situation started to improve in 2011 due to higher MNC profits, increased economic growth, higher commodity prices, and some attractive asset bargains (UNCTAD 2012b, pp. 2, 13–14). However, in 2012, global FDI flows dropped due to the dampening effect of persistent economic and political risks (UNCTAD 2013a, p. 1).

With respect to the political factors shaping global FDI trends, this chapter already has discussed how states embraced a large number of wide-ranging agreements and policies from 2003 onward to improve their appeal as investment destinations. These measures incontrovertibly created an environment conducive to greater FDI flows. Furthermore, the global liberalization trend continued into the second decade of the twenty-first century. Nevertheless, starting in 2009, diverse factors ranging from sensitivities about selling strategic resources to environmental concerns to displeasure with international arbitration led states to enact tighter policies to the extent that the percentage of stricter relative to liberalizing measures hit heights not seen since 1992. Concurrently, countries also began to take a stance towards IIAs and BITs that was more cautious and/or state friendly (UNCTAD 2010, pp. 18–23; UNCTAD 2011a, pp. 11–12; UNCTAD 2012b, pp. 84–92). While it is difficult to blame this new situation for the decline in FDI seen from 2008–12, it is quite conceivable it limited its recovery.

Recent Global FDI Features and Factors

In 2013, global IFDI hit $1.47 trillion. The next year, it fell to $1.23 trillion (UNCTAD 2014a, pp. 3, 10; UNCTAD 2015b, pp. 2, 18). There is some optimism final FDI figures for 2015 will show a rebound from the decline witnessed in 2014 due to modest, economic growth in the USA, China's continued search for resources and assets (e.g., brands, intellectual property, and technology), and its One Belt, One Road (OBOR) initiative, which calls for massive Chinese OFDI, and the stabilization of Europe (coupled with its improving investment environment, abundant investment bargains, and cheap currency). However, economic challenges or problems in China, Russia, and developing countries like Brazil, which have to do with factors such as weak commodity prices, changing economic development patterns, and other issues will generate countervailing winds restraining FDI growth (EY 2015; fDi Intelligence 2015; Jones 2015).

In 2013, the USA was the largest sender of FDI, pouring $328 billion overseas. It was followed by the EU ($285 billion), Japan ($136 billion), China ($101 billion), Russia ($87 billion), and Hong Kong ($81 billion). Top EU outward investors included Germany ($30 billion), Sweden ($33 billion), and Italy ($31 billion). The next year, USA OFDI totaled $337 billion, Hong Kong's ran $143 billion, and China's was $116 billion. The next five largest outward investors were Japan ($114 billion), Germany ($112 billion), Russia ($56 billion), Canada ($53 billion), and France ($43 billion) (UNCTAD 2014a, pp. 3, 5; UNCTAD 2014b, p. 7; UNCTAD 2015b, p. 8). Over the past two years for which complete statistics are available, the data continue to show the importance of the developing world for global OFDI. In 2013, developed countries accounted for 63.8 percent of global OFDI while developing (primarily East and Southeast Asia economies) and transition economies accounted for 29.2 and 7.0 percent. For 2014, the developing country share almost reached 34.6 percent while the developed country share fell to 60.8 percent. Transition economies remained relatively inconsequential, representing less than 5.0 percent of total global OFDI (UNCTAD 2014a, p. 3; UNCTAD 2015b, pp. 6, 30, A3–A6).

In 2013, PE FDI was but a shadow of its pre-2008 GFC grandeur, totaling just $171 billion, due to reasons ranging from an unattractive investment environment to increased regulatory scrutiny to cost control pressures. Nevertheless, it still remained a vital source of M&A-related FDI. SWF FDI "continued to expand in terms of assets, geographical spread, and target industries" (UNCTAD 2014a, p. 8). Still, in 2013, it just totaled $6.7 billion (ibid; UNCTAD 2014b, pp. 17–19). In contrast, UNCTAD estimates that SOE FDI in 2013 ran about $160 billion, which constituted a significant portion of global FDI flows. SOE foreign direct investors were heavily oriented towards strategic sectors where they held very strong positions in their home countries. Examples include the extractive industries, telecommunications, and financial services (UNCTAD 2014a, pp. 8–9; UNCTAD 2014b, pp. 20–2). In 2014, PE investors soared in relevance, exploiting huge cash balances and low interest rates to strike around $200 billion of M&A deals "mainly in transactions involving large companies" (UNCTAD 2015b, p. ix). In 2014, SWFs spent $16 billion, though they were restrained in their overseas investment activities by low oil prices and weak export markets. In 2014, SOE FDI in the form of M&A and greenfield investment fell to $118 billion. The main reasons were that SOE investors focused on consolidating/digesting past investments and faced various host-country restrictions (ibid., pp. 14–17).

In 2013, the largest FDI hosts in regional terms were, in order, the EU ($333 billion), the USA ($230 billion), East Asia (excluding Japan) ($221 billion), Latin America ($186 billion), Southeast Asia ($126 billion), and the CIS ($94 billion). Of note, almost 70 percent of CIS IFDI consisted of FDI flows to Russia. The next year, the EU remained in the lead, receiving $258 billion. East Asia (excluding Japan) assumed second place, garnering $248 billion, while Latin America vaulted into third place, with IFDI totaling $159 billion. The fourth spot was held by Southeast Asia which took in FDI worth $133 billion. The USA fell to fifth place, receiving just $92 billion. The CIS received FDI worth $42 billion, a significant drop YoY.[7] In 2013, FDI flows to developed and developing countries were roughly the same, with the former receiving

$697 billion and the latter $671 billion. In 2014, the amount of FDI hosted by developed countries plunged to $499 billion while developing countries received $681 billion, showing a huge change from historical ratios. In 2013, FDI to transition economies constituted about 7 percent of total global IFDI. However, in 2014, transition economies hosted less than 4 percent of total global IFDI (UNCTAD 2014b, pp. 2; UNCTAD 2015b, p. 30).

Turning to host countries, the USA was the top FDI recipient in 2013, taking in $187 billion, while China received about two-thirds as much FDI ($124 billion). The next leading FDI recipients, in order, were Hong Kong ($74 billion), Canada ($71 billion), Russia ($69 billion), Singapore ($65 billion), Brazil ($64 billion), Australia ($54.2 billion), the UK ($48 billion), and France ($43 billion). In 2014, China and Hong Kong surged into first and second place, receiving, respectively, FDI totaling $129 and $103 billion. The USA slipped to third place, but still hosted $92 billion of FDI. The next seven places among the top ten were occupied by the UK ($72 billion), Singapore ($68 billion), Brazil ($63 billion), Canada ($54 billion), Australia ($52 billion), Chile ($23 billion), and Spain ($23 billion). Russia declined to 16th place.[8] Clearly, there are "old favorites" as far as FDI destinations are concerned. Nevertheless, the direction of FDI flows is dynamic as shown by constant shifts in both the ranking and composition of the top ten FDI recipients.

As for the sectoral destination of FDI, in 2013, "services continued to account for the largest shares of announced greenfield projects and M&A deals", totaling $558 billion (UNCTAD 2014b, pp. 9–10). With respect to services, M&A was disposed towards the finance, business services, and information and communication subsectors (ibid., p. 216). Investment in the manufacturing sector was the next largest sectoral destination, hitting $391 billion, with the largest investment proportions flowing into the food, beverages, and tobacco, chemicals and chemical products, and electrical and electronic equipment subsectors (ibid., pp. 9–10, 216). In 2013, primary sector FDI hit $71 billion, with investment suppressed by low commodity prices and the troubled situation of companies in the extractive industry (ibid., pp. 9–10). Turning to 2014, service FDI again dominated, but not as much as the prior year. In fact, services FDI (greenfield plus M&A) was slightly less than 2013, running $554 billion. The greatest amounts of service FDI flowed into the finance, business services, and construction subsectors. In 2014, manufacturing FDI, which hit $458 billion, showed healthy growth, especially in areas like chemicals and chemical products, electrical and electronic equipment, food, beverages, and tobacco, machinery and equipment, and motor vehicles and transport. Primary sector FDI also grew, registering $82 billion (UNCTAD 2015b, pp. 12–14, A14).

There is not much to say about the economic factors behind the annual IFDI results for 2013, which showed a 11.5 percent increase YoY, but, in absolute terms, were lower or nearly lower than IFDI figures for 2006–8 and 2010–12 (see Table 2.1). Generally speaking, increased economic stability, rising commodity prices, bargain hunting, low interest rates, and a recovery in corporate profits after the initial shock of the 2008 GFC all fueled greater global investment activity, though not all regions fared equally well. However, there were limits to the global recovery of FDI because of continuing economic weakness in many parts of the world. In 2014, the FDI situation took a turn for the worse "because of the fragility of the global economy, policy uncertainty for investors, and elevated geopolitical risks" despite GDP and trade growth (ibid., pp. ix, 2).

Reflecting on the global political drivers of FDI, the environment became relatively less welcoming in 2013, though there was some improvement in 2014. On the positive side, the number of liberalization/promotion measures (e.g., sector openings, liberalization of ownership caps, privatization initiatives, investment incentives, and creation of special economic zones) was almost three times the number of restrictive/regulatory measures (e.g., new entry regulations, investments review rejections, and new ownership caps). Furthermore, states concluded more BITs, IIAs, and IIAs with pre-establishment provisions and there was notable progress on mega-regional trade pacts with substantive investment provisions such as the Trans-Pacific Partnership (TPP). Still, the number of restrictive/regulatory measures remained at high levels with governments imposing, *inter alia*, new restrictions on divestments, operations, business closures, and headquarter relocations (UNCTAD 2014a, p. 18; UNCTAD 2014b, pp. 106–19; UNCTAD 2015b, pp. xi, 102–18). These restrictions likely dampened or muted investor sentiments.

FDI Cases: The USA, China, and Russia

This section briefly covers recent FDI trends relating to the USA, China, and Russia, starting with the USA. As previously noted, the USA was the largest FDI host globally in 2013. While primary sector-related FDI in the USA plummeted for reasons similar to those that had battered global primary sector FDI, foreign investors, especially Japanese companies, made significant investments in the US manufacturing and service sectors in 2013. In 2014, US IFDI totals plummeted. This had little to do with economic or political conditions, but rather linked to an immense divestment by Vodafone which resulted when Verizon bought out Vodafone's investment in its operations in the USA. In 2013 and 2014, the USA was a huge outward investor, sending substantial amounts of money into Canada, among other destinations (UNCTAD 2014b, pp. 77–81; UNCTAD 2015b, pp. 70–5). Preliminary assessments indicate that the situation with respect to FDI inflows into the USA in 2015 will be much better with foreign investors motivated to take stakes in American assets due to improved economic conditions there (OECD 2015, pp. 1–4, 8).

China was the leading FDI host in East Asia in 2013 and 2014 and the world's leading FDI recipient in 2014, when it received $128 billion. One of the most noteworthy developments in regards to China's IFDI figures was a continuing shift to investments in services like retail, transport, and finance and a shift away from low value added manufacturing FDI. FDI in services first surpassed manufacturing in 2011 and hit 55 percent in 2014. In 2013 and 2014, China was a very large outward investor, sending $101 billion and $116 billion abroad, with

Chinese companies such as China National Offshore Oil Company, Shuanghui, and Lenovo concluding numerous multi-billion dollar investment transactions.[9] While resource investing remained important, Chinese investors put greater emphasis on the services and infrastructure sectors. Supportive government policy, regional integration, the quest to lower costs, OBOR, and favorable growth rates all provided fuel to continuing OFDI by Chinese firms (UNCTAD 2014b, pp. 46–51; UNCTAD 2015b, pp. 39–45). Analysis suggests China's IFDI totals for 2015 will exceed those in 2014 while OFDI also seems to be running at a healthy clip based on the latest systematic study (OECD 2015, pp. 3, 8–9; 'FDI inflows jump 7.9% to US$114b' 2015).

In 2013, Russian IFDI flows experienced healthy growth due to, among other things, firming commodity prices and a major investment by BP in Rosneft, which was part of BP's compensation for selling its 50 percent stake in TNK-BP to Rosneft. As well, Russia's market size, strong Sino-Russian relations, and Russia's 2012 WTO entry (and subsequent liberalization measures) encouraged greater FDI in Russia's financial, automobile, and natural sectors. In 2013, Russian OFDI figures registered impressive results. This was a function of the aforementioned Rosneft purchase of BP's TNK-BP stake, Russian investors buying downstream energy and value added manufacturing assets, and Moscow's adoption of measures to support Russian OFDI (UNCTAD 2014a, pp. 15; UNCTAD 2014b, pp. 22, 70–6). Russia's 2014 IFDI and OFDI totals were much less impressive. Relevant factors include economic sanctions, low commodity prices, the financing challenges of Russian banks, weak Russian ruble, capital flight, and an inability or unwillingness by foreign companies to invest in Russia. A bright spot was Chinese investment, with Chinese companies investing so much that China rose to become Russia's fifth largest investor in 2014 (Kuchma 2015; UNCTAD 2015b, pp. 65–70). OECD analysis suggests that IFDI and OFDI for 2015 will be much better than 2014. Still, one must be cautious as major European players remain reluctant to or are limited in investing in Russia (OECD 2015, pp. 4, 8–9; Rapoza 2015).

Global Developments, FDI Futures, and Implications for Russia

In this conclusion, I briefly consider several ongoing global economic developments and their potential implications for global FDI trends. For reasons of space, there are many salient issues such as regional integration, the continued increase in BITs and IIAs, and political tensions/problems with potential FDI effects that cannot be covered in any meaningful fashion. The focus, then, solely will be on global economic growth, commodity prices, and China. Following a discussion of these issues, I turn specifically to speculating about the case of Russia and FDI.

As of now, the direction of the global economy remains uncertain. The USA, the EU, and Japan all are growing slowly or not growing at all, with fiscal and debt burdens continuing to weigh on their economic prospects and manufacturing activity. For a myriad of reasons, China, a large source of global growth in recent years, has slowed significantly, though its 7–8 percent growth rate remains the envy of many. Numerous African, Latin American, and Central Asian countries are confronting severe economic challenges, partly as a result of China's slow-down, which has reduced commodity prices as well as export demand. Political tensions or problems relating to territorial and maritime issues, domestic political and ideological divisions, and terrorism remain pervasive in Africa, the Middle East, portions of Eastern Europe, South Asia, and Southeast Asia. All of this will weigh negatively on MNC, PE, SWF, and SOE FDI volumes, though low borrowing costs, huge cash holdings, investment bargains, currency depreciations (which facilitate asset acquisitions), and progress in regional and sub-regional integration initiatives such as the TPP should offset the restraining effect of these forces somewhat (Conference Board 2015; Hannon 2015; Finley, Cascione & Karunakar 2015).

In the near term, there is little reason to expect commodity prices to recover meaningfully. A big part of this is the global politico-economic situation just described. For their part, energy prices specifically will be pressured by the deci-sion of Saudi Arabia and other OPEC members to focus on maintaining market share rather than price levels, falling energy import requirements in China and the USA (which can supply a huge amount of its own energy needs now through shale oil production), Iran's re-emergence as a major player in global energy markets, warmer weather, and other variables. Going forward, low energy prices coupled with a related tightening of financing for energy-based investment will discourage investments in the energy sector and limit the investment resources of energy-based SWFs, SOEs, and firms. Many of the dynamics, especially excess production, affecting the energy sector also can be found in other commodity sectors, with similar negative effects on prices and investment prospects (Egan 2015; Friedman 2015; Gilblom, Lehane & Lee 2015).

China's economic situation will have important ramifications for global FDI patterns generally, as well as specifically in regards to China. Looking at FDI flows into China, we should expect China's slowing growth rate, more aggressive policy stance towards foreign companies, and rising manufacturing costs to depress IFDI.[10] Still, the fact China has the world's second largest economy, huge sectoral opportunities in areas such as finance, medical, and retail, and is shifting to a consumption, innovation-oriented economy undoubtedly will lure many foreign investors. Turning our attention to OFDI, there is every reason to expect Chinese firms to continue to send massive amounts of money abroad in search of resources, markets, brands, technology, and to support the OBOR initiative. This said, the relative balance among Chinese OFDI sectoral destinations may shift in tandem with China's evolving economic development model as witnessed in the case of Chinese OFDI flowing into Africa (Dasgupta 2015).

What does all of this mean for Russia? Unimpressive global economic growth, weak commodity prices, and China's changed economic situation certainly will have serious effects on FDI flows into Russia. These "depressing" factors will be offset somewhat by the country's market size, income, low cost, talented work-force and low energy costs. Moreover, Chinese companies, which, as noted, have become important investors in Russia are likely to continue to sink money in Russia because of the very warm state of Sino-Russian relations bilaterally and globally. Even so, Chinese investments will be limited by Russia's weak economic situation, bureaucracy, financial issues inside Russia, local concerns about the economic, environmental, and social impact of Chinese investment, and infrastructure shortcomings. Reflecting about Russian OFDI, the global economic situation and weak commodity prices coupled with sanctions, higher borrowing costs, and other factors are likely to constrain Russian OFDI in the near term (Kuchma 2015; Rapoza 2015; Schuman 2015).

Conclusion

This chapter offers background information on global FDI trends from 2003 to the present to give context to and a foundation for appreciating the other analyses in this book. It reviews global FDI trends from 2003–14, examining *inter alia* FDI origins, geographic and sectoral destinations, and key FDI players. It also probes the economic and political factors that influenced global FDI patterns during this period of time. The chapter also supplies a focused analysis of the IFDI and OFDI situation with respect to the USA, China, and Russia, concentrating specifically on 2013 and 2014. The penultimate section of the chapter offers observations about the global economic situation, commodity prices, and China's economic condition, the potential implications of these facts for future global FDI trends, and speculates about how these global economic variables will influence Russia's FDI situation.

An analysis of global FDI trends reveals several interesting facts. First, the story of global FDI trends after 2003 was one of constant increases until the GFC, a shock from which global FDI flows have yet to recover. Second, while the USA, the EU, and Japan specifically and developed world generally continue to dominate as FDI home countries, the developing world, above all China, has become far more important as a source of FDI. Third, new sources of FDI have appeared with SWFs and PE investors becoming important players affecting global FDI patterns. Fourth, service sector FDI has been dominant, though the GFC did impact its importance relative to manufacturing FDI. In terms of causal factors, the quest for natural resources, globalization, good economic growth, low borrowing costs, and supportive government policies at the global, regional, and national levels helped drive FDI to new heights while the absence of these factors, offset somewhat by bargain asset prices, led to stagnant or reduced global flows. Of note, while governments continue to support more FDI, their policies reflect less enthusiasm than before.

As of the writing of this chapter, the overall global economic situation remains poor, China's economic future uncertain, and commodity prices severely depressed. Such conditions as well as troubled political conditions in a number of regions such as the Middle East and Latin America do not augur well for a significant recovery in FDI. However, FDI should be stabilized somewhat by low borrowing costs, attractive investment opportunities, currency depreciations, the huge cash holdings of investors, and positive developments in regional economic integration initiatives such as the TPP and the Association of Southeast Asian Nations Economic Community. Unfortunately for Russia, the troubled state of the global economy and the EU coupled with low commodity prices and economic sanctions make it difficult to be sanguine about its near term prospects regarding FDI. It will take renewed economic growth, a recovery in commodity prices, and a stabilization of political tensions for global FDI and Russia's FDI to resume the upward path on which they embarked at the beginning of 2000.

Notes

1 All figures in this chapter are given in US dollars (USD, $).
2 Consult the UNCTAD *WIR* series for the relevant data.
3 The *WIR* has been published since the early 1990s and is considered one of the most authoritative and comprehensive sources of data on foreign direct investment.
4 The period 2003–12 was selected for two reasons. First, the data for this period is complete and relatively static (i.e., not subject to regular revision). Second, this ten-year timeframe gives us an opportunity to reflect upon FDI trends and drivers over a longer period where the distortive effects of idiosyncratic factors are less relevant.
5 Hong Kong was returned to the People's Republic of China in July 1997, but continues to be treated as a separate economic entity in diverse ways.
6 For discussion, relevant materials include UNCTAD (2005, pp. 8–10), UNCTAD (2006a, p. 9), UNCTAD (2007a, pp. 9–10) and UNCTAD (2008, p. 3).
7 Author's compilation using UNCTAD *WIR* Annex Tables downloaded at http://unctad.org/en/Pages/DIAE/World%20Investment%20Report/Annex-Tables.aspx
8 See Endnote 7.
9 Blanchard (2011) provides background on the rise of Chinese OFDI, its drivers, and relevant debates.
10 One piece focusing on investor concerns about China's contemporary stance towards foreign investment is Blanchard 2014.

Bibliography

Blaine, H.G. (ed.) 2009, *Foreign Direct Investment*, Nova Science, New York, NY.
Blanchard, J.M. 2011, 'Chinese MNCs as China's new long march: a review and critique of the Western literature', *Journal of Chinese Political Science*, vol. 16, no. 1, pp. 91–108.
Blanchard, J.M. 2014, 'Distrust about China's antitrust campaign', *The Diplomat*, 28 September, viewed 28 September 2014, http://thediplomat.com/2014/09/distrust-about-chinas-antitrust-campaign
Bora, B. (ed.) 2002, *Foreign Direct Investment: Research Issues*, Routledge, London.
Chen, J. (ed.) 2000, *Foreign Direct Investment*, Macmillan, Houndmills.
Conference Board 2015, 'Global Economic Outlook 2016: the global economy in a holding pattern', https://www.conference-board.org/publications/publicationdetail.cfm?publicationid=5045
Dasgupta, S. 2015, 'Chinese investment in Africa falls by 40%', *VOA*, 25 November, viewed 26 November 2015, http://www.voanews.com/content/chinese-investment-to-africa-falls-by-40-percent/3072974.html
Egan, M. 2015, 'Copper, aluminum, and steel collapse to crisis levels', *CNN Money*, 9 December, viewed 15 December 2015, http://money.cnn.com/2015/12/09/investing/oil-prices-metals-crash-crisis-levels

EY 2015, 'European Attractiveness Survey 2015', viewed 15 December 2015, http://www. ey.com/Publication/vwLUAssets/EY-european-attractiveness-survey-2015/$FILE/ EY-european-attractiveness-survey-2015.pdf

'FDI inflows jump 7.9% to US$114b' 2015, *ShanghaiDaily*.com, 12 December, viewed 12 December 2015, http://www.shanghaidaily.com/business/finance/FDI-inflows-jump-79-to-US114b/shdaily.shtml

fDi Intelligence 2015, 'The fDi Report 2015: global greenfield investment trends', http:// report.fdiintelligence.com/

Finley, R.S., Cascione, S. & Karunakar, R. 2015, 'Prospects still slim for major global economic pickup', *Reuters*, 18 December, viewed 18 December 2015, http://www. reuters.com/article/us-global-economy-idUSKBN0U120820151218

Friedman, N. 2015, 'What went wrong in oil-price forecasts?', *The Wall Street Journal*, 10 December, viewed 10 December 2015, http://www.wsj.com/articles/what-went-wrong-in-oil-price-forecasts-1449794306

Gilblom, K., Lehane, B. & Lee, J. 2015, 'When's winter coming? Balmy December sinks global energy prices', *Bloomberg Business*, 18 December, viewed 18 December 2015, http://www.bloomberg.com/news/articles/2015-12-18/when-s-winter-coming-balmy-december-sinks-global-energy-prices

Gordon, K. & Pohl, J. 2015, 'Investment treaties over time: treaty practice and interpretation in a changing world', *OECD Working Papers on International Investment*, viewed 1 December 2015, http://dx.doi.org/10.1787/5js7rhd8sq7h-en

Hanon, P. 2015, 'Economic growth to steady after China, Brazil slowdowns, OECD indicators suggest', *The Wall Street Journal*, 8 December, viewed 8 December 2015, http:// www.wsj.com/articles/economic-growth-to-steady-after-china-brazil-slowdowns-oecd-indicators-suggest-1449573424

Hernandez, V. & Nieto, M.J. 2015, 'The effect of the magnitude and direction of institutional distance on the choice of international entry modes', *Journal of World Business*, vol. 50, no. 1, pp. 122–32.

Jones, C. 2015, 'FDI into Europe surges over a third in year, poll says', *Financial Times*, 27 May.

Kalotay, K. 2010, 'Patterns of inward FDI in economies in transition', *Eastern Journal of European Studies*, vol. 1, no. 2, pp. 55–76.

Kuchma, A. 2015, 'Russia is facing record capital and investment outflow', *RBTH*, 29 January, viewed 5 December 2015, http://rbth.com/business/2015/01/29/russia_is_facing_record_capital_and_investment_outflow_43261.html

Moody, A. (ed.) 2007, *Foreign Direct Investment and the World Economy*, Routledge, Abingdon, UK.

Moosa, I.A. 2002, *Foreign Direct Investment: Theory, Evidence, and Practice*, Palgrave, Houndmills.

Moran, T.H. 1978, 'Multinational corporations and dependency: a dialogue for dependentistas and non-dependentistas', *International Organization*, vol. 32, no. 1, pp. 79–100.

Moran, T.H. 2006, *Harnessing Foreign Direct Investment for Development*, Brookings Institution Press, Washington, DC.

OECD 2015, *FDI in Figures*, viewed 5 December 2015, http://www.oecd.org/daf/inv/ investment-policy/FDI-in-Figures-October-2015.pdf

Petras, J. & Veltmeyer, H. 2007, *Multinationals on Trial: Foreign Investment Matters*, Ashgate, Aldershot.

Rapoza, K. 2015, 'Russia getting more money from Asia as sanctions scare Europeans', *Forbes*, 15 November, viewed 5 December 2015, http://www.forbes.com/sites/

kenrapoza/2015/11/15/russia-getting-more-money-from-asia-as-sanctions-scare-europeans

Schuman, M. 2015, 'Thaw in China–Russia relations hasn't trickled down', *The New York Times*, 15 December, viewed 18 December 2015, http://www.nytimes.com/2015/12/16/business/international/thaw-in-china-russia-relations-hasnt-trickled-down.html

Shaver, J.M. 2013, 'Do we really need more entry mode studies?', *Journal of International Business Studies*, vol. 44, no. 1, pp. 23–7.

UNCTAD 1999, *World Investment Report (WIR) 1999: Foreign Direct Investment and the Challenge of Development* (overview), United Nations, New York & Geneva.

UNCTAD 2000, *World Investment Report (WIR) 2000: Cross-Border Mergers and Acquisitions and Development* (overview), United Nations, New York & Geneva.

UNCTAD 2001, *World Investment Report (WIR) 2001: Promoting Linkages* (overview), United Nations, New York & Geneva.

UNCTAD 2003, *World Investment Report (WIR) 2003: FDI Policies for Development* (overview), United Nations, New York & Geneva.

UNCTAD 2004, *World Investment Report (WIR) 2004: The Shift Towards Services* (overview), United Nations, New York & Geneva.

UNCTAD 2005, *World Investment Report (WIR) 2005: Transnational Corporations and the Internationalization of R&D* (overview), United Nations, New York & Geneva.

UNCTAD 2006a, *World Investment Report (WIR) 2006: FDI from Developing and Transition Economies* (overview), United Nations, New York & Geneva.

UNCTAD 2006b, *World Investment Report (WIR) 2006: FDI from Developing and Transition Economies* (full), United Nations, New York & Geneva.

UNCTAD 2007a, *World Investment Report (WIR) 2007: Transnational Corporations, Extractive Industries and Development* (overview), United Nations, New York & Geneva.

UNCTAD 2007b, *World Investment Report (WIR) 2007: Transnational Corporations, Extractive Industries and Development* (full), United Nations, New York & Geneva.

UNCTAD 2008, *World Investment Report (WIR) 2008: Transnational Corporations and the Infrastructure Challenge* (overview), United Nations, New York & Geneva.

UNCTAD 2009a, *World Investment Report (WIR) 2009: Transnational Corporations, Agricultural Production, and Development* (overview), United Nations, New York & Geneva.

UNCTAD 2009b, *World Investment Report (WIR) 2009: Transnational Corporations, Agricultural Production, and Development* (full), United Nations, New York & Geneva.

UNCTAD 2010, *World Investment Report (WIR) 2010: Investing in a Low-Carbon Economy* (overview), United Nations, New York & Geneva.

UNCTAD 2011a, *World Investment Report (WIR) 2011: Non-Equity Modes of International Production and Development* (overview), United Nations, New York & Geneva.

UNCTAD 2011b, *World Investment Report (WIR) 2011: Non-Equity Modes of International Production and Development* (full), United Nations, New York & Geneva.

UNCTAD 2012a, *World Investment Report (WIR) 2012: Towards a New Generation of Investment Policies* (overview), United Nations, New York & Geneva.

UNCTAD 2012b, *World Investment Report (WIR) 2012: Towards a New Generation of Investment Policies* (full), United Nations, New York & Geneva.

UNCTAD 2013a, *World Investment Report (WIR) 2013: Global Value Chains: Investment and Trade for Development* (overview), United Nations, New York & Geneva.

UNCTAD 2013b, *World Investment Report (WIR) 2013: Global Value Chains: Investment and Trade for Development* (full), United Nations, New York & Geneva.

UNCTAD 2014a, *World Investment Report (WIR) 2014: Investing in the SDGs: An Action Plan* (overview), United Nations, New York & Geneva.

UNCTAD 2014b, *World Investment Report (WIR) 2014: Investing in the SDGs: An Action Plan* (full), United Nations, New York & Geneva.

3 Maturing Strategies of Russian Multinational Companies

A Historical Perspective

Wladimir Andreff

Introduction

This chapter examines the relationships between Russia and outward foreign direct investment (OFDI), and consequently strategies of Russian multinational companies (MNCs) in a historical perspective. From an economic standpoint, Dunning's Investment Development Path (IDP) model[1] (Dunning 1981; Dunning & Narula 1998) fits with a long-term analysis of both OFDI and inward foreign direct investment (IFDI) and MNCs' evolving strategies, despite the evolution being disrupted over six decades by restrictive rules of a communist regime. Zubkovskaya and Michailova (2014) have used Dunning's Organization, Location and Internalization (OLI) paradigm, though not his IDP model, to trace Russian MNCs' development from the 1990s on, with a shorter historical perspective than here. Before 1914, Russia primarily hosted inward FDI, a flow which was definitely phased out in 1932. Together with OFDI by some Soviet state-owned enterprises in the post-World War II period, the long century from 1881–1987 roughly fits with the first stage of IDP model in Russia/the Soviet Union.

One of Gorbachev's important reforms consisted of reopening the USSR to IFDI. FDI inflows suddenly started growing fast, as expected in the second stage of the IDP model, and was then boosted by the economic transformation of former Soviet republics into transition economies; however, their attractiveness – including that of Russia – appeared to be lower than expected in the 1990s, until 1998 (Andreff 1999). Nevertheless, IFDI flowing into Russia accelerated substantially while some Russian companies became MNCs from scratch. Then Russian firms' OFDI recovered when the deepest transformational recession (Kornaï 1994) ended. Substantial OFDI development running alongside a boosted IFDI exactly exhibits what the second stage of IDP model is all about.

The next historical sequence covers the 2000–7 boom of Russian OFDI, growing faster than IFDI, a typical aspect of the third stage in the IDP model. In 2007, the Russian OFDI value came close to that of IFDI; Russia was on the brink of the fourth stage of the IDP model characterized by OFDI roughly balancing IFDI. However, the expansion of Russian MNCs was disturbed by global financial crisis (GFC) bursting out; though Russian OFDI instability increased, its pace remained the fastest growing in the world, in particular compared to other BRICs' OFDI. Finally, the policy of Russian Government (the Russian State) towards Russia's MNCs has been significant.

In the past two years, as a reaction to Western sanctions, the Russian Government has taken sanctions as well, but they did not target Russian OFDI. Now, Western sanctions, in weakening the Russian domestic economy, may affect some Russian firms, including their capacity to invest abroad. However, the consequences of sanctions are very much blurred as regard how much they actually weaken the Russian economy and its subsequent OFDI, since they are overwhelmed by the huge impact of a dramatic drop in world oil prices. To disentangle both effects would require robust econometric testing when enough data is available.

First Stage: From FDI in Czarist Russia to Soviet "Red Multinationals", 1881–1987

In its first stage of Dunning's IDP, from 1881–1914, Russia was an FDI net importer, being not developed enough an economy to significantly invest abroad. In 1913, FDI inflow amounted to ₽553 million – a third of total capital investment in the Russian industry this year – and was markedly larger than OFDI in the balance of payments. France (31 percent of total), England (24 percent), Germany (20 percent), Belgium (14 percent), and the USA (5 percent) were the primary sources of IFDI (Bovykin 1990). As to French FDI in Russia, Pereire brothers invested in Russian railways with the Grande Société des chemins de fer russe. Rothschild invested in Russian oil through the company Bnito in 1886. In 1889, the stock value of French FDI in Russia was 219 million French francs, primarily set in mining and metallurgy, then in petroleum, banking, pharmaceutical products, and textiles (Girault 1972). Twenty-nine Belgian tramway companies had also invested in Russia between 1880 and 1914; they were under the control of seven financial groups: Empain, Fraiteur, Société Générale Belge d'Entreprises Electriques, Compagnie Mutuelle des Tramways, Société Générale de Tramways et d'Application d'Electricité, Thys, Union des Tramways. Other Belgian companies had developed electricity production in Russia such as Compagnie Générale Auxiliaire d'Entreprises Électriques and Éclairage Électrique de Saint-Pétersbourg.

The other way round, Russian enterprises began to invest abroad in the last two decades of the nineteenth century (Bulatov 1998, 2001), in China, Mongolia, and Persia. From 1886–1914, Russia's cumulative capital exports amounted to about ₽2.3 billion. In 1914, the current value of Russian OFDI stock reached $3.8 billion, far below the British ($18.3 billion), the French ($8.7 billion), and the US ($7.1 billion) ones, but ahead of Canadian OFDI of $3.7 billion (Wilkins 1990). Before 1914, a few Russian banks had settled agencies in Western Europe while a number of foreign banks had shares in the capital of Russia's domestic banks. Linked to French purchases of Russian state bonds, the French banking industry had spread into Russia (Andreff & Pastré 1981): in 1914, Société Marseillaise de

Crédit Industriel et Commercial held a 21 percent share in the Bank of Azov on Don, Paribas a 37 percent share in the Bank of Siberia in Saint Petersburg, Crédit Mobilier a 57 percent share in the Bank for Private Trade in Saint Petersburg, and Société Générale a 65 percent share in the Russian-Asian Bank (Girault 1973). During the interwar period, the USSR withdrew OFDI, though not all of it. Trading subsidiaries were established in Afghanistan, Iran, Mongolia, and Turkey to sustain foreign trade. Some Soviet companies invested in the West such as the Russian Wood Agency in London (1923), the Anglo-Soviet Shipping in London (1923), Amtorg in New York (1924), Moscow Narodny Bank in London, and Eurobank in Paris. However, the IDP model was disrupted on the IFDI side. The USSR hosted IFDI by enacting the 1923 law on concessions; but the period open for negotiating concessions was closed in 1932 (Albin 1989). After that, practically, foreign investors were prohibited from taking stakes within the borders of the Soviet Union.

In the wake of Brezhnev's economic reforms, some foreign companies were able to circumvent the former prohibition creating an entry barrier against IFDI. However, as expected in IDP model, a much lower OFDI developed as well.[2] In 1979, 30 Soviet foreign trade organizations – for example, Almazjuvelirexport, Avtoexport, Energomashexport, Exportles, Sovfracht, Sovinflot, Soyuzchimexport, Soyuzneftexport, Stankoimporthad, Techmashexport, and Traktorexport – invested abroad in 105 Western-based companies (Hill 1986). The first British subsidiary of a Soviet company dates back to the 1950s; in 1980 there were nine subsidiaries with a £907 million turnover and £15 million fixed assets which accounted for less than 0.1 percent of total overseas investment in the UK. Twenty-nine Soviet companies held subsidiaries in West Germany in 1982 in the services industry as well as three banks. Some well-known Soviet investors abroad were: Nafta, owning an oil distribution network in the UK and the Netherlands; Scalda-Volga, holding a 95 percent share in an assembly line in Belgium; and Anglo-Soviet Shipping Company, being based in London. Soviet OFDI was involved in insurance companies in London and Vienna and in a steel plant and trade companies in France. In North America, Soviet enterprises held joint ventures such as Satra Corporation in New York. Foreign subsidiaries of Soviet companies were mostly settled in services; they were few and operated on a small scale in terms of turnover and investment. They also held 34 subsidiaries in developing countries[3] in 1982 (Zaleski 1986).

Various estimates of OFDI from Council for Mutual Economic Assistance (CMEA) countries were published (McMillan 1987), the last one for 1990 in a United Nations study (UNTCMD 1992): out of Eastern Europe's OFDI stock, amounting to $1,226 million, $699 million were held by Soviet enterprises in industrial subsidiaries and $13 million by Soviet banks. However, overall Soviet OFDI was lower than 0.1 percent of worldwide stock in 1990. Soviet enterprises had started investing again abroad in the 1960s and the 1970s: 23 subsidiaries in the pre-1965 period, 13 in 1965–9, 76 in 1970–9, and 49 in 1980–90 – 161 overall out of 863 foreign subsidiaries of all socialist MNCs. In 1990, they were located in 35 countries, mostly in Western developed countries: five in Spain, six in

Australia and the Netherlands, seven in Norway and Switzerland, eight in Sweden, nine in Austria and the USA, ten in Finland, 11 in Canada and Italy, 12 in Belgium, 15 in the UK, 16 in France, and 27 in Germany. Most of them were operating in trade and financial services, and only nine in manufacturing industry.

Soviet MNCs attracted considerable attention in the 1970s. The United Nations Centre on Transnational Corporations was entrusted to collect information on FDI from CMEA countries, although official CMEA doctrine was to deny the existence of anything that could look like a socialist MNC. The parent companies of so-called "red multinationals" (Hamilton 1986) were state-owned enterprises involved in foreign trade and business. They preferred investing in trade, banking, finance, and other services rather than in manufacturing industry. In developing countries, red multinationals were more concentrated in raw materials and power consumption. However, when located abroad, Soviet firms usually hired local manpower supervised by expatriate managers, and they often owned a majority stake or the whole stock of their foreign subsidiaries (Andreff 1982). Specific to red multinationals when compared to other MNCs was a slower growth of their OFDI during the 1980s. Centrally planned economies, such as the USSR, created systemic hindrances to OFDI by state-owned enterprises until Gorbachev's Perestroika. Other obstacles to OFDI from the Soviet Union were ideological motives of political leaders, foreign trade restrictions, hard currency shortages, the low quality of tradable goods, central authorities' interference in the firms' investment decision processes, and mandatory fulfillment of the domestic plan before any foreign expansion. Finally, being state-owned, they had no ownership advantages (or even had disadvantages) over local companies in host countries.

Banking cooperation between Soviet and Western banks has been active both ways since the late 1960s, with a rather strong presence of foreign banks in Moscow.[4] The other way round, the Moscow Narodny Bank had subsidiaries in London, Singapore, and Beirut. Several Soviet banks had subsidiaries in Western Europe: North European Commercial Bank (Eurobank) in Paris, Voskhod Commercial Bank in Zurich, East–West Bank in Frankfurt, Russian-Iranian Bank in Teheran, Danube Bank in Vienna, and East–West United Bank in Luxembourg.

With Gorbachev's Perestroika, a 1987 decree adopted by the Council of Ministers of the USSR reopened the country to joint ventures with foreign partners, allowing them to take a maximum 49 percent ownership share in a joint venture based in the Soviet Union. This was not attractive enough to Western MNCs (Andreff & Andreff 1997; Andreff 1999); a new decree authorized full ownership of foreign subsidiaries in 1989 while the legal framework for OFDI was settled by a decree "On development of economic activity by Soviet organizations abroad" (18 May 1989) followed by the 26 June 1991 law "On investment activity in the Russian Republic" (Mizobata 2014). This legislation was kept by the Russian Federation but, due to the breakup of the USSR, the new legal framework was hardly enforced in practice before 1992.

A Transition: From Recovery to Fast-Growing Russian Outward FDI, 1990–9

From December 1990–3, two opposite series of facts were witnessed, the first one being a collapse of former Soviet OFDI. Soviet MNCs declined markedly. OFDI from the newly independent Russian Federation was cut to practically nothing in 1991–3, according to UNCTAD data that exclude capital flight. Former Soviet MNCs had been facing constraints that dried up their liquidity and their capacity to finance their subsidiaries abroad; the latter became under-capitalized and could not survive without new capital transfers from parent companies between 1990 and 1993. Some Soviet MNCs went bankrupt, some were disbanded and taken over by a private investor, and others were disintegrated into a number of smaller privatized firms; all divested or closed down their foreign subsidiaries. They slowed down their OFDI dramatically and almost ceased investing abroad. Stabilization policy, a credit crunch, and a harsher shortage of hard currency compelled Russian firms to adjust so that no more money was available for investing abroad. Managers in public and privatized enterprises were accused of asset stripping to by-pass firms abroad, a behavior that raised popular resentment against OFDI. Legislation was much less favorable to OFDI than IFDI in the early years of transition due to fear of "crown jewels" sales to foreign investors. Public opinion was hostile to OFDI associated with capital flight. The expansion of Russian MNCs abroad has often been interpreted as capital runaway, if not an exodus, towards more friendly and stable, less risky foreign investment climates than Russian domestic market (Bulatov 1998; Kalotay 2004a; Vahtra & Liuhto 2004). Round-tripping FDI was exemplary of such strategy.

A second fact observed in 1991–3 is that various companies spontaneously emerged as newly being multinationals, the so-called "born multinationals" (Liuhto 2001). The breakup of the Soviet Union into new independent states generated per se a number of firms whose assets were divided among two or more successor states. An inherited division of labor across former Soviet republics organized by nation-wide state-owned enterprises gave rise to MNCs overnight. Many Soviet firms had their headquarters in Moscow and subsidiaries in other former Soviet republics so that the latter's transformation into autonomous successor states by the same token transformed these companies into multinationals overnight after the outset of transition. Of course, these firms continued producing and investing away from Russia in Commonwealth of Independent States (CIS) after 1991. Various research projects carried out by the Pan-European Institute (PEI) at the Turku School of Economics showed that most of former giant Soviet firms became major Russian MNCs. The number of their foreign subsidiaries jumped overnight to several thousands (Liuhto & Jumpponen 2001), instead of 161 in 1990 (Table 3.1).

Economic recovery took hold in Russia by end of the 1990s. Improved economic environment and resumed entrepreneurial confidence triggered an investment boom in the domestic economy, in particular after 1998, and fueled decisions to invest abroad. In fact, a new OFDI wave took place in newly privatized as well as in still state-run firms which resumed their foreign investment

Table 3.1 OFDI from Russia, 1994–2013 ($ millions and percent)

	1994	1997	1999	2000	2004	2007	2008	2009	2010	2011	2012	2013
OFDI stock ($ millions)	386	6,410	8,586	20,141	81,974	255,211	202,837	248,894	433,655	362,101	413,159	501,202
FDI outflow ($ millions)	101	3,184	2,144	3,177	9,601	45,916	55,663	43,281	52,616	66,851	48,822	94,907
FDI outflow/GFCF* (%)	0.2	3.8	6.5	7.3	9.2	16.8	15.0	16.1	16.0	19.0	11.1	21.1
OFDI stock/GDP (%)	0.1	1.5	2.3	7.8	14.0	19.8	12.0	20.4	28.4	19.5	20.5	24.1
OFDI/IFDI stock (%)	18.9	44.6	51.9	79.8	83.2	75.4	94.9	98.6	102.5	79.2	81.2	87.1

Source: UNCTAD 1992 onwards

Note: *GFCF = gross fixed capital formation

business, first in neighboring countries. In 1994, Russia's OFDI stock reached $386 million and jumped to $8.6 billion in 1999, being multiplied by 22 in five years; FDI outflow was multiplied by 21. OFDI grew faster from Russia than from any other CIS or Central Eastern European country (CEEC) over 1994–9, and even faster than OFDI from the three other BRICs: multiplied by 2.0 from Brazil, by 1.6 from mainland China, and by 2.1 from India. Since they were lagging behind, Russian MNCs benefited from a catching up advantage compared to other BRICs' MNCs (Andreff 2016). Econometric testing (Andreff 2003) showed that Russian OFDI had some characteristics of the IDP model's second stage in 1994–9, which was confirmed in a further study (Kalotay 2004b).

However, Russian MNCs still looked more or less like MNCs from developing countries and their major features differentiated them from MNCs based in developed countries. They were not all or not primarily in private ownership; still a significant number of them were state-owned. They had a modest size compared to Western and Japanese MNCs. The bulk of their OFDI was located in neighboring and border countries or in the same geographical region – that is, first and foremost in CIS and CEECs. The number of countries hosting their foreign subsidiaries was comparatively low. Each of these Russian MNCs had only settled a small number of subsidiaries abroad. They had primarily invested abroad in the primary sector and heavy manufacturing industries inherited from the Soviet planned economy while MNCs from developed countries were privileging the tertiary sector for their OFDI. However, some of these features were used as specific competitive advantages to challenge MNCs from developed countries through market-seeking OFDI targeted at new markets. Only few Russian MNCs were investing abroad with an efficiency-seeking objective – looking for lower unit labor cost abroad – since their domestic production costs translated in hard currency were comparatively low after the transition shock.

Due partly to the emergence of born multinationals and partly to the attractiveness of former business and trade area, the initial geographical orientation of Russian OFDI was geared towards the "near abroad" – that is, CIS member states. Studies confirmed a significant involvement of Russian FDI in Belarus, Kazakhstan, and Ukraine (Blyakha 2009; Yeremeyeva 2009). The next most important host countries were the CEECs as former CMEA members in which Russian companies still enjoyed familiarity with local business conditions. Then the EU incumbent members followed, which, in a short lapse of time, have taken their place among the significant host countries for Russian OFDI. Such geographical distribution was specific to the first decade of Russian companies' expansion abroad.

Maturing Strategies of Russian Multinationals: The 2000–7 Booming Expansion

Empirical evidence since 2000 leans towards the conclusion that Russia's OFDI has reached the third IDP stage with a high outward to inward FDI ratio, higher than 75 percent, and even higher than 100 percent – as in developed economies – in

2010; a fast-growing OFDI to GDP ratio from below 7 percent until 1999 to more than 20 percent since 2009; an even faster growing ratio between FDI outflow and domestic investment from nearly 7 percent in 1999 to 21 percent in 2013. Over 2000–7, Russian OFDI definitely was the fastest growing among BRICs' OFDI and in the world (Andreff 2016).

Industrial distribution of this first wave of front-running Russian OFDI was concentrated on few industries and inherited from the top pecking order of heavy industries in the former Soviet planned economy. Russian MNCs were over-represented in metallurgical industries and still are, with a 32.5 percent share for iron, steel, and non-ferrous metals in 2009 (Table 3.2), and then in traditional manufacturing industries like refining and chemicals. Cases in point are Gazprom (gas and oil), Itera, Lukoil, Novatek, Tatneft in the oil industry; Alrosa, Evraz, Koks, Mechel, Metalloinvest, MMK, NMLK, Norilsk Nickel, Novolipetsk Steel, Rusal, Severstal, and TMK in the metallurgical industry; Borodino, OMZ, and Renova in machinery; AvtoVAZ, GAZ, KAMAZ, and UAZ in the automobile industry; and in various industries, Investlesprom (paper-wood), Eurocement and LSR Group (building materials), Eurochem (chemical fertilizers), Acron (agro-chemistry), Gloria Jeans and Vostok-service (clothing), Kalina (perfumes, cosmetics), Alterwest, Russian Solod, Russian Wine Trust, SGI Group and WimmBillDann, (agro-food industry), and Inter RAO UES (electricity).

Data collection by the Central Bank of Russia distinguishes OFDI that flows straightforwardly to foreign countries from round-tripping OFDI – that is, investment by Russian enterprises and citizens in offshore companies, in particular in tax havens, with a view to reinvesting the same capital later on in Russia;[5] since

Table 3.2 Industrial Distribution of OFDI from Russia, 2009 ($ millions and percent)

Mining and quarrying, of which:	1,318	3.0%
Crude oil and gas extraction	306	0.7%
Metal ores extraction	894	2.0%
Manufacturing industries, of which:	18,732	42.0%
Food and beverages	118	0.3%
Refining petroleum products	3,263	7.3%
Printing and media recording	154	0.3%
Chemicals	81	0.2%
Iron and steel	7,467	16.7%
Non-ferrous metals	7,062	15.8%
Nuclear power equipment	57	0.1%
Transportation equipment	125	0.3%
Electricity, gas, steam, water supply	184	0.4%
Construction	4	0.0%
Services, of which:	24,578	55.0%
Trade and repairing, of which:	17,341	38.9%
Wholesale trade of fuels	14,078	31.5%
Transportation and communication	1,899	4.3%
Finance	3,277	7.3%
Real estate	2,055	4.6%
Total	44,628	100.0%

Source: Rosstat 2009

Table 3.3 Major Host Countries for Russian OFDI Stock, 2011 ($ millions and percent)

Host country	Russian FDI	%	Host country	Russian FDI	%
Cyprus	121,596	33.6	St Kitts & Nevis	2,681	0.7
Netherlands	57,291	15.8	Kazakstan	2,514	0.7
British Virgin Islands	46,137	12.8	Bermuda	2,497	0.7
Switzerland	12,679	3.5	France	1,989	0.5
Luxembourg	11,599	3.2	Ireland	1,849	0.5
United Kingdom	10,662	2.9	Isle of Man	1,546	0.4
United States	9,501	2.6	Serbia	1,496	0.4
Jersey	7,035	1.9	Lithuania	1,464	0.4
Germany	6,692	1.8	Czech Republic	1,463	0.4
Gibraltar	5,701	1.6	Italy	1,435	0.4
Bahamas	5,481	1.5	Armenia	1,417	0.4
Belarus	4,663	1.3	Sweden	1,414	0.4
St. Vincent and Grenadines	4,421	1.2	Vietnam	1,078	0.3
Ukraine	4,395	1.2	Montenegro	1,072	0.3
Austria	4,229	1.2	Finland	1,038	0.3
Turkey	3,654	1.0	India	982	0.3
Spain	3,535	1.0	Uzbekistan	947	0.3
Bulgaria	2,748	0.8	Canada	850	0.2

Source: Central Bank of Russia 2016

Russian OFDI located in tax havens still represents a significant share among host countries (Table 3.3), round-tripping has not ceased yet.[6] The Bahamas, Bermuda, the British Virgin Islands, Cyprus, Gibraltar, the Isle of Man, Jersey, Luxembourg, Saint Kitts and Nevis, and Saint Vincent, and the Grenadines are still highly ranked among the major host countries for Russian OFDI; together they attracted about 58 percent of overall OFDI in 2011. Most of them are well known for staging circular investment.

In recent years, more non-European countries have appeared among the major host areas of Russian MNCs, namely Canada, India, the United Arab Emirates, and the USA. Since 2005, Russian MNCs have made noticeable acquisitions in developing countries, focusing on Africa and Asia. Russian MNCs are somewhat losing their specificity as companies from emerging countries supposed to achieve most of their OFDI on an "intra-regional" base in countries located in the same region of the world as their home country.[7] Thus, some Russian MNCs are on the brink of a global strategy in which foreign subsidiaries are located anywhere in the world where their profitability is higher. The only exception so far is Latin America – with none of the first 30 host countries of Russian OFDI – due to its remote location from Russia and institutional barriers such as absent bilateral non-double taxation and investment treaties with Russia.

Apart from tax havens, the major host countries of Russian MNCs now exhibit one of the three following characteristics: (1) they belong to major export markets for Russian products (Austria, France, Germany, Spain, Turkey, and the UK); (2) they share a common culture and use Russian as business language in the CIS;[8] and (3) a few markets are located at a remote trade distance from Russia (Canada and the USA).

Another new trend is that Russian OFDI started booming in the 2000s in a more modernized part of the manufacturing industry, transportation and communication services (telecommunications, finance, and related media recording), with the Sistema group, which owns MTS in telephone production and Sitronics in telecommunications equipment; RTI Systems in aerospace and missiles production; the Alfa Group, Altimo, Megafon and Vimpelcom in telecommunications; Korolev Rocket and Space Corporation Energia (aeronautics); and NPO Mashinostroyenia (military equipment). Services have become the first sector of Russian OFDI expansion (a 55 percent share in 2009), in contrast with services underdevelopment under former central planning. Russian insurance and financial companies and banks such as Alfa-bank, Bank of Moscow, Gazprombank, Sberbank, and VTB have developed and internationalized. Such MNCs exemplify a recent industrial diversification of Russian OFDI which spreads over high tech industries and services resulting from the modernization of some segments in the Russian manufacturing industry which became more deeply rooted after 1999.

A rather frequent strategy of Russian MNCs can be stylized as market-seeking OFDI, relaying earlier export. This strategy pertains to traditional markets such as the CIS; it is also the rationale for Russian OFDI in Western markets, where Russian firms face tough competition and are strongly challenged when entering. Those Russian MNCs which invest abroad in mining, oil, and gas industries have adopted both market-seeking and resource-seeking approaches and attempted to take over their most needed suppliers abroad by means of trans-border mergers and acquisitions (M&As). Russian OFDI in the CIS is basically resource-seeking when geared towards oil, gas, and mining. The same strategy applies to the fairly recent Russian OFDI in Africa, though it is mitigated here with a motive of accessing new consumer markets. Russian MNCs have not yet adopted an efficiency-seeking strategy, although they could have envisaged it in lower unit labor cost CIS and developing countries. Finally, Russian companies have conducted an asset-seeking strategy based on M&As, with a view to acquiring Western technology and R&D intensive units.

Since 1997 the share of the primary sector has been steady at around 60 percent of all trans-border M&A deals while the share of the manufacturing industry has been below 25 percent (Table 3.4). The proportion of M&As in Europe (CEECs included) peaked in 1997–2000, whereas that in the CIS climaxed in 2001–4. The first asset acquisitions appeared in developing countries in 2005 and the share of non-European (primarily North American) developed countries is around 20–25 percent of total M&A deals. The financial crisis impacted M&As undertaken by Russian MNCs downwards. While the overall number of trans-border M&A deals was 114 in 2007 and 119 in 2008, it fell to 102 in 2009 and 70 in 2010 (Filippov 2011).

One major objective for trans-border M&As by Russian MNCs is to take over European and North American firms. From 2005–10, M&As have primarily targeted entry in high tech industries linked to natural resources in Canada, Italy, South Africa, Switzerland, and the USA. Trans-border M&As are less frequent in the near abroad, whose firms are of smaller size and less attractive in terms of high

Table 3.4 Trans-border Mergers and Acquisitions Achieved by Russian Companies, Industrial and Geographical Distribution, 1992–2008 ($ millions and percent)

Industry	1992–6	1997–2000	2001–4	2005–8
Total	511 (100.0)	1,700 (100.0)	5,498 (100.0)	55,850 (100.0)
Primary sector	45 (8.8)	1,098 (64.6)	2,980 (54.2)	33,485 (60.0)
Manufacturing industry	451 (88.3)	146 (8.6)	661 (12.0)	13,430 (24.0)
Services	15 (2.9)	456 (26.8)	1,857 (33.8)	8,935 (16.0)
Region				
CIS countries	.	61 (3.6)	1,233 (22.4)	9,039 (16.2)
Europe	311 (60.9)	1,237 (72.8)	3,069 (55.8)	29,888 (53.5)
Other developed countries	200 (39.1)	402 (23.6)	1,196 (21.8)	13,712 (24.6)
Developing countries	.	.	.	3,210 (5.7)

Source: Adapted from Vahtra 2010

tech assets. A few exceptions are the VimpelCom-Kyivstar, Gazprom-Beltransgaz, and Evraz-SukhayaBalka deals. With the lasting crisis some M&As occurred such as Nezavisimaya Transportnaya acquiring Pervaya Gruzovaya in 2011, Tele 2 Russia Holding taking over VTB, and Rosneft merging TNK-BP in 2013.

As regard overall Russian OFDI, investing directly in R&D is significant sign of a step forward towards a more global strategy. For instance, Sistema entered the stock equity of an Indian company in the mobile telecommunications industry in 2008 and then attempted to acquire a German firm involved in microelectronics, Infineon, in 2009. Similarly, Sberbank attempted (but failed) to participate into the purchase of Opel, a General Motors subsidiary, during the bankruptcy proceeding of this company, with a view to capturing its high technology. In the iron and steel industry, Evraz, Severstal, and Rusal have invested a great deal of money in technological development in their foreign subsidiaries whereas, in the oil industry, Lukoil and TNK-BP have acquired foreign firms with a view to upgrading their own technological level. This spread of trans-border M&As by Russian MNCs in high tech industries was backed and supported by the highest Russian authorities, even up to then-President Medvedev (Filippov 2010).

A few Russian MNCs seem to have actually turned to a global strategy recently, not only as far as their geographical orientation is concerned, but also from all perspectives (Andreff 1999). One of them consists in integrating all their value chain on a world scale; the different sequences of the production and trade process (input purchase, supply, production, products delivery, sales, and after-sale services) are allocated in various countries depending on profitability criteria. In recent years, this tendency was observed with some Russian MNCs. With a view to global value chain integration, the latter have often bought or merged assets located abroad, which is a second dimension of global strategy. The third one is global scope for asset-seeking OFDI, through M&As, into technological assets required for R&D and it often makes for a decisive step forward on the path to globalizing an MNC's strategy; this is where some Russian MNCs are today. The fourth dimension of global strategies lies in strategic alliances. Russian MNCs have formed strategic alliances with foreign partners – often other MNCs – since 2000: on average 40 per year with a peak of 89 in 2007. This among the most representative evidence of evolving towards a global strategy and a sign of maturing strategies in some Russian MNCs. Still a few Russian MNCs are on the brink of switching to the above-defined genuine global strategy; some cases in point are Renova, TMK, and, to some extent, Gazprom, Lukoil, and NLMK.

Russian OFDI Muddling through the Global Financial Crisis since 2008

The financial crisis has triggered a collapse of world FDI outflows, first of all from developed countries; but it has slowed down the growth of OFDI stock less worldwide, according to UNCTAD data. As against this worldwide trend, Russian OFDI was harshly affected by the crisis, with a 21 percent cut in its stock value in 2008, due to both divestments from abroad and foreign asset deprecia-tion. Moreover, the corporate debt of large Russian firms rose (up to $110 billion in 2009). MNCs like Rusal, Norilsk Nickel, TMK, and Sistema were among the most indebted Russian companies. However, Russian OFDI stock grew again by 23 percent in 2009 and 74 percent in 2010, fueled by new investments abroad, foreign asset appreciation and likely capital flight; it lost 17 percent in 2011 and recovered in 2012 (+14 percent) and 2013 (+21 percent). Ruble depreciation since 2014 has been bad news for further OFDI expansion. These figures exhibit that crisis entailed a much higher instability in OFDI from Russia, namely higher than with other BRICs' OFDI (Andreff 2016).

Nevertheless the overall Russian OFDI growth trend has not been compro-mised by its hectic evolution in recent years; it was twice as large in 2013 than 2007 despite the crisis impact. The crisis shock has been dramatic, not radical. Russian MNCs were born in such an unstable domestic business and institutional environment, surrounded by transformational recession, then they went through the 1998 Russian financial crisis. From these sequences they have learned a lot about how adapt to financial crash and credit crunch. This underlies their resil-ience to adverse economic effects in GFC, but due to its instability Russian OFDI took one step backward compared to other BRICs' OFDI. Its OFDI stock made India the world's 34th largest outward investor in 2007 whereas Brazil had reached the 19th rank the same year as against Russia the 12th, and mainland China the 23rd. In 2013, Brazil was the 19th most important source of OFDI worldwide and India the 31st, as against Russia being the 16th and China the 12th. During the crisis, all the BRICs have climbed this ranking based on UNCTAD data, except Russia.

A more negative impact of the crisis on OFDI is that a number of MNCs have divested from abroad. Selling the assets of foreign subsidiaries can help finance a parent company in financial distress. An MNC can always take the crisis as an excuse for cutting down some less profitable activities located abroad. This obvi-ously happened to Russian MNCs' foreign subsidiaries (Table 3.5), whose foreign direct divestment was primarily concentrated in the EU and CIS

Table 3.5 Significant Divestment Deals by Russian Companies, 2008–10

Vendor	Foreign assets located in:	Industry	Acquiring firm based in:
2008			
Arbat Prestizh	Ukraine	Perfumes, cosmetics	Ukraine
N Trans	Estonia	Seaport operator	Netherlands
Lukoil	Poland	Gas stations	Poland
Gazprom Media	Moldova	Media services	USA
Nakhodka Re	Ukraine	Reinsurance services	USA
2009			
TMK	USA	Metallurgy	USA
Atomredmetzoloto	Kazakhstan	Uranium mining	Netherlands
Rolf GK	Netherlands	Car dealer	Japan
Bryansk Machine Building	Ukraine	Machine building	Ukraine
AvtoVAZ	Finland	Car manufacturing	United Kingdom
Managing company Estar	Ukraine	Steel manufacturing	Ukraine
Gidromashservis	Ukraine	Electric engine manuf.	Ukraine
Antanta PIO Global Invt. Group	Ukraine	Holding company	Ukraine
Basic Element	Austria	Holding company	Austria
Nutritek	Estonia	Food	Estonia
Veritas SPA	Italy	Services	Italy
Millhouse LLC	Virgin Islands	Asset management	Virgin Islands
2010			
Farmstandart	Latvia	Pharmaceuticals	Latvia
Gazprom	Cayman Islands	Oil, gas	Ireland
Baltika	Kazakhstan	Beer brewery	Kazakhstan
Petrovsky Bank	Bosnia Herzegovina	Banking	Bosnia Herzegovina
Ingosstakh	Austria	Insurance services	Belgium
Russian Alcohol Group	Georgia	Alcohol production	Georgia
Mirax Group	Turkey	Construction services	Turkey
Kavitatsionnye Tekhnologii	Ukraine	Railway wagons	Ukraine

Source: Adapted from Filippov 2011

countries, Ukraine in particular. Russian divestment also occurred in tax havens. Two examples are Millhouse, a Russian-owned asset management fund (Roman Abramovich's property), which divested from the company Primerod International Ltd, located in the British Virgin Islands, in 2009, and Gazprom, which sold its holding ZGG Cayman Holding in the Cayman Islands in 2010.

Russia's Multinationals and Russian State Policy

Beyond a nice typology of Russian MNCs that Liuhto and Vahtra (2007) put forward by crossing the level of a firm's transparency and existing state control over the company,[9] a last focus must be put on the role of the Russian Government interfering in strategies of Russian MNCs. Before the current crisis of the late 2000s, Russian MNCs were described as a form of soft power which had replaced the military power of the Russian regime, in particular throughout the near abroad. Under Yeltsin, the government was proactive through privatization in creating privately owned companies in monopoly situations,[10] which swiftly transformed into MNCs though not really promoting OFDI. Under Putin, the Russian Government has shifted its objectives towards promoting OFDI, mostly in the service of national strategic goals. Russia started conducting a national champions' policy providing support to companies investing abroad in key industries.

Since 2000, the government has reinforced its role in the economy due to swifter expansion of state-owned enterprises and partial renationalization in some industries. Both state participation in the stock equity of some Russian MNCs and their internationalization strategy have increasingly been influenced by Russia's foreign policy. In 2007, seven state corporations were launched, the CEOs of which were appointed directly by the president of the Russian Federation. These corporations are in charge of industrial restructuring through gathering activities into industrial trusts under public control in aeronautics, shipbuilding, the nuclear energy, new technologies, and banking. They started internationalizing by acquiring technological assets abroad while the pressure of presidential administration on them accentuated. Their strategies serve both domestic industrial policy and Russia's foreign policy. In 2008, when Dmitry Medvedev, a former Gazprom CEO, was elected President of the Russian Federation, and Igor Sechin, a former Rosneft CEO, was appointed Deputy Prime Minister, the relationships between the government and its state-owned MNCs tightened a lot. The dividing line between government and business became more blurred. In a meeting with Russian CEOs from manufacturing industry in 2007, Putin enjoined them to invest more abroad. Thus Russian MNCs, whether privately or state owned, are incited by the state to go on internationalizing. In 2008, then-President Medvedev appealed Russian companies to "copy China" by expanding overseas and undertaking a global spread of their foreign assets, though the government had not yet developed a consistent policy frame for assisting Russian MNCs' global expansion like in China.

The hydrocarbons industry and its MNCs have, especially, been a tool to serve Russia's international relationships, including through controlling the network of oil and gas pipes. Indeed, many Russian MNCs achieve their OFDI for the sake of national economic interest as intended by the highest governmental authorities. This raises questions about their internationalization as a tool for Russia regaining political hegemony (Driga & Dura 2013). Russian state-owned MNCs are often heavily influenced by or incited to stick to major objectives of Russia's foreign policy, though less than Chinese MNCs. Expansionist objectives of Russian MNCs are not autonomous *vis-à-vis* government willingness to be a global player in the world economy. Russian political influence is a push factor of Russian investment expansion – for instance, in Central Asia; the Russian Government tries to help Russian MNCs in Asia and Africa as well.[11] The strongest concerns about possible political interference in Russian MNCs and the quality of their corporate governance have been expressed in the Czech Republic, Hungary, Poland, and Spain.

Conclusion

Reading the history of Russia's OFDI through the lens of the IDP model is fruitful. However, this background economic rationale has been disturbed by several exogenous shocks for the Russian economy. The first and major one was the adoption of communist restrictive rules against OFDI for 70 years. The next one was the post-communist transition which, after some time, boosted Russian companies' investment abroad. Throughout this process, strategies of Russian MNCs have been maturing. The effects of a third shock – the 2008 GFC and its aftermath – are still lasting and hindering Russia's OFDI or at least destabilizing it into an uneven growth path.

As regard the future, WTO accession of the Russian Federation in August 2012 should have triggered a new impetus for both OFDI from Russia and more transparent strategies in Russian MNCs. But hindrances and destabilizing factors have been exacerbated in 2014–15: the ongoing ruble depreciation should trigger OFDI downwards, but the fall might be partly compensated by capital flight OFDI (Kalotay 2015). Sanctions and embargoes – a fourth exogenous shock – have fueled domestic recession and severed capital flight in recent months; a similar aftermath of sanctions and embargoes might well affect OFDI in turn. This remains to be checked with forthcoming statistics without forgetting that, in the long run, Russian OFDI should align again on its IDP expansion path.

Notes

1 In the first stage of its economic development, a country hosts very few FDI and does not invest at all abroad. In the second stage, it becomes attractive to IFDI and achieves its very first OFDI, being a net FDI importer. In the third stage, due to its new technological competences and low unit labour cost, the country attracts very significant IFDI and its MNCs start to substantially invest abroad even though the country still remains net FDI importer. In the fourth stage, a country is assumed to be a developed one and invests more outwards than it is invested by IFDI; its FDI balance becomes positive. In the fifth and last stage, the now post-industrial country roughly reaches a balance between its inward and outward FDI.

2 An accepted estimate of OFDI by all CMEA countries (Zaleski 1983) was $724 million in 1978, excluding OFDI in banking, assessed to be another $325 million. The overall amount was slightly over $1 billion, i.e. 0.3 percent of the worldwide OFDI stock in 1978 (Andreff 1987).

3 Located in Argentina, Cameroon, Ethiopia, India, Iran, Lebanon, Libya, Mexico, Morocco, Nigeria, Peru, and Singapore.

4 Crédit Lyonnais was the first bank to open a subsidiary in the Soviet Union and Chase Manhattan Bank the first US bank to do so.

5 This so-called circular investment, transferred through FDI in order to come back to Russia is analyzed in detail by Pelto, Vahtra and Liuhto (2003).

6 Since the 2008-onward crisis round-tripping and trans-shipping FDI received in offshore economies has accelerated again to reach up to two-thirds of Russian OFDI. Its final destination is the CIS, the CEECs, and, primarily, the Russian Federation herself.

7 However, the same evolution of investing far beyond an intra-regional base, in developed countries, is witnessed with Chinese and Indian MNCs as well, which is

not without raising new challenges to the standard international trade and investment theory that are tackled in Andreff and Balcet (2013).

8 In 2014, Russian OFDI stock still was respectively $9.9 billion in Ukraine, $9.1 billion in Kazakhstan, $8.3 billion in Belarus, $3.8 billion in Uzbekistan, $3.1 billion in Armenia, $1.4 billion in Azerbaijan, $1.0 billion in Tajikistan, $0.7 billion in Kyrgyzstan, $0.5 billion in Georgia, and $0.4 billion in Moldova (EDB 2015).

9 Thus, four types of Russian MNCs come out, respectively coined "Non-Transparent Patriots" for companies under tight state control, most often in strategic industries linked to natural resources; "Transparent Patriots" refer to companies which disclose their financial accounts though they are in partial or overall state ownership; "Non-Transparent Independents" are those companies that are not (or only slightly) controlled by the state but whose corporate governance misses transparency; "Transparent Independents" are actually privately owned and their strategies are not clearly influenced by the state or any political considerations.

10 Resulting in a number of oligarchs being at the head of significant Russian MNCs (Kuznetsov 2007).

11 There is a more extensive discussion of the relationship between Russian MNCs and their home government in Panibratov (2012).

Bibliography

Albin, A.J. 1989, 'Joint venture law in the Soviet Union: the 1920s and the 1980s', *Northwestern Journal of International Law & Business*, vol. 9, no. 3, pp. 633–57.

Andreff, M. & Andreff, W. 1997, 'Foreign direct investment in Russia and CIS countries: employment and attractiveness', *Economic Systems*, vol. 21, no. 4, pp. 354–9.

Andreff, W. 1982, *Les multinationales hors la crise*, Le Sycomore, Paris.

Andreff, W. 1987, *Les multinationales*, La Découverte, Paris.

Andreff, W. 1999, 'The global strategy of multinational corporations and their assessment of Eastern European and CIS countries', in V. Tikhomirov (ed.), *Anatomy of the 1998 Russian Crisis*, Contemporary Europe Research Centre, University of Melbourne, Melbourne.

Andreff, W. 2003, 'The newly emerging TNCs from economies in transition: a comparison with Third World outward FDI', *Transnational Corporations*, vol. 12, no. 2, pp. 73–118.

Andreff, W. 2016, 'Outward foreign direct investment from BRICs countries: comparing strategies of Brazilian, Russian, Indian and Chinese multinational companies', *European Journal of Comparative Economics*, vol. 12, no. 2, pp. 79–131.

Andreff, W. & Balcet, G. 2013, 'Emerging multinational companies investing in developed countries: at odds with HOS?', *European Journal of Comparative Economics*, vol. 10, no. 1, pp. 3–26.

Andreff, W. & Pastré, O. 1981, 'La genèse des banques multinationales et l'expansion du capital financier international', in C-A. Michalet (ed.), *Internationalisation des banques et des groupes financiers*, Editions du CNRS, Paris.

Blyakha, N. 2009, *Russian Foreign Direct Investment in Ukraine*, Pan-European Institute, University of Turku, Turku.

Bovykin, V.I. 1990, 'Les emprunts extérieurs russes', *Revue d'Economie Financière*, vol. 14, pp. 81–92.

Bulatov, A.S. 1998, 'Russian direct investment abroad: main motivations in the post-Soviet period', *Transnational Corporations*, vol. 7, no. 1, pp. 69–82.

Bulatov, A.S. 2001, 'Russian direct investment abroad: history, motives, finance, control and planning', *Economics of Planning*, vol. 34, no. 3, pp. 179–94.

Central Bank of Russia 2016, *Russian Federation: Outward Foreign Direct Investment of Nonbanking Corporations, by Country*, viewed 14 February 2016, http://www.cbr.ru/eng/statistics/?PrtId=svs

Driga, I. & Dura, C. 2013, 'Restoring the economic power of Russia through OFDI expansion', *Economia Seria Management*, vol. 16, no. 2, pp. 227–41.

Dunning, J.H. 1981, 'Explaining the international direct investment position of countries: towards a dynamic or development approach', *WeltwirtschaftlichesArchiv*, vol. 119, pp. 30–64.

Dunning, J.H. & Narula, R. 1998, 'The investment development path revisited: some emerging issues', in J.H. Dunning & R. Narula (eds.), *Foreign Direct Investment and Governments: Catalysts for Economic Restructuring*, Routledge, London.

EDB 2015, *Monitoring of Mutual Investments in the CIS 2015*, Eurasian Development Bank, Centre for Integration Studies, report 32, Saint Petersburg.

Filippov, S. 2010, 'Russian companies: the rise of new multinationals', *International Journal of Emerging Markets*, vol. 5, no. 3/4, pp. 307–32.

Filippov, S. 2011, *Russia's Emerging Multinational Companies Amidst the Global Economic Crisis*, UNU-MERIT Working Paper Series, 2011-003, United Nations University, Maastricht.

Girault, R. 1972, 'Conjoncture et investissement international. Les placements français en Russie: un exemple à la fin du XIXe siècle', *Revue Economique*, vol. 23, no. 5, pp. 889–918.

Girault, R. 1973, *Emprunts russes et investissements français en Russie, 1887–1914*, Armand Colin, Paris.

Hamilton, G. (ed.) 1986, *Red Multinationals or Red Herrings? The Activities of Enterprises from Socialist Countries in the West*, Frances Pinter, London.

Hill, M. 1986, 'Soviet and Eastern European company activity in the United Kingdom and Ireland', in G. Hamilton (ed.), *Red Multinationals or Red Herrings? The Activities of Enterprises from Socialist Countries in the West*, Frances Pinter, London.

Kalotay, K. 2004a, 'Will foreign direct investment take off in the Russian Federation?', *Journal of World Investment & Trade*, vol. 5, no. 1, pp. 119–38.

Kalotay, K. 2004b, 'Outward FDI from Central and Eastern European countries', *Economics of Planning*, vol. 37, no. 2, pp. 141–72.

Kalotay, K. 2015, 'The impact of the new ruble crisis on Russian FDI', *1st World Congress of Comparative Economics*, 25–27 June, Rome.

Kornaï, J. 1994, 'Transformational recession: the main causes', *Journal of Comparative Economics*, vol. 19, no. 1, pp. 39–63.

Kuznetsov, A.V. 2007, *Prospects of Various Types of Russian Transnational Corporations*, Pan-European Institute, University of Turku, Turku.

Liuhto, K. 2001, *Born International: The Case of the Latvian Shipping Company*, Lappeenranta University of Technology, Lappeenranta.

Liuhto, K. & Jumpponen, J. 2001, 'Russian direct investment abroad: where does Russian business expansion abroad lead?', in K. Liuhto (ed.), *Ten Years of Economic Transformation*, vol. II, Lappeenranta University of Technology, Lappeenranta.

Liuhto, K. & Vahtra, P. 2007, 'Foreign operations of Russia's largest industrial corporations: building a typology', *Transnational Corporations*, vol. 16, no. 1, pp. 117–44.

McMillan, C.H. 1987, *Multinationals from the Second World*, Macmillan, London.

Mizobata, S. 2014, *Emerging Multinationals in Russia*, Kyoto Institute of Economic Research, discussion paper no. 899, Kyoto University, Kyoto.

Panibratov, A. 2012, *Russian Multinationals: From Regional Supremacy to Global Lead*, Routledge, London.

Pelto, E., Vahtra, P. & Liuhto, K. 2003, *Cyp-Rus Investment Flows to Central and Eastern Europe: Russia's Direct and Indirect Investments via Cyprus to CEE*, Pan-European Institute, University of Turku, Turku.

Rosstat 2009, *Ob inostrannyh investitsijah v Rossii v 2009 godu*, viewed 14 February 2016, http://www.gks.ru

UNCTAD 1992 onwards, *World Investment Report (WIR) 1992: Transnational Corporations as Engines of Growth*, United Nations, New York & Geneva.

UNTCMD 1992, United Nations, Transnational Corporations and Management Division, *The East–West Business Directory 1991/1992*, United Nations, Transnational Corporations and Management Division, New York: United Nations, Sales No. E.92.II.A.20.

Vahtra, P. 2005, *Russian Investments in the CIS: Scope, Motivations and Leverage*, Pan-European Institute, University of Turku, Turku.

Vahtra, P. 2010, *A Dawn for Outward R&D Investments from Russia?*, Pan-European Institute, University of Turku, Turku.

Vahtra, P. & Liuhto, K. 2004, *Expansion or Exodus? Foreign Operations of Russia's Largest Corporations*, Pan-European Institute, University of Turku, Turku.

Wilkins, M. 1990, 'Investissement étranger et financement de la croissance américaine (XIXe siècle–début du XXe)', *Revue d'Economie Financière*, vol. 14, no. 2, pp. 67–79.

Yeremeyeva, I. 2009, *Russian Investments in Belarus*, Pan-European Institute, University of Turku, Turku.

Zaleski, E. 1983, 'Les multinationales des pays de l'Est', in A. Cotta & M. Ghertman (eds.), *Les multinationales en mutation*, Presses Universitaires de France, Paris.

Zaleski, E. 1986, 'Socialist multinationals in developing countries', in G. Hamilton (ed.), *Red Multinationals or Red Herrings? The Activities of Enterprises from Socialist Countries in the West*, Frances Pinter, London.

Zubkovskaya, A. & Michailova, S. 2014, 'The development of Russian multinational enterprises from the 1990s to the present', *Organizations and Markets in Emerging Economies*, vol. 5, no. 2(10), pp. 59–78.

4 Investment Relations between Russia and the USA

Alexey Kuznetsov

Background of Investment Relations between Russia and the USA

Russia's economic relations with the USA are highly politicized. Although political and other non-economic factors are important for Russia's trade and investment ties with other countries, too, the political dialogue with the USA is crucial. The politicization of the bilateral economic relations has been a typical problem throughout all periods of the USSR/Russia–USA relationship, including the more dangerous episodes of the Cold War or Putin's presidency, Gorbachev's Perestroika, or the liberal reforms of Yeltsin's presidency. Still, the USA and Russia have developed ways to overcome excessive political influence for the sake of pure economic interests.

Several periods in Russia–USA investment relations can be distinguished. First, positive changes in the investment relations between the USSR and the USA became apparent at the end of the 1980s. A partial liberalization of the Soviet economy was connected with unsuccessful attempts at technological modernization. Regardless, attracting inward FDI via joint ventures (JVs) was one of the government's liberalization/modernization instruments. Companies from the USA as well as Western Europe became the main participants in these JVs as they tried to realize their market-seeking motives (Zimenkov 1999).

The second period of intensifying investment relations was connected with post-Soviet reforms in Russia, with many US companies beginning to expand their investments in Russia during the 1990s. As an example of this expansion, Philip Morris made its first investment in Russia in 1992, though it already had started to sell licenses to Soviet cigarette factories in 1977. Another large American investor, PepsiCo, followed the same path. It conquered the Russian market during the Soviet period with exports and franchising and subsequently established its own plant in Russia in 1997. Thereafter, it invested several billion US dollars in new plants and acquisitions.

The legal foundations of Russia–USA economic relations were laid during the second period. For example, the 1990 bilateral agreement on trade relations came into force in Russia in 1992. Importantly for our purposes, despite the agreement, there was continued discrimination against some Russian goods such as metals during the 1990s. This discrimination forced some Russian steel companies to undertake market-seeking FDI in the USA at the beginning of the 2000s. In 1992, the two countries concluded the Russia–USA double taxation treaty and a bilateral investment agreement. However, the latter deals only with the guarantees of US governmental agencies (Soglasheniye... 1992), and therefore a full-fledged bilateral investment treaty between Russia and the USA is still lacking, which is a major problem for private Russian investors who cannot use international instruments of the Multilateral Investment Guarantee Agency (MIGA) on US territory. As a consequence, Russian companies do not receive any official guarantees against the confiscation of their US assets for political reasons.

The post-transformation recovery of the Russian economy in the beginning of the 2000s stimulated the dawn of the third period of investment relations. These relations assumed a more mutual character because Russian transnational companies (TNCs) undertook significant FDI in North America. Despite this FDI expansion, there was no progress during the 2000s on the legislative front as far as regulating Russia–USA FDI was concerned, a contrast to positive legislative developments with the EU and some emerging economies.

The investment motives of Russian companies in the third period were mainly market-seeking, including the goal of overcoming US trade protectionism in the steel industry. Simultaneously, Russia's modest energy trade with the USA led Russian oil and gas companies to invest, albeit in insignificant amounts, in the USA. In contrast, US companies developed their FDI operations in Russia, though they were not as important players in the Russian economy as their European counterparts. Modest FDI flow from the USA to Russia also can link to moderate trade relations – that is, the USA constitutes just 4 percent of Russian foreign trade turnover. Regardless, there are some US companies that have established import-substituting production in Russia, the most well-known US company being the Ford plant which began its car production near Saint Petersburg in 2002. As in the previous period, market-seeking and resource-seeking motives dominated the drivers of US corporations in Russia (PBN Company 2005, 2006; Ketchum 2012).

The global economic crisis of 2007–9 and its fallout slowed down large Russian companies' investment in the USA. Long before the Ukrainian crisis, several Russian steel companies and even some oil and gas corporations started to suffer from a lack financial resources to expand their overseas activities. As for a "second echelon" of the Russian TNCs, they are not as active in North America as in the EU or in the post-Soviet space, because the "neighborhood effect", including cultural proximity, has a weak role. Furthermore, according to the Uppsala school, Russian firms, with a few exceptions such as those in the information technology sector, usually embrace gradual internationalization. The USA, though, is not a typical place for Russian businesses to take their initial overseas investment expansion steps (Johanson & Vahlne 1977; Kuznetsov 2009).

In addition, Russia and the USA have different legal systems; Russia has a codified legal system whereas a case law system prevails in the USA. Moreover, these two countries have different standards of accounting. When Russian companies use international accounting standards, they prefer International Financial Reporting Standards (IFRS) instead of the US Generally Accepted Accounting Principles (GAAP). However, there is one positive cultural factor in the Russia–USA FDI relations – that is, English is the most popular foreign language in Russia.

A new period in the Russia–USA investment relations began approximately in 2009–10. It represented the stagnation of mutual FDI flows. The stagnation resulted from economic considerations of investors and fundamental political processes.

In 2010–15, US corporate investment in Russia remained at a low level due to problems in realizing all four main types of FDI motives described by Dunning (2000). Despite problems, however, the size of the Russian market continues to attract US businesses, as indicated by much firm-level evidence. For instance, Procter & Gamble deems its Russian subsidiary one of the most dynamic among the company's global businesses. Similarly, Philip Morris views Russia as the second largest tobacco market after China. Russia's current macroeconomic situation, however, is a deterrent to market-seeking FDI. For example, Ford suffers from problems after years of a booming Russian automobile market. Furthermore, US investors with resource-seeking or strategic asset-seeking motives frequently encounter barriers in Russia where national security concerns have become emphasized once again. The most evident cases with security concerns link to the oil and gas industry, where large foreign TNCs have begun to lose control over their Russian units. As for efficiency-seeking FDI motives, Russia is at a competitive disadvantage against emerging markets, which have lower labor costs.

Political tensions harm bilateral Russia–USA FDI flows. The Ministry of Foreign Affairs of the Russian Federation describes the current situation as a "difficult period" because Russia's estimates related to the Ukrainian crisis vary considerably from those of the USA. However, the first serious frictions – for example, the conflict around Schneerson Library and the "Magnitsky Act" – already appeared in 2010–12 (Ministry of Foreign Affairs of the Russian Federation 2015). The current "sanctions war" between the USA and Russia is only an episode in a fundamental changing global order, which is shifting from a unipolar world under American dominance towards a polycentric world with several global powers including Russia (Dynkin & Ivanova 2012).

Literature Review

In contrast to EU–Russia or CIS–Russia FDI flows, USA–Russia investment relations are not central to FDI studies in Russia. Probably, the most adequate explanation for the aforementioned situation can be found in the regional integration agenda, which is rather popular in FDI studies in Russia. Russia–USA investment relations have never been a part of corporate integration in contrast to Russia's corporate integration with the EU or countries in the post-Soviet space, which may explain the lesser interest of FDI scholars in the Russia–USA FDI relationship.

Despite a lesser academic interest, some interesting articles on Russia–USA FDI relations exist. In fact, US FDI in Russia has been investigated since the end of the 1990s (e.g. Zimenkov 1999). A few case studies of US FDI in some Russian regions can be found as well (e.g. Kuznetsova 2006). The first detailed information on Russian FDI in the USA emerged in the scientific literature in the middle of the 2000s (e.g. Vahtra & Liuhto 2004). However, an article dedicated to Russian FDI in the USA appeared only at the beginning of the 2010s (Pichkov 2011). Thereafter, several studies on Russia–USA FDI flows have been published (Borisov & Frye 2012; Zimenkov 2013).

These contributions usually present information on the legal environment surrounding Russia–USA investment relations, empirical facts about FDI, and some general conclusions on the nature of these relations. It should be stressed that the aforementioned experts tended to see positive effects ranging from high salaries to developing traditions of corporate social responsibility flowing from the US business presence in Russia. Negative perceptions towards the USA are less typical among FDI studies in Russia, though they are quite prevalent in studies dealing with military aspects of the USA/NATO–Russia relations or the US role in globalization – for example, in connection with the dollarization of the Russian economy (e.g. Bratersky 2011).

In this chapter, we aim to investigate Russia–USA FDI relation using well-known theoretical frameworks, which can aid us to comprehend the specifics of Russia–USA relations. Special attention is paid to investor motivations. Despite the post-communist specifics of the investment climate, including political rent-seeking motives (e.g. Kuznetsov 2009), "classic" TNCs usually invest on the basis of various combinations of the motives described earlier by Dunning (2000).

Whereas Dunning's theory explains mainly "why" firms undertake FDI, the ideas of the Uppsala school are more appropriate to answer to the question of "where" FDI occurs (Johanson & Vahlne 1977). Although the "neighborhood effect" is not that relevant for the Russia–USA FDI relationship because of the large distance between the economic centers of these countries, some geographically determined models of foreign investment expansion can be found (e.g. Kuznetsova *et al.* 2007).

For example, the expansion of US companies with mass produced goods or services (e.g. fast food restaurants) can be explained with the help of the hierarchic-wave model of spatial FDI diffusion. Originally, this model was introduced to explain the diffusion of innovations, but in the beginning of the 1990s it was applied to illuminate FDI as well (Schlunze 1992). According to this model, foreign investors from distant countries prefer to commence their spatial expansion in the host country from the capital city – that is, in Russia's case it would be Moscow. Thereafter, they may establish subsidiaries in other significant cities, such as Saint Petersburg, Kazan, or Nizhny Novgorod, as well as in towns around the capital city. Thereafter, they may establish subsidiaries in cities with less hierarchic rank and in areas surrounding several of the largest cities, etc. In Russia's case, the shift from initial FDI in the European part of Russia to FDI in the Urals and thereafter in Siberia have been observed earlier (Kuznetsov 2007).

The hierarchic-wave model is not universal. It can be simplified by economy of scale. If the company needs two to three plants to conquer the whole Russian market, we are able to notice some spatial FDI diffusion from Central Russia or Northwest Russia to the Volga region or the Urals, and thereafter to North Caucasus and Siberia.

The initial point of FDI expansion can be distorted by the "neighborhood effect". This is shown by Saint Petersburg's popularity as an initial location for many European investors to conduct FDI in Russia. However, earlier cooperation ties or M&A deals may distort the location choice, as the logic of hierarchic-wave diffusion is based on the need to learn. Put differently, cooperation or the acquisition of existing business networks may support foreign investors with necessary information for FDI, and thus foreign firms can be found in rather unexpected Russian regions for newcomers.

Foreign investors in high tech and medium tech manufacturing may make their location choices under a large set of factors where theoretical models can hardly be identified. It is also difficult to find any model of FDI diffusion in the oil and gas industry and some other natural resource-based sectors, where foreign companies usually invest in those enterprises that the state regulations permit.

Methodology

The main methodological challenge for this study relates to the quality of the data. There are plenty of sources, but, despite the availability of data, it remains difficult to obtain an accurate picture. The Central Bank of Russia (the Bank of Russia), the Federal State Statistics Service (Rosstat), and the US Bureau of Economic Analysis (BEA) present varying figures, which can be explained both by methodological differences (mainly in tracking of FDI via offshores) and by defaults in collecting FDI information.

For example, Rosstat, Russia's main statistical body, tries to collect some figures on FDI and other indicators of companies under foreign control. However, its FDI statistics have poor quality because they are based on the "1 Invest" form, which is sent to a small number of investors. However, other Rosstat information on US investors is reliable. For instance, Rosstat publishes data on the number of enterprises with US capital in Russia and its regions.

To surmount data problems, we compare data from various official sources with expert estimates and information from corporate websites, our main task being to identify tendencies. For example, although the precise figures differ, the use of multiple sources provides with a good basis for claiming that there was a decrease in Russia–USA FDI flows after 2010. Beyond this, data disparities provide a good reason for in-depth research.

There are no lists concerning the leading US investors in Russia or Russia's largest investors in the USA. Therefore, a researcher needs to search for other company rankings. The list of the largest US companies in Russia in terms of turnover is the most appropriate initial point for investigating US FDI, although some companies on this list will be exporters without significant FDI in Russia.

As for Russian investors in the USA, it is appropriate to investigate all Russia's leading TNCs because there are only a few dozen of them in contrast to thousands of US TNCs. Russia's largest TNCs often publish figures on their long-term (non-current) foreign assets in different countries. The USA or the USA plus Canada frequently form a separate geographical category in the financial reports of the Russian companies which helps us to discover the main Russian investors in the USA.

It is of utmost importance to pay attention to regional contrasts within the Russian Federation and the USA. Both these countries are extremely large in terms of territorial size and consist of numerous regions which manifest different economic features – for example, developed post-industrial economies, natural resource, less developed agrarian regions, etc. As a result of these regional disparities, some features of the center–periphery model can be found in their FDI geography. Models of FDI diffusion can be validated through the history of a company's spatial expansion, though a researcher will have to conduct scrupulous investigations of earlier annual and financial reports and various media sources. Several cases validate only some aspects of these models but a large set of investors reflects some interesting regularities in the geographical FDI distribution. Explanations for location choices can also be found in the Russian statistics – that is, evidence of the dominance of Moscow and its gradual decrease in the FDI geography.

US FDI in Russia: Recent Trends and Structure

Central Bank of Russia data and "parallel" statistics by the BEA can be considered as the most reliable sources on US FDI in Russia because they follow the international standards created by the OECD and the IMF. However, information from some US companies indicates both the Central Bank of Russia and the BEA underestimate the US business presence in Russia.

Despite significant divergences between data sources, both aforementioned organizations show a major decrease in the US FDI stock in 2010, a recovery during 2012–13, and a significant drop in 2014. However, according to the Central Bank of Russia, net US FDI flows in Russia remained positive during the whole period (Table 4.1). This may also mean that large changes in the US FDI stock are mainly connected with changes in the valuation of assets – that is, predominantly due to the fluctuation of the Russian Ruble exchange rate.

Table 4.1 US Direct Investment in Russia, 2009–14 ($ millions)

	2009	*2010*	*2011*	*2012*	*2013*	*2014*
US FDI stock*	20,763	10,040	11,285	13,389	13,140	9,263
US FDI stock**	13,875	5,203	2,784	3,520	18,583	2,775
US FDI net inflows**	2,296	435	276	285	485	708

Sources: *Bureau of Economic Analysis 2015; **Central Bank of Russia 2016d, 2016e

According to Rosstat, in 2014, there were 755 enterprises with US capital in Russia, which accounted for 3.2 percent of all foreign firms in Russia. In fact, the USA ranked eighth after three trans-shipping and round-tripping destinations (Cyprus, the British Virgin Islands, and the Netherlands), three neighboring countries (Ukraine, Belarus, and China), and Germany (Rosstat 2015b). The quantity of Russian enterprises with US capital has remained relatively stable in recent years: the number was 746 in 2012 and 770 in 2013 (Rosstat 2015a).

In 2014, 31 percent of enterprises with US capital (235 firms) operated in Moscow. Saint Petersburg occupied second place with 16 percent (124 firms). The aforementioned figures show that the concentration of US enterprises in Russia's "capital areas" was higher than the concentration of foreign firms on average. The shares of Moscow and Saint Petersburg among all foreign firms was 21 percent and 9 percent respectively.

The Moscow region, the Sakhalin region, and the Republic of Tatarstan were the next most popular regions for US investors (51, 26, and 21 firms respectively). The Krasnodar krai, the Leningrad region, the Novosibirsk region, the Primorye krai, the Rostov region, the Sverdlovsk region, the Samara region, the Vladimir region, and even the city of Sevastopol had from 17 to nine enterprises with US capital in 2014.

Enterprises with US capital were absent only in 20 out of Russia's 85 regions. It seems that US investors prefer not to invest in the regions with a high concentration of ethnic minorities – for example, the Chechen Republic, the Republic of Ingushetia, the Republic of North Ossetia, the Republic of Marii El, the Republic of Buryatia, etc. In 2014, apart from national republics and autonomous regions, only the Belgorod region, the Bryansk region, the Pensa region, and the Kamchatka krai had not registered any companies having US capital.

Rather recently, the Central Bank of Russia started to publish more detailed FDI statistics. These statistics show that Moscow and the Moscow region are the main recipients of US FDI (Table 4.2). In general, the regional concentration of the US FDI stock is rather high in comparison with the leading European investors. However, the statistics also indicate that US companies do not play a strategic role in any Russian regions, Moscow included. However, there are a few significant manufacturing projects by US investors in some regions of the European part of Russia as well as oil and gas projects in Sakhalin.

McDonald's is geographically the most widely spread US company in Russia. It has more than 540 restaurants in over 50 Russian regions. It is important to mention here that McDonald's did not use franchising in Russia during 1990–2013, and, as a consequence of its investment-driven strategy, its FDI stock in Russia exceeds $1 billion. McDonald's is the best example of the hierarchic-wave of spatial FDI diffusion. Its first restaurant was opened in Moscow in 1990. During the 1990s, McDonald's opened 38 new restaurants in Moscow and 32 restaurants in other cities and towns, including the Moscow region. McDonald's entered Saint Petersburg, Russia's second largest city, in 1996. A bit later, the company established restaurants in other large cities in the European part of Russia, Nizhny Novgorod (1997), Kazan and Samara (1999), and Rostov-on-Don

Table 4.2 Regional Distribution of US FDI Stocks in Russia, January and July 2015 ($ millions and percent)

Region	US FDI stock, 1st January 2015			US FDI stock, 1st July 2015		
	$ millions	*Share of US FDI stock in Russia, percent*	*Share of USA in total FDI stock of the region, percent*	*$ millions*	*Share of US FDI stock in Russia, percent*	*Share of USA in total FDI stock of the region, percent*
Russia total	2,775	100.0	0.8	2,860	100.0	0.7
Moscow city	1,339	48.3	0.7	1,270	44.4	0.7
Moscow region	1,059	38.2	9.7	1,203	42.1	9.4
Sverdlovsk region	116	4.2	1.7	86	3.0	1.1
Republic of Tatarstan**	41	1.5	2.3	99	3.5	4.9
Saint Petersburg	31	1.1	0.1	34	1.2	0.2
Leningrad region**	24	0.9	0.8	25	0.9	0.8
Sakhalin region*	21	0.8	0.1	13	0.5	0.0
Rostov region	14	0.5	1.6	14	0.5	1.7
Kaliningrad region	11	0.4	2.1	12	0.4	2.4
Yamalo-Nenets Autonomous District**	7	0.3	0.1	7	0.2	0.1
Other regions	112	4.0	0.1	97	3.4	0.1

Source: Central Bank of Russia 2016c

Notes
* According to the Bank of Russia, the main investors in the Sakhalin region came from the Bahamas (about 60 percent) and Bermuda (more than 37 percent). Due to information from companies, the same underestimation of US FDI stocks is typical for some other regions, including the Republic of Tatarstan, Saint Petersburg, the Rostov region, the Ryazan region, the Orenburg region, etc.
** In these cases the Bank of Russia gives some general information for North America

(2001). McDonald's started to conquer the Urals and Siberia only in the 2000s. Regions in Western Siberia are still the easternmost regions with the McDonald's restaurants in Russia.

In addition to official statistics, it is necessary to utilize company or firm-level data for our analysis. The case of ExxonMobil in the Sakhalin region exemplifies this. ExxonMobil is an operator of the large oil and gas project Sakhalin-1, in which it has a 30 percent stake. The share product agreement for the project was signed in 1995 and the agreement came into force a year later. Oil and gas production started in 2005. According to the Institute of World Economy and International Relations (IMEMO), this US company has invested about $5 billion in the Sakhalin region (Kuznetsov *et al.* 2015). However, Exxon Neftegas Limited, based in the Bahamas, is formally the official investor. In fact, Sakhalin-1 did not receive any direct investment from the USA, but all the capital came from the Bahamas, as the Central Bank of Russia registers only the last country in the investment chain. Another illustrative example is connected with oil and gas industry in the Yamalo-Nenets Autonomous District. An unsuccessful attempt of US participation is linked with US sanctions against Russia. It is still the only major divestment by US firms in Russia in 2014.[1]

Firm-level analysis is essential for understanding the industrial structure of the US FDI stock in Russia and the main motives of the US investors. According to Expert Agency, food and beverages companies dominate among US corporations operating in Russia (Khanferyan, Mindich & Zherdev 2015), although the leader in terms of turnover is tobacco giant Philip Morris (Table 4.3), which has invested $1.5 billion in Russia. Also Mars and Mondelez International have both invested more than $1 billion in Russia. The largest US acquisition in Russia touched the food industry as well, when PepsiCo bought WimmBillDann for more than $5 billion in 2010–11.

US food companies demonstrate the simplified hierarchic-wave model of spatial FDI diffusion. For instance, Mars opened its first trade subsidiary in Russia in Moscow in 1991, and thereafter it built a plant in Stupino, in the Moscow region, in 1994–5. Later, Mars established a factory in Novosibirsk in 2002 and another one in the Ulyanovsk region in 2007. Simultaneously, the company expanded further within the Moscow region.

Mondelez International, former Kraft Foods, offers another example. The company's trade subsidiary was founded in Moscow in 1994. Its new or acquired plants are located in the Vladimir and the Novgorod regions, both of which are

Table 4.3 Largest Russian Companies Under Control of US Investors, Ranked by Turnover, as of the End of 2014 ($ millions)

Rank among Russia's largest companies	Company	Industry	Turnover, $ millions
49	Philip Morris	Tobacco	5,036.7
56	PepsiCo*	Beverages	4,414.0
76	Procter & Gamble	Wholesale trade (chemicals)	3,371.6
109	Apple	Wholesale trade (information technologies)	2,488.5
128	Mars	Food	2,082.0
143	Ilim (International Paper owns 50 percent)	Pulp and paper	1,846.8
159	Mondelez	Food	1,622.9
180	Ford Sollers (Ford owns 50 percent)	Motor vehicles	1,422.0
189	McDonald's	Food and restaurants	1,370.7
197	General Motors	Motor vehicles	1,332.0
222	Johnson & Johnson	Wholesale trade (pharmaceuticals)	1,128.6
228	Cargill	Food	1,090.9

Source: Khanferyan, Mindich and Zherdev 2015

Note: *It needs to be stressed here that Coca-Cola HBC Eurasia is a subsidiary of a Greek company, even if the majority of experts considers it as a significant US investor in Russia

not that far away from the capital city.[2] After many years of operations in Russia, Mondelez International decided to invest in a new factory in Novosibirsk, Siberia.

BEA FDI statistics confirm the dominance of the food industry in the US FDI stock in Russia. According to its data, at the end of 2014, 43.4 percent of the US FDI stock in Russia was concentrated in manufacturing. The food industry represents two-thirds of this proportion. Both the aforementioned figures are extraordinarily high for US investors, as the average share of manufacturing in the US total outward FDI stock was only 13.5 percent while the share of food industry in US FDI in manufacturing was only a tenth (Hansen & Limés 2015).

Although the main shares of US FDI in global manufacturing consist of chemicals, computers and electronics, and transportation equipment, these sectors represent a relatively modest amount of US FDI in Russia. Nevertheless, a car producer, Ford, became a pioneer of a new industrial cluster near Saint Petersburg in 2002. Thereafter, Ford established two plants with Russian Sollers in the Republic of Tatarstan in 2012–14. In turn, General Motors established a joint venture with Avtovaz and EBRD in 2001 and opened a new assembly plant in Saint Petersburg in 2008. However, the aforementioned unit was closed in 2015 because of a dramatic decrease of sales during the current economic crisis. Both these US car producers have invested several hundred million US dollars in Russia. None of the cases manifest even the most simplified form of hierarchic-wave spatial FDI diffusion. However, this is not a surprise when we keep in mind Ford established its first trade office in Russia more than a century ago (in 1907) and its first industrial ties were developed already at the beginning of the 1930s.

Several well-known industrial companies from the USA have established large wholesale units in Russia, and their turnover frequently exceeds that of their industrial plants in Russia. For instance, Procter & Gamble has four plants in Russia in the Tula region, the Nizhny Novgorod region, the Moscow City, and Saint Petersburg, but a significant part of its turnover in Russia is connected with imports. In fact, Procter & Gamble can be found among Russia's largest companies by turnover, although its FDI stock in Russia is only about $300 million. According to the BEA (2015), wholesale trade occupied almost 16 percent of the US FDI stock in Russia at the end of 2014.

Some fresh FDI projects in manufacturing can be found in the "second echelon" of business. For instance, Armstrong invested more than $50 million in the production of ceiling plates in the Alabuga (Yelabuga) Special Economic Zone in the Republic of Tatarstan during 2013–14. This new factory's production replaces deliveries of Armstrong's construction materials from the USA to Russia. Although Armstrong already began its exports to Russia in 1993, it became economically feasible for the company to start production in Russia to reduce costs. Another illustrative example links to Guardian Industries. Its first glass production unit in the Ryazan region was founded in 2008 while its second factory in the Rostov region began operations in 2012–13. Investments in each facility exceeded $200 million. It needs to be stressed here that the FDI projects of both Armstrong and Guardian Industries were not picked up by the Central

Bank of Russia, although they were noticed by the Russian Ministry of Economic Development (Portal vneshneekonomicheskoy deyatel'nosti 2014).

Russia's financial sector is another potential recipient of US FDI. However, even Citibank is far behind its European counterparts such as Société Générale, UniCredit, or Raiffeisenbank. In contrast to many European and Asian banks, the subsidiaries of other US banks, including Morgan Stanley and Goldman Sachs, do not rank among Russia's 100 largest banks. Probably, US banks have lost their competitive edge in the Russian market due to a lack of confidence (political tensions) and the absence of the "neighborhood effect". It seems that Russian companies use European and Asian banks as they have close trade relations with these countries. Similarly, Russian citizens prefer European and Asian banks because they usually go as tourists to home countries of these banks.

All the above-mentioned facts show that the market-seeking motives still prevail in the operations of US companies in Russia. Although strategic asset-seeking motives could have attracted more US technology companies into Russia, Boeing is a rare example among US high tech companies investing in Russia. Boeing established its first R&D center in Moscow in 1993 and a manufacturing JV with VSMPO (Ural Boeing Manufacturing) in 2009. Well-known negative characteristics of the Russian investment environment have probably been the main reasons for US high tech corporations' cautiousness about investing in Russia.

We assume market-seeking motives will continue to play a key role in shaping US FDI in Russia in the future. Additional possibilities may emerge from the development of the Eurasian Economic Union. The best example is John Deere, which invested $45 million in the Orenburg region during 2005–14. John Deere Orenburg supplies agricultural machinery both in Russia and in Kazakhstan. Moreover, US companies can press their European competitors in some sectors such as retail trade. So far Wal-Mart Stores has made several unsuccessful attempts to enter the Russian market, though it managed to register a small subsidiary in Russia in 2008.

The "sanctions war" between Russia and Western countries and Russia's negative attitude towards the NATO will limit the operations of the US companies with resource-seeking and strategic assets-seeking motives in Russia. Correspondingly, US pressure on its own companies is also evident. For example, ConocoPhillips stopped its FDI activities in 2015 although it had been a large investor in Russia (in Polyarnoye Siyaniye in the Arkhangelsk region) since 1992. It needs to be pointed out that ConocoPhillips' problems in the Russian market started before the Ukrainian crisis and that it was these financial problems that forced the firm to sell its 20 percent stake in Lukoil as well as its 30 percent share in their JV Naryanmarneftegaz.

The future of efficiency-seeking American FDI will be determined by changes in the Russian investment climate rather than current political tensions between the USA and Russia. In other words, such firms care most about issues such as the ease of obtaining construction permits, trading across borders, getting electricity, or protections for minority investors than political issues.

Table 4.4 Russian Direct Investment in the USA, 2009–14 ($ millions)

	2009	2010	2011	2012	2013	2014
Russian FDI stock *	8,416	5,689	6,025	5,943	6,237	5,278
Russian FDI stock **	10,532	9,825	9,145	10,557	21,547	14,507
Russian FDI net inflows **	1,634	1,060	1,625	688	739	1,654

Sources: *Bureau of Economic Analysis 2015; **Central Bank of Russia 2016a, 2016b

Special Features of Russian FDI in the USA

Although there were some examples of Soviet FDI in the USA, such as Amtorg Trading Corporation, Russian FDI in the USA really boomed between 2003 and 2008. All FDI statistics show only nominal development in the expansion of Russian investment in the USA after 2009 (see Table 4.4).

The main Russian TNCs FDI projects in the USA connect to the steel industry. Usually, Russian steel companies have expanded their investments because of market-seeking motives. In terms of specific firms, Evraz, NLMK, and TMK are among the leading investors (Table 4.5). Although Severstal has had production operations in Michigan since 2004 and established the largest Russian greenfield project in the USA (in Columbus, Mississippi, in 2007), it decided to exit the US market. The main reason for its divestments was the low profitability of its US assets in comparison with the Russian assets, which were significantly modernized in the middle of the 2000s.

Mechel and Norilsk Nickel have also left the USA. However, their divestments do not link to problems associated with the US investment climate, but rather to the financial problems of their parent companies. It should be stressed here that both these companies went to the USA because of resource-seeking motives: Mechel owned Bluestone Coal from 2009–14 while Norilsk Nickel controlled palladium and platinum mining company Stillwater between 2003 and 2010.

Russian oil and gas TNCs have not been active in the USA, though Lukoil has developed a petroleum station network in the USA since 2000. However, it has decreased the number of its petroleum stations lately, and nowadays the US share in its foreign non-current assets is just about 1 percent.

Probably, US protectionism against foreign state-controlled companies is one of the most adequate explanations for the reluctance of the Russian state-owned companies to invest in the USA. State-controlled Rosneft, Russia's fourth largest TNC in terms of foreign assets, can be taken as an example. Rosneft tried to buy an international oil trading company from Morgan Stanley for approximately $400 million but the deal was blocked by US authorities in 2014. US protectionism can be observed in manufacturing as well when a target industry has strategic importance. For example, we may remember "sanctions" against Russian aircraft companies and their connection with US "suspicions" about nuclear non-proliferation.

Despite US protectionism, we were able to find some Russian FDI in US manufacturing. One example includes Rostselmash, the famous Russian producer of agricultural machinery, which owns several plants in the USA. In addition,

Table 4.5 Russia's Top 20 Non-financial TNCs Ranked by Foreign Assets, 2014 ($ billions and percent)

Company	Industry	Foreign assets, $ billions 2013	Foreign assets, $ billions 2014	Share in total assets, 2014, %	Foreign non-current assets, $ billions 2013	Foreign non-current assets, $ billions 2014	Share of the USA in non-current assets, 2014, %
1 Gazprom	Oil and gas	40.1	36.0	13	31.6	27.8	0
2 Lukoil	Oil and gas	32.6	32.9	29	25.7	26.3	1
3 VimpelCom	Telecommunications	36.8	30.4	74	30.5	23.3	0
4 Rosneft	Oil and gas	8.4	9.4	6	6.6	7.1	0
5 Evraz	Steel	8.7	5.3	46	4.6	3.7	40
6 Sovcomflot	Transportation	5.3	5.3	83	4.3	4.3	0
7 Rusal	Non-ferrous metals	3.7	2.8	19	3.0	2.2	0
8 Russian Railways	Transportation	3.2	2.8	4	1.9	1.6	0
9 TMK	Steel	2.6	2.5	44	1.7	1.5	≈60*
10 Zarubezhneft	Oil and gas	2.4	2.4	67	2.0	2.0	0
11 Atomenergoprom	Nuclear	2.8	2.4	6	2.2	1.8	0
12 Sistema	Conglomerate	3.0	1.7	8	2.0	1.1	0
13 Nordgold	Non-ferrous metals	1.7	1.6	73	1.1	1.0	0
14 Inter RAO	Electricity	1.6	1.6	15	1.1	1.0	0
15 EuroChem	Chemicals	1.5	1.4	23	1.1	1.0	0
16 NLMK	Steel	1.6	1.3	12	1.1	0.8	≈30**
17 Transneft	Transportation	1.5	1.1	3	1.0	0.8	0
18 MMK	Steel	1.1	1.0	12	0.9	0.7	0
19 Polymetal	Non-ferrous metals	0.2	1.0	35	0.2	1.0	0
20 Norilsk Nickel	Non-ferrous metals	0.6	0.7	5	0.3	0.4	0
Top 20 (2014)	–	**159.4**	**143.6**	**17**	**122.9**	**109.4**	**3**

Sources: Kuznetsov 2016; author's calculations based on companies' financial reports

Notes

* TMK publishes only total information for the USA and Canada. In North America, there are 12 plants (including one in Canada) and five other enterprises (including two in Canada). The share of the region is 73 percent

** NLMK does not publish exact figures on the geography of its foreign non-current assets. It has nine foreign plants (including three in the USA) and some trading enterprises in Europe

EuroChem, a producer of fertilizers, bought Ben-Trei Fertilizer Company in the USA in 2015 and announced its plans to build a new factory in Louisiana.

Due to the leading position of the USA in information technology, some distinguished Russian companies such as Kaspersky Laboratory, Luxoft, Mail.ru Group, and Yandex, have established subsidiaries in the USA. California and New York are the most attractive sites for them due to the large market as well as an abundance of high-qualified staff, particularly Silicon Valley.

All in all, Russian FDI in the USA is relatively diversified geographically. Pennsylvania is the most popular state among Russian TNCs. We may find subsidiaries of Lukoil, NLMK, and TMK in this region due to its market size and geographical proximity to New York and other economic centers. However, Russia's leading investor Evraz has not opened any plants in Pennsylvania, but it has established its steel division headquarters in Chicago, Illinois, manufacturing facilities in Oregon and Colorado, and its vanadium headquarters in Connecticut and a plant in Arkansas. Its steel mill in Delaware was closed in 2014. Among all Russian investors in the USA, TMK has the most diversified geography, with 11 factories in Arkansas, Iowa, Kentucky, Nebraska, Oklahoma, Pennsylvania, and Texas, as well as its US headquarters in Houston, Texas.

When we analyze the presence of Russian investments in the USA, we should not forget Russian FDI in US real estate. Although we have identified several large real estate deals of Russian oligarchs and their family members in the USA, the majority of the real estate investment belongs to Russia's upper-middle class. The USA is the most popular destination for Russian citizens outside Europe.[3] However, the long distance between the Russian Federation and the USA narrows the range of geographical options, and hence the Russians prefer three states, namely California, New York, and Florida. Florida appears to be the most frequent location because of its real estate prices, which are lower than average prices in Moscow or some other large cities in Russia (Petegirich 2015). Russians usually buy new buildings in the USA but in other aspects their preferences differ significantly (Levitova 2010).

The USA is not an attractive market for several Russian TNCs due to its geographic distance, legislative peculiarities (case law tradition, extraterritorial legislation, etc.), and political risks, which have increased in 2014–15. Therefore, some of Russia's state-controlled TNCs, such as Gazprom, Sovcomflot, or Russian Railways, will most probably ignore the USA.

It seems that some private Russian companies have had major difficulties competing in the US market and thus they prefer to invest in other countries. Russian telecommunications companies and banks can be taken as examples here. Alfa Capital Markets, established in 2001, is Russia's only significant private financial subsidiary in the USA. Russia's first state-controlled bank VTB Capital entered the USA in 2012 when it founded a branch in New York. Currently, its US unit suffers from the political pressure due to US "sanctions".

The USA only occupies 11th place as a market for Russian exports, and therefore the outlook for further Russian investment in the USA is not that bright when we keep in mind that market-seeking motives prevail as far as the USA is concerned and that FDI tends to follow export flows. Moreover, high political risks associated with the USA will cool Russian investors with non-commercial FDI motives. In this context, we should remember that "insuring" assets from probable confiscation in Russia used to be a frequent motive for Russian businesses to invest abroad. Due to the ongoing "sanctions war", the probability of losing assets in the USA is higher than in Russia, and therefore Russian businesses nowadays prefer to stay in Russia instead of investing in the USA. Another example of non-commercial motives is related to the acquisition of the status of being a "global investor". Recently, the USA and several other Western countries have disappointed Russian investors. As a result, US assets have become a burden for a Russian business's image at home.

The *coup d'état* in Ukraine caused a significant decrease in the Russian FDI stock in Ukraine, which unwittingly supported the US leadership. In fact, the decrease in Russian FDI in the Ukraine has been larger than the drop in Russian FDI in the USA. Even if no dramatic drop in Russian FDI in the USA has occurred so far, the USA will probably lose its leading place as a recipient of the Russian FDI since the growth opportunities offered by Belarus and Kazakhstan due to the economic integration of the Eurasian Economic Union are more encouraging than those offered by the USA.

Conclusions

The USA and Russia are important investors but their bilateral investment ties are not particularly intensive, especially when we compare Russia–USA FDI flows with investments between the EU and the USA or capital flows between the EU and Russia. Moreover, there is no evidence that the situation will change for the better soon.

Problems in the political dialogue between Russia and the USA have always obstructed contacts on the business level. However, the current situation is difficult even in comparison with earlier periods of political tensions. Despite the tensions, both the Russian companies in the USA and, especially, US enterprises in Russia have numerous incentives to develop the bilateral FDI relationship. In doing so, they could support the stability of American food and tobacco FDI in Russia as well as Russian steel FDI in the USA.

Despite the presence of US investors in several sectors of the Russian economy, there is a real problem of fully fledged participation of the Russian firms in the US-dominated global value chains. As for Russian TNCs, they can be equal partners to the US companies only in a limited number of industries, such as information technology or in natural resource-based sectors.

Notes

1 It is impossible to track the investing company. Probably, the investment was connected with new Arctic gas projects and it was conducted through a round-tripping or trans-shipping of Russian capital via a third country.
2 Since the year 2000, the company has also produced coffee in the Leningrad region. However, beverage assets of Mondelez merged with DE Master Blenders 1753 in 2014. Jacobs Douwe Egberts, with headquarters in the Netherlands, became a new owner of Mondelez's plant in Gorelovo, the Leningrad region (Jacobs Rus).
3 According to OECD Benchmark Definition, all investments in real estate are regarded as FDI if they give control over 10 percent, including investments in dachas abroad, etc. (OECD 2008).

Bibliography

Borisov, K. & Frye, T. 2012, 'Perspectives of Russian–American investment cooperation: tendencies, mechanisms of support, recommendations', *Russian Analytical Digest (RAD)*, no. 119, pp. 16–23, Center for Security Studies (CSS), viewed 10 January 2016, https://www.irex.org/sites/default/files/u93/Borisov-Eng.pdf

Bratersky, M.V. 2011, 'Miroviye finansi v rossiysko-amerikanskih otnosheniyah', *SShA i Kanada: ekonomika, politika, kul'tura*, no. 8, pp. 3–15.

Bureau of Economic Analysis 2015, *Balance of Payments and Direct Investment Position Data*, viewed 15 January 2016, http://bea.gov/iTable

Central Bank of Russia 2016a, Russian Federation: Outward Foreign Direct Investments by Russian Residents, by Geographical Allocation, 2007–2015 (Balance of Payments Data, outflows minus inflows), viewed 15 July 2016, http://www.cbr.ru/eng/statistics/credit_statistics/direct_investment/inv_out-country_e.xls

Central Bank of Russia 2016b, Russian Federation: Outward Foreign Direct Investment Positions by Geographical Allocation in 2009–2015, viewed 15 July 2016, http:// www.cbr.ru/eng/statistics/credit_statistics/direct_investment/dir-inv_out_country_1_e.xlsx

Central Bank of Russia 2016c, Pryamiye investitsii v Rossiyskuyu Federatsiyu iz-za rubezha: ostatki po sub'yektam Rossiyskoy Federatsii v razreze instrumentov i stran partnerov, viewed 15 July 2016, http://www.cbr.ru/statistics/credit_statistics/direct_investment/dir-inv_in_country_3.xlsx

Central Bank of Russia 2016d, Russian Federation: Inward Foreign Direct Investment, by Geographical Allocation, 2007–2015 (Balance of Payments Data, inflows minus outflows), viewed 15 July 2016, http://www.cbr.ru/eng/statistics/credit_statistics/inv_in-country_e.xlsx

Central Bank of Russia 2016e, Russian Federation: Inward Foreign Direct Investment Positions by Geographical Allocation in 2009–2015, viewed 15 July 2016, http://www.cbr.ru/eng/statistics/credit_statistics/direct_investment/dir-inv_in-country_1_e.xlsx

Dunning, J.H. 2000, 'The eclectic paradigm as an envelope for economic and business theories of MNE activity', *International Business Review*, vol. 9, no. 2, pp. 163–90.

Dynkin, A. & Ivanova, N. (eds.) 2012, *Russia in Polycentric World*, Ves Mir, Moscow.

Hansen, N.R. & Limés, R. 2015, *US Direct Investment Abroad for 2012–2014. Detailed Historical-Cost Positions and Related Financial Transactions and Income Flows*, Bureau of Economic Analysis, viewed 15 January 2016, http://www.bea.gov/scb/pdf/2015/09%20September/0915_outward_direct_investment_detailed_historical_cost_positions.pdf

Johanson, J. & Vahlne, J-E. 1977, 'The internationalization process of the firm: a model of knowledge development and increasing foreign market commitments', *Journal of International Business Studies*, vol. 8, no. 1, pp. 23–32.

Ketchum 2012, *Investitsionniy klimat Rossii 2012*, viewed 20 January 2016, http://www.analitika.kz/docs/Russia_Investment_Climate_2012RU.pdf

Khanferyan, V., Mindich, D. & Zherdev, F. 2015, *Reyting krupneyshih kompaniy Rossii RAEX-600*, Expert, Moscow, viewed 20 January 2016, http://raexpert.ru/ratings/expert400/2015/

Kuznetsov, A. 2007, *Internatsionalizatsiya rossiyskoy ekonomiki: investitsionniy aspect*, URSS, Moscow.

Kuznetsov, A. 2009, 'Dvizhushchiye sili internatsionalizatsii rossiyskogo biznesa', *Mirovoye Razvitiye*, no. 5, pp. 5–14.

Kuznetsov, A. 2010, 'Inward FDI in Russia and its policy context', *Columbia FDI Profiles*, viewed 15 January 2016, http://ccsi.columbia.edu/files/2014/03/Profiles_Russia_IFDI_Final_November_30_2010.pdf

Kuznetsov, A. 2016, 'Foreign investments of Russian companies: competition with West European and East Asian multinationals', *Herald of the Russian Academy of Sciences*, vol. 86, no. 2, pp. 77–85.

Kuznetsov, A., Kvashnin, Y., Nevskaya, A. & Chetverikova, A. 2015, *EAEU and Eurasia: Monitoring and Analysis of Direct Investments*, EDB Centre for Integration Studies, Saint Petersburg.

Kuznetsova, O., Kuznetsov, A., Turovskiy, R. & Chetverikova, A. 2007, *Investitsionniye strategii krupnogo biznesa i ekonomika regionov*, URSS, Moscow.

Kuznetsova, Y. 2006, 'Amerikanskiy capital v ekonomike Samarskoy oblasti v 1996–2005 godah', *Vestnik Samarskogo Gosudarstvennogo Universiteta*, no. 10-1, pp. 94–100.

Levitova, A. 2010, 'Rossiyane v N'yu-Yorke predpochitayut novostroyki s mramornim pod'yezdom', viewed 20 January 2016, http://realty.rbc.ru/experts/02/11/2010/562949979131787.shtml

Ministry of Foreign Affairs of the Russian Federation 2015, *Rossiysko-amerikanskiye otnosheniya*, viewed 20 January 2016, http://www.mid.ru/maps/us/-/category/10498/?currentpage=double

OECD 2008, *OECD Benchmark Definition of Foreign Direct Investment*, 4th edition, viewed 20 January 2016, http://www.oecd.org/daf/inv/investmentstatisticsandanalysis/40193734.pdf

PBN Company 2005, *Rossiya kak ob'yekt investitsiy*, viewed 20 January 2016, http://federalbook.ru/files/FS/Soderjanie/FS-17/III/Sharonov%202.pdf

PBN Company 2006, *Rossiya kak ob'yekt investitsiy*, viewed 20 January 2016, http://www.sras.org/files/textedit/pbn2006_fullreport_rus.pdf

Petegirich, O. 2015, *Amerikanskaya mechta: tri tochki prityazheniya glya russkogovoryashchih pokupateley nedvizhimosti*, viewed 20 January 2016, http://prian.ru/pub/30801.html

Pichkov, O. 2011, 'Pryamiye investitsii rossiyskih kompaniy v SShA', *Vestnik Akademii*, no. 2, pp. 5–7.

Portal vneshneekonomicheskoy deyatel'nosti 2014, *Osnovniye itogi investitsionnogo sotrudnichestrva Rossii s SShA*, viewed 20 January 2016, http://ved.gov.ru

Rosstat 2015a, *Regioni Rossii: Sotsial'no-ekonomicheskiye pokazateli 2015*, Moscow.

Rosstat 2015b, *Rossiyskiy statisticheskiy ezhegodnik 2015*, Moscow.

Schlunze, R.D. 1992, 'Spatial Diffusion of Japanese Firms in West Germany and West Berlin from 1955 to 1989', *Geographical Review of Japan*, Series B, vol. 65, no. 1, pp. 32–56.

Soglasheniye... 1992, *Mezhdu Pravitel'stvom Rossiyskoy Federatsii i Pravitel'stvom Soyedinyonnih Shtatov Ameriki o sodeystvii kapitalovlozheniyam*, Washington, DC, viewed 10 January 2016, http://www.consultant.ru/document/cons_doc_LAW_154506/

Vahtra, P. & Liuhto, K. 2004, *Expansion or Exodus?: Foreign Operations of Russia's Largest Corporations*, Pan-European Institute, University of Turku, Turku.

Zimenkov, R. 1999, 'Pryamiye investitsii SShA v ekonomiku Rossii', *SShA i Kanada: economika, politika, kul'tura*, no. 6, pp. 3–15.

Zimenkov, R. 2013, 'Torgovo-ekonomicheskiye otnosheniya SShA so stranami BRICS', *SShA i Kanada: economika, politika, kul'tura*, no. 4, pp. 25–40.

5 Do Formal Institutions Really Matter for Foreign Direct Investments to the Russian Federation?

The Case of FDI Flows from the European Union to Russia

Sergei Sutyrin and Olga Trofimenko

Introduction

Being proponents of institutional theory, we endeavor to use its key ideas to analyze investment cooperation between the Russian Federation (RF) and the European Union (EU). Our chapter specifically covers foreign direct investments (FDI) from the EU to Russia. EU companies have long experience investing in the country. Indeed, the first substantial FDI projects took place already in the nineteenth century. Businessmen from Belgium, Germany, Sweden, and other European countries were quite active in exploring opportunities arising from the country's industrialization and need for infrastructure development (telegraph, telephone, tram lines, electrification, etc.).

After the nationalization resulting from the 1917 revolution, Russia received no FDI inflows for almost 70 years. A new era of international investment cooperation began with the economic liberalization initially launched by Mikhail Gorbachev in the second half of the 1980s. FDI dramatically expanded after the collapse of the USSR in 1991. More recently, over the last decade until 2014, the RF was among the fastest-growing host and home countries for FDI in the world. The EU was one of Russia's most important FDI partners, both as a source of investment and as a recipient of Russian FDI.

This chapter aims to test whether or not the institutional environment really influenced FDI flows to Russia generally and EU FDI flows to Russia in particular. The authors identify key institutional changes in the Russian economy and analyze whether these changes led to substantial changes in FDI inflows. At the same time, the chapter considers key macroeconomic indicators that might have affected the process under review. In addition, it compares investment inflows to Russia against the global FDI trends. This allow us to see if the RF is a "trend-taker" or a "trend-maker" in terms of international investment inflows. On the basis of these comparisons, we draw some conclusions and identify key future research questions.

EU–Russia Investment Cooperation: An Institutional Approach

In market economies, individual companies are the ultimate players in international trade and investment activities. While developing respective strategies, they have to take into account both domestic and international rules and regulations such as trade and investment policies at home and in host countries/territories. The influence of these policies on corporate behavior has widely been discussed in the economic literature (e.g. Rugman & Verbeke 1990). Appreciating their high importance, Peng, Wang and Jang (2008) summarized the ideas developed in the academic community on the impact of formal and informal institutions on corporate strategies.

Even though the institution-based view (IBV) considers political, legal, and societal dimensions as part of the institutional environment (Peng, Wang & Jang 2008), this study will focus mainly on the first two, which are closely related and indeed often inseparable. The authors argue that the societal dimension (at least in the context of a present study) is relatively stable and thus cannot influence investment strategies to the same extent as the political and legal ones. According to the World Economic Forum (2014, p. 4), "the institutional environment is determined by the legal and administrative framework within which individuals, firms, and governments interact to generate wealth". Following this approach, the chapter probes the impact of these factors on European investments in Russia. Cultural distance is neglected.

The institutional environment changes over time. EU–Russia investment cooperation has been evolving against a background of EU enlargement and the EU's development of its common internal rules and other regulatory changes, aiming largely at securing the overall interests of the EU. This is witnessed on the Russian side, too. Changes in Russian regulations towards FDI quite often have been tied to Russia's need for investment in certain economic sectors or to the need, as perceived by the Russian Government, to establish/maintain or restore control in strategic industries.

In the case of Russia, it also might be reasonably argued that investors have been confronting so-called "institutional upheaval", defined as "a rapid and pervasive change in the norms and values that underlie and legitimate economic activity, which results in fundamental change in a society's political system, its legal and regulatory frameworks, its economic system, and its financial infrastructure" (Newman 2000, p. 603). Institutional upheaval is a wholesale change of major aspects of an institutional environment and governance systems, accompanied by extreme uncertainty, and ambiguity (Roth & Kostova 2003).

At the beginning of transition period in the early 1990s, Russia opened itself to FDI. Having serious economic problems and ambitious development goals, it tried to influence FDI inflows and outflows by introducing a plethora of rules and norms. An additional transformation took place when Russia began, at the end of the 1990s, to negotiate its accession to the World Trade Organization (WTO). On the one hand, it aimed to benefit from its non-member status prior to accession, introducing with respect to inward FDI WTO-inconsistent requirements. On the other hand, it introduced some changes to bring domestic regulation directly or indirectly dealing with foreign investments into compliance with WTO rules.[1]

According to the WTO, "strong political will at the highest levels and commitment to the process of trade facilitation are often identified as the most important success factors of any trade facilitation reform. Political will frequently represents the overarching factor upon which most of the other success factors rest and depend" (World Trade Organization 2015, p. 10). The same argument could be made about the performance of national and international institutions influencing capital flows – for example, during the Asian financial crisis of 1997–8,

> marked by massive flight of short-term capital and large-scale sell-offs of foreign equity holdings, has at the same time been accompanied by a wave of inward direct investment. This inward investment to some extent reflects policy changes, as Asian governments, under pressure from the IMF and in any case desperate for cash, have dropped old policies unfavorable to foreign ownership. (Krugman 2008)

– a clear illustration of political will and its influence on FDI. Elsewhere, Sutyrin *at al.* (2012) addressed Russian institutional reforms in the context of the WTO accession, looking at, among other things, the energy, financial, agriculture, and automobile sectors, internal taxes, and other areas.

Dunning and Lundan (2008) examined how an institutional dimension could be incorporated into the three components of the Ownership, Location, and Internationalization (OLI) paradigm. In their study, they proposed to separate institutional factors from other influences on the performance of MNEs. At the same time, some authors declared the existence of certain institutions – for example, bilateral investment treaties (BITs) produce an increase in investment flows (Neumayer & Spess 2005). Others disagree arguing that BITs *per se* do not have any substantial effect, if any, on FDI (Hallward-Driemeier 2003; Tobin & Rose-Ackerman 2003).

When researching FDI in transition economies, we must take into account the privatization process as an institutional issue. The policy implications of privatization-related inward FDI have been discussed by many researchers including Kalotay and Hunya (2000) and Hunya (1997). These authors underlined the overall positive effects of privatization-related FDI in Central and Eastern Europe. They argued that predictable and sound policies could contribute to a maximization of both FDI and privatization revenues. Even though, at the moment, this issue is not a crucial one in Russian context, it should be taken into consideration especially due to the fact that Russia maintains certain limitations on the foreign companies' participation in privatizations as described in "Schedules of Specific Commitments on Services" ('Services schedules and MFN exemptions of Russian Federation' 2012) or the Federal Law *On the Order of Foreign Investment in Companies with Strategic Impact on the National Security of the Russian Federation* (FZ-54 2008) and its amendments.

Since the beginning of the 1990s, Russian companies started gradually invest-ing abroad. Later on, via round-tripping, they bolstered Russia's FDI. Up to 2014, Russian TNCs accounted for the bulk of FDI projects originating from transition economies (UNCTAD 2014, p. xxi). The peak of officially reported FDI flows from Russia was reached in 2013 with $87 billion, followed by the decline in 2014 to $56 billion (UNCTAD 2015, p. 8). Many researchers – for example, Lisitsyn *et al.* (2005), Liuhto and Vahtra (2007), Liuhto and Jumpponen (2008), and Kalotay *et al.* (2014) – have paid attention to these developments. The contemporary economic and political trends influencing FDI were addressed by Liuhto (2015) in the case of the challenges of Russia–EU economic cooperation and Kalotay (2015) in the case of the depreciation of the Russian ruble.

Methodology

The study is based upon some key ideas from institutional theory. In particular, with respect to investment, the latter claims that, in general, institutions might either constitute powerful barriers to or provide significant incentives for compa-nies investing in certain countries. The impact of the institutional environment varies depending upon its transparency and stability, as well as changes in regula-tion and political movements. The study investigates investment cooperation between the EU and Russia taking into consideration key changes in their insti-tutional environments pertaining to capital flows.

In addition to the institutional approach, we draw upon the theory of rational expectations for our analysis. Huang (1997, p. 174) shows that "FDI decisions are based upon all available past information, while most of this information is contained in the past investment experience." The authors try to figure out how expectations of foreign investors influence FDI inflows to Russia.

The authors use the data sets of several institutions, namely the Russian Statistical Service (Rosstat), the Central Bank of Russia (CBR), Eurostat, and UNCTAD. In many instances, these data, due to well-known imperfections of FDI statistics, do not match each other. Hence, relative comparisons are an integral part of the study. The difference in FDI statistics from Rosstat and CBR is rather substantial (Table 5.1). Taking into account the fact that the most up-to-date FDI statistics are offered by the CBR, which relies on the OECD *Benchmark Definition of Foreign Direct Investment* (OECD 2008) and the IMF's *Balance of Payments Manual* (IMF 2009), the authors, where appropriate, use the data, provided by the CBR. For a proper comparison, the data from UNCTAD are also used, taking into consideration that in assessing FDI flows the organization takes the data provided

Table 5.1 Annual FDI Inflow to the Russian Federation, 2008–14 ($ millions)

	2008	2009	2010	2011	2012	2013	2014
Rosstat	27,027	15,906	13,810	18,415	18,666	26,118	n.a.
CBR	74,783	36,583	43,168	55,084	50,588	69,219	20,958

Sources: Central Bank of Russia 2015; Rosstat 2015

by national central banks. As comprehensive, reliable, and comparable information on EU investments to Russia does not exist, the authors, where necessary, deal with total amounts of FDI inflows. They believe this approach is an appropriate one, as investors from EU countries with the share of over 70 percent (European Commission 2015) are trend-makers for FDI inflows to the country.

In addition to analyzing the impact of formal institutions, the authors investigate key trends in EU–Russian investment cooperation, highlighting the economic factors influencing FDI flows. The authors use correlation analysis and scatter diagrams to illustrate key findings.

To illustrate the business behavior of foreign investors, the authors present information about two Finnish companies that have been operating on the Russian market for several years: Valio and Stockmann. Finnish Valio is one of few foreign firms expanding production and planning to increase FDI in Russia despite the pressure of economic sanctions. Stockmann represents the other side of the coin: it sold its department stores in Russia. Data about these two companies is mainly based on the information available on their websites and in their annual reports.

Research Findings

European Investments in Russia: General Trends

Inward investment to Russia is dominated by ten particularly active states with almost 84 percent coming from a limited amount of players. Seven out of the top ten investors in Russia are EU countries. Indeed, this region plays a critical role in overall capital inflows to Russia. All in all, the share of EU member states in the Russian inward FDI (IFDI) stock according to Eurostat (2014) is about 75 percent. Figure 5.1 depicts the EU's leading investing countries to the Russian Federation.

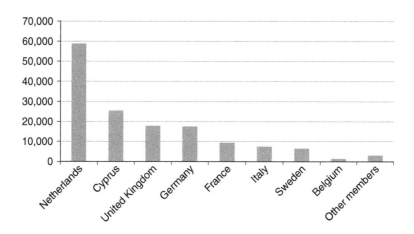

Figure 5.1 Direct Investment Stocks of Selected EU Countries in Russia, as of the End of 2014 (€ millions)

Source: Eurostat 2015

According to Eurostat, the Netherlands and Cyprus are key EU investors in Russia. In some publications Luxemburg also is listed among the leaders (ibid.), mainly due to the activity of special purpose entities (SPEs)[2] registered there; having said that, the information on the investments coming from this country to Russia is not always directly available: it is marked as confidential in the Eurostat database (Eurostat 2015). The bulk of these financial resources is Russian capital that previously was withdrawn (legally or illegally) from the Russian Federation.

Some countries such as Malta and Romania have never participated in meaningful investments projects in Russia. More generally, inflows from almost one third of EU member states are rather low, due to the modest investment activities of these countries' companies, a lack of international experience, and other logics (ibid.). Regardless of the different levels of individual member states FDI to Russia, the EU as a whole is a very important source of FDI for Russia. During the past several years, it represents the vast majority of inflows (Figure 5.2).

The sectoral composition of the EU's investments in Russia corresponds to the general picture. EU member states are among largest actors in all kind of FDI sectors. For example, in 2013, investments from Cyprus dominated FDI in fuel extraction and energy resources, France and the UK were active in manufacturing industries, Luxemburg and the Netherlands prevailed in food processing, and companies from Finland focused on construction.

The bulk of EU investments (around 75 percent) flows to the services sectors, out of which financial and insurance FDI worth €61.5 billion accounted for more than 60 percent (Eurostat 2014). In addition to services, mechanical engineering is perceived as one of the most attractive and promising industries. All in all, the EU's investments to Russia have gradually diversified. Whereas oil and gas sectors initially were the most appealing ones, over the course of time capital

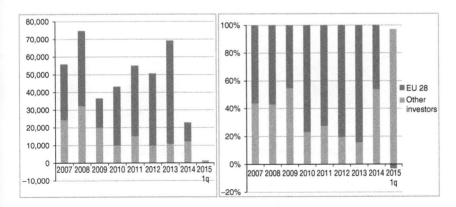

Figure 5.2 Annual FDI Flow to the Russian Federation, 2007–1Q/2015 ($ millions and percent)

Source: Central Bank of Russia 2015

flows to other fields have started to increase. Among other causes, one of the reasons for this includes gradual changes in Russian legislation concerning FDI.

European Investments in Russia: The Role of Formal Institutions

In this chapter, the authors use the widely shared definition of formal institutions as a set of laws, regulations, and conventions that create a legal environment for FDI. Normally, institutions result from several levels of regulation, namely multilateral, bilateral, national, and regional ones. Figure 5.3 combines the data on FDI inflows to the RF and key steps of formal institutions development.

At the multilateral level two documents should be mentioned, namely the Seoul Convention (1985) that created the International Agency on Investments Guarantees and the Washington Convention on the Procedures of Investment Dispute Settlement between States and Foreign Residents (1966). Even though Russia signed both of them, so far it has not ratified the latter. Beyond this, none of those conventions has been used to settle conflicts between Russia and foreign investors. Figure 5.3 does not demonstrate any FDI growth that could be related to those conventions.

As a WTO member, Russia is no longer (with some exceptions that will be terminated in 2018) allowed to apply policies that contravene the WTO Agreement on Trade-Related Investment Measures (TRIMs) and other agreements. At the same time, given that more than a half of the EU's FDI goes into services, the fact that

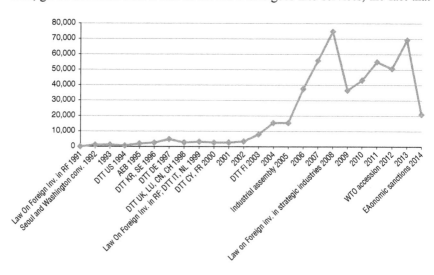

Figure 5.3 Institutional Development and Annual FDI Inflows to Russia, 1991–2014 ($ millions)

Sources: ConsultantPlus 2015; Federal Tax Service of Russia 2015; UNCTADSTAT 2015

Note: Information on DTTs is on the year of coming in force

AEB = Association of European Business; CH = Switzerland; CN = China; CY = Cyprus; DE = Germany; DTT = Double Tax Treaty; FI = Finland; FR = France; IT = Italy; KR = Republic of Korea; LU = Luxemburg; NL = The Netherlands; RF = Russian Federation; SE = Sweden; UK = United Kingdom; US = United States

Russia secured limitations on market access and national treatment in a large number of its sectors and sub-sectors should not be ignored. Figure 5.3 shows moderate FDI growth in 2012 after Russia's accession to the WTO. It is an open question, though, whether this process was really stimulated by the country's membership. Moreover, economic theory and empirical studies tell us that trade liberalization (e.g., tariffs cutting, other things being equal) might discourage FDI as exporting becomes easier (see, for example, Nobakht & Madani 2014).

Sutyrin and Kolesov (2015) analyzed positive and negative changes in dynamics of foreign trade and GDP growth for individual national economies after their accession to the WTO. The study of 29 non-GATT states that successfully acceded to the WTO between 1995 and 2012 revealed not just an absence of any general trend, but also surprisingly small difference between the number of countries that experienced positive and negative dynamics. A similar approach was applied to the impact of WTO accession on IFDI. Despite varying relations between FDI and foreign trade, foreign investments might be expected to grow (resulting from internationally recognized rules application and higher level of transparency), as well as following the principles of General Agreement on Trade in Services (GATS), Agreement on Trade-Related Aspects of Intellectual Property Rights (TRIPs) and TRIMs. Meanwhile, analysis revealed that the annual growth rate of the inward FDI stock after the accession for individual countries fluctuated between minus 11.7 percent and plus 56.0 percent; positive dynamics in annual rate took place in 11 cases out of 21, negative dynamics in the remaining ten.

At the bilateral level, Russia signed a set of Double Tax Treaties (DTTs) and BITs. In total, Russia has 80 DTTs, with all EU members covered. These treaties have been in force for some countries since the mid-1990s (Poland), but for the bulk of EU countries since the beginning of the 2000s (Federal Tax Service 2015). The existence of DTTs allows foreign companies and individuals tax burden optimization. BITs also cover a wide range of countries. Russia/the USSR signed BITs with many current EU members, such as Belgium, France, Germany, Italy, Luxemburg, and the Netherlands in 1989. BITs were concluded much later with some other counties like Finland (1996) (ConsultantPlus 2015). The treaties provide additional guaranties to foreign investors – for example, in the case of nationalization. As it is shown on Figure 5.3, there was no significant FDI inflow growth as a result of the aforementioned agreements.

At the national/federal level, Russia gradually modified its civil, tax, and customs codes – the latter in parallel with Russia's WTO accession negotiations and the Eurasian integration process. The law specifically designed to regulate foreign investments in Russia was adopted in 1991 and modified in 1999. There is no need to list all other legal acts influencing FDI inflows (e.g., the 1990 Federal Law on Banks and Banking, the 1992 Federal Law on Insurance Activities, etc.). It is sufficient to mention that being initially introduced in the beginning of the 1990s, they gradually evolved, as a rule, in the direction of promoting greater liberalization. Figure 5.3 clearly shows that introduction of two basic laws on FDI hardly led to substantive positive changes in investment flows, which remained rather low until 2005.

A substantial change in FDI regulation resulted from the Federal Law *On the Order of Foreign Investment in Companies with Strategic Impact on the National Security of the Russian Federation*. It considerably restricted investments into several "strategic sectors". Foreign investors were not allowed to acquire controlling stakes in Russian oil and gas companies. Instead, they were encouraged to participate in joint projects (FZ-54 2008). In line with this, Shell and Gazprom, at the very beginning of 2014, created a joint venture aimed at extracting of shale oil in Western Siberia (Shell 2015). The law per se did not have any serious negative effect on extractive industries: it was actively discussed prior the adoption and foreign investors managed to adjust.

Another important factor influencing inward investment was the introduction of Russian Government Decision No166 *On Alterations in the Customs Tariff of Russian Federation with Regard to Spare Parts Imported into the Country for Industrial Assembly*, issued on 29 March 2005 ('Government Decision No166' 2005). The document fixed zero import duties on almost all spare parts and components entering the territory of the country to be used in industrial assembly of vehicles on the territory of the Russian Federation. For some products, customs duties were reduced substantially. In addition, the government introduced prohibitive import duties on second-hand automobiles, together with preserving high import duties on new cars at 25 percent level. The goal was to provide additional incentives for foreign companies to invest in car assembling enterprises. This led to the increase of FDI into the sector, with the total amount of foreign investments in Russian automotive sector growing to $4.2 billion by 2012 (Samofalova 2007). In particular, companies like BMW, PSA Peugeot Citroën, and Renault-Nissan established new production lines in the country.

The economic sanctions imposed on Russia, especially those of European countries, clearly influenced investment cooperation and had an impact equivalent to institutional upheaval. Indeed, in a very short period of time, the "rules of the game" have changed substantially due to the EU imposing several types of restrictions against Russia "over the Ukraine crisis" from March 2014. These sanctions have poisoned the general atmosphere for investment and have had specific effects. For example, there is a prohibition on investing in Crimea. EU citizens and EU-based companies cannot buy real estate or entities there, finance local companies, or supply related services. In addition, they may not invest in infrastructure projects.

The general idea of the European measures, among other things, is to hamper the access of Russian business entities to external financial resources. In addition, the EU imposed a ban on the supply of dual-purpose goods and equipment for geological prospecting and the extraction of mineral resources from shelf deposits. The latter made the maintenance of existing/the initiation of new oil and gas extraction projects impossible. Under the circumstances, it is logical enough to expect declines in FDI inflows.

At the same time, Russia's retaliatory sanctions of August 2014 did not aim at similarly impacting investment cooperation in a negative way. Case 1 illustrates the point.

Case 5.1 Impact of the Russian import ban on Valio Oy: every cloud has its silver lining

Economic sanctions are traditionally regarded as a factor that restrains international cooperation in many fields, including investment. At the same time, under certain conditions, they can have an opposite effect. A Russian food embargo that prohibits, among other things, imports of milk and dairy products might stimulate production and investment growth in Russia.

Valio Oy is the leading Finnish producer of milk and dairy products. The bulk of production premises is located in Finland. It also owns two factories in Estonia and one in Ershovo, the Moscow region (producing melted cheese Viola and slicing and packing hard cheese). The total volume of investments to the project in Russia exceeded €60 million (Valio 2015). Regardless the existence of production facilities, the company was one of the leading exporters of dairy products to the Russian Federation. The Russian market was a very important destination: Valio exported to Russia about 20 percent of its total production (that accounted for 49 percent of the company's total exports) (RBC 2015).

Since the Russian Government imposed so-called "anti-sanctions" on 7 August 2014, most product lines became the subjects of embargo.

In order to retain the market share, the company had to undertake urgent measures – in particular, expanding production in Russia. In October 2014, Valio announced the start of milk and cream production using the facilities of its partner company Galaktika. In January 2015, Valio launched the production of yoghurt and cheese at the premises of German-owned factory Ehrmann in the Moscow region. Another company, Kochmeister Rus, became a platform for contract butter production. Manufacturing at Valio's own factory in Ershovo has increased as well. All in all, the company plans to double its output compared to the pre-sanctions period, even though it admits that it is not possible to substitute with local production all the various lines existing before sanctions.

There are certain obstacles that do not allow Valio to increase its production in Russia rapidly. The company is very sensitive to the quality of milk; therefore, only a selected number of suppliers in Russia meets the requirements. In addition, some products, such as lactose-free cheese, are produced by Valio in Finland only, largely due to some peculiarities and complexity in technology. There is no need to initiate a relatively costly process of transferring this production to Russia: the embargo does not cover lactose-free products. In the short run, the utilization of partners' facilities to increase production in Russia allowed Valio to compensate partly decrease of its market share. But the company would like to restore and to retain its market share. In particular, in the future it might localize production of hard cheese. In order to reach this goal, the company is planning to build a new factory. Under the circumstances, Russia might expect new investments from the EU (RBC 2015).

All in all, one sees the gradual development of formal institutions regulating FDI inflows to Russia. Most of the efforts relate to the goal of achieving a certain level of liberalization and enhancing investments into desired sectors. The existing institutional environment is far from perfect, but, taking into consideration the fact it was created against the background of the system that did now allow any FDI, one might argue, a certain level of success has been achieved. In most cases, institutional developments did not have any direct positive impact on FDI. Figure 5.3 clearly shows that the introduction of the two basic laws on FDI, DTTs, and BITs with key investing countries did not result in any substantial investment expansion. The impact of Russia's WTO accession on FDI inflows also is unclear. Rapid IFDI growth took place after 2005 and could be connected to industrial assembly programs. At the same time, a rather modest amount of inflows in the automotive industry ($4.2 billion by 2012 compared to total amount of investments in Russian economy) suggests other factors had greater impact on the process. In 2014, when economic sanctions were imposed, the institutional environment had a seriously negative effect on FDI.

To sum up, no individual specific institutional change exerted a powerful impact on FDI, including EU investments, to Russia. Nevertheless, we argue that altogether they create the necessary environment that is generally favorable for foreign investments. In addition, due to certain inertia of business processes, there must be a natural lag between creation of new institutions and company's decisions to invest. Complementing institutional analysis with that of macroeconomic indicators could provide more comprehensive understanding of IFDI flows into Russia.

FDI from the EU to Russia

Role of the Macroeconomic Factors

First of all, we would like to analyze whether investment inflows to Russian corresponded with global and regional trends. Figure 5.4 shows a high level of correlation between FDI inflows to Russia and global FDI outflows without the EU (0.89). The correlation between FDI inflows to Russia and the EU's FDI outflows is small (0.47), but this is in line with the correlation between the EU's FDI outflows and the rest of the world (0.44) (Figure 5.5). This is due to high activity levels in EU companies in 1997–2000, followed by a peak in 2007 and a gradual slowdown since 2008.

For almost 15 years (i.e., 1999–2013), one may observe substantial GDP growth in Russia. In its turn it influenced, for example, real income growth and market size positively. Under the circumstances, inward investments to Russia demonstrated a high level of correlation with the country's GDP, current prices (0.89). Figure 5.6 shows this clearly. The correlation coefficient between IFDI and GDP is even higher if calculated with the exclusion of 2014 (0.95).[3] A similar picture appears if we consider GDP per capita.

Figure 5.7 shows relationship between FDI inflows to Russia and average income per capita. The dependence between two categories is an exponential one – FDI

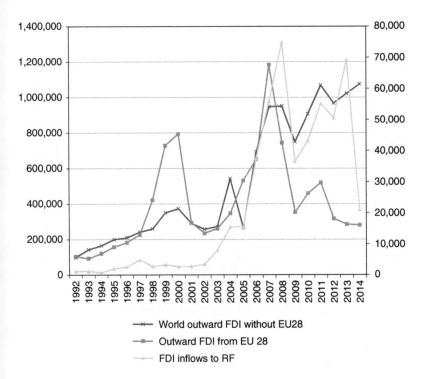

Figure 5.4 The Development of FDI Flows, 1992–2014 ($ millions; current prices and current exchange rates)

Source: UNCTADSTAT 2015

Note: World OFDI without EU 28 and OFDI from EU 28 – left axis; FDI inflows to RF – right axis

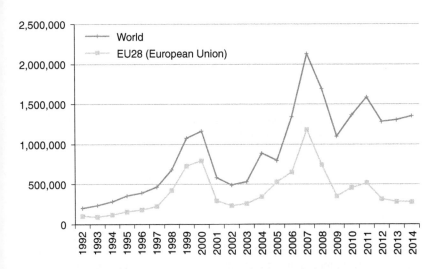

Figure 5.5 The Development of Annual FDI Outflow, 1992–2014 ($ millions; current prices)

Source: UNCTADSTAT 2015

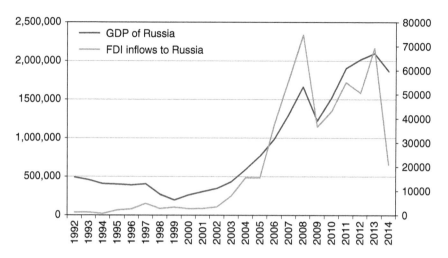

Figure 5.6 The Development of the Russian GDP and FDI Inflow to Russia, 1992–2014
(\$ millions; current prices and current exchange rates)

Source: UNCTADSTAT 2015

Note: GDP of Russia – left axis, FDI inflows to Russia – right axis

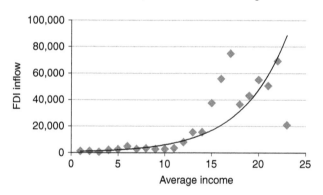

Figure 5.7 FDI Inflow to Russia and Average Income Per Capita in the Russian Federation,
1992–2014 (\$ millions and ₽ thousands)

Sources: Rosstat 2015; UNCTADSTAT 2015

Note: FDI inflow to Russia (\$ millions; current prices), average monthly income per capita in the
Russian Federation (₽ thousands)

grew faster than income. This is in line with the theory of rational expectations:
companies make decisions based on available information, previous experiences,
as well as expectations about future prospects. Average monthly income per
capita was gradually increasing in Russia (in rubles) regardless of the GDP
contraction in 2009 and economic slowdown starting from 2012. Since the end of

2014, the Russian ruble sank substantially (almost double drop between January 2014 and January 2016). In combination with negative forecasts for Russia's GDP growth for 2015–16, this resulted in loss of positive perception of the market prospects for some of foreign investors. Case 2 illustrates the point.

Current Trends and Future Prospects

The authors argue that the FDI decline in 2014 was the result of two simultaneously existing and interconnected factors: institutional (a general worsening of Russian image worldwide and political tensions influencing companies' performance[4]) and economic (the decrease of oil prices, the depreciation of Russian ruble,[5] market shrinking, inflation, and federal budget deficit). Moreover, expectations of foreign investors regarding the prospects of the Russian market, at least in the short run, tend to prevent new FDI.

A survey on the prospects of European companies in Russia done jointly by the Association of European Business (AEB) and market research company Growth from Knowledge (GfK) in the beginning of 2015 revealed some somber

---

Case 5.2   Stockmann in Russia

Stockmann is a Finnish retail company operating in 16 countries, including its home market, Sweden, the Baltic States, Saudi Arabia, and the United Arab Emirates. The second largest revenue source after Finland for several years appeared to be the RF, with a 25 percent share in 2012 (Stockmann 2012, p. 19).

Stockmann was one of the first foreign retailers to enter the Russian market: the first shop in Moscow was opened in 1989.With several brands (Stockmann, Lindex, and Seppälä), the company was present in 16 different cities, including Moscow, Saint Petersburg, and Yekaterinburg, with 76 shops (ibid., p. 15). The profitability was a challenge for many years. In 2012, the company reported operating profit growth in Russia as the result of the ruble strengthening (ibid., p. 30). When analyzing risks and opportunities in Russia, the company noted already in 2012 that consumer behavior and purchasing power depended a lot on energy prices, especially oil prices (ibid., p. 35).

Starting from 2013, Stockmann's financial results in Russia deteriorated. The stagnation of economic growth in the country in 2014 and weak national currency significantly reduced the company's revenue in euros, regardless of some growth in the ruble. All in all, there was a loss of €34.2 million (Stockmann 2014, p. 12). Poor economic results forced Stockmann to adjust to new conditions and, in 2015, it announced an intention to sell most of its stores in Russia. By February 2016, the €5-million deal was settled (Lenta.ru 2016).

estimates. The results of the study showed general worsening of the so-called Business Sentiment Index, with positive giving way to neutral ones. All in all, 5 percent of companies under the review directly and 16 percent indirectly were the subject of the EU/US sanctions against Russia. Russia's retaliatory measures directly influenced 2 percent of EU companies directly, 7 percent partly, and 38 percent indirectly. Respondents named bureaucracy, legislative restrictions, a lack of qualified personnel, and the unreliability of value chains among major barriers to sustainable development of their businesses in Russia. Nevertheless, long-term expectations appeared to be relatively positive (Association of European Business 2015).

Regardless of current negative trends, in many instances the Russian market still offers substantial opportunities for European investors. Russia has an urgent need for infrastructure investments such as the modernization of Baikal-Amur Mainline (BAM) and Trans-Siberian railroads. Urbanization processes and the World (Football) Cup 2018 are expected to create an additional demand for foreign capital. Moreover, having substantial social and defense expenditures, Russia has to ensure their financing in the state budget. The current version of the Russian state budget presumes a certain level of government debt, a part of which should be covered from privatization. European investors might participate in these projects.

In informal conversations, representatives of some European companies mention that they receive better than ever treatment from local authorities. Officials understand that in order to overcome existing challenges caused by negative external factors,[6] they should try to do their best to keep foreign investors in the country. In turn, many European businesses support the restoration of the pre-sanction regime. For example, the AEB declared that it opposed measures against Russia (Interfax 2014). Moreover, companies have been looking for opportunities to bypass existing restrictions. According to Philippe Pegorier, Chairman of AEB in Russia, European business is interested in maintaining its existing investment stakes in the Russian economy despite mutual sanctions. According to Pegorier, business could adjust to new conditions, particular taking resources from European-owned factories in China and India (RBC 2014). FDI flows to Russia also may go via companies under the European ownership but registered in jurisdictions that do not participate in economic sanctions.

In short and even medium run, European direct investments to Russia most probably will decline, mainly due to the fact that investors do not believe the Russian economy will experience a substantial recovery over the next couple of years. Instead, they anticipate economic slowdown. Expected decrease in government procurements caused by budget constraints might have additional negative effects on inward foreign investments. As sensibly argued by Kalotay (2015, p. 32),

> the deteriorating prospects of the Russian economy will hit again most of the forms of FDI, especially market-seeking inbound FDI and natural-resource-based outbound FDI. Potential exceptions can be identified in privatization

deals, which depend more on government decisions, natural-resource-seeking inward FDI, which will react more to international market prices of raw materials, and exodus capital.

Conclusions

European capital accounts for about three-quarters of total investments in Russia. In many cases, Russian capital, previously withdrawn from the country, mimics European capital and is returning. At the same time, the share of Russia in the EU's outward FDI stock is low: about 3 percent (Eurostat 2014, 2015). Investments from the EU to Russia can be found in almost all economic sectors, with a predominance in wholesale and retail trade, manufacturing, and extractive industries. Russian trade policy measures with regard to FDI and import regulation stimulated capital flows in some sectors.

Generally speaking, the analysis presented herein shows that the institutional environment is far from being a key determinant of FDI flows to Russia generally and EU FDI flows to Russia specifically. Nevertheless, this is not entirely the case when there is institutional upheaval, which took place twice in the history of contemporary Russia: in the beginning of the 1990s, when the legal environment for FDI inflows was introduced, and, in 2014, after certain (including investment) restrictions were imposed against Russia. In the first case, institutional upheaval did not lead to any substantial FDI inflows for several years – until 1997. Legislative changes were accumulated and, by the end of the decade, the key elements of institutional environment favorable for FDI were created. In the second case, political tensions led to the decay of investment activities.

Russia, in general, has moved to improve formal institutions related to FDI through its negotiations to join the WTO, legal and economic reforms connected to the process, as well as (unfortunately terminated) negotiations on OECD accession.

Assessing the impact of formal institution on the EU's FDI flows to Russia, one could sensibly argue that a proper institutional environment is a necessary, but not a sufficient precondition. Analysis of the key institutional changes shows that only a few of them had more or less significant direct effect on FDI. In most cases, the strategies of foreign investors are mainly influenced by the pull and push factors related to market-seeking, efficiency-seeking, and resource-seeking motives.

All in all, institutional factors should be studied together with general factors related to the economy. Typically, the existence of a certain kind of institutional environment has only a supplemental or supportive effect. This said, the presence of certain institutions gives a clear sign with regard to general attitude of a given country towards foreign capital. The influence of institutions can be really huge in time of institutional upheaval. Quick and radical changes in legislation, especially restrictive ones, including embargos and all kinds of other bans, have a serious negative effect on FDI, at least in the short run.

The interdependency of institutional and economic factors is of clear significance. Current economic crisis might *ceteris paribus* stimulate the Russian

Government to undertake new reforms in line with international trends of regulation. As the Global Competitiveness Report states,

> the importance of a sound and fair institutional environment has become all the more apparent during the recent economic and financial crisis and is especially crucial for further solidifying the fragile recovery, given the increasing role played by the state at the international level and for the economies of many countries. (World Economic Forum 2014, p. 4)

The present study is limited by a lack of proper comparable statistics on EU–Russia investment cooperation and information for certain time periods. The chapter presented a picture of the influence of formal institutions on the EU's FDI flows to Russia. Further studies could cover reverse capital flows. Moreover, special attention could be paid to the influence of institutional factors on the investment activities of SMEs. Taking into consideration their limited resources, one might expect a higher influence of institutional environment for this group of companies. Last, but not least, having similar economic and institutional conditions, different companies generate different results in terms of profit, turnover, and market share. The abilities of companies to adjust to altered conditions should not be forgotten in FDI studies.

Notes

1 Many other components of the WTO system are of clear relevance to investments. In one of the reports, the WTO ambitiously claimed: "Because the benefits which the WTO brings to the world economy come primarily via the impact of the WTO on investment decisions, it is no exaggeration to say that investment is at the heart of the WTO" (World Trade Organization 1996).
2 A special-purpose entity is a legal entity "established to perform specific functions limited in scope or time,... having no or few non-financial assets and employees, little or no production or operations and sometimes no physical presence beyond a 'brass plate' confirming its place of registration, related to another corporation, often as a subsidiary and often resident in a territory other than the territory of residence of the related corporation... its core business function consists of financing its group activities or holding assets and liabilities of its group, that is the channeling of funds from non-residents to other non-residents, and with only a minor role for managing and directing activities" (Eurostat 2013).
3 Exclusion of 2014 does not change substantially the correlation between the Russian GDP and outward investments from Russia.
4 A very clear impact of prohibitions used was the direct and indirect ban that many CEOs received from the US Government prior to the Saint Petersburg Economic Forum 2014, where many investment contracts were usually signed. They had to skip their scheduled trips to Russia and assign staff of lower level to attend (Forbes 2014).
5 According to Kalotay (2015), all types of FDI, privatization-related, natural resource-seeking, market-seeking, efficiency-seeking, and round-tripped capital, were hit by the rapid change of the exchange rate of the Russian ruble.
6 In addition to sanctions, decline of oil prices, substantial capital outflows, and some others are commonly named in this context.

Bibliography

Association of European Business 2015, *Strategies and Prospects of AEB Member Companies in Russia*, viewed 15 September 2015, http://gtmarket.ru/news/2015/06/16/7205

Central Bank of Russia 2015, *Foreign Direct Investments to Russian Federation*, viewed 15 November 2015, http://www.cbr.ru/statistics

ConsultantPlus 2015, *Mezhdunarodnye dogovory Rossijskoj Federacii o pooshchrenii i vzaimnoj zashchite kapitalovlozhenij i investicij*, viewed 10 October 2015, www.consultant.ru

Dunning, J. & Lundan, S. 2008, 'Institutions and the OLI paradigm of the multinational enterprise', *Asia Pacific Journal of Management*, vol. 25, no. 4, pp. 573–93.

European Commission 2015, *Countries and Regions: Russia*, viewed 20 November 2015, http://ec.europa.eu/trade/policy/countries-and-regions/countries/russia/

Eurostat 2013, *Eurostat Statistics Explained: Glossary*, viewed 20 March 2016 http://ec.europa.eu/eurostat/statistics-explained/index.php/Glossary:Special-purpose_entity_(SPE)

Eurostat 2014, *Foreign Direct Investment Between the European Union and BRIC*, viewed 20 November 2015, http://epp.eurostat.ec.europa.eu/statistics_explained/index.php/Foreign_direct_investment_between_the_European_Union_and_BRIC#cite_note-2

Eurostat 2015, *EU Direct Investment Positions, Breakdown by Country and Economic Activity (BPM6) [bop_fdi6_pos]*, viewed 2 March 2016, http://ec.europa.eu/eurostat/web/balance-of-payments/data/database

Federal Tax Service of Russia 2015, *Primenjaemye soglashenija ob izbezhanii dvoinogo nalogooblozhenija*, viewed 10 October 2015, https://www.nalog.ru/rn77/about_fts/international_cooperation/mpa/dn/

Forbes 2014, *Peterburskij ehkonomicheskij forum – 2014*, viewed 10 October 2015, http://www.forbes.ru/sobytiya-package/vlast/257657-peterburskii-ekonomicheskii-forum-2014

FZ-54 2008, *On the Order of Foreign Investment in Companies with Strategic Impact on the National Security of the Russian Federation*, The Federal Assembly of the Russian Federation, Moscow.

'Government Decision No166' 2005, *On Alterations in the Customs Tariff of Russian Federation with Regard to Spare Parts Imported into the Country for Industrial Assembly*, The Government of the Russian Federation, Moscow.

Hallward-Driemeier, M. 2003, *Do Bilateral Investment Treaties Attract Foreign Direct Investment? Only a Bit... and They Could Bite*, World Bank Policy Research Paper WPS 3121, World Bank, Washington, DC.

Huang, G. 1997, *Determinants of United States: Japanese Foreign Direct Investment: A Comparison Across Countries and Industries*, Garland, New York & London.

Hunya, G. 1997, 'Large privatization, restructuring and foreign direct investment', in S Zecchini (ed.), *Lessons from the Economic Transition: Central and Eastern Europe in the 1990s*, Kluwer Academic, Boston.

IMF 2009, *Balance of Payments and International Investment Position Manual 2009*, 6th edition (BPM6), International Monetary Fund, Washington, DC.

Interfax 2014, *Evropejskie kompanii nazvali RF strategicheskim partnerom vopreki sankciyam*, viewed 1 November 2015, http://www.interfax.ru/business/396449

Kalotay, K. 2015, 'The impact of the new ruble crisis on Russian FDI', *Baltic Rim Economies*, no. 1, pp. 31–2.

Kalotay, K. & Hunya, G. 2000, 'Privatization and FDI in Central and Eastern Europe', *Transnational Corporations*, vol. 9, no. 1, pp. 40–66.

Kalotay, K., Éltető, A., Sass, M. & Weiner, C. 2014, *Russian Capital in the Visegrad Countries*, Centre for Economic and Regional Studies of the Hungarian Academy of Sciences, Institute of World Economics, Working Paper 210, Budapest.

Krugman, P. 1998, *Fire-sale FDI*, viewed 9 November 2015, http://web.mit.edu/krugman/www/FIRESALE.htm

Lenta.ru 2016, *Stockmann prodal ubytochnye torgovye centry v Rossii*, viewed 1 February 2016, https://lenta.ru/news/2016/02/01/stockmann/

Lisitsyn, N., Sutyrin, S., Trofimenko, O. & Vorobieva, I. 2005, *Outward Internationalisation of Russian Leading Telecom Companies*, Pan-European Institute, University of Turku, Turku.

Liuhto, K. 2015, 'The economic dependence of EU member states on Russia', in A. Pabriks & A. Kudors (eds.), *The War in Ukraine: Lessons for Europe*, The Centre for East European Policy Studies, University of Latvia Press, Rīga.

Liuhto, K. & Jumpponen, J. 2008, 'International activities of Russian Corporations: where does Russian business expansion lead?', *Russian Economic Trends*, vol. 10, no. 3–4, pp.19–29.

Liuhto, K. & Vahtra, P. 2007, 'Foreign operations of Russia's largest industrial corporations: building a typology', *Transnational Corporations*, vol. 16, no. 1, pp. 28–36.

Neumayer, E. & Spess, L. 2005, 'Do bilateral investment treaties increase foreign direct investment to developing countries?', *World Development*, vol. 33, no. 10, pp. 1567–85.

Newman, K. 2000, 'Organizational transformation during institutional upheaval', *Academy of Management Review*, vol. 25, no. 3, pp. 602–19.

Nobakht, M. & Madani, S. 2014, 'Is FDI spillover conditioned on financial development and trade liberalization: evidence from UMCs', *Journal of Business and Management Sciences*, vol. 2, no. 2, pp. 26–34.

OECD 2008, *Benchmark Definition of Foreign Direct Investment*, 4th edition, viewed 15 September 2015, www.oecd.org/publishing/corrigenda

Peng, M., Wang, D. & Jang, G. 2008, 'An institutional-based view of international business strategy: a focus on emerging economies', *Journal of International Business Studies*, vol. 39, no. 5, pp. 920–36.

RBC 2014, *Evropejskij biznes gotov sohranit' dolyu investicij v Rossii*, viewed 10 November 2015, http://www.rbc.ru/rbcfreenews/20140919144858.shtml

RBC 2015, *Molochnaya adaptaciya: kak Valio i «Svalya» kompensiruyut poteri ot sankcij*, viewed 10 November 2015, http://www.rbc.ru/business/14/04/2015/5527a3b59a79471 93d322534

Rosstat 2014, *On Foreign Investments in Russian Federation in 2013*, viewed 19 October 2014, http://www.gks.ru/wps/wcm/connect/rosstat_main/rosstat/ru/statistics/enterprise/investment/foreign/

Rosstat 2015, *Srednedushevye dohody naseleniya*, viewed 10 November 2015, http://www.gks.ru/wps/wcm/connect/rosstat_main/rosstat/ru/statistics/population/level/#

Roth, K. & Kostova, T. 2003, 'Organizational coping with institutional upheaval in transition economies', *Journal of World Business*, vol. 38, no. 4, pp. 314–30.

Rugman, A. & Verbeke, A. 1990, 'American trade policy and corporate strategy', *World Competition: Law and Economic Review*, vol. 13, no. 4, pp. 79–90.

Samofalova, O. 2007, *Inostrannye avtogiganty zavershily ekspansiuy v Russiuy*, viewed 10 October 2015, http://www.rb.ru/article/inostrannye-avtogiganty-zavershili-ekspansiyu-v-rossiyu/5014407.html

'Services schedules and MFN exemptions of Russian Federation' 2012, viewed 1 September 2015, https://www.wto.org/english/thewto_e/countries_e/russia_e.htm

Shell 2015, *Projects of Shell in Russia*, viewed 10 October 2015, http://www.shell.com.ru/aboutshell/shell-businesses/shell-businesses-russia.html

Stockmann 2012, *Annual Report*, viewed 1 February 2016, http://www.stockmanngroup.com/en/annual-reports

Stockmann 2014, *Annual Report*, viewed 1 February 2016, http://www.stockmanngroup.com/en/annual-reports

Sutyrin, S. & Kolesov, D. 2015, 'Impact of accession to the WTO on Russian economy: analysis of international background', in K. Kumo & I. Korgun (eds.), *Foreign Economic Relations and Regional Growth in North East Asia: Russia's WTO Accession and Its Effects*, The Institute of Economic Research, Hitotsubashi University, Tokyo.

Sutyrin, S., Lomagin, N., Sherov-Ignatiev, V., Trofimenko, O., Kapustkin, V., Nazarova, M. & Lisitsyn, N. 2012, *Russia's Accession to the WTO: Major Commitments, Possible Implications*, viewed 10 October 2015, International Trade Center, www.intracen.org

Tobin, J. & Rose-Ackerman, S. 2003, *Foreign Direct Investment and the Business Environment in Developing Countries: The Impact of Bilateral Investment Treaties*, William Davidson Institute Working Paper 587, viewed 10 October 2015, http://deepblue.lib.umich.edu/bitstream/handle/2027.42/39973/wp587.pdf

UNCTAD 2009, *World Investment Report (WIR) 2009: Transnational Corporations, Agricultural Production, and Development*, United Nations, New York & Geneva.

UNCTAD 2014, *World Investment Report (WIR) 2014: Investing in the SDGs: An Action Plan*, United Nations, New York & Geneva.

UNCTAD 2015, *World Investment Report (WIR) 2015: Reforming International Investment Governance*, United Nations, New York & Geneva.

UNCTADSTAT 2015, *Foreign Direct Investment: Inward and Outward Flows and Stock, Annual, 1980–2014*, viewed 10 October 2015, http://unctadstat.unctad.org/wds/ReportFolders/reportFolders.aspx

Valio 2015, *Proizvodstvo Valio v Rossii*, viewed 10 November 2015, http://www.valio.ru/production-valio-in-russia/

World Economic Forum 2014, *The Global Competitiveness Report 2014–2015*, Geneva.

World Trade Organization 1996, *Trade and Foreign Direct Investment*, viewed 10 October 2015, https://www.wto.org/english/news_e/pres96_e/pr057_e.htm

World Trade Organization 2015, *World Trade Report 2015*, New York & Geneva.

6 Investment Relations between Sweden and Russia

Torbjörn Becker[1]

Introduction

Sweden and Russia have a long history of trade and investment but over time the nature and level of investments have shifted as the political and economic circumstances have changed. Kragh (2014a) provides a very long-term perspective on trade and investments between the two countries dating back to the Vikings, as well as an overview of the Swedish companies that were exporting to and investing in Russia from the middle of the nineteenth century and over the Swedish manufacturing boom in the early twentieth century. A striking fact is that, in 1915, Russia accounted for 30 percent of Swedish exports of engineering products, equivalent to the exports to Norway, Germany, and Great Britain combined. Many Swedish firms were, at the time, also investing in Russia, including ASEA, (Electro)Lux, LM Ericsson, Nordiska Kompaniet (NK), the Nobel brothers, and Svenska Kullager Fabriken (SKF). All of this, of course, came to an abrupt end in 1917 when the Bolsheviks came to power and private assets were confiscated. According to estimates reported in Kragh (2014b), the assets seized from (at least) 148 Swedish companies and 401 households amounted to around 6 percent of Swedish GDP at the time.

Fast forward to the next significant boom of Swedish FDI in the 1980s, when Swedish investments abroad increased by 500 percent in real terms between 1980 and 1987. Swedenborg, Johansson-Grahn, and Kinnwall (1988) provide a detailed account of survey data from the Research Institute of Industrial Economics between 1965 and 1986. The top three Swedish multinationals in terms of employment were at the time Electrolux, SKF, and Ericsson – well-known investors in Russia at the beginning of the twentieth century as described above. The FDI boom continued through the 1990s as is shown in Hakkala and Zimmermann (2005), where the above data is extended to 2003. In the mid-2000s, Finland overtook the USA as the largest recipient of Swedish FDI. At the same time, Russia did not enter the top 20 list of countries in terms of affiliate turnover and employment, but entered in 15th place in terms of exports by Swedish MNEs. By the early 2000s, Swedish FDI started to flow to Russia again at a significant rate and, by the end of 2014, Russia accounted for around 2 percent of the stock of Swedish FDI.

Investments from Russia to Sweden have not been significant, although Russia's global investments have increased substantially. In 2014, Russia ranked in sixth place in outward foreign direct investment (OFDI) flows and 17th in terms of FDI stocks according to UNCTAD data reported in Liuhto (2015). A comprehensive survey of Russian OFDI and discussion of how Russia became a significant investor abroad is provided in Liuhto and Majuri (2014). In a study of OFDI from the Russian steel industry, Fortescue and Hanson (2015) argue that the driving forces behind these investments have been both psychological and political, in addition to the more regular business-related factors. They also conclude that the OFDI strategies in the steel sector have not been very successful due to poor timing and debt dependence. None of the investments by Russian firms studied in their article went to Sweden, consistent with the overall picture of limited investment flows from Russia to Sweden.

This chapter will contrast the investment relations of the past with the more recent experience of the last decade and a half. More specifically, it will provide a detailed analysis of bilateral investment data between Sweden and Russia, and discuss some of the difficulties we face with data on bilateral economic links in an era of globalization, movable multinationals, and tax havens. Several hypotheses regarding bilateral capital flows from a growing academic literature will then be compared to the actual data on investments between Sweden and Russia before some policy-related comments are made to conclude the chapter.

Theoretical and Methodological Framework

The academic literature on the determinants of capital flows goes back a long time to the early models of trade and factor mobility and has since developed both in macro and micro models. This chapter will not provide an overview of this large and growing literature, but Lizondo (1990) presents an extensive overview of the early models of FDI. Markusen and Maskus (2001) give a more detailed exposé of general equilibrium models of MNEs, while Dunning (2001) presents a detailed history of how his Ownership, Location and Internationalization (OLI) framework has developed over time. The empirical investigations are to a large extent based on extensions of the gravity model that has been used to explain trade (see Anderson 2010) and has lately received theoretical underpinnings also from studies of FDI (see, e.g., Bergstrand & Egger 2007; Kleinert & Toubal 2010). A number of key hypotheses from this literature will guide the investigation of investments between Sweden and Russia.

In particular, this study will address the following questions:

- Has FDI been moving in line with standard macro and finance variables as suggested by risk/return arguments regarding international capital flows?[2]
- Do investment flows follow trade flows or has FDI replaced exports over time?[3]

- Are FDI flows more stable than portfolio investments, and does FDI provide more international risk sharing in this sense?[4]
- What type of FDI (horizontal, vertical, export-platform, complex) dominates investments between Sweden and Russia and do investments come in the form of greenfield investments or merger and acquisition (M&A)?[5]
- Are the observed flows and levels of FDI between Sweden and Russia consistent with predictions from previous empirical studies?[6]

In addition to answering these research questions regarding investment flows, the answers can also be relevant to policy makers considering various strategies to influence trade and investment as part of a more extensive growth strategy.

Swedish–Russian Data

Macro-Level Data

To put the discussion of investment flows in perspective, Figure 6.1 shows some basic statistics on the relative size and importance of the two countries in 2014. The left panel takes a Swedish perspective and relates trade and investment to and from Russia to total Swedish trade and investment. The highest bar in the chart, at around 5 percent, is the share of Swedish imports that come from Russia. At around 2 percent we have the bars representing Swedish exports and FDI to Russia, as well as Russia's share of world GDP. The share of Swedish portfolio investment going to Russia is less than 0.5 percent – in line with the Russian stock market's weight in the financial markets index provider MSCI's All Country World Index (ACWI). However, Russian investments in Sweden account for a negligible share of foreign investments in Sweden.

The right panel shows the corresponding data from a Russian perspective. Sweden accounts for around 1 percent of total Russian trade, with a higher share

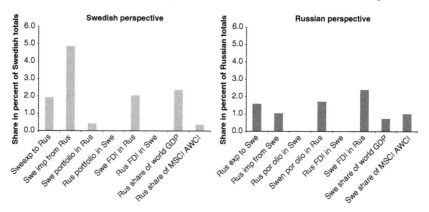

Figure 6.1 The Relative Importance of Sweden and Russia for Each Other, 2014 (percent)
Source: Author's calculations based on data of CBR 2015; SCB 2015

in terms of Russian exports than imports. On the investment side, Swedish investment in Russia is around 2 percent of foreign investments in the country, with a slight overweight on FDI compared to portfolio investments. Although Sweden is not a large country in terms of world GDP, its share in the MSCI AWCI of around 1 percent is higher than Russia's share. Nevertheless, there is little investment traveling in any form from Russia to Sweden.

Investment flows in both directions have increased since the end of the 1990s, but exactly by how much depends on what data source we look at. In general, international investment flows are part of the balance of payments statistics, which is included in the regular official statistics. In Sweden, the central bank (the Riksbank) has commissioned Statistics Sweden (SCB) to produce and publish the statistics, while in Russia, the data is available from the Central Bank of Russia's (CBR's) website. Bilateral FDI data is also available from, among others, the OECD and the UNCTAD. In general, the OECD reports the data coming from the country that receives investment inflows, while the UNCTAD country pages take both inflows and outflows from the respective countries official data. The IMF is also leading the Coordinated Direct Investment Survey (CDIS) to improve quality of direct investment data, but the data starts only in 2009. Here we will only compare the official SCB and CBR data.

Another important twist regarding international capital flows is that they are on a regular basis routed through tax havens. This is less of a problem when we look at aggregate inflows and outflows from a country that is not a tax haven, but can lead to a very skewed picture when we want to understand bilateral flows between, for example, Sweden and Russia. To illustrate, according to the IMF's CDIS for 2014, the top five list of countries making direct investment in Russia are all tax havens, bar Germany in fifth place, while Cyprus leads this ranking and is the top country in terms of receiving direct investments from Russia. The two countries making most direct investments in Sweden are the Netherlands and Luxemburg. The Netherlands also tops the list of countries in the world receiving direct investment, well ahead of the USA in second spot. It is not a very brave assumption that this is a result of tax and other regulatory concerns. The only comfort in looking at investment flows between Sweden and Russia is that the observed flows are most likely real and not part of a tax haven story since neither country is known as a haven. However, some of the bilateral flows may still be routed through tax havens, which means that the official macro data on flows can be viewed as lower bounds.

The bilateral data on FDI from Sweden to Russia from SCB shows very little action until 2004, when there is a recorded flow of around $500 million; after that flows come and go with a record year in 2013 of around $1.5 billion (Figure 6.2). The data from CBR starts a few years later but in general shows flows that are at least two to three times larger than the Swedish data between 2008 and 2012. Then, in 2013, when the Swedish data chronicles a record year, the Russian data shows a very significant net outflow of Swedish FDI. Looking at the CBR data on stocks of FDI in Russia, the data for flows in 2013 is not easier to understand. However, the stock data shows a massive decline of Swedish FDI in 2014, at a

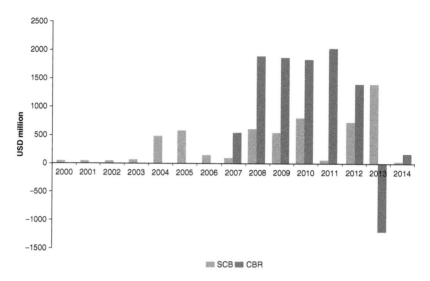

Figure 6.2 FDI Flows from Sweden to Russia, 2000–14 ($ millions)

Sources: CBR 2015; SCB 2015

scale that does not seem realistic, so it is unclear if the flow or stock data from the CBR is more reliable.

FDI flows from Russia to Sweden were virtually non-existent according to official statistics until around 2008 and, even after that, the flows in the peak year 2011 only amount to around $500 million (Figure 6.3). Again, the data sources are very inconsistent, and the Swedish data show net outflows in almost all of the years. The Russian data also has a large negative net flow in 2013, similar to what was recorded for Swedish flows to Russia.

In addition to the official balance of payments data, there are company-level data on greenfield FDI as well as M&As from private sources (fDi Intelligence from the *Financial Times* for FDI data and MergerMarket on M&As). This data has the benefit of being collected by the same institution for both countries, and Figure 6.4 shows the country aggregates. The dominant type of flow by a wide margin is greenfield investments from Sweden to Russia ("Swe inv Rus"). There are also smaller but non-trivial M&A flows going in the same direction ("Swe buy Rus"), while flows from Russia to Sweden are virtually non-existent until 2015. We will have a closer look at the details of the company-level data below.

The annual average flows for the years 2007–14 are shown in Figure 6.5 to compare the macro data and the company-level data. The data are not fully compatible since the company data is gross investment flows whereas the balance of payments data are net flows ("net" in the sense that money sent back to the home country from the affiliate in the foreign country is deducted from any new investments done in the foreign country).

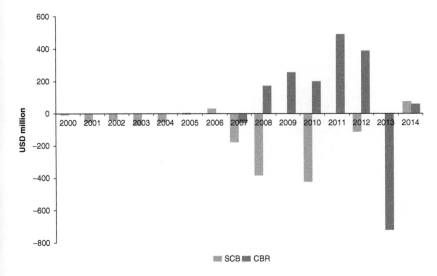

Figure 6.3 FDI Flows from Russia to Sweden, 2000–14 ($ millions)

Sources: CBR 2015; SCB 2015

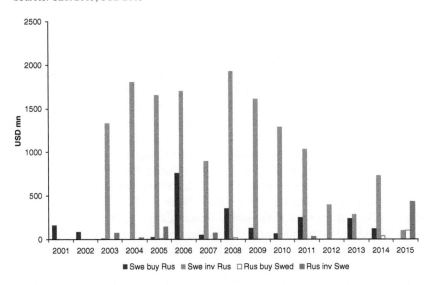

Figure 6.4 Investment Flows Based on Company Data, 2001–15 ($ millions)

Sources: fDi Markets 2015; MergerMarkets 2015

Given the discrepancy that arises because of net versus gross flows, it is not surprising that (gross) company flow data is higher than the (net) balance of payments data for Sweden. However, the difference between CBR and SCB is even larger than between company data and CBR data. The reported average

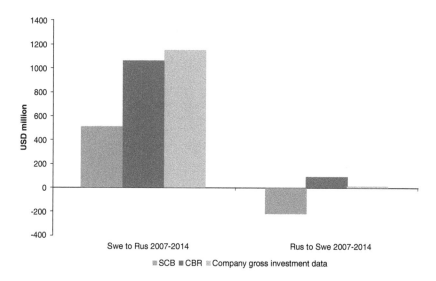

Figure 6.5 Annual Average FDI Flows from Different Sources, 2007–14 ($ millions)

Source: Author's calculations based on data of CBR 2015; fDi Markets 2015; MergerMarkets 2015; SCB 2015

annual FDI flows from Sweden to Russia vary from SCB's $522 million in net flows to the company data on gross flows of close to $1.2 billion. Russian flows to Sweden are small in comparison to the flows in the other direction and the different data sources do not even have the same sign on the flows.

There are also significant portfolio investments from Sweden to Russia, but the bilateral portfolio data is only available in terms of stocks and not flows (Figure 6.6) and flows cannot be derived simply by taking changes in stocks due to valuation effects. The stock of Swedish portfolio investments in Russia is almost exclusively made up of equity investments. After a very rapid increase in portfolio investments until 2006, there was a trend break in 2007 and then a dramatic decline in 2008 at the time of the global financial crisis (GFC). Much of this is most likely related to valuation effects since the stock market in Russia as in other places fell significantly that year, but Russia also suffered significant capital outflows in 2008 after the military intervention in Georgia. The fact that the share of Swedish portfolio equity invested in Russia went down from over 3 percent to around 1.5 percent in 2008, when almost all stock markets around the globe fell, suggests that there was more to the decline in Russia than valuation effects. However, the rebound in 2009 still points to a significant valuation effect, while the downward trend since 2010 is a combination of portfolio outflows and a relatively poor performing stock market in Russia. In 2014, Russian equity investments were back at around 1 percent of total Swedish portfolio equity abroad, similar to its share in 2002 before the rapid increase and still above Russia's 0.4

Figure 6.6 Swedish Portfolio Investments in Russia, 2001–14 ($ millions)

Source: Author's calculations based on data of SCB 2015

percent share of the MSCI AWCI. However, the total share of Swedish portfolio investments in Russia is just above 0.4 percent since debt instruments and funds are over half of Swedish portfolio investments in other countries but virtually non-existent in Russia.

Company-Level Data

Now we will have a more detailed look at the company-level data. There are issues also here with the labels "Swedish" or "Russian" companies. Many companies can have their main operation in one country but legally be incorporated in a different country, or started in one country but then, over time, the majority shareholdings are with investors in another country. Most of the companies included here seem to receive a reasonable country label, but one significant data point on M&A (close to $1 billion in 2012) has been excluded from the study that was classified as Swedish by MergerMarket since the acquiring company making the investment in Russia was a Swedish subsidiary of the Danish brewery Carlsberg. At the same time, IKEA is a company founded in Sweden and with major activity in Sweden, and a major investor in Russia, as we will see, and left in the dataset despite being legally a foundation based in the Netherlands since 1982. This is somewhat arbitrary but most people when asked would call IKEA a Swedish company. In short, there is no perfect way of giving multinational companies a country label in a globalized economy, although scholars often use the location of a company's headquarters to determine its nationality.

The data reported in this section cover the period January 2001–August 2015, or half a year longer than the macro data reported earlier. The first years have few investments recorded but in 2003 there was a significant increase in flows from Sweden to Russia, with recorded flows going from $85 million in 2002 to $1.3 billion. For most of the years, and consistent with the macro data, Russian flows to Sweden are small and only a fraction of the flows in the other direction until 2015, when there is one significant Russian investment at the same time as flows from Sweden to Russia are at their lowest since 2002.

During this period, 67 Swedish companies made greenfield FDI in Russia and 22 did M&As (Table 6.1). The greenfield investments covered 202 transactions worth together close to $15 billion. IKEA was the single largest investor, with 59 investments worth $6.5 billion, which was almost six times the recorded investments of Tele2 in second place. Comparing the list of companies doing greenfield

Table 6.1 Company Data on FDI, January 2001–August 2015 ($ millions and € millions)

Gross company level FDI from Sweden to Russia

		Greenfield FDI		
	# firms	# transactions	total amount ($ millions)	avg. amount ($ millions)
Total	67	202	14,801	73
Top 10 companies:				
IKEA		59	6,507	110
Tele2		28	1,072	38
CastorX Capital		1	1,000	1,000
Volvo		12	971	81
Svenska Cellulosa Aktiebolaget (SCA)		4	708	177
Scania		3	688	229
Petrosibir (Shelton Petroleum)		1	401	401
Oriflame		6	375	63
Baltic Construction Company (BCC)		1	375	375
NCC (Nordic Construction Company)		2	200	100

		M&A		
	# firms	# transactions	total amount (€ millions)	avg. amount (€ millions)
Total	22	28	698	39
Top 10 companies:				
Nordea AB		2	246	246
Tele2 AB		5	173	35
Lundin Mining AB		1	97	97
Hilding Anders International AB		1	52	52
Auriant Mining AB		2	43	43
Teleca AB		1	18	18
Orkla Svenska AB (Procordia Food AB)		1	15	15
Kontakt East Holding AB		1	13	13
Scancem AB		1	11	11
Seco Tools AB		1	10	10

Table 6.1 Continued

Gross company level FDI from Russia to Sweden

	Greenfield FDI			
	# firms	# transactions	total amount ($ millions)	avg. amount ($ millions)
Total	8	9	767	85
All 8 companies:				
Lukoil		1	431	431
Golden Telecom		1	124	124
Planet Fitness		1	76	76
Kaspersky Lab		1	73	73
Rosatom		1	31	31
PlayFon		2	17	8
ABBYY		1	11	11
Reksoft		1	4	4

	M&A			
	# firms	# transactions	total amount (€ millions)	avg. amount (€ millions)
Total	5	5	85	28
All 5 companies:				
Steenord Corp		1	63	63
International Marketing & Sales Group Plc		1	14	14
VSMPO Avisma Corporation Public Stock Company		1	8	8
Baltic Reefers Ltd.		1	n.a.	n.a.
Simeos Mediacom, LLC		1	n.a.	n.a.

Source: Author's calculations based on data of fDi Markets 2015; MergerMarkets 2015

investment with those on the M&A list, only Tele2 enters close to the top on both lists. Thirteen of the M&A transactions do not report the amount involved and these amounts are missing in Table 6.1. For example, the total value of Nordea's investments is higher than the €246 million shown in the table since one of their two M&As has no recorded deal value. For the aggregate numbers on M&A displayed in the previous section, missing values are estimated (guessed) by using the average value of the transactions that do have recorded deal values. For individual companies with few investments, this type of estimate (guess) makes less sense and is therefore not presented here.

Russian companies were not very active investors in Sweden, with a total of eight companies making nine greenfield investments and five additional companies each making one M&A transaction during this time period. The total amounts were $767 million of greenfield investments and $85 million of M&A deals. A single investment by Lukoil accounts for half of all the recorded investments. In short, and in line with expectations, more Swedish MNEs have been interested in investing Russia than the other way around.

Research Findings

The data above has shown that investments going from Sweden to Russia dominate the flows going in the other direction by a very significant margin. This is in line with the hypothesis that capital moves from countries with higher income levels to countries with lower income levels, as well as the hypotheses that flows go to larger markets with many potential customers and to markets with natural resources that are important inputs to certain MNEs. In addition to these general conclusions, this section will discuss the more specific research questions outlined above.

Capital Flows and Standard Macro Indicators of Risk and Return

The first question to address is whether investments from Sweden to Russia have been moving in line with standard macro and finance variables as suggested by risk/return arguments. In Figure 6.7, FDI stocks and gross flows are plotted with Russian GDP, oil prices and the RUB/SEK exchange rate, where all variables are expressed as an index set to 100 in 2005. It is clear that the stock of Swedish FDI in Russia has grown very much in line with the development of Russian GDP, which in turn has shown a very high correlation with international oil prices (see Becker 2014). Over the period, there has been a downward trend in the exchange rate that shows less of a correlation with the other variables. Note that these data

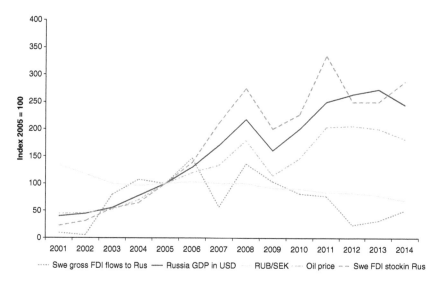

Figure 6.7 Russian Macro Data and Swedish FDI Trends, 2001–14 (index 2005 = 100)

Source: Author's calculations based on data of IMF 2015; SCB 2015

end in 2014 since the investment data for 2015 is not yet available, but we know that in 2015, there was a sharp decline in both oil prices, the exchange rate, and also in Russian GDP. Another observation here is that the stock of FDI follows GDP closely, while the flow of FDI experienced a downward break after the GFC that still remains. FDI flows are, of course, connected to the stock of FDI, but this chart shows quite clearly that it will matter which variables are used when running regressions between FDI and, for example, GDP and many gravity equations use GDP to explain FDI flows rather than stocks.

Swedish investors make investments in many countries and Figure 6.8 shows the share of total Swedish FDI invested in some major emerging market countries (Brazil, China, and Russia), as well as some of the markets closer to Sweden (Poland and the three Baltic countries, namely Estonia, Latvia, and Lithuania), in order to get some perspective on the investments going to Russia. The first observation is that the shares of these countries have all grown quite rapidly between 2000 and 2014, with shares doubling or even tripling in this time period. What is also noteworthy is that although the three BRIC countries included here get a lot of attention in the general discussion, the three Baltic countries combined account for the largest share of Swedish investments in these countries by some margin, while the share invested in Poland is similar to Russia or Brazil.

There are also estimates of the returns on FDI from SCB, and, in Table 6.2, the mean returns and standard deviations of returns are presented for the above set of countries as well as for the total stock of outstanding Swedish FDI. Although the numbers are likely relatively rough estimates of returns, they confirm the general view that emerging markets offer higher returns that are more volatile than the

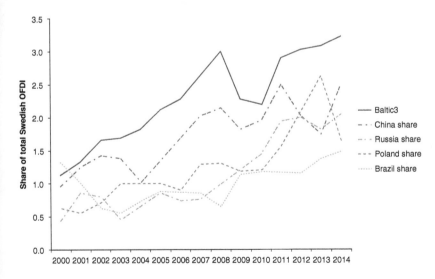

Figure 6.8 Swedish FDI Stocks in Key Emerging Markets, 2000–14 (percent)

Source: Author's calculations based on data of SCB 2015

Note: Baltic3 is sum of Estonia, Latvia, and Lithuania

Table 6.2 Returns in Percent on Swedish FDI, 2005–14

	Mean	*St. dev.*	*Mean/St. dev.*
Total	10.2	2.2	4.7
Total excl. Russia	10.0	2.2	4.6
Russia	22.6	6.8	3.3
China	18.9	6.7	2.4
Brazil	26.1	12.2	1.9
Poland	9.9	6.2	1.1
Baltic3	16.7	7.3	1.9

Source: Author's calculations based on data of SCB 2015

Note: Baltic3 is the sum of returns in SEK of Estonia, Latvia, and Lithuania divided by the sum of the FDI stock in SEK of the three countries

overall portfolio. When returns are normalized by the standard deviation, the total portfolio shows the highest risk adjusted return, despite the fact that the mean return in Russia is twice as high. This does not mean that investment in Russia is not of interest overall, and comparing the total portfolio with and without investments in Russia, the portfolio that includes Russia generates a slightly higher risk adjusted return. This data and calculations provide some indication of why investing in Russia and other emerging markets is of interest to Swedish investors.

Portfolio investments from Sweden to Russia also seem closely correlated with returns in Russia. This is seen in Figure 6.9, which displays the Russian RTS index and the stock of Swedish portfolio investments in Russia, where again both

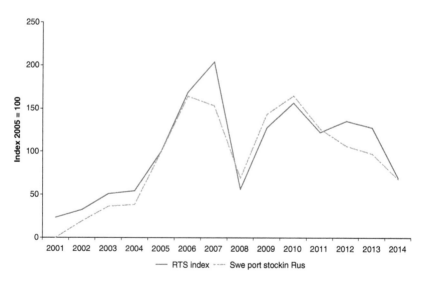

Figure 6.9 Swedish Portfolio Investments and the Russian Stock Market, 2001–14 (index 2005 = 100)

Sources: Moscow Exchange 2015; SCB 2015

variables are normalized to 100 in 2005. As discussed above, Swedish portfolio investments in Russia are almost exclusively in equity, so the close correlation with the RTS index is in line with both investors going to markets with a rising stock market and the fact that the stock of portfolio will automatically move in line with the stock market due to the valuation effect. However, there are clear signs in the chart that portfolio investments have been reduced in the last couple of years, since the investment stock also declined in 2012–13 when the RTS index was stable.

FDI versus Portfolio Investments

The above analysis of FDI and portfolio flows is also relevant for the academic literature on different types of capital flows and in particular how FDI and portfolio flows differ in terms of volatility and from an international risk-sharing perspective. A first hypothesis that has been forwarded in different models and forms is that FDI is more stable than portfolio flows and provides more risk sharing and would therefore be preferable for emerging market countries. In Figure 6.10, both stocks and shares of Swedish FDI and portfolio investments in Russia are shown. The trends all move in tandem until 2006; both stocks and Russia's share of total Swedish investments all move up sharply with the shares of FDI and portfolio investments being at almost the same exact level in 2006. After that, the stocks and shares of portfolio investments fell sharply for two years before recovering temporarily in 2009–10 but then continued on a downward path. FDI stocks show much less volatility over the time period, and in 2014 Russia accounted for 2 percent of the stock

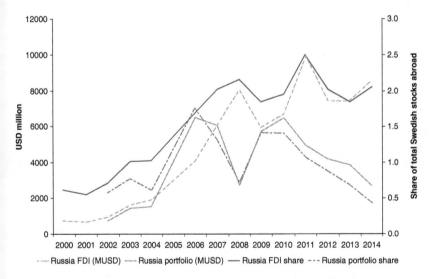

Figure 6.10 Swedish FDI Versus Portfolio Investments, 2000–14 ($ millions)

Source: Author's calculations based on data of SCB 2015

of Swedish OFDI. In the same year, the share of portfolio investments had fallen to less than 0.5 percent.

Again, some of this is due to the fact that portfolio flows respond more strongly to valuation effects since shares are valued in the market all the time while this is not the case for FDI. However, the same valuation logic applies in all countries that receive investments from Sweden, so the decline in Russia's share of total portfolio investments cannot be attributed to a general decline in stock markets around the globe but includes a significant Russia specific component as well. In short, the Swedish–Russian experience seems to support the hypothesis that FDI is a more stable form of international capital flows that is more likely to stay also in times of economic turbulence in the host country and provides more international risk sharing.

Another argument that has been used to explain whether investments tend to come as FDI or portfolio flows is the quality of institutions in the host country. As already discussed, both FDI and portfolio flows moved in line with the general macroeconomic development in the first five years in the figure before the trends diverge quite distinctly. If the hypothesis regarding the impact of institutions on the composition of capital flows is relevant here, we should be able to observe some institutional changes or other news that may affect the sentiment of portfolio investors at the time of the diverging flows.

There were several political and security-related events in 2006 and 2007 in Russia – increased tensions with Georgia; the death of former agent Litvinenko and related diplomatic disputes with the UK; democracy demonstrations in Saint Petersburg and Moscow; and missile defense arguments with the USA – but it is not clear to what extent any particular event was key to the shift in investor sentiment and a trend break in portfolio flows. Some governance indicators measured by the World Bank, such as voice and accountability, regulatory quality, and control of corruption did deteriorate somewhat from 2005–7. In terms of corruption, Russia went from 121 to 143 from 2006–7 on Transparency International's list, which is one deteriorating institutional factor that could lead to fewer portfolio flows according to both theoretical models and empirical estimations.

FDI versus Trade

A key issue in the early literature on FDI was whether capital flows would replace trade or be a complement and potentially even support more trade. For the case of Swedish investments to Russia, there is a strong positive correlation between trade and the stock of FDI (Figure 6.11). The significant drop in gross investment flows in 2007 seem a bit off in terms of the trend in exports and is to a large extent a result of IKEA not making any recorded investments in that year, while making investments of well over $1 billion both in 2006 and 2008. The sharp decline in exports in 2009 at the peak of the GFC and contraction of the Russian economy was associated with a decline in both the stock and gross flow of FDI. Although the gross FDI flows have been smaller since the 2009 crisis, the stock of FDI is still moving in parallel with exports and would support the general view that FDI is more likely a complement rather than a substitute for trade.

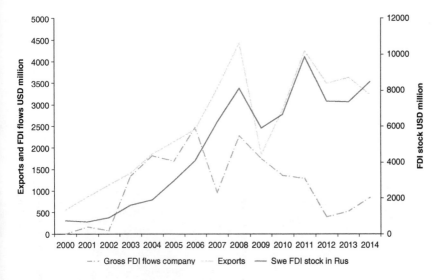

Figure 6.11 Swedish Exports Versus FDI, 2000–14 ($ millions)

Source: Author's calculations based on data of SCB 2015

FDI versus Trade in Different Sectors

From Figure 6.12, it is clear that both exports and investments from Sweden to Russia are far more diversified than the flows in the other direction.[7] The composition also suggests that investments and trade go hand-in-hand in many cases as also the Swedish macro numbers above suggested. This is also clear with the major flows from Russia to Sweden; the main exports to Sweden are oil and petrochemicals and the largest investment from Russia to Sweden is Lukoil's investment in a warehouse in Gothenburg to get closer to its customers for marine lubricants. Although ships from many countries come to Gothenburg, so the country of the final customer in Gothenburg is not necessarily Swedish, this would fit the general idea of horizontal FDI. The other Russian investments in Sweden are focused on the ICT sector and gaining access to one of the world's most dynamic environments for both development and consumer testing of ICT products and services. These investments have multiple purposes for the investing companies and are more complex in nature than pure horizontal or vertical FDI as they exploit a market with both knowledge and customers that help the companies develop their international strategies.

The exports and investments from Sweden to Russia are more diverse as shown by data and have the potential to include a wider range of classifications of FDI. However, a closer look seems to suggest that a large share of investments going to Russia is relatively straightforward horizontal FDI and most of the other investments fall rather squarely in the vertical class of FDI. IKEA is, by a wide margin, the largest Swedish investor in Russia and is basically investing in a retail infrastructure that makes it possible to sell its goods to Russian consumers. This

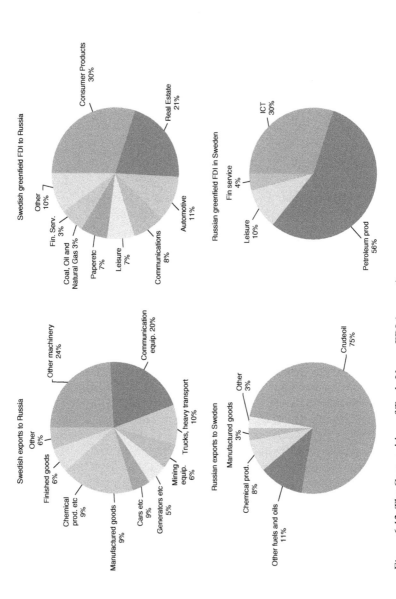

Figure 6.12 The Composition of Trade Versus FDI (percent)

Source: Author's calculations based on data of fDi Markets 2015; MergerMarkets 2015; SCB 2015

Note: Export shares are for 2014 while FDI shares are based on cumulative company flows from January 2003 to August 2015

does not mean that all of its investments fall in the category of consumer products since IKEA develops shopping malls (that are classified as real estate investments) and also has some manufacturing of goods in Russia. Despite these multifaceted investments, IKEA's investments are basically about gaining access to the Russia market, and in line with the horizontal FDI hypothesis. Also investments by telecommunications companies, in a wide sense, and financial institutions fall in the category of horizontal FDI and gaining access to a large Russian market. There are also significant investments in the automotive sector that could potentially fall in different categories of FDI. However, tariffs and other trade obstacles suggest that this is again largely about gaining access to the Russian market rather than making Russia an integral part of international production chains. Finally, construction firms and real estate investors also fall in the horizontal FDI box.

There are also Swedish firms that are in natural resource sectors that make significant investments in Russia to gain access to Russia's enormous natural resources. However, the natural resource-related vertical FDI only account for around 10 percent of total investments by Swedish firms in Russia. This is likely due to a combination of the relatively small scale of this sector among Swedish MNEs and the regulatory and business environment in Russia in natural resource intensive industries. Overall, vertical, export-platform and more complex reasons for FDI seem to be far behind market-seeking horizontal investments when it comes to FDI from Sweden to Russia.

Predicted versus Actual Investments between Sweden and Russia

The final question to address is whether observed FDI flows are in line with empirical models. Many different empirical models have been estimated in the recent past with the general structure including some version of traditional gravity variables and then augmenting the empirical model with a wide set of explanatory variables to study the effect of more specific factors. Many of the extra indicators turn out to have relatively modest effects on the level of investments even if they are statistically significant, and most of the variables are not robust in the sense of clearing the hurdle of a Bayesian selection process as discussed above. The empirical predictions presented here therefore focus on the most basic specifications from three recent studies that look at bilateral FDI from high income to lower income countries. Two articles, Bevan, Estrin, and Meyer (2004) and Frenkel, Funke, and Stadtmann (2004), include Russia in the sample of countries while Bellak, Leibrecht, and Damijan (2007) do not but still focus on FDI to transition countries in Central and Eastern Europe (CEE). Both the articles that include Russia have a Russia dummy that is estimated to be negative and significant from both a statistical and economic perspective (Table 6.3).

By applying the estimated models to relevant Swedish and Russian data, we obtain predicted bilateral flows from Sweden to Russia that can be compared to the actual average FDI flow of $396 million. In short, all models predict much larger flows ($1.1, $1.5, and $8.1 billion respectively) than the observed net FDI flows from Sweden to Russia. However, the annual average gross FDI flow based

Table 6.3 Prediction of FDI Flows from Sweden to Russia Based on Empirical Estimates, 2001–14 ($ millions)

Actual annual average FDI flow 2001–14 = $396 million

Bevan, Estrin, and Meyer (2004)		Frenkel, Funke, and Stadtmann (2004)		Bellak, Leibrecht, and Damijan (2007)	
Dep. var: FDI		Dep.var: log(FDI)		Dep.var: ln(FDI)	
	Coeff.		Coeff.		Coeff.
GDP home	0.02449	log(GDPhome)	0.036	ln(GDPhome)	0.332
GDP host	1.20838	log(GDPhost)	0.021	ln(GDPhost)	1.2
Distance	−0.03643	log(Distance)	−0.016	ln(GDP/cap home)	3.133
Relative ULC	68.76288	Russia dummy	−0.068	ln(GDP/cap host)	−0.404
Common border	307.7798	Constant	8.606	ln(Distance)	−0.922
Russia dummy	−401.5899			Constant	−55.893
Constant	−156.1672				
Transition index	48.97338				
Predicted FDI ($ millions)	**1058**	**Predicted FDI ($ millions)**	**1451**	**Predicted FDI ($ millions)**	**8127**

Source: Author's calculations based on data of CBR 2015; EBRD 2015; SCB 2015

on company data is $1.2 billion, which is right in the middle of the estimates generated by the empirical models that include Russia. One obvious problem with the estimate in the study that does not include Russia is that the coefficient on host country GDP is very large (and Russia has a very large GDP compared with the CEE countries included in the study) while there is no negative Russia dummy that reduces the impact of the predicted FDI flow.

In sum, the empirical models that include standard gravity model variables differ along many dimensions, including in what forms the models are estimated (levels, natural logs, or logs), what countries are included and what time period the data cover. Although the models are qualitatively similar, the quantitative estimates are quite divers and generate large differences in predicted values for bilateral flows between two specific countries. It is therefore difficult to answer with any precision the question of whether the bilateral flows from Sweden to Russia are "too small" or "too large". However, it does seem that there is empirical support for Russia being different in a sense of receiving less FDI than standard gravity models would predict given the negative dummies and huge flow the empirical model without Russia generated here. It cannot be concluded with any greater certainty if this is due to Russia having a much larger GDP than most other countries included in empirical studies or if it depends on Russia-specific institutional factors but this could be a topic for future studies.

Conclusions

Swedish investments to Russia have to a large extent been motivated by gaining access to a market of over 140 million customers that, for a relatively long time, have experienced very significant increases in real disposable incomes. Although Russia is still a large market with many customers, real incomes have fallen recently and the general macroeconomic outlook is not favorable in light of low international oil prices and continued sanctions and counter-sanctions. Russia thus faces the challenge of attracting foreign companies that can help diversify and modernize the economy at a time when the domestic environment is not very attractive to foreign companies. The companies that are already there may have too much to lose to move out of Russia, but it will be hard to convince new companies to enter the Russian market at this point in time.

The policy options from a Russian perspective can be viewed as focusing on sticks or carrots to attract more foreign investments: sticks in the sense of sanctions and tariffs to make it harder to export to Russia so any company that wants to have access to the Russia market is "forced" to move inside the (potentially expanded) sanctions and tariff barriers; carrots could instead be preferential tax treatments or major reforms of the institutional factors that are viewed as impediments to investments today (for example, corruption, rule of law, and government efficiency). Most economists would argue that the latter set of reforms would generate the largest long-term gains to the Russian economy, not only from foreign investments, but also from potential Russian investors and entrepreneurs. However, these reforms are also the most complicated to implement without potentially rocking the whole power structure in Russia and are likely not first in line to be implemented by policy makers.

Looking at flows from Russia to Sweden, it is probably less of an issue on the minds of Swedish policy makers. The Swedish economy is going relatively well; is already viewed as one of the world's most competitive; and has a particularly high potential in the ICT sector that has already seen some Russian investments. It is also hard to change the fact that Sweden is a relatively small country with a relatively inflexible labor and housing market that makes investments in many sectors other than ICT rather unattractive. Dealing with these inflexibilities is high on the policy agenda in Sweden, but, as in Russia, some of the most needed reforms are the ones that are hardest to actually implement for policy makers.

Notes

1 The author would like to thank Kari Liuhto and Sergei Sutyrin for their patience, careful reading, and many useful comments, and Roman Bobilevs for help with data. Special thanks to Magnus Runnbeck and Jens Wernborg at Business Sweden for help with company-level data. A slightly more extensive version of this chapter is available as SITE Working paper no. 35.
2 For a discussion of theories that assume perfect markets, see Lizondo (1990). Froot and Stein (1991) discuss the importance of exchange rate movements, while Portes and Rey (2005) look at capital flows with frictions that generate predictions in line with gravity models.
3 This question has a very long history in the trade and factor mobility literature. In a more recent contribution, Helpman, Melitz and Yeaple (2004) develop a model with heterogeneous firms to explain how MNEs chose to serve foreign markets, while Helpman (2006) provides a good overview of the topic more generally.
4 Albuquerque (2003) argues that FDI is preferred over portfolio investments when there is a high risk of expropriation and that FDI is more stable and better for risk sharing. Daude and Fratzscher (2008) focus on how FDI and portfolio investments respond differently to frictions and institutional factors, while Fratzscher and Imbs (2009) discuss how institutions in the host country can increase the transaction costs for FDI and reduce diversification benefits of the home country.
5 The early focus on horizontal versus vertical FDI has been expended more recently by export-platform investments (Ekholm, Forslid & Markusen 2007) and more complex patterns of trade and investment when more countries and types of capital are included in the standard models (Baltagi, Egger & Pfaffermayr 2007). Nocke and Yeaple (2007) show that the nature of firm heterogeneity determines what type of FDI is chosen.
6 There is a growing number of articles that estimate empirical models of bilateral FDI that can be used to generate predictions of investments between Sweden and Russia. One empirical issue is that the list of explanatory variables keeps growing with each new study. There are two recent articles (Eicher, Helfman & Lenkoski 2012; Blonigen & Piger 2014) that use Bayesian techniques to see what variables are statistically robust, and one general conclusion is that standard gravity variables such as GDP and distance always do well.
7 Becker (2015) provides a more detailed analysis of bilateral trade flows.

Bibliography

Albuquerque, R. 2003, 'The composition of international capital flows: risk sharing through foreign direct investment', *Journal of International Economics*, vol. 61, no. 2, pp. 353–83.

Anderson, J. 2010, *The Gravity Model*, Working Paper 16576, National Bureau of Economic Research, Cambridge, MA.

Baltagi, B.H., Egger, P. & Pfaffermayr, M. 2007, 'Estimating models of complex FDI: are there third-country effects?', *Journal of Econometrics*, vol. 140, no. 1, pp. 260–81.

Becker, T. 2014, *A Russian Sudden Stop or Just a Slippery Oil Slope to Stagnation?*, Centrum Balticum, Turku.

Becker, T. 2015, *Russia's Economic Troubles: A Perfect Storm of Falling Oil Prices, Sanctions and Lack of Reforms*, SIEPS, European Policy Analysis, 2015:9, Stockholm.

Bellak, C., Leibrecht, M. & Damijan, J.P. 2007, *Infrastructure Endowment and Corporate Income Taxes as Determinants of Foreign Direct Investment in Central- and Eastern European Countries*, KU Leuven LICOS Discussion Paper, No. 193, Leuven.

Bergstrand, J.H. & Egger, P. 2007, 'A knowledge-and-physical-capital model of international trade flows, foreign direct investment, and multinational enterprises', *Journal of International Economics*, vol. 73, no. 2, pp. 278–308.

Bevan, A., Estrin, S. & Meyer, K. 2004, 'Foreign investment location and institutional development in transition economies', *International Business Review*, vol. 13, no. 1, pp.43–64.

Blonigen, B.A. & Piger, J. 2014, 'Determinants of foreign direct investment', *Canadian Journal of Economics*, vol. 47, no. 3, pp. 775–812.

CBR 2015, *Central Bank of Russia: Statistics*, viewed 30 December 2015, http://cbr.ru/Eng/statistics/

Daude, C. & Fratzscher, M. 2008, 'The pecking order of cross-border investment', *Journal of International Economics*, vol. 74, no. 1, pp. 94–119.

Dunning, J.H. 2001, 'The eclectic (OLI) paradigm of international production: past, present and future', *International Journal of the Economics of Business*, vol. 8, no. 2, pp. 173–90.

EBRD 2015, *European Bank for Reconstruction and Development, Transition Indicators per Country*, viewed 30 December 2015, http://www.ebrd.com/what-we-do/economic-research-and-data/data/forecasts-macro-data-transition-indicators.html

Eicher, T.S., Helfman, L. & Lenkoski, A. 2012, 'Robust FDI determinants: Bayesian Model Averaging in the presence of selection bias', *Journal of Macroeconomics*, vol. 34, no. 3, pp. 637–51.

Ekholm, K., Forslid, R. & Markusen, J.R. 2007, 'Export-platform foreign direct investment', *Journal of the European Economic Association*, vol. 5, no. 4, pp. 776–95.

fDi Markets 2015, *Financial Times database*, viewed 30 December 2015, http://www.fdimarkets.com

Fortescue, S. & Hanson, P. 2015, 'What drives Russian outward foreign direct investment? Some observations on the steel industry', *Post-Communist Economies*, vol. 27, no. 3, pp. 283–305.

Fratzscher, M. & Imbs, J. 2009, 'Risk sharing, finance, and institutions in international portfolios', *Journal of Financial Economics*, vol. 94, no. 3, pp. 428–47.

Frenkel, M., Funke, K. & Stadtmann, G. 2004, 'A panel analysis of bilateral FDI flows to emerging economies', *Economic Systems*, vol. 28, no. 3, pp. 281–300.

Froot, K.A. & Stein, J.C. 1991, 'Exchange rates and foreign direct investment: an imperfect capital markets approach', *The Quarterly Journal of Economics*, vol. 106, no. 4, pp. 1191–217.

Hakkala, K. & Zimmermann, D. 2005, *Foreign Operations of Swedish Manufacturing Firms: Evidence from the IUI Survey on Multinationals 2003*, Working Paper Series 650, Research Institute of Industrial Economics, Stockholm.

Helpman, E., 2006, 'Trade, FDI, and the organization of firms', *Journal of Economic Literature*, vol. 44, no. 3, pp. 589–630.

Helpman, E., Melitz, M. & Yeaple, S. 2004, 'Export versus FDI with heterogeneous firms', *American Economic Review*, vol. 94, no. 1, pp. 300–16.

IMF 2015, *International Monetary Fund, World Economic Outlook, October 2015 database*, viewed 30 December 2015, http://www.imf.org/external/ns/cs.aspx?id=28

Kleinert, J. & Toubal, F. 2010, 'Gravity for FDI', *Review of International Economics*, vol. 18, no. 1, pp. 1–13.

Kragh, M. 2014a, 'Doing business in Russia? Swedish perspectives from the Varangians to Vladimir Lenin', in A. Husebye (ed.), *Doing Business in Russia: Sources to Swedish Business History in Russia, 1850–1920*, Centre for Business History, Bromma.

Kragh, M. 2014b, 'Patterns of Swedish–Russian Trade and Investments (1840s–1920s)', in M. Kragh (ed.), *Swedish Business History in Russia, 1850–1917*, Centre for Business History, Bromma.

Liuhto, K.T. 2015, 'Motivations of Russian firms to invest abroad: how sanctions affect the Russian outward foreign direct investment?', *Baltic Region*, vol. 4, no. 26, pp. 4–19.

Liuhto, K.T. & Majuri, S.S. 2014, 'Outward foreign direct investment from Russia: a literature review', *Journal of East–West Business*, vol. 20, no. 4, pp. 198–224.

Lizondo, J.S. 1990, *Foreign Direct Investment*, IMF Working paper, WP 90/63, Washington, DC.

Markusen, J.R. & Maskus, K.E. 2001, *General-Equilibrium Approaches to the Multinational Firm: A Review of Theory and Evidence*, Working Paper No. 8334, National Bureau of Economic Research, Cambridge, MA.

MergerMarkets 2015, *Merger Market Group*, viewed 30 December 2015, http://mergermarketgroup.com

Moscow Exchange 2015, *RTS index*, viewed 30 December 2015, http://moex.com/en/index/RTSI

Nocke, V. & Yeaple, S. 2007, 'Cross-border mergers and acquisitions vs. greenfield foreign direct investment: The role of firm heterogeneity', *Journal of International Economics*, vol. 72, no. 2, pp. 336–65.

Portes, R. & Rey, H. 2005, 'The determinants of cross-border equity flows', *Journal of International Economics*, vol. 65, no. 2, pp. 269–96.

SCB 2015, *Statistics Sweden, Statistical Database*, viewed 30 December 2015, http://www.statistikdatabasen.scb.se

Swedenborg, B., Johansson-Grahn, G. & Kinnwall, M. 1988, *Den svenska industrins utlandsinvesteringar 1960–1986*, Industriens Utredningsinstitut, Almqvist och Wiksell International, Stockholm.

7 Russian FDI in Finland

Empirical Evidence from a Knowledge-Driven Investment

Kari Liuhto and Elisa Aro[1]

Introduction: The Historical Development of Russian Direct Investment in Finland

In 1809, as an outcome of the Napoleonic wars, all of Finland was annexed to Russia, and Finland became an autonomous part of the Russian Empire. A significant share of Finland's external trade, roughly 40 percent between 1827 and 1917, took place with the Russian mainland. Historical evidence of Russian investment in Finland is scarce; however, it is a well-known fact that some Russian businessmen[2] moved to Finland and reached salient positions in the country. For example, Russian merchants represented a quarter of all merchants in the new capital city of Finland, Helsinki, in 1879 (Shenshin 2008).

After Finland gained its independence from Russia in December 1917 as a consequence of the Bolshevik revolution, Finland's trade with Soviet Russia slumped and remained at a low level until World War II. After the war, bilateral trade relations started to pick up, and some Soviet subsidiaries were established in Finland. At the end of the Soviet era, around a dozen Soviet corporations operated in Finland (McMillan 1987). Examples of such include Konela (a sales unit of Soviet automobiles), Saimaa Lines (shipping), Suomen Petrooli, and Teboil (oil industry).

After the disintegration of the USSR in 1991, Russia inherited the Soviet subsidiaries in Finland. Despite the Soviet heritage, the Russian total FDI stock in Finland remained modest. In 1995, when Finland joined the EU, Russia's total investment in Finland was merely €241 million and accounted for approximately 4 percent of Finland's inward FDI stock. Even if Russia's investment in Finland did not decline markedly, its share descended to below 1 percent of Finland's inward FDI stock by the year 2000, due to a substantial investment inflow from other countries to Finland. In the past few years, Russia's share has slowly started to increase again (Table 7.1).

By the year 2000, nearly 2,000 firms with Russian participation were registered in Finland (Jumpponen 2001). Seven years later, their numbers reached approximately 3,000 (Ollus 2008) – that is, Russian enterprises then represented over 1 percent of Finland's total enterprise population. Despite their large number, the bulk of these Russian firms did not employ anyone and only a few have started industrial production in Finland.

Table 7.1 The Development of Russian FDI Stock in Finland, 1995, 2000, 2005, 2010–14 ($ millions and percent)

	1995	2000	2005	2010	2011	2012	2013	2014
Russia's OFDI stock, $ millions*	3,015	20,141	146,679	366,301	361,750	406,295	501,202	431,865
Russia's FDI stock in Finland, $ millions**	n.a.	n.a.	n.a.	1,151	948	1,309	1,382	1,280
Finland's share in Russia's OFDI stock, %**	n.a.	n.a.	n.a.	0.31	0.26	0.32	0.29	0.33
Russia's FDI stock in Finland, € millions***	241	240	378	503	634	583	887	1,138
Russia's share in Finland's IFDI stock, %***	3.88	0.92	0.81	0.78	0.92	0.80	1.38	1.47

Sources: *UNCTAD 2001, 2006, 2011, 2012, 2013, 2014, 2015; **Central Bank of Russia 2015; ***Bank of Finland 2014; Statistics Finland 2015

At the end of 2013, 27 subsidiaries of Russian corporations were registered in Finland. Their total turnover was €3.5 billion and they employed nearly 700 persons. Their significance in the Finnish economy was rather modest: 0.3 percent of the total personnel and 4.7 percent of the total turnover of all foreign subsidiaries in Finland (Statistics Finland 2015). Despite their marginal role in the Finnish economy, a handful of Russian-owned companies, such as Teboil, Gasum, Norilsk Nickel Harjavalta, RAO Nordic, and Nizhnekamsneftekhim, can be found among the largest corporations in Finland (Table 7.2).[3]

The roots of Teboil date back to the Soviet era, when Sojuznefteexport bought the enterprise from two private Finnish businessmen in 1948. In 2005, Russia's largest private oil company, Lukoil, acquired Teboil from another Russian oil company, Nafta Moskva, previously Sojuznefteexport. In 2014, Teboil covered a fifth of the Finnish retail oil market (Petroleum & Biofuels Association – Finland 2015).

Although Finland began importing gas from the USSR in 1974, Gasum was established 20 years later to handle the natural gas supply in Finland. In 2014, natural gas provided nearly a tenth of Finland's total energy consumption, and Gasum was fully responsible for that supply (BP 2015). In December 2015, Gazprom, a Russian state-controlled corporation, sold its 25 percent ownership to the Finnish Government, which resulted in Gasum no longer being a Russian-owned company (Gasum 2015).[4]

Since 2007, Norilsk Nickel Harjavalta (NNK) has been owned by one of Russia's richest tycoons, Vladimir Potanin. In February 2014, speculation was raised that NNK might resell the unit. However, in April 2014, Potanin indicated that he intends to keep the Harjavalta plant in Finland at least until 2016 ('Norilsk Nickel' 2014).

RAO Nordic is owned by Inter RAO, a Russian state-controlled company. It is Russia's leading electricity exporter and importer and is a Russian electricity trader in Finland. Although Russia's share of Finland's electrical energy supply has diminished over recent years, it nonetheless accounted for nearly 5 percent of the Finnish total electricity supply in 2015 (Finnish Energy Industries 2016).

Nizhnekamsneftekhim's headquarters are located in Tatarstan, Russia; it is one of Russia's largest petrochemical producers. In 1997, the company established a subsidiary in Finland, Nizhex Scandinavia, which is one of the corporation's sales units in the EU. Some Russian-owned firms, such as Yandex, have not been included in this list yet. In 2015, Yandex, a Russian Internet company, opened a data center in Finland. Media reports suggest that Yandex has invested approximately €80 million in its plant and the company employs some 20 people. The firm plans to at least double its investments in Finland (Sajari 2015). Yandex has invested in Finland via its Dutch subsidiary; hence the Yandex investment cannot be regarded as a direct investment by Russia to Finland ('Datakeskuksen hukkalämpö…' 2014).

Another Russian state-owned firm worth mentioning is RosAtom, since it plans to conduct Russia's largest investment in Finland ever. RosAtom has

Table 7.2 Five Russian-owned Firms Among Finland's 500 Largest Corporations, 2014 (€ millions and percent)

Rank on the basis of turnover	Name(owner; ownership share)	Entry of Russian-capital	Industry	Turnover,€ millions	Change from 2013, %	Profit,€ millions	Gross invest-ments,€ millions	Staff
32.	Teboil(Lukoil; 100 percent)	1948	Oil business	2,132	–7	28	12	232
62.	Gasum(Gazprom; 25 percent until December 2015)	1994	Gas business	1,079	–6	–10	38	319
79.	Norilsk Nickel Harjavalta(Norilsk Nickel, 100 percent)	2007	Metal business	768	1	n.a.	n.a.	254
162.	RAO Nordic(Inter RAO; 100 percent)	2002	Electricity trading	347	–15	6	0	55
406.	Nizhex Scandinavia (Nizhnekamskeneftekhim; 100 percent)	1997	Chemicals trading	122	–37	0	n.a.	10

Source: 'Talouselämä 500' 2015, pp. 36, 38, 42, 52

recently become a major owner, 34 percent, in Fennovoima. This €6 billion nuclear power plant is to be constructed by 2024 (Fennovoima 2016).

In addition to the aforementioned investments, an acquisition of the Hartwall Areena and the Finnish ice-hockey team, Jokerit, by Gennady Timchenko and Arkady and Boris Rotenberg[5] needs to be addressed here, since their acquisition, together with the RosAtom investment, has received the largest media coverage of Russian investments in Finland (Viita 2013; 'Sanctioned Russian...' 2014; Farchy 2015). Moreover, the trio's investment is worth mentioning since it has been conducted in a rather specific service sector – the sports industry. At the end of 2014, Boris and Arkady Rotenberg sold their shares to Boris' son Roman, who is a Finnish citizen (Raeste 2014).

To sum up, despite sanctions, Russian corporations have shown a continued interest in investing in Finland. RosAtom's investment, worth roughly €2 billion, will multiply Russian FDI stock in Finland.

Objective and Accomplishment of Research

The research process began in June 2015 and proceeded as follows: (1) identification of the research problem/objective; (2) a literature review on empirical studies related to the topic – that is, Russian investments in Finland;[6] (3) an analysis of relevant statistics;[7] (4) expert interviews (experts at Statistics Finland and the Bank of Finland); (5) selection of the case company; (6) a review of available public information on the case company; (7) selection of the theoretical framework; (8) execution of empirical study (November 2015); (9) analysis of empirical findings; and (10) writing and finalization (December 2015–April 2016).

The authors decided to study knowledge intensive Russian investments abroad, since there is little research on this phenomenon (Filippov 2011; Panibratov 2011; Liuhto & Majuri 2014). The main objective of this research is to analyze the internationalization of knowledge intensive Russian firms. Five sub-objectives of this study are based on the Ownership, Location, and Internationalization (OLI) paradigm (Dunning 1977) and its extension (Eden 2003). This chapter aims to answer the following five questions: why (motives), where (location), how (mode), who (capability), and when (timing). An interview guide was based on the themes of the theoretical framework that addressed the aforementioned five main questions of the internationalization of a firm.

Case methodology was applied in this research. Since the authors wanted to gain in-depth insights into the internationalization process of a Russian company, a case study best served the purpose of the research (Yin 2003). The case selection used the following criteria. The investment had to fulfill the definition of an FDI[8] and the chosen company needed to be regarded as a knowledge intensive firm. Finland was selected as the research context, since the country is one of the leading knowledge intensive economies in the world (Dahlman, Routti & Ylä-Anttila 2006). Even if there are more than 3,000 registered enterprises with Russian participation in Finland, only a handful of them met the selection criteria; therefore, Arctech Helsinki Shipyard was chosen as the case company. Selection of a shipbuilding corporation is also interesting from a historical perspective, as Finland used to produce a great number of ships for the USSR from after World War II until the disintegration of the Soviet Union in 1991.

Data was collected by interviewing the Finnish CEO of the case company operating in Finland. The company's CEO was interviewed on 20 November 2015. The interview was conducted by telephone. There are some challenges related to telephone interviews that we needed to pay attention to. First, one of the major challenges is that the interviewer cannot visually observe the body language and reactions of the respondent, which means that relevant non-verbal information may be missed. Second, it is more difficult to maintain the interview on the telephone than it would be in face-to-face interviews (Bryman & Bell 2015). However, the aforementioned weaknesses did not hamper this research.

The interview was recorded and transcribed after the interview. The data was analyzed similarly to that described by Bryman and Bell (2015), initially writing marginal notes on the transcript and categorizing the data according to the five themes associated with the aforementioned five questions. The models and taxonomies presented in the theoretical framework were utilized to guide the analysis and to categorize the data.

The major limiting factor in our research is that the authors did not have the opportunity to interview the executive management of the Russian parent company. Since the responses lack the Russian investor's perspective, the findings of this chapter need to be treated with this limitation in mind.

Five Questions Relevant to a Firm's Internationalization

The OLI paradigm developed by Dunning (1993) has probably become the most cited FDI theory. The paradigm, which was evolved over the course of time, aims at combining several leading theories of internationalization. It summarizes three types of advantages that multinational enterprises (MNEs) identify when they make decisions on foreign expansion: ownership (O), location (L) and internalization (I) advantages. The paradigm can be associated with three underlying questions that include: "why" the international activity is initiated; "where" to internationalize; and "how" the internationalization occurs. Eden (2003) suggests that the paradigm could be broadened to involve two additional questions that are essential when analyzing the internationalization process: "who"; and "when". These five questions are essential when categorizing factors that affect the internationalization of a firm and its FDI decisions.

Why

The taxonomy of four main types of foreign activity of MNEs characterizes the most frequent internationalization motives, and hence aids us answering the question "why" (Dunning 1993):

(1) Resource-seeking motives (supply-oriented FDI) are the underlying objective for obtaining access to resources at a lower real cost than in the home country

or for obtaining resources that are unavailable in the home country, and which the enterprise lacks. Enterprises may seek, for instance, physical resources or less expensive labor;

(2) Market-seeking motives (demand-oriented FDI) arise from the enterprise's interest in satisfying a foreign market or markets. Market-seeking investments may aim at holding a competitive position in existing markets or exploiting new markets due to market size, market growth, the need for following suppliers or customers abroad, the need for product and marketing adaptation, lower production and transaction costs or physical presence on competitive markets;

(3) Efficiency-seeking motives involve exploitation of a more efficient division of labor and taking advantage of the benefits obtained by production in various countries. The efficiency-seeking enterprise, thus, aims to effectively combine foreign and domestic assets; and

(4) Strategic asset or capability-seeking motives stem from the interest to increase such strategic assets and capabilities that the investing enterprise lacks or wishes to enhance, which would be essential to its strategy. These kinds of investment motives are especially common in technological as well as information and knowledge intensive service sectors.

Where

The question "where" may be answered by looking at location advantages. When deciding upon the localization of the investment, several variables may be involved in an enterprise's contemplations. The crucial question is whether a particular location provides advantages over another. These advantages are specific to a location in terms of their origin and use, although all enterprises can have access to them (Dunning 1993). Wilson and Baack (2012) utilize a framework of location determinants based on the Dunning's paradigm. The determinants are grouped into four types in a similar way as Dunning's taxonomy of the four main motivations. Wilson and Baack apply the key determinants to study advertisements of several countries that promote themselves as the best location choice for FDI. For a more detailed description, see Wilson and Baack (ibid., p. 104).

How

Buckley and Casson (1998) present 12 entry strategies with several variants making a distinction between production and distribution activities. The model by Pan and Tse (2000) differs from Buckley and Casson's model in that it presents a hierarchical perspective on the entry modes. As the model of Pan and Tse is used in this study, a closer description is needed. Pan and Tse divide entry modes into non-equity modes and equity modes. They consider both direct and indirect exports and contractual agreements, such as licensing and alliances, as non-equity modes. Correspondingly, Pan and Tse name equity joint ventures (JVs) (minority, majority and 50–50 JVs) and wholly owned subsidiaries, such as greenfield investments and acquisitions, as examples of equity modes. For a more detailed description of the model, see Pan and Tse (ibid., p. 538).

Who

Potentially the question of "who" can be handled by analyzing the resources enterprises have in order to achieve a deeper understanding of the kinds of resources and capacities a firm possesses for investing in foreign markets. The resource-based view (RBV) examines sources of sustained competitive advantage of a firm. The RBV suggests that a firm may obtain a competitive advantage over its competitors when its resources are heterogeneously distributed and these resources are immobile or, at least, not perfectly mobile (Barney 1991). The resources may include, for instance, physical, human, and organizational capital resources. Therefore, if an enterprise has valuable resources that are difficult to imitate, the enterprise is in a better position to gain a competitive advantage over its competitors and is better equipped to enter foreign markets and engage in new investments.

Several researchers have developed models based on the RBV. The model by Ekeledo and Sivakumar takes into account firm specific resources in relation to the choice of entry mode by a firm. Analyzing its resources, a firm contemplates whether it possesses sufficient competitive advantages to establish a full-control mode (sole ownership) in the foreign market or whether it needs enhancement of resources in the form of a shared-control mode. The degree of control varies depending on which mode is chosen, affecting the level of authority the firm has in the enterprise (Ekeledo & Sivakumar 2004). In this study, the model is used to analyze the strategic issues behind the internationalization process and to contemplate whether it was in the interest of the company to protect its competitive advantages or enhance its resources. Furthermore, the firm specific resources may aid in resolving how the case company evaluated its internal resources and what kind of impact they had on the decision to invest abroad. The home- and host-country factors are excluded from this study. For a more detailed description of the model, see Ekeledo and Sivakumar (ibid., p. 74).

When

The timing of the internationalization is an essential question for the enterprises. The gradual entry into foreign, unfamiliar markets may prove to be less risky, since market knowledge of the more unfamiliar countries can be acquired gradually (Johanson & Vahlne 1977). However, first-movers often have better prerequisites for positioning advantages in the market (Carpenter & Nakamoto 1989), which is why a rapid internationalization strategy is often related to the first-mover advantages (Tuppura *et al.* 2008). In practice, the greater these advantages are, the faster internationalization strategy companies want to follow in order to be among the first ones in the market and gain maximum benefit from the first-mover advantages.

Yet, a risk-free investment or first-mover advantages may not be the only determining factors when it comes to the timing and speed of foreign expansion. A model developed by Oviatt and McDougall (2005, p. 541) presents factors which affect the speed. The starting point of the model is the entrepreneurial opportunity that the enterprise discovers. Thereafter, four types of forces have influence on the speed of internationalization:

(1) Enabling forces: transportation, communication, and digital technology, which enable rapid and more cost-efficient internationalization;
(2) Motivating forces: presence of competitors or potential competitors;
(3) Mediating forces: the way in which the enterprise interprets the opportunity as well as the aforementioned enabling and motivating forces; and
(4) Moderating forces: market knowledge, the intensity of knowledge in the product or service offering, and international network that have moderating influence on the speed of internationalization.

The models described above aid in explaining FDI choices of enterprises and in categorizing main reasons behind the choices. However, it is worthwhile to notice that the decision-making process of managers related to FDI choices is complex and the investment decisions may be subject to bias that even the managers may not recognize (Buckley, Devinney & Louviere 2007).

Case: Arctech Helsinki Shipyard

A Description of the Case Company and Its Parent Company

Arctech Helsinki Shipyard originated in 1865, when Helsinki Shipyard was founded. Several changes occurred in the ownership of Helsinki Shipyard before Korean-owned STX Finland Oy and Russian United Shipbuilding Corporation (USC)[9] signed a 50–50 JV agreement. With this agreement, Arctech Helsinki Shipyard was founded in December 2010. In December 2014, USC acquired the remaining half of the company for the estimated sum of €20 million ('Russian state…' 2014).

Arctech Helsinki Shipyard is a company specializing in Arctic shipbuilding. The company manufactures icebreakers, ice-going LNG tankers, and other types of Arctic offshore and special vessels. Shortly after its inception, Arctech Helsinki Shipyard delivered two vessels to Sovcomflot, the largest shipping company in Russia. In 2014, the deliveries were followed by the icebreaking, multipurpose, emergency, and rescue vessel Baltika. At this point, the company has had orders for six icebreaking vessels, including the *Polaris*, which was christened in December 2015 (Arctech 2015). The value of order book in the first quarter of 2016 was some €700 million (Mustamäki 2016; Repo 2016).

In 2014, the turnover of Arctech Helsinki Shipyard was slightly over €50 million, and the company had an operating loss of €30 million. Since 2011, the company has run at a loss, varying from €16 million in 2011 to €30 million in

2014 ('Arctech Helsinki Shipyard' 2015). Arctech Helsinki Shipyard employed nearly 600 in the beginning of 2016 (Mustamäki 2016).

USC, the parent company of Arctech Helsinki Shipyard, was founded in 2007. USC is a state-owned corporation. The corporation has three shipbuilding and three repair centers in Russia: (1) the Western Shipbuilding and Repair Center in Saint Petersburg; (2) the Northern Shipbuilding and Repair Center in Severodvinsk; and (3) the Far Eastern Shipbuilding and Repair Center in Vladivostok (Doing business in St. Petersburg 2015). USC designs and constructs military and civil ships as well as commercial vessels and offshore equipment ('Company overview...' 2015). USC manufacturers a major portion of the products of the whole shipbuilding industry in Russia, accounting for 80 percent of all shipbuilding projects (Doing business in St. Petersburg 2015).

Research Findings

Why

According to the CEO of Arctech Helsinki Shipyard, USC did not have a specific internationalization strategy agenda when the investment opportunity was first taken into consideration. Instead, the initiative for the investment spontaneously came from the owner of the Helsinki Shipyard, STX Finland. The shipyard in Helsinki did not have any orders at that time and, to avoid closing the shipyard, establishment of a JV was introduced. The investment was promoted to USC as the possibility of acquiring Arctic expertise needed for an eventual rapid expansion of oil and gas drilling in Russia.

The main motive of USC for investing in a JV located in Finland was to make use of the Arctic knowledge residing in the shipyard owned by STX Finland. This mainly involved issues, such as expertise in Arctic shipbuilding and industrial engineering. It was in the interest of USC to transfer this acquired expertise to the Russian shipyards. This was especially important at that time, since the Arctic business was booming. Furthermore, the respondent stated that USC could provide a more versatile product offering after the investment, and added that the civil and Arctic shipbuilding had been somewhat limited beforehand. For example, the civil shipbuilding sector in Russia has not traditionally been a priority and has been an underdeveloped sector, which could be better capitalized on due to the investment.

The access to knowledge was a critical motive, but it is also worthwhile to refer to the public statement given by Aleksey Rakhmanov, Managing Director of USC, at the time when the investment was publicized. Rakhmanov stated as follows: "we have obtained not only full access to technical documentation and the know-how but also to the people who can share this knowledge. The company has efficient assets, but the advantage of the asset is in its human potential" (Arctech 2014).

To sum up, looking at the taxonomy provided by Dunning (1993), the main motivation for the investment of the Russian parent company consisted of strategic asset- or capability-seeking motives.

Where

According to the CEO of Arctech Helsinki Shipyard, the choice of country did not have a major impact on the investment decision, though the proximity of the location of the shipyard to Saint Petersburg in Russia may have simplified the decision-making process. In this context, one should keep in mind that there is a major shipbuilding concentration in Saint Petersburg.

Another location factor that may have had some impact on the investment decision is related to the Finnish suppliers. There are several Finnish suppliers in the industry that USC had previously utilized. According to the CEO, however, this did not play a significant role in terms of the investment decision, but might have helped entering the Finnish market. It was easier for the Russian company to enter the Finnish market where the other suppliers were present, compared to other markets.

It can be concluded that, in this case, the location determinants do not stand out as decisive reasons for making an investment decision. The fact that no other specific location determinants clearly emerge from the data, except for the proximity of the shipyard, may be explained by the notion that USC primarily contemplated the investment possibility in terms of the activity of the shipyard. For instance, it was more important for the investor to know that the shipyard delivers ships according to plan, than to contemplate location factors. Moreover, taking into account the main motive for the investment of USC, acquiring Arctic shipbuilding expertise, it may be stated that the firm specific advantages were more prominent than the location specific advantages.

How

In the case of Arctech Helsinki Shipyard, the investment process involved two phases. First, USC engaged in an equity JV with STX Finland, a subsidiary of the Korean-owned STX Europe, buying 50 percent of the shares. The JV agreement was signed in December 2010 and with this deal a new company, Arctech Helsinki Shipyard, was founded. Nevertheless, a long-term vision of a wholly owned Russian company already existed at that time. In fact, clauses on how to reach 100 percent ownership were included in the agreement. In 2014, USC bought the remaining 50 percent from STX Finland and, thus, Arctech Helsinki Shipyard became a wholly owned subsidiary of USC. Hence, looking at the model of Pan and Tse (2000), both of the investments represented equity modes, starting from an equity JV and ending in a wholly owned company through an acquisition.

Who

According to the CEO of Arctech Helsinki Shipyard, USC had not previously invested in foreign firms, but the capacity to engage in an FDI was rather good from the beginning and the JV agreement could be quickly signed. The reason for initiating the investment from a JV agreement is twofold. First, according to the respondent, it was easier for both parties, the seller and buyer, to start the collaboration with a JV with equal 50 percent ownership. The second reason is associated with the aforementioned Arctic expertise: it was reasonable to take part in the JV in order to utilize this expertise. Shortly after the JV agreement had been signed, contracts for the two shipbuilding projects to Russia were also signed. Acquiring Arctic expertise was critical to USC at this stage, since without the JV, USC alone would not have obtained these orders. Therefore, the Russian parent company aimed at enhancing resources with the JV agreement, which is in line with the research findings of Ekeledo and Sivakumar (2004), according to which shared-control modes are adopted when an enterprise needs a complementary resource.

However, while the agreement was signed and collaboration started, it was natural that the previously mentioned clauses for a possible 100 percent ownership were put into practice shortly thereafter. The internal resources of USC, in terms of required expertise, had improved due to the JV with ownership of Arctech Helsinki Shipyard being a logical step in the investment process. However, a more critical issue, in this context, is the ability of the seller to continue with its operations. According to the CEO of the case company, after the JV agreement was signed, the financial position of STX Finland deteriorated and its interest in continuing shipbuilding in Europe started to decline. Consequently, it was also logical for the seller to make use of the opportunity and sell the remaining shares.

When

In terms of the speed of the investment, it can be concluded that the investment process occurred rapidly. The respondent stated the first contracts for the equity JV were made in just over six months. By the closing date of the deal, investment negotiations had taken a total of one year. At that time, no schedule existed for 100 percent ownership, even if it was clear on both the seller's and buyer's sides that this would be the ultimate goal. There are several reasons why the first investment took place in 2010 and why the process was fast-paced. First, STX Finland wanted to avoid closure of the shipyard and safeguard its future, which is why the company was eager to sell part of its shares. The need to look for a new owner occurred in a period when Arctic business was rapidly growing, which contributed to a positive investment decision.

Looking at the speed of the investment through Oviatt and McDougall's (2005) model, a mediating factor which affected the speed is related to the way in which USC interpreted this emerging opportunity; acquiring Arctic expertise from its JV partner was strategically important for USC, at that time. The timing of new investments might not be as ideal at present, as the respondent mentioned: there is still a demand for Arctic projects, but growth is not as fast as it was back then. Also changes in the political climate in Russia have had an impact on the production of Russian companies and it is now a preferred strategy to produce the products in Russia instead of producing them abroad. Moreover, falling oil prices and the sanctions on Russia further complicate the business. However, the respondent noted that the sanctions mainly complicate the financing and bank actions of the company. Second, at the same time that the JV agreement was on the agenda, the aforementioned shipbuilding contracts to Russia were discussed. According to the respondent, the contracts may have sped up the investment. The model of Oviatt and McDougall (ibid.) includes enabling forces that influence the speed of investment, such as digital technology. In this case, instead of the technology, the shipbuilding contracts functioned as enabling factors that contributed to the speed. Nevertheless, there is no clear evidence that other factors presented in the theoretical model would have had an effect on the speed of this investment.

The main empirical findings show that the time specific issues are crucial in the whole internationalization process of USC. The seller's wish to sell the company occurred in a period when Arctic business was booming. The emerging opportunity became essential for USC as it needed to obtain Arctic expertise at that time. Therefore, enhancing resources through a JV was a logical solution for the company and an efficient start for the foreign expansion. Moreover, the two shipbuilding orders accelerated the investment process as USC, alone, would not have received the orders. For these reasons, it can be concluded that the complementary question "when", proposed by Eden (2003), arises as a critical factor in this particular case (Table 7.3).

Conclusions

Finland is a marginal FDI target for Russian corporations. Only 0.3 percent of the Russian outward FDI stock has been placed in Finland. Moreover, Russia's role as a foreign investor in the country is small, around 1.5 percent of all of the FDI Finland has received so far. Such a modest investment flow from Russia to Finland is rather surprising, since Finland and Russia are neighboring countries, trade relations between them quite intensive[10] and Fenno-Russian political relations, despite sanctions, function rather well.

Russian investments in Finland are below potential. We assume that Russian investments in Finland will grow should Russia continue reforming its economic structures, since the complementarity between the Finnish and the Russian economies would thus be more easily achieved. The recent development supports the aforementioned conclusion, as Russian FDI in Finland has increased despite the prevailing sanctions against Russia. Russian FDI stock in the country will multiple within the next ten years, should RosAtom's pledged investment worth some €2 billion be finalized.

Table 7.3 A Summary of the Main Empirical Findings

Case	Why	Where	How	Who	When
Acquired Finnish company: Arctech Helsinki Shipyard Investing Russian company: United Shipbuilding Corporation (USC)	Strategic asset or capability-seeking: Arctic expertise in shipbuilding A more versatile product offering of the case company	Unexpected appearance of investment opportunity determined the location. Though the geographical location did not play a major role, geographical proximity and earlier business contacts supported the investment process in Finland.	First, 50–50 JV with STX Finland Thereafter, acquisition: 100 percent ownership to USC	Investing company's good financial capacity to invest rapidly. The company did not have prior experience on acquisitions in foreign markets.	Mediating factors: the emerging opportunity essential for USC at the time Growth of Arctic business Enabling factors: two shipbuilding projects ordered to Russia

In addition to growth, the Russian investments in Finland have become more diversified, since Russian firms not only operate in natural resource-dominated sectors, but have also moved towards more knowledge intensive sectors. As an example, one may take the fresh, indirect investment of Yandex via the Netherlands in Finland and the direct investment of United Shipbuilding Corporation in the Arctech Helsinki Shipyard, the case company of this study.

The main findings of the empirical study are as follows:

(1) The main motivation for the investment of the Russian company consisted of strategic asset- or capability-seeking motives, i.e. the motivation to acquire Arctic shipbuilding expertise.

(2) The target country (Finland), per se, did not have a major impact on the investment decision. Rather an unexpected appearance of an investment opportunity determined the location of this Russian outward investment. Here, one should acknowledge that the Arctic shipbuilding knowledge is relatively concentrated in the hands of a few major players.

(3) The investment process involved two phases: USC engaged in a 50–50 JV with STX Finland, a subsidiary of the Korean-owned STX Europe, in December 2010; four years later, USC bought the remaining shares from STX Finland, resulting in Arctech Helsinki Shipyard becoming a wholly owned subsidiary of USC.

(4) The financial readiness of USC to engage in an FDI was rather good from the beginning and hence the JV agreement could be quickly signed. After the JV agreement was signed, the financial situation of STX Finland deteriorated and its interest in continuing shipbuilding in Europe started to decline. Consequently, it was also logical for the seller to make use of the opportunity and sell the remaining shares.

(5) The timing of the new investments was ideal as Arctic business was experiencing rapid growth concurrent to when a new owner was needed for the shipyard in Helsinki. The investment timing would be more problematic now that changes in the political climate have had an impact on the production of Russian companies resulting in a preferred strategy to produce ships in Russia, instead of producing them abroad. Moreover, falling oil prices and the sanctions on Russia also complicate business.

In conclusion, evidence from the case company shows that the investment by USC in Finland was not carefully planned in advance, but rather that USC management seized the opportunity, when Korean STX drifted into financial difficulties. The case also shows that the East–West investment cooperation may continue, though at a slower space, despite Western sanctions against Russia. Furthermore, the chapter implies that the internationalization of Russian corporations is gradually losing its peculiar characteristics, which results in an increasing applicability of theories on the internationalization of a firm to the internationalization of Russian enterprises.

To end, United Shipbuilding Corporation reminds us of Czar Peter the Great (aka Peter I or Pyotr I), who traveled incognito as artilleryman Pyotr Mikhailov to the Netherlands and England to learn about advanced shipbuilding at the end of the seventeenth century. Approximately three centuries later, United Shipbuilding Corporation has arrived in Finland to acquire the Arctic shipbuilding expertise. It seems that centuries may change but Russia's need to acquire state of the art knowledge from the Western world remains.

Notes

1 The authors wish to express their gratitude to the Foundation for Economic Education (Liikesivistysrahasto) for its financial support (Grant 8-4699).
2 The Sinebrychoff family, for example, moved to the eastern part of contemporary Finland by the end of the eighteenth century and opened a brewery in the Helsinki region in the early decades of the nineteenth century.
3 Ollus (2008) provides a list of the 20 largest Russian corporations in Finland in 2007. Some of these companies have been sold or liquidated due to financial difficulties or even illegalities ('Sekom-yhtiöiden…' 2014).
4 Despite Gazprom's recent exit, we presented Gasum here, as it was one of the most significant Russian-owned companies in Finland until December 2015.
5 Each one of this businessman trio has faced Western sanctions ('Ukraine crisis' 2014).
6 A small number of relevant studies, such as Jumpponen (2001), Vahtra (2007), Ollus (2008) and Jumpponen, Ikävalko, and Karandassov (2009), has been published earlier. Due to a lack of space, they are not analyzed in this article.
7 Several Finnish, Russian, and international organizations provide statistics dealing with Russian OFDI. These statistics do not offer exactly the same information. For a more detailed discussion on the statistical differences, see Norring (2015).
8 FDI is an investment, which aims at gaining effective voice in the management of the enterprise to be invested in. It has been proposed that the investment needs to represent at least 10 percent of equity ownership in order to be identified as an FDI (UNCTAD 2015).
9 The USA added United Shipbuilding Corporation to its financial sanctions list in July 2014 (Saul 2014).
10 In 2015, Russia represented 8.5 percent of Finland's foreign trade (Customs Finland 2016) and Finland 1.9 percent of the foreign trade of Russia (Customs Russia 2016).

Bibliography

Arctech 2014, *Arctech Helsinki Shipyard to Russian Ownership*, 30 December, viewed 8 February 2016, http://arctech.fi/arctech-helsinki-shipyard-to-russian-ownership/
Arctech 2015, *Arctech We Make You Break the Ice*, viewed 28 December 2015, http://arctech.fi
'Arctech Helsinki Shipyard' 2015, *Talousanomat*, viewed 17 February 2016, http://yritys.taloussanomat.fi/y/arctech-helsinki-shipyard-oy/helsinki/2366464-3/
Bank of Finland 2014, *Suorat sijoitukset ulkomailta Suomeen*, Bank of Finland.
Barney, J.B. 1991, 'Firm resources and sustained competitive advantage', *Journal of Management*, vol. 17, no. 1, pp. 99–120.
BP 2015, *BP Statistical Review of World Energy*, British Petroleum.
Bryman, A. & Bell, E. 2015, *Business Research Methods*, 4th edition, Oxford University Press, Oxford.

Buckley, P.J. & Casson, M.C. 1998, 'Analyzing foreign market entry strategies: extending the internalization approach', *Journal of International Business Studies*, vol. 29, no. 3, 539–61.

Buckley, P.J., Devinney, T.M. & Louviere, J.J. 2007, 'Do managers behave the way theory suggests? A choice-theoretic examination of foreign direct investment location decision-making', *Journal of International Business Studies*, vol. 38, no. 7, pp. 1069–94.

Carpenter, G.S. & Nakamoto, K. 1989, 'Consumer preference formation and pioneering advantage', *Journal of Marketing Research*, vol. 26, no. 3, pp. 285–98.

Central Bank of Russia 2015, *Russian Federation: Outward Foreign Direct Investment Positions by Instruments and Geographical Allocation in 2009–2014*, viewed 8 February 2016, http://www.cbr.ru/Eng/statistics/credit_statistics/direct_investment/dir-inv_out_country_1_e.xlsx

'Company overview of OJSC United Shipbuilding Corporation' 2015, *Bloomberg Business*, 3 December, viewed 8 February 2016, http://www.bloomberg.com/resea rch/stocks/private/snapshot.asp?privcapId=50042758

Customs Finland 2016, *Monthly Statistics on the Foreign Trade of Goods, December 2015*, viewed 1 March 2016, http://www.tulli.fi/en/releases/ulkomaanka uppatilastot/tilastot/kktilastot/201512/index.html

Customs Russia 2016, Внешняя торговля Российской Федерации по основным странам за январь-декабрь 2015 г., viewed 27 February 2016, http://www.customs.ru/index2.php?option=com_content&view=article&id=22580&Itemid=1976

Dahlman, C.J., Routti, J. & Ylä-Anttila, P. 2006, *Finland as a Knowledge Economy: Elements of Success and Lessons Learned*, World Bank Institute, Washington, DC.

'Datakeskuksen hukkalämpö lämmittää jopa koko Mäntsälän' 2014, *The Finnish Broadcasting Company YLE*, 24 October, viewed 8 February 2016, http://yle.fi/uutiset/datakeskuksen_hukkalampo_lammittaa_jopa_koko_mantsalan/7550739

Doing business in St. Petersburg 2015, *Shipbuilding*, viewed 16 December 2015, http://www.doingbusiness.ru/?option=com_k2&view=item&id=284:shipbuilding-cluster&Itemid=427

Dunning, J. 1977, *Trade, Location of Economic Activity and the Multinational Enterprise: A Search for an Eclectic Approach*, Macmillan, London.

Dunning, J. 1993, *Multinational Enterprises and the Global Economy*, Addison-Wesley, Harlow.

Eden, L. 2003, 'A critical reflection and some conclusions on OLI', in J. Cantwell & R. Narula (eds.), *International Business and the Eclectic Paradigm: Developing the OLI Framework*, Routledge, London.

Ekeledo, I. & Sivakumar, K. 2004, 'International market entry mode strategies of manu-facturing firms and service firms: a resource-based perspective', *International Marketing Review*, vol. 21, no. 1, pp. 68–101.

Farchy, J. 2015, 'US frustrates Russian oligarchs' cat and mouse over sanctions', *Financial Times*, 9 August, viewed 8 February 2016, http://www.ft.com/intl/cms/s/0/3a5326d0-3ce4-11e5-bbd1-b37bc06f590c.html

Fennovoima 2016, *Fennovoima*, viewed 8 February 2016, http://www.fennovoima.fi/en/

Filippov, S. 2011, 'Emerging Russian multinationals: innovation, technology, and interna-tionalization', *Journal of East–West Business*, vol. 17, no. 2–3, pp. 184–94.

Finnish Energy Industries 2016, *Energy Year 2015*, viewed 8 February 2016, http://energia.fi/en/statistics-and-publications

Gasum 2015, 'Gasum now 100% in Finnish ownership, Gasum', viewed 8 February 2016, http://www.gasum.com/Corporate_info/News/2015/gasum-now-100-in-finn-ish-ownership/

Johanson, J. & Vahlne, J-E. 1977, 'The internationalization process of the firm: a model of knowledge development and increasing foreign market commitments', *Journal of International Business Studies*, vol. 8, no. 1, pp. 23–32.

Jumpponen, J. 2001, "Made in Russia' in Finland: preliminary empirical findings', in K Liuhto (ed.), *East Goes West: The Internationalization of Eastern Enterprises,* Lappeenranta University of Technology, Lappeenranta.

Jumpponen, J., Ikävalko, M. & Karandassov, B. 2009, *Venäläisvetoinen yrittäjyys Suomessa,* Lappeenranta University of Technology, Lappeenranta.

Liuhto, K.T. & Majuri, S.S. 2014, 'Outward foreign direct investment from Russia: a literature review', *Journal of East–West Business*, vol. 20, no. 4, pp. 198–224.

McMillan, C.H. 1987, *Multinationals from the Second World: Growth of Foreign Investment by Soviet and East European State Enterprises,* Macmillan, London.

Mustamäki, E. 2016, 'Arctic shipbuilding: case: Arctech Helsinki Shipyard', in K. Liuhto (ed.), *The Baltic Maritime Cluster in the Baltic Sea Region and Beyond,* Centrum Balticum, Turku.

'Norilsk Nickel to keep the Harjavalta plant until at least 2016' 2014, *Interfax*, 29 April.

Norring, A. 2015, *Suomen ja Venäjän välisten suorien sijoitusten tilastot,* Bank of Finland, Helsinki.

Ollus, S-E. 2008, *Venäläinen kapitalismi ja Suomi,* Finnish Business and Policy Forum EVA, Helsinki.

Oviatt, B.M. & McDougall, P.P. 2005, 'Defining international entrepreneurship and modeling the speed of internationalization', *Entrepreneurship: Theory and Practice*, vol. 29, no. 5, pp. 537–53.

Pan, Y. & Tse, D.K. 2000, 'The hierarchical model of market entry modes', *Journal of International Business Studies*, vol. 31, no. 4, pp. 535–54.

Panibratov, A. 2011, 'From national leaders to global players: evidence from Russian MNEs in the high technology sector', in M. Marinov & S. Marinova (eds.), *Internationalization of Emerging Economies and Firms*, Palgrave Macmillan, London.

Petroleum & Biofuels Association – Finland 2015, *Finnish Oil Market 2014*, viewed 8 February 2016, http://www.oil.fi/en

Raeste, J-P. 2014, 'Jokerien ja Hartwall-areenan omistuksissa muutoksia: Roman Rotenberg osti isänsä ja setänsä osuuksia', *Helsingin Sanomat*, 10 October, viewed 12 August 2016, http://www.hs.fi/talous/a1412829294589

Repo, H. 2016, 'Helsingin telakka alkaa tehdä tankkereita', *Tekniikka & Talous*, 11 March, 2016, pp. 10–11.

'Russian state company buys out Helsinki shipyard' 2014, *The Finnish Broadcasting Company YLE*, 31 December, viewed 8 February 2016, http://yle.fi/uutiset/russia n_state_company_buys_out_helsinki_shipyard/7713509

Sajari, P. 2015, 'Yandexin palvelinkeskus Mäntsälässä on otettu käyttöön – huomattava laajennus jo suunnitteilla', *Helsingin Sanomat*, 19 June, viewed 8 February 2016, http://www.hs.fi/talous/a1434677933826

'Sanctioned Russian billionaires sell Finnish hockey team' 2014, *Moscow Times*, 10 October, viewed 8 February 2016, http://www.themoscowtimes.com/business/article/sanctioned-russian-billionaires-sell-finnish-hockey-team/509269.html

Saul, J. 2014, 'Russian Artic oil shipping ventures to struggle as sanctions bite', *Reuters*, 6 November, viewed 8 February 2016, http://www.reuters.com/article/shipping-arctic-sanctions-idUSL5N0SP3YU20141106

'Sekom-yhtiöiden johdolle syytteet törkeistä talouspetoksista' 2014, *The Finnish Broadcasting Company YLE*, 11 April, viewed 8 February 2016, http://yle.fi/uutiset/sekom-yhtioiden_jodolle_syytteet_torkeista_talouspetoksista/7185975

Shenshin, V. 2008, *VENÄLÄISET JA VENÄLÄINEN KULTTUURI SUOMESSA: Kulttuurihistoriallinen katsaus Suomen venäläisväestön vaiheista autonomian ajoilta nykypäiviin*, University of Helsinki, Helsinki.

Statistics Finland 2015, *Statistical Databases*, viewed 8 February 2016, http://pxweb2.stat.fi/database/StatFin/databasetree_fi.asp

'Talouselämä 500' 2015, *Talouselämä*, no. 21, pp. 36–55.

Tuppura, A., Saarenketo, S., Puumalainen, K., Jantunen, A. & Kyläheiko, K. 2008, 'Linking knowledge, entry timing and internationalization strategy', *International Business Review*, vol. 17, no. 4, pp. 473–87.

'Ukraine crisis: Russia and sanctions', 2014, *BBC*, 19 December, viewed 8 February 2016, http://www.bbc.com/news/world-europe-26672800

UNCTAD 2001, *World Investment Report (WIR) 2001: Promoting Linkages*, United Nations, New York & Geneva.

UNCTAD 2006, *World Investment Report (WIR) 2006: FDI from Developing and Transition Economies*, United Nations, New York & Geneva.

UNCTAD 2011, *World Investment Report (WIR) 2011: Non-Equity Modes of International Production and Development*, United Nations, New York & Geneva.

UNCTAD 2012, *World Investment Report (WIR) 2012: Towards a New Generation of Investment Policies*, United Nations, New York & Geneva.

UNCTAD 2013, *World Investment Report (WIR) 2013: Global Value Chains: Investment and Trade for Development*, United Nations, New York & Geneva.

UNCTAD 2014, *World Investment Report (WIR) 2014: Investing in the SDGs: An Action Plan*, United Nations, New York & Geneva.

UNCTAD 2015, *World Investment Report (WIR) 2015: Reforming International Investment Governance*, United Nations, New York & Geneva.

Vahtra, P. 2007, *Suurimmat venäläisyritykset Suomessa*, Pan-European Institute, University of Turku, Turku.

Viita, K. 2013, 'Putin allies buy Finnish hockey team to play for Russian title', *Bloomberg*, 28 June, viewed 8 February 2016, http://www.bloomberg.com/news/articles/2013-06-28/putin-allies-buy-finnish-hockey-team-to-play-for-russian-title

Wilson, R.T. & Baack, D.W. 2012, 'Attracting foreign direct investment: applying Dunning's Location Advantages Framework to FDI advertising', *Journal of International Marketing*, vol. 20, no. 2, pp. 96–115.

Yin, R.K. 2003, *Case Study Research: Design and Methods*, 3rd edition, Sage, California.

8 Russian Indirect Investment in the Estonian Information and Communications Technology Sector

Alari Purju

Introduction: Foreign Direct Investment into Estonia

Foreign direct investment (FDI) constituted 10–25 percent of annual capital formation in Estonia during 2000–14. During the last two years of the analyzed period, capital inflows decreased substantially, the main reason being that Nordic banks, which were important investors into Estonia, moved a large amount of their capital out of Estonia in 2013 and 2014, depleting the large inflows of earlier years. Figure 8.1 presents data on total FDI inflows into Estonia as well as FDI from Russia for the period 2000–14, by which time the amount of annual Russian FDI flows into Estonia had risen to €114 million.[1] The larger relative importance of Russian FDI in 2013 and 2014 had much to do with the substantial decrease of FDI from the Nordic countries.

Estonia's total amount of accumulated FDI stock at the end of 2014 was €16,235 million. Figure 8.2 shows the sources of this FDI by country. The largest proportions belong to Sweden, with €4,241 million (27 percent of total FDI), and Finland, with €3,568 million (23 percent). Russia's share is 5 percent, with €860 million. The Russian share could be higher than the official figures indicate because earlier studies have already demonstrated that some Russian companies prefer to invest through third countries – for example, through Cyprus or the Netherlands – because they feel their investments will receive a better welcome if they are not seen as coming from Russia but third countries (Kilvits, Purju & Pädam 2005, p. 71) or because they want to take advantage of certain tax benefits.

The latter feature is not a unique characteristic of Russian FDI. Developed country multinational enterprises (MNEs) also try to optimize their taxes when they insert an affiliate in a country with favorable or low corporate tax regime (e.g., Ireland or the Netherlands) into transactions between their subsidiaries in different countries. For this reason it is rather complicated to deduce precisely inward foreign direct investment (IFDI) figures flowing from a particular country – for example, the amount of Russian capital coming to Estonia through FDI from the Netherlands. One exception could be made with Cyprus due to its almost full reliance on Russian and, to a lesser degree, Azeri, Kazakh, and Ukrainian capital (Pelto, Vahtra & Liuhto 2004,

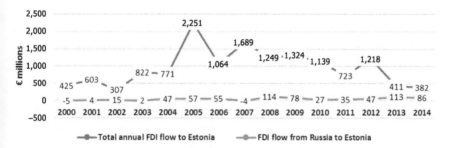

Figure 8.1 Annual FDI Flow into Estonia, 2000–14 (€ millions)

Source: Bank of Estonia 2015

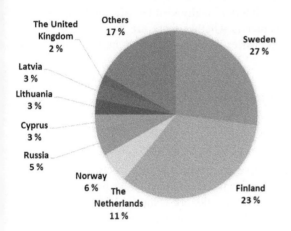

Figure 8.2 Percent of IFDI Stock in Estonia by Home Country, as of the End of 2014

Source: Bank of Estonia 2015

p. 13; Kalotay 2013, p. 58). Indeed, another study argues that FDI from Cyprus could be used as a more or less acceptable proxy for trans-shipped FDI from Russia (Kalotay *et al.* 2014, p. 6). At the end of 2014, FDI stock from Cyprus in Estonia totaled €552 million. If Cypriot FDI is regarded as Russian indirect investment, the Russian capital stock in Estonia was some €1,400 million at the end of 2014 and Russia was the fourth largest source of IFDI for Estonia after Sweden, Finland, and the Netherlands.

In terms of the sectoral division of FDI, FDI in financial and insurance activities (€4,364 million or 26.9 percent of total FDI stock) represented the largest share of Estonia's total FDI stock at the end of 2014. The next largest IFDI sectors were real estate (€2,858 million or 17.6 percent), wholesale and retail trade (€2,372 million or 14.6 percent), manufacturing (€2,119 million or 12.0 percent), professional scientific and technical activities (€1,335 million or 8.2

percent), and transport and storage (€899 million or 5.5 percent). The information and communications technology (ICT) activities received only €343 million or 2.1 percent. Swedish FDI was concentrated in the financial and insurance sector while Russian outward foreign direct investment (OFDI) went into transport and storage, real estate, and manufacturing. Estonia's IFDI in ICT is very small and seems usually small in light of the sale of Skype initially to eBay and later to Microsoft. However, Skype and other successful ICT companies were never registered in Estonia, or at least their headquarters were not, so these investments were recorded as having taken place in other countries. In the case of Skype, the location of its headquarters is Luxembourg (Skype 2015).

The objective of this research is to analyze internationalization of a Russian ICT firm taking into account theories of OFDI. I have chosen Estonia as the case study for examining Russian ICT OFDI partly for the reason that this sector has been successful and is internationally visible. One important research question addressed in this chapter is whether there are any specific features related to modern network industries such as ICT that have an impact on investment from Russia.

Network Industry Concept and FDI in ICT: Theoretical Background

Network Industry Concept

Network industries refer to businesses that benefit from the network effect. This is when the value of goods or a service increases when others purchase the same goods or services. More generally, networks are comprised of complementary components which encompass wholesale and retail networks, information networks, and services such as the Yellow Pages, Yahoo, and Google (Economides 2006, p. 96). Traditional network industries in transportation (airlines, railroads, roads, and shipping) and delivery services (postal services), which feed on these, and new network industries (telecommunications and computers) merit separate discussion. Economides emphasizes that many of the features of traditional network industries apply to virtual networks, which is a collection of compatible goods that share a common technological platform. All computers running Windows 95 can be thought of as a virtual network. Compatible computer software and hardware make up a network, as do computer operating systems and compatible applications (ibid.). Further, the network of networks and ecosystem, converging entire industries and technologies into complex, interwoven and global economic structures, entered the discussion (Moore 2006, p. 72). Knowing that this industry functions on a networking principle and new technologies and products could be consumed globally and benefits would come from the network effect, a very practical question arises of how networking is taking place in practice? How is it linked to location issues of companies in the sector and how is it reflected in FDI decisions of opening subsidiaries or purchasing companies in other countries to support typical development strategies in the sector?

Tahvanainen and Steinert provide an interesting description of how global technology start-ups access modern business ecosystems. They examine the principles that shape start-ups' networking efforts, the practices start-ups employ to identify relevant partners and establish connections with them, and the practices start-ups utilize to attract and commit partners to their cause and network. They found that firms need to embrace and learn how to exploit serendipitous networking opportunities to gain access to stakeholders.[2] Recognizing serendipity as a complementary mode to more strategic approaches will grant entry into the dimension of the unknown unknowns. The full exploitation of serendipity necessitates a great deal of flexibility with regard to the start-ups' initially designed product or service concepts, strategies, and business plans because in the serendipitous mode these are often re- and co-designed with newly encountered stakeholders. They also found that offshore governmental agency nodes could play a decisive role in accelerating and facilitating the integration of foreign newcomers into a local ecosystem (Tahvanainen & Steinert 2013, pp. 3–5).

Their conclusions are based on the Silicon Valley experience in the USA and give a good summary of how this network industry works. Participation in networks is a two-directional avenue, giving newcomers access to networks and allowing larger companies to screen new business ideas and products. That probably is one reason why even medium-sized ICT companies often have offices in different countries. The other is a very specialized labor market. Nikulainen and Pajarinen (2013) describe how ICT industry restructuring took place in Finland and what the characteristics were of labor mobility and knowledge spillovers. They report that the decline of Nokia and the subsequent restructuring of the Finnish ICT labor market with regional spillovers created possibilities for ICT companies to hire specialists in the region. Access to qualified labor could be one reason for Russian OFDI into the ICT sector of the Baltic Sea region.

ICT Networks and FDI

The most general impact of the ICT sector on an economy is on the level of GDP and the GDP growth rate. The annual report of the World Bank underlines three specific channels through which ICT has these effects: inclusion, efficiency, and innovation. It promotes the inclusion of firms in the world economy by enabling more firms to trade new products to new destinations. It raises efficiency by allowing firms to make better use of their capital and labor. It enhances innovation by enabling firms to exploit scale effects through online platforms and services that compete with conventional business models in retail, transport, accommodation, and banking, to name but a few. These three mechanisms thus boost growth by expanding trade, increasing capital and labor utilization, and intensifying competition (World Bank 2016, p. 50). Of course, greater growth creates a potential for greater investment, including FDI.

There are several more direct relations between ICT and FDI. Research in development economics argues that a higher level of ICT services has a positive impact on FDI coming from particular country. Addison and Heshmati (2003) investigated the causal relationship between FDI, GDP growth, trade openness, and ICT. Their main findings were that democratization and ICT increase FDI inflows to developing countries. The article concluded that more assistance should be given to poorer countries to help them to adopt ICT and to break out of their low ICT equilibrium trap (ibid.). Soper *et al.* (2012) argued more recently that the direct impact of ICT investments on future levels of institutionalized democracy in emerging societies is shown to partially explain the observed relationship between ICT investments and future FDI in those societies.

In the current digital transformation of industry and society, the integration of the existing embedded systems with new Internet-based standards, platforms, systems, devices, and services is a major trend. The convergence of these instruments permits emergence and utilization of new types of device and service platforms (Porter & Happelman 2014). The role of FDI in this digital transformation is the third aspect of interrelationship between FDI and ICT sector development.

Investment in the ICT sector can come from private or public sources and be domestic or foreign. This analysis examines private funding, specifically in the form of FDI, which can come from the same company in another country (which, for example, creates a subsidiary in the host country) or from a specialized financial institution like a venture capital firm in another country.[3] In this context, international investment by a venture capital firm, which is accompanied by equity financing and involves the acquisition of at least a 10 percent stake is considered FDI.[4] In addition to venture capital, other types of private capital investment are growth investment, rescue/turnaround investment, replacement capital, and buyouts (EVCA 2014, p. 44).

The specific features of private capital investment are that the securities held by the investor cannot be sold in an anonymous market like a stock exchange. At the same time, the market has two very crucial characteristics for investors: information asymmetry and moral hazard (Denis 2004, p. 303). Information asymmetry is expressed in a wide gap in between the information held by entrepreneurs and that held by investors. It is difficult for outside investors to get a clear idea of the potential of the technological innovation while the entrepreneurs, very often being authors of the innovation, understand the potential better and can use this information for making decisions, which are useful for them with extra cost for outside investors. Moral hazard can occur for the reason that the entrepreneurs have raised funds from outside investors and can spend the money on other activities not related to the developing the particular project. Information asymmetry and moral hazard as market failures make the choice of financial instruments in projects financed by venture capital critical.

The financial instruments that give access to a firm's financial capital are the cash shares, capital contributions shares, common shares, priority or preference shares with financial advantages (such as dividend guarantees) or non-financial advantages (i.e., the right to name administrators or voting rights in certain financial operations), or shares with double voting rights. Securities that do not give voting rights, such as priority shares without voting rights or investment certificates, are not used by investors because they want to benefit from their voting rights (Rédis 2010, p. 32). It thence transpires that there are very strong incentives for venture capital to make investment in one or another form of share ownership with voting rights. This is a reason why it could be assumed that if these investments are made between the countries, and acquired ownership in a foreign company is at least 10 percent of value of its total share capital, the investment qualifies as FDI.

Specific feature of FDI in ICT sector links to the network industry phenomenon. The interest of MNEs dominating or owning certain technological platforms (Apple and Microsoft) widens the network potential of the new company and these companies get easier access to investments of international venture capital companies or can be bought by these dominating MNEs. From a FDI statistical standpoint venture capital companies and sometimes MNEs use very sophisticated financial networks going through low corporate tax countries and thus financial transfers related to these purchases are very hard to record. For example, all private investments into the Estonian economy (including venture capital, growth, rescue/turnaround, replacement capital, and buyout) were €28 million in 2013 and €40 million in 2014, but only a single company TransferWise raised from the venture capital market €58 million (EVCA 2015, p. 21).[5] That makes the case study method a very valuable method for examining FDI in the ICT sector.

Russian OFDI in ICT Companies

Research on Russian OFDI understandably has concentrated on Russian transnational companies in the natural resource sector. This discussion, which delves into the reasons for OFDI from Russia, contains valuable information about and insights into this process (Heinrich 2004; Kalotay 2005; Kuznetsov 2010; Holtbrügge & Kreppel 2012; Liuhto & Majuri 2014).

The ICT sector is a very dynamic, global business with its own specific features. The classical approach to Russian OFDI based on the experience of more traditional sectors probably underestimates the dynamics of the ICT industry and the importance of participation in international ICT community and in networks, which create new technical platforms for the industry. This could become a more powerful reason for Russian OFDI in the ICT sector even when direct economic sanctions imposed on Russian business people and the reciprocal actions of the Russian Government do not directly impact Russian ICT companies.

For the current study, the discussion of the internationalization of the service industry through OFDI is more interesting. Liuhto (2015, pp. 9–10) provides a list of the most frequent motivations of Russian firms investing abroad. Drawing upon this list, we can derive arguments for ICT companies from Russia to invest abroad. One factor is the pressure of increasing global competition, especially regarding the products and services of modern network industries. A second factor could be the acquisition of advanced Western technology, which in modern network industries is connected directly with different types of networking.

A third driver could be the factors of risk aversion, the acquisition of real estate, or the establishment of a firm abroad in order to get a "Golden Visa", all quite interrelated, especially when one thinks about Russia's current political situation.

Regarding Russian OFDI in the ICT sector, Latukha and Panibratov (2013) identify reasons why Russian ICT firms are interested in internationalization. Their study suggests the internationalization motives of these firms may be primarily explained by their highly skilled labor force and low labor cost opportunities. They claim that the technological sophistication of Russian companies and that of their foreign competitors in the high tech sectors is almost the same and thus partnership internationalization strategies are appropriate. Their study shows that strategic priorities of internationalizing Russian ICT firms are focused on the acquisition of customers rather than on acquisition of technologies. They also argue that these firms' internationalization endeavors succeeded in turbulent economic and financial times when the companies prioritized the exploration of investment opportunities rather than escaping from home-country limitations.

Filippov (2011a, 2011b) also studied the internationalization of the Russian ICT firms. He found many were entirely self-financed and grew without any government assistance. As well, many were SMEs, which had gradually accumulated experience after the 1990s and started venturing abroad. Several companies became tightly integrated into world markets and found success selling their product abroad. His conclusion is that innovation and use of comparative advantage is important in this process. Often this internationalization is organic in terms of the establishment of greenfield subsidiaries rather than acquisition of foreign firms.

Djankov (2015) describes the risks of doing business in Russia after economic sanctions were implemented due to Putin's assertive foreign policy towards Ukraine. Though the number of directly affected people and industries is small in terms of numbers, these sanctions have significant indirect negative effects. They have effectively dried up the supply of fresh capital to the Russian economy. Large state-owned companies or companies with close ties to politicians have managed to substitute expensive (high interest rate) private financing for state support in the form of access to state-owned banks or special import-substitution schemes promoted by some Russian ministries. Private businesses without political ties, however, have experienced severe financial constraints. The subsequent ruble devaluation has exacerbated the credit crunch as bank loan interest rates spiked in early 2015 to over 20–25 percent. Djankov also argues that economic sanctions have been a reason for surge of super wealth in Russia because when the Russian ruble was substantially devalued in December 2014, the super rich could afford to shift their assets into foreign currency such that many of their assets did not decline in value. The faith of this wealth depends on political favor and encourages capital flight (ibid., p. 3).

These political tensions and macroeconomic problems probably increase uncertainties and inclination of Russian business leaders to avoid long-term capital investment, which, in turn, produces insufficient investment in innovation. Altogether, this reflects a lack of trust in the Russian business environment and could be an additional factor supporting OFDI by Russian ICT companies.

Research Method

The Russian company Parallels Holding Inc. and its Estonian subsidiary Parallels Software Estonia OÜ were chosen for the reason that this is a global ICT company in a niche area. The case study method was applied because this gives in-depth insights into the internationalization process of the company. The investment had to fulfill the definition of FDI. As investment for the Estonian subsidiary came from Cyprus and the subsidiary is fully owned by the companies registered in Cyprus, we have taken it as a proxy for Russian FDI.

The case study describes different stages of the company's shift from a purely Russian company to a global MNE. It is based on a semi-structured interview with a vice president of the company and took place in Enterprise Estonia in Tallinn on 7 December 2015. The semi-structured interview instrument asks questions about the company's background, business strategy, products/applied technology, potential markets, and partners. One set of questions concerns the views of the company about new locations as available resources, places for product development, or finances for widening business. The role of business environment in initiating FDI is also covered. Interviews with representatives of the Faculty of Information Technology at the Tallinn University of Technology and Enterprise Estonia and open sources provided additional information for the case study.

The general theoretical foundations of Russian OFDI often build upon wider frameworks for FDI or internationalization such as the eclectic approach and Dunning's taxonomy (Dunning 1993). The paradigm has been broadened according to Eden's (2003) suggestion to incorporate questions "who" and "when" to the initial three questions "why", "where" and "how". Liuhto and Aro (2016) also applied this widened approach to OFDI from Russia.

The Case Company: Parallels Software Estonia OÜ

The Case Company and Its Parent Company

Several computer programmers, including Nikolay Dobrovolsky, founded Parallels in 1999 in Moscow. Dobrovolsky was the CEO of the company.[6] The idea was to develop a domestic virtual machine technology for Internet page developers, which makes test and use of operational systems possible. In 2004 Russian venture fund Runa Capital invested in the company and became a majority shareholder. In 2007 Runa Capital initiated the merger of Parallels with another company controlled by its SWsoft, headed by CEO Serguei Beloussov.[7] The new Parallels Holding was formed in 2008.[8] The headquarters of Parallels Holding Ltd is in Seattle (USA) with Serguei Beloussov having assumed the chairmanship.

A majority of the shares of Parallels Holding Ltd belong to Serguei Beloussov and his financial partner Ilya Zubarev. In 2014, the other owners of Parallels Holding Ltd, which include founders and employees, held 25 percent of shares and another 25 percent belonged to venture capital funds such as Bessemer, Insight VP, Intel Capital, and Almaz Capital Partners. Parallels' market is divided between the USA (40 percent), Europe (39 percent), Japan (20 percent), and Russia (1 percent) (Software Russia 2014).

The company has development centers in Moscow and Novosibirsk (Russia). It acquired 2X Software in February 2015. The next month, it rebranded their service provider business unit to Odin. Parallels has more than 800 employees across the USA, Europe, and Asia and had a consolidated turnover of over €130 million in 2014 (Parallels 2015). The company is a global leader in cross-platform solutions. Parallels products include a desktop for Mac, a solution for running Windows on Mac without rebooting. This company, with 78 percent market share, was a global leader in 2014 and its software is used by more than 50 percent of Fortune 200 companies. The company has the following other products: Parallels Desktop for Mac Business Edition (a solution to deliver Windows and Windows applications to employees with Macs), Parallels 2X Remote Application Server (delivers applications and virtual desktops to any device and operating system), Parallels Access (tool for remote access to someone's computer), and Parallels' Mac Management for Microsoft System Centre Configuration Manager (Parallels 2015).

Parallels Software Estonia OÜ was incorporated in December 2014 by Cyprus-registered company Parallels (Cyprus) Limited, with €2,500 recorded in the Estonian Commercial Register on 12 November 2014. Another owner is CPH Software Ltd, registered in Cyprus with €2,500 since 3 September 2015. The company received a €583,000 grant from Enterprise Estonia,[9] which is close to half of the €1.2 million initial payment under the program of technical support centers,[10] which takes the form of compensation for training costs of employees. The company promised to create a center with 60 ICT system developers with an annual turnover of €2.6 million. The company presented to Enterprise Estonia a business plan ; the main cost article is covering the training-related expenditures of new developers.

According to the grant rules, the agreed expenditures are compensated afterwards. The company rents office space in the Ülemiste Centre, near Tallinn Airport, which is the location of several Estonian ICT companies, such as Helmes AS and Nortal AS. Parallels Software Estonia OÜ aims to employ half of its staff from the European Union and another half from Russia and other countries of the Commonwealth of Independent States (CIS).

Research Findings

Why

Parallels Inc. was looking for a location in the Baltic Sea region for its new development center. Representatives of Enterprise Estonia contacted them and came to meet them when they had a contact day in Riga, Latvia. The active role of Enterprise Estonia was important in attracting Parallels to Estonia. The main idea behind this new development center in the Baltic Sea region was that the company needed new product developers and wanted to hire specialists internationally. Estonia and Latvia have large Russian-speaking populations and programming and other ICT skills are popular among Russian-speaking youth in both countries, which means they would provide a potential hiring pool of specialists. Parallels also expected that several foreign experts who would not go to Russia would consider going to Tallinn or Riga, where they would constitute the second potential pool of specialists. Good service level in capitals of the Baltic States and relatively close location to the Russian development centers also deserve mention. The positive attitude of Enterprise Estonia and personal contacts between venture capitalists were also important. A more general driver is that the creation of development centers around the world is a very common ICT company networking-based strategy.

Where

Estonia has a reputation as the birthplace of some globally renowned ICT firms, such as Skype. In addition, the Estonian Government has been vocal about and supportive of the development of public services in e-format.[11] Starting in 2014, Estonia offered an e-citizenship, which Nikolay Dobrovolsky acquired in 2015. With good ICT infrastructure, Estonia was considered a good place by Parallels for the launching and testing of new products. Closeness to the ICT community in the Ülemiste Centre is an advantage. In addition, Tallinn is considered a good living environment for Russian-speaking people because there are Russian-language kindergartens, schools, and cultural attractions. In addition, the Ülemiste Centre corporate location is only a five-minute drive from the Tallinn Airport which made it easy to get a flight to/from the place of work. Also wider regional contacts in the Baltic Sea region are targeted.

How

As noted, the founder of Parallels Software Estonia OÜ is a Cyprus-registered company Parallels (Cyprus) Limited; another owner is CPH Software Ltd, which also is registered in Cyprus. In the Estonian Commercial Register, member of management board Yakov Zubarev is registered (Äriregister 2015).[12] It is a greenfield investment with no Estonian partner or purchased Estonian ICT company. Making investment into another country, the company compares advantages and possible risks of different options such as greenfield investment, takeover of local company with majority shareholding for OFDI company, minority shareholding in some Estonian company for OFDI company. From a corporate governance point of view there is a trade-off between spread ownership, bringing into the company a wider spectrum of human resources, and concentrated ownership, making control over activities of specialists and sensible technical information easier. The full ownership of OFDI signals that the control argument is stronger in case of Parallels Holding Ltd.

Another aspect is related to the dominating global market position of Parallels in a particular niche. That advantage assumes closeness to the business ecosystems of Apple and Microsoft. Keeping in mind this argument, the purpose of widening the business is, first of all, (human) resource-seeking. However, the company is looking also for new ideas and tries to introduce participation in networks. Nikulainen and Pajarinen (2013) and Tahvanainen and Steinert (2013) describe networking as a two-directional avenue, giving newcomers access to networks and making for larger companies' screening of new business ideas and products possible. Parallels' current market position keeps it quite closed for that kind of cooperation but that could change if the company develops its contacts further in the region.

Who

The firm plans to widen its service development activities into new areas. The core team of the subsidiary is planned to move to Tallinn from development centers in Russia. Additionally, the goal is to hire local specialists and specialists from other European states so that the company can widen its human resource base. However, the company offers training possibilities for potential local employees in other development centers in Russia.

Another human resource development plan is targeting universities in Estonia and also in other Baltic States. The company is ready to dispatch some of its employees to teach classes at universities and is ready to organize and finance research laboratories for students. They also offer internships at the company and the possibility of working in close teams, with the best graduates having a chance to join the company.

When

The timing of investment into Estonia is related to the general strategy of the Parallels Holding Ltd. One idea behind this widening is screening for other business opportunities and products. Timing was also influenced by development of interesting ICT tools and environment by the Estonian Government. Estonian capability for such kinds of projects signals also the availability of quite substantial ICT sector potential. Parallels also wanted to be part of that development.

Uncertainty related to the political stage in Russia and political relationships between Russia and the USA and Russia and the European Union is one factor in the introduction of a new development center. Parallels is not directly affected by these relationships, though they have indirect influence by shaping the preferences of potential employees.

Conclusions

Russia's official share of the total FDI stock into Estonia at the end of 2014 was 5 percent. In actuality, the Russian share of Estonian IFDI share is higher because, as some earlier studies demonstrated, some Russian companies prefer to invest through the third countries. The main reason for such investing strategies was that Russian investors expected that their investments would be more welcome if they did not come directly from Russia but from third countries.

The Russian company Parallels Holding and its Estonian subsidiary Parallels Software Estonia OÜ were chosen as a case study for this chapter for the reason that it is a global ICT company in a niche area. As investment for the Estonian subsidiary came from Cyprus and the subsidiary is 100 percent owned by the companies registered in Cyprus, we take it as a proxy for Russian FDI. It is a greenfield investment with no Estonian partner or Estonian ICT company purchased. From a corporate governance point of view there is a trade-off between spread ownership bringing into company wider spectrum of human resources and concentrated ownership making the control over activities of specialists and sensible technical information easier. The full ownership of OFDI signals that the control argument is stronger.

The main idea behind this new development center in the Baltic Sea region was that the company needed new product developers and wanted to hire specialists internationally. Estonia and Latvia have large Russian-speaking populations and programming and other ICT skills are popular among Russian-speaking youth in both countries, which means they would provide a potential hiring pool of specialists. Parallels also expected that several foreign experts who would not go to Russia would consider going to Tallinn or Riga, where they would constitute the second potential pool of specialists.

The core team of the subsidiary is planned to move to Tallinn from development centers in Russia. Additionally, the goal is to hire local specialists and specialists from other European states so that the company can widen its human resource base. However, the company offers training possibilities for potential local employees in other development centers in Russia. Estonia's good ICT infrastructure meant that Parallels considered the country a good place for launching new products and testing them. Also important was relatively close location to Russian development centers.

One idea behind this widening is screening for other business opportunities and products. Timing was also influenced by development of interesting ICT tools and environment by the Estonian Government. Estonian capability for such kinds of projects signals also the availability of quite substantial ICT sector potential. Parallels also wanted to be part of that development.

Another human resource development plan is targeting universities in Estonia and also in other Baltic States. The company is ready to dispatch some of its employees to teach classes at universities and is ready to organize and finance research laboratories for students. They also offer internships at the company and the possibility of working in close teams, with the best graduates having a chance to join the company.

Uncertainty related to the political stage in Russia and political relationships between Russia and the USA and Russia and the European Union is one factor in the introduction of a new development center. There is a threat that political tensions would be an obstacle in free movement of specialists between Russia and other locations of the company.

For the ICT industry is very important to participate in the international ICT community and in networks, which create new technical platforms for the industry. The current case study demonstrated that this is a dominant reason for OFDI from Russia in the ICT sector.

The case study demonstrated also the complicated dilemma for an ICT company in a foreign country. The company is targeting participation in the network with the goal of potentially screening new business ideas and products. Its dominant position in a particular market segment keeps it quite closed for other possible partners. Networking-based cooperation could increase if the company develops its contacts further in the region.

The complicated financial pattern of OFDI of ICT companies needs special investigation and a case method could add a lot of additional information to this study field. There is definitely a need for deeper research.

Notes

1 The negative figure of Russian FDI in 2000 and 2007 is due to the fact that value of loss of capital related to FDI was larger than value of incoming capital in these years.
2 Serendipity: literary, the natural ability to make interesting or valuable discoveries by accident (*Longman Dictionary of Contemporary English* 2015).
3 The OECD definition of FDI is applied, according to which FDI is a category of investment that reflects the objective of establishing a lasting interest by a resident enterprise in one economy (direct investor) in an enterprise (direct investment enterprise) that is resident in an economy other than that of the direct investor. The lasting interest implies the existence of a long-term relationship between the direct investor and the direct investment enterprise and a significant degree of influence on the management of the enterprise. The direct or indirect ownership of 10 percent or more of the voting power of an enterprise resident in one economy by an investor resident in another economy is evidence of such relationship (OECD 2014).
4 Venture capital is, strictly speaking, a subset of private equity and refers to equity investments made to support the pre-launch, launch, and early stage development phases of a business. In statistical analysis, EVCA adds together under total venture capital seed money, start-up, and later-stage venture capital investment (EVCA 2015, p. 44).
5 One example is Skype, which was released in 2002. In 2005, eBay acquired Skype for $2.6 billion. In 2009, Silver Lake, Andreessen Horowitz, and Canada Pension Plan Investment Board announced acquisition of 65 percent of Skype for $1.9 billion, valuing the business at $2.75 billion. Microsoft later acquired Skype in 2011 for $8.5 billion (Wired 2009; Horowitz 2011). Headquarters of Microsoft's Skype is in Luxembourg, but most of the development team and 44 percent of the overall employees of the division are still situated in Tallinn and Tartu, Estonia (Skype 2015). Another example is GrabCAD, a community for connecting engineers with CAD-related work, which was founded by Estonian developers in 2009 and moved to the USA in 2011. In 2014, the American 3D printing company Stratasys acquired it for an estimated $100 million. TransferWise, the peer to peer international money transfer company founded by two Estonians, raised $58 million funding in a round led by Silicon Valley venture capital fund Andreessen Horowitz. It has moved its headquarters to London (Bershidsky 2015; Kaminska 2015; Newton 2015; Äripäev 2015).

6 Nikolay Dobrovolsky, creator of ParallelsDesktop software for Mac, received a prestigious Young Global Leaders award, bestowed each year by the World Economic Forum in Davos. In Russia, Nikolay Dobrovolsky won the nomination "The Best Innovative Manager of the Zvorykin Award" in 2008 (Marchmont 2012).
7 Serguei Beloussov is a citizen of Singapore (Beloussov 2015).
8 In April 2009, an investment company Almaz Capital Partners bought 5 percent in Parallels for $11 million, which sets the value of the entire company at $220 million. There was a plan of IPO in 2010 but financial crisis was one reason why this plan was not realized (Newspepper 2010).
9 Enterprise Estonia is a public organization whose goal is to support innovation and development in Estonia. The agency implements the EU structural funds in Estonia. During the EU's new 2014–20 funding period the budget of Structural Funds is €3.5 billion of which €588.1 million is implemented by Enterprise Estonia. Enterprise Estonia had budget of €104.8 million in 2015 and total number of employees is 300 (Enterprise Estonia 2015).
10 It is one of the largest support schemes of Enterprise Estonia. Other companies which received support in 2015 were Kuhne+Nagel AS IT centre development Project, Ramirent Baltic AS for development of group's financial centre in Tallinn, Upitech OÜ for development of e-healthcare services centre in Tallinn (company is registered in the Netherlands but has Estonian owners), Orkla Accounting Centre OÜ, and JELD-WEN Eesti AS for developing a support services centre in Estonia (Enterprise Estonia 2015; Äripäev 2015).
11 The Estonian Government started to actively develop the ICT sector. The government is also the fourth important employer for the ICT specialists. The e-Estonia digital society project and development of respective infrastructure X-road connects all the decentralized components of the system. Key elements of e-Estonia are electronic ID cards, introduced in 2002 and carried by more than 93 percent of the Estonian residents by 2014. Electronic ID cards are regularly used as a national ID cards for legal travel within the EU and Schengen area. They function also as national health insurance cards, as a proof of identification when logging into bank accounts from a home computer, as customer loyalty cards, for digital signatures, for e-voting, for assessing databases to check one's medical records, to file taxes (e-Estonia 2015). In 2012, the European IT Agency opened its doors in Tallinn. The city is also home of NATO's Cyber Defence Centre of Excellence.
12 Yakov (Jack) Zubarev is President and General Manager of Parallels Holding Ltd (Parallels 2015).]

Bibliography

Addison, T. & Heshmati, A. 2003, *The New Global Determinants of FDI Flows to Developing Countries*, WIDER, United Nations University, Helsinki.
Äripäev 2015, 'Financial Times põrmustas TransferWise'l', 29 December.
Äriregister 2015, viewed on 20 December 2015, https://ariregister.rik.ee/ettevotja
Bank of Estonia 2015, viewed 20 December 2015 http://statistika.eestipank. ee/?lng=eng#listMENU/1873/treeMENU /MAKSEBIL_JA_INVPOS/146
Beloussov 2015, viewed 20 December 2015, https://www.techinasia.com/acronis-serguei-beloussov-singaporean-story
Bershidsky, L. 2015, 'Estonia's overhyped Silicon Valley', *Bloomberg View*, viewed 10 March 2015, https://www.bloomberg.com/view/articles/2015-03-05/estonia-s-over-hyped-silicon-valley
Denis, D.J. 2004, 'Entrepreneurial finance: an overview of the issues and evidence', *Journal of Corporate Finance*, vol. 10, no. 2, pp. 301–26.

Djankov, S. 2015, *Russia's Economy Under Putin: From Crony Capitalism to State Capitalism*, Peterson Institute for International Economics, Washington, DC.

Dunning, J. 1993, *Multinational Enterprises and the Global Economy*, Addison-Wesley, Harlow.

Economides, N. 2006, 'Competition policy in network industries: an introduction', in D.W. Jansen (ed.), *The New Economy and Beyond: Past, Present and Future*, Edward Elgar, Cheltenham.

Eden, L. 2003, 'A critical reflection and some conclusions on OLI', in J. Cantwell & R. Narula (eds.), *International Business and the Eclectic Paradigm: Developing the OLI Framework*, Routledge, London.

e-Estonia 2015, *e-Estonia. The future is now*, viewed on 20 December 2015, https://issuu.com/eas-estonia/docs/e-estonia_thefutureisnow

Enterprise Estonia 2015, *Ettevõtluse Arendamise Sihtasutus, EAS*, viewed 20 December 2015, http://www.eas.ee/en/eas/overview

EVCA 2015, *Central and Eastern Europe Statistics 2014: An EVCA Special Paper*, The European Private Equity & Venture Capital Association, Brussels.

Filippov, S. 2011a, 'Emerging Russian multinationals: innovation, technology and internationalization', *Journal of East–West Business*, vol. 17, no. 2–3, pp. 184–94.

Filippov, S. 2011b, 'Innovation and R&D in emerging Russian multinationals', *Economics, Management and Financial Markets*, vol. 6, no.1, pp. 182–206.

Heinrich, A. 2005, 'Russian companies in old EU member states: the case of Germany', *Journal of East–West Business,* vol. 11, no. 3–4, pp. 41–59.

Holtbrügge, D. & Kreppel, H. 2012, 'Determinants of outward foreign direct investment from BRIC countries: an explorative study', *International Journal of Emerging Markets*, vol. 7, no. 1, pp. 4–30.

Horowitz, B. 2011, 'Why the Skype investment worked', *Fortune*, 20 May, viewed 20 December 2015, http://fortune.com/2011/05/10/why-the-skype-investment-worked.htm

Kalotay, K. 2005, 'Outward foreign direct investment from Russia in global context', *Journal of East–West Business*, vol. 11, no. 3–4, pp. 9–22.

Kalotay, K. 2013, 'The 2013 Cyprus bailout and the Russian foreign direct investment platform', *Baltic Rim Economies*, no. 3, pp. 58–9.

Kalotay, K., Éltetö, A., Sass, M. & Weiner, C. 2014, *Russian Capital in the Visegrád Countries*, Centre for Economic and Regional Studies of the Hungarian Academy of Sciences – Institute of World Economics, Budapest.

Kaminska, I. 2015, 'TransferWise vs the banks', *Financial Times Alphaville*, 22 December.

Kilvits, K., Purju, A. & Pädam, S. 2005, 'Russia's foreign direct investments in new EU member states: the case of the Baltic States', *Journal of East–West Business*, vol. 11, no. 3–4, pp. 61–73.

Kuznetsov, A. 2010, *Industrial and Geographical Diversification of Russian Foreign Direct Investments*, Pan-European Institute, University of Turku, Turku.

Latukha, M. & Panibratov, A. 2013, 'Servicing local customers for entering foreign markets: internationalization of Russian IT firms', in M. Marinov & S. Marinov (eds.), *Emerging Economies and Firms in the Global Crises*, Palgrave Macmillan, London.

Liuhto, K.T. 2015, 'Motivations of Russian firms to invest abroad: how sanctions affect the Russian outward foreign direct investment?', *The Baltic Region*, vol. 26, no. 4, pp. 4–19.

Liuhto, K. & Aro, E. 2016, 'Russian FDI in Finland: empirical evidence from a knowledge-driven investment', in K. Liuhto, S. Sutyrin & J-M. Blanchard (eds.), *The Russian Economy and Foreign Direct Investment*, Routledge, London.

Liuhto, K. & Majuri, S. 2014, 'Outward foreign direct investments from Russia: a literature review', *Journal of East–West Business*, vol. 20, no. 4, pp. 198–224.

Longman Dictionary of Contemporary English 2015, viewed 29 December 2015, http://www.longman.com/ldoce

Marchmont 2012, *Creator of ParallelsDesktop Receives Young Global Leaders Award*, 11 March, viewed 22 December 2016, http://marchmontnews.com/Technology-Innovation/Volga/18373-Creator-ParallelsDesktop-receives-Young-Global-Leaders-award

Moore, J.F. 2006, 'Business ecosystems and the view from the firm', *Antitrust Bulletin*, vol. 51, no 1, pp. 31–75.

Newspepper 2010, 'Russian software developer Parallels prepares IPO', viewed on 22 December 2015, http://newspepper.su/news/2010/12/16/russian-software-developer-parallels-prepares-ipo/

Newton, R. 2015, 'Tallinn, Estonia: Baltic city's global digital ambitions', *Financial Times*, 11 August.

Nikulainen, T. & Pajarinen, M. 2013, *Industry Restructuring in the ICT Sector: What Does Labour Mobility Tell Us About Skill Relatedness and Knowledge Spill-Overs?*, ETLA, Helsinki.

OECD 2014, *Glossary of Foreign Direct Investment: Terms and Definitions*, Organisation for Economic Co-operation and Development, viewed 20 January 2016, http://www.oecd.org/daf/inv/investment-policy/2487495.pdf

Parallels 2015, viewed 10 October 2015, http://www.parallels.com

Pelto, E., Vahtra, P. & Liuhto, K. 2004, 'Cyp-Rus investment flows to Central and Eastern Europe: Russia's direct and indirect investments via Cyprus to CEE', *Journal of Business Economics and Management*, vol. 5, no. 1, pp. 3–13.

Porter, M. & Heppelmann, J. 2014, 'How smart connected products are transforming competition', *Harvard Business Review*,92, no. 11, pp. 64–88.

Rédis, J. 2010, 'ICT start-ups venture capital and funding', *Problems and Perspectives in Management*, vol. 8, Special Issue, pp. 30–7.

Skype 2015, viewed 29 December 2015, http://www.skype.com/et/about.html

Software Russia 2014, viewed 20 December 2015, http://software-russia.com/in_focus/media/how-parallels-beat-apple-and-vmware

Soper, D.S., Demirkan, H., Goul, M. & St.Louis, R. 2012, 'An empirical examination of the impact of ICT investments on future levels of institutionalized democracy and foreign direct investment in emerging societies', *Journal of the Associations of Information Systems*, vol. 13, no. 3, pp. 116–49.

Tahvanainen, A. & Steinert, M. 2013, *Network! Network! Network! How Global Technology Start-Ups Access Modern Business Ecosystems*, ETLA, Helsinki.

Wired 2009, *EBay Sells 65 percent of Skype for 1.9 billion, Andreessen Among Investors*, viewed 20 December 2015, http://www.wired.com/2009/09/andreessen-among-buyers-of-skype-new-york-times/

World Bank 2016, *World Development Report 2016: Digital Dividends*, World Bank, Washington, DC.

9 Political Risk of Western Oil and Gas Investments in Russia
Review of Media Coverage on ExxonMobil and Total in the Russian Arctic

Hanna Mäkinen and Eini Haaja[1]

Introduction

Extant research on political risk in the Russian oil and gas industry and Arctic energy resources is relatively scarce.[2] However, the oil and gas industry is of strategic importance for Russia, and the sector's development affects the political risk faced by foreign investors. While foreign investors continue to participate in hydrocarbon extraction in Russia despite the earlier risk experiences encountered by foreign corporations and the turbulence in East–West political relations, further research is needed on the constituents and dynamics of political risk in the Russian energy sector.

The main objective of this chapter is to analyze the sources of political risk in two mega projects exploiting natural resources in Russia – ExxonMobil's investments in the Kara Sea project and Total's investments in the Yamal liquefied natural gas (LNG) project – from the perspective of the Western media coverage of these projects. Given the current turbulent political situation caused by the crisis in Ukraine and the related sanctions imposed by Western countries on Russia, particular attention is paid to the potential impact of this situation on the political risk faced by foreign investors.

Theoretical Framework for Analyzing Political Risk

Political risk is created by a foreign investor's uncertainty about general instability in the host country's political system in the future and/or future acts by the host government that would cause loss to the investor. Political risk is conventionally distinguished from market risk, which derives from uncertainty about future changes in cost, demand, and competition in the market (Root 1987, p. 130).

Extant literature proposes various models explaining the sources and effects of political risk for foreign direct investment (FDI) (e.g. Robock 1971; Simon 1984; Root 1987; Alon & Martin 1998; Schmidt 2001; Alon & Herbert 2009). However, general models for political risk are rarely practical enough for analyzing individual investment projects; for instance, Salonen (1987) calls for more context specific definitions. Therefore, researchers have also presented industry specific political risk constructs, such as Lax (1983) and Laaksonen (2010) for the oil and gas industry. While the construct by Lax (1983) embraces governmental, socio-cultural, economic, and industry specific dimensions, the construct by Laaksonen (2010) limits the focus of analysis to government-driven sources of political risks and joins them with the possible effects of political risk on business. The political risk construct for an FDI by Laaksonen (2010) was originally developed in light of the Shtokman project based on earlier political risk models (see Table 9.1).[3] In this study the construct is revisited based on the Kara Sea and Yamal LNG projects.

The micro-level sources of political risk consist of internal and external industry-level, firm-level, and project-level issues. The internal industry-related sources include domestic gas reserves and production, and the strength of the national gas company. Both concepts refer to the business environment in the host country's gas industry and the bargaining power that the host government may have against a foreign investor directly or through a state-owned gas

Table 9.1 The Political Risk Construct for an FDI into a Gas Field Project

Micro sources of political risk	
Internal	*External*
Industry • Domestic gas reserves and production • Strength of the national gas company	• World petroleum market conditions
Firm • Bargaining advantages • Position in the world industry • Dependence of a foreign firm on the local market vs the level of firm diversification	• Political/economic relationship between the host and the home government • Company dealings with host government
Project • Level of technology transfer • Exports generated by the project • The size of the project • Extent of natural resource seeking	• Congruence with governmental goals • Ownership/contractual relationship between the firm and the host

$$\Downarrow$$

Effects of political risk on business	
Ownership/control risk	*Operations risk*
• Coerced contract renegotiation • Contract revocation • Intervention • Coerced sale • Nationalization	• Price controls • Foreign staff limits • Import/export requirements • Restrictions on repatriation of dividends, royalties, interest, fees, or capital • Discrimination

Source: Modified from Laaksonen 2010, p. 53

company. The world petroleum market conditions may have an effect on the host government's actions regarding the industry (Lax 1983; Laaksonen 2010).

The firm-level issues affect the investor's bargaining power against the host government (Laaksonen 2010). First, these sources include bargaining advantages, such as technology, managerial skills, services, and capital. If the investor is able to offer the host country what it needs, the host government is less likely to intervene in the investor's operations in the host country. Second, the company's position in the global market also affects its bargaining power. When it comes to the external firm-level sources, one issue is the relationship between the host and the home government. A company represents its home country and, depending on the relations between the two countries, is likely to gather either goodwill or hostility from the host government. Company dealings with the host government, in turn, refer to the company's individual relations with the host country (Lax 1983; Alon & Herbert 2009; Laaksonen 2010).

In terms of the project-level issues, the level of technology transfer refers to the need or even dependence of the host country on technology inflows from abroad, which reduces the level of political risk. The exports generated by the project and the size of the project relate to the contribution of the project to the national economy, which is a risk-reducing phenomenon. The extent of natural resource-seeking suggests the project's potential to exploit the host country's natural resources, which might cause the state to set regulative restrictions/obligations to the foreign investor. Congruence with governmental goals, in turn, refers to the fact that projects that are at odds with the host government's policies or priorities tread on thin ice. Ownership or contractual relationships between the firm and the host refers to the governance structure of the project. If the ownership of the project is primarily held by the foreign investor, the host government may consider the business relationship exploitive, and often such majority positions are not preferred or acceptable (Schmidt 2001; Alon & Herbert 2009; Laaksonen 2010).

All of these sources may lead to ownership/control risk effects or to operational risk effects. On the one hand, ownership or control risk effects consist of the host country coercing renegotiation or unilateral revocation of the contract between the host government and the investor, intervening to temporarily seize foreign-owned property, and coercing the sale or nationalization of foreign-owned property. Operations risk, on the other hand, affects an investor's everyday operations in the host country, comprising of price controls of the project's products, foreign staff limitations, requirements related to imports and/or exports, and restrictions on repatriation of dividends, royalties, interest, fees, or capital. Political risk may also materialize through discrimination – for instance, in terms of taxes and compulsory subcontracting (Robock 1971; Root 1987).

In general, political risk refers to the probability that the political risk sources will lead to the presented effects, which again may result in an inadequate return on investment for the foreign investor. Laaksonen (2010) highlights that political risk is dynamic and in constant change, and if the investor, at the focal point of time, perceives the risk probability and uncertainty regarding the project's future acceptable in relation to the expected rate of return, then it is worth proceeding with the project.

Methodology

This research was conducted as a qualitative case study (e.g., Yin 1994) on two foreign energy companies, ExxonMobil and Total, participating in the oil and gas projects in the Kara Sea and the Yamal Peninsula in the Russian Arctic. The aim of the chapter was to analyze political risk in international energy projects in the Russian Arctic. The Kara Sea and Yamal LNG projects were selected as they are the only ongoing international energy projects in the region that were in progress when the sanctions came into force. As the focus of the study is on the potential impact of the turbulent political situation and sanctions on political risk faced by foreign investors, Chinese companies participating in the Yamal LNG project were excluded from the analysis, as China does not participate in the sanctions imposed by the EU and the USA on Russia.

News media is a major source of information and has significant influence as the shaper of public opinion in the Western world, thus it also affects the perceptions of Western companies on political risk. Consequently, the focus of the research was narrowed down to how Western media targeting the general public covers these projects. Hence, two English-language newspapers, the *Financial Times*[4] and the *Moscow Times*,[5] were selected as the data sources as they target the general public and, simultaneously, comprehensively report on the Kara Sea and Yamal LNG projects. Moreover, both newspapers can be considered to influence Western public opinion on Russia-related issues, the *Financial Times* due to its broad circulation[6] and the *Moscow Times* as one of the few English-language newspapers published in Russia. The researchers also had access to their electronic archives, allowing systematic data collection. Interviews with the representatives of the investor companies and the host and home governments were not conducted as accessing the companies and governments, and engaging in open discussions with their representatives on such a sensitive topic was not considered realistic in the context of this study.

The perspective of both the *Financial Times* and the *Moscow Times* has to be taken into account when estimating the reliability of the material. The *Financial Times*, on the one hand, is considered center-right/liberal[7] and pro-EU.[8] The *Moscow Times*, on the other hand, has been criticized for being biased towards the West when covering Russian-related issues.[9] Hence, there is reason to expect that the Western perspective of both newspapers also influences their coverage on the Kara Sea and Yamal LNG projects. However, as the researchers were aware of this possible bias and viewed the material critically, and as the particular focus of the research was not on the factual information of these projects, but on how Western media targeted for the general public reports it, this was not considered an obstacle to this work. Hence, the main limitation of this study relates to the selection of two newspapers as the primary data source, by which other potential source materials were excluded from the analysis; however, the clear definition of the source material was necessary for the systematic data collection and analysis conducted in this study. As the data for this study was solely comprised of articles in two relevant newspapers, further studies should broaden the view by including data from other sources, such as discussions with the investor companies and the host and home governments.

The newspaper articles used were systematically collected by text searching two key words, "Kara Sea" and "Yamal", from the electronic archives of both the *Financial Times* and the *Moscow Times*, from 1 January 2011 to 31 December 2015, thus allowing the research to follow the whole timeframe of the ExxonMobil–Rosneft and Total–Novatek joint ventures (JVs) through to the completion of this chapter. Searching with the key word "Kara Sea" returned 55 articles from the *Financial Times* and 57 articles from the *Moscow Times* that were related to the ExxonMobil–Rosneft JV in the Kara Sea during the selected timeframe. Respectively, searching with the key word "Yamal" returned 53 articles from the *Financial Times* and 86 articles from the *Moscow Times* that were relevant in terms of the Yamal LNG project. The data analysis was based on a qualitative document analysis, which combines elements of content analysis and thematic analysis and is particularly applicable to qualitative case studies (see, e.g., Bowen 2009). Since political risk is not a new research phenomenon, the study builds on a predetermined theoretical framework aiming at theory elaboration (Eisenhardt 1989). The data was coded and grouped under the themes of industry-, firm-, and project-level sources of political risk, following the political risk construct presented in Table 9.1.

ExxonMobil in the Kara Sea Project

The Russian oil company, Rosneft, launched the project in the Kara Sea in the Russian Arctic shelf in 2010, after obtaining licenses to explore three blocks with estimated recoverable resources of 6.3 billion tons of oil and 14,600 billion cubic meters (bcm) of natural gas, in the area (Rosneft 2015). In August 2011, Rosneft and ExxonMobil signed an agreement to jointly develop these three blocks, after a deal between Rosneft and BP on exploration in the same area collapsed (Gorst, Clover & Crooks 2011). However, ExxonMobil had to leave the project in September 2014, just after the drilling of the first well had started, due to the sanctions imposed by the USA on the Russian oil industry[10] following the crisis in Ukraine. Shortly thereafter, Rosneft confirmed an oil discovery, but the Kara Sea project has remained frozen ever since (Farchy & Crooks 2014; Adams, Crooks & Farchy 2015).

As regards the industry-level sources of political risk, Russia's proven oil reserves are among the ten largest in the world, and Russia is the world's second largest oil producer, after Saudi Arabia (BP 2015). State-controlled Rosneft dominates the Russian oil sector, being both Russia's top oil producer (EIA 2015) and politically well–connected (Hille 2014a). In addition, the Russian Government retains control over Arctic energy projects, as according to the Subsoil Law,[11] only companies having a majority of state ownership and more than five years' experience in the industry are allowed to drill the Russian continental shelf, with Gazprom and Rosneft holding the majority of these licenses. Foreign companies can enter the Russian offshore energy projects only as minority partners in JVs with Russian state-owned companies (Panin 2014a). Consequently, the bargaining power of the Russian Government in the case of these projects remains extremely strong.

Although Russia has been a strong energy power for a long time, some challenges related to the future of Russian oil production exist. As the West Siberian oil fields, currently accounting for the majority of Russian oil production, are being depleted, Russia is being forced to compensate the declining output by turning to resources that are more challenging and costly to develop, such as Arctic offshore and shale resources, and, for this, it needs foreign expertise in their extraction. The development of new fields is extremely important to Russia due to the dependence of its economy on oil, which accounts for 40 percent of federal budget revenues. However, Russia is also currently experiencing economic difficulties due to the low world market price of oil, and the market situation has made the costly Arctic offshore oil projects less lucrative for energy companies (Chazan & Farchy 2014; 'Sanctions or...' 2014; Milne, Adams & Crooks 2015).

When it comes to the firm-level sources of political risk, ExxonMobil has several advantages strengthening its bargaining power against the host government. The development of Arctic offshore resources requires special technological knowledge and it is unlikely that Rosneft, although experienced in conventional oil production, would be able to develop these resources without Western energy companies. Along with a deal with ExxonMobil, one of the world leaders in Arctic underwater drilling technology, Rosneft was given access to ExxonMobil's technology to exploit these deepwater resources and experience in managing complex projects (Crooks 2011b). Moreover, ExxonMobil has enough capital to operate such a project and a certain degree of political clout ('BP defeat...' 2011). ExxonMobil is the world's largest publicly traded energy company, having a strong position on the world energy business and a high level of operational diversification. ExxonMobil is not dependent on the Russian market, which strengthens its bargaining power. However, having a presence in the Russian Arctic is still important to ExxonMobil, in the search for future growth prospects (Crooks 2011b; ExxonMobil 2015).

In terms of the political and economic relations between the host and the home government, the agreement between Rosneft and ExxonMobil was sealed in 2011, but tensions between Russia and the USA had already started to increase in 2012, shortly after Vladimir Putin was re-elected as the President of Russia. Relations have further worsened since the Ukrainian crisis. Thus, the host–home relationship constitutes a clear source of political risk. In fact, ExxonMobil had to suspend its JV with Rosneft, in the fall of 2014, due to the economic sanctions, and the project has remained on hold ever since.

When it comes to company dealings with a host government, ExxonMobil is described as generally taking a hard line against troublesome countries. This corporate policy is also reflected in ExxonMobil's long-lasting dispute with the Russian Government and Gazprom over gas exports from the Sakhalin I project. Crooks (2011a) describes ExxonMobil's corporate culture as stubborn and disciplined. However, in this case, the mutual benefits that the deal brought to both companies (Crooks 2011a) may have reduced the political risk related to the company dealings with the host government. Nevertheless, the relationship between ExxonMobil and the Russian Government is, at least publicly, presented as good. An example of this is the signing ceremony of the ExxonMobil–Rosneft partnership agreement, where then Prime Minister Putin and ExxonMobil's CEO Rex Tillerson praised their strategic partnership (Gorst, Clover & Crooks 2011).

Regarding the project-level sources of political risk, Russia is clearly in need of foreign technology inflows in order to develop the Arctic hydrocarbon resources. As ExxonMobil has world-class technological knowledge of Arctic underwater drilling (Pfeifer & Belton 2011), cooperation with ExxonMobil is necessary for Russia, which reduces the level of political risk. When it comes to the size of the Kara Sea project and the exports it will generate, some uncertainty is involved. The blocks ExxonMobil and Rosneft are exploring in the Kara Sea are on the frontier in the sense that neither oil nor gas has ever been produced there before (Crooks 2011b). Nevertheless, the project is extremely important to Russia due to the depletion of old fields and the need to compensate for this by exploring new regions. Whereas the contribution of the Kara Sea project to the national economy reduces the political risk, the extent of natural resource-seeking is a risk-increasing factor due to the strategic importance of the oil sector and Russia wanting to control these operations.

In terms of the congruence of the project with governmental goals, the situation with the Kara Sea project has changed since ExxonMobil and Rosneft agreed on joint development of the region's resources. The Kara Sea project has remained on hold since ExxonMobil's retreat and is likely to be postponed even further. It is considered unlikely that Rosneft could proceed with the project alone, and, due to low oil prices, the project is not even economically viable. In the beginning of the JV, the project was clearly congruent with the goals of the Russian Government, but at the end of 2015, both the will and the ability of Russia to implement the project remains unclear (Amos 2014; Milne, Adams & Crooks 2015; 'Russia turns…' 2015).

Finally, as regards the ownership or contractual relationship between the firm and the host, Russia wants to retain control over strategically important oil and gas projects, which, in the case of deposits located in the Russian continental shelf, is also assured by the Subsoil Law. The $3.2 billion agreement between ExxonMobil and Rosneft involves joint explorations in the three blocks in the Kara Sea and one block in the Black Sea, with Rosneft holding a 66.7 percent equity stake in the JVs, and ExxonMobil, the remaining 33.3 percent. As a part of the agreement, Rosneft was given minority stakes in some of ExxonMobil's projects, and the companies agreed to establish an Arctic research and design center in Saint Petersburg (Crooks 2011b). The estimations on the costs of the Kara Sea project range from $200 billion to $600 billion ('Exxon–Rosneft deal'

2012; 'Exxon halts...' 2014). It seems that, in return for one third of the royalties over some two decades, ExxonMobil was expected to provide the lion's share of the financial resources, do most of the work, and share its expertise and some of its international assets with Rosneft (Aris 2011). Given that the partnership agreement is rather beneficial for Rosneft and the control over the project remains in Russia, the firm–host contractual relationship does not constitute a serious source of political risk.

Total in the Yamal LNG Project

The Yamal LNG project, implemented by the Russian gas company Novatek, is based on the resources of the Yuzhno-Tambeyskoye natural gas field on the coast of the Ob Bay, with estimated natural gas reserves of 926 bcm (Novatek 2014). Located in an isolated Arctic area, which is ice-bound for up to nine months a year, the project requires special drilling technologies. In addition, the project includes logistical challenges, necessitating the construction of infrastructures for transportation of equipment and people, as well as for opening a new LNG sea transportation route via the Northern Sea Route to Asia (Total 2015b).

In March 2011, Total agreed to purchase a 20 percent stake in the Yamal LNG project and a 12 percent stake in Novatek, which could be increased to 19.4 percent within three years (Belton 2011). In fall 2013, the China National Petroleum Corporation (CNPC) joined the Yamal LNG project with a 20 percent stake, and, in fall 2015, China's Silk Road Fund (SRF) signed a framework agreement on the acquisition of a 9.9 percent equity stake in the project. The closure of the deal with SRF will leave Novatek with a 50.1 percent stake in the $27 billion JV ('China signs...' 2013; Raval, Farchy & Stothard 2014; Hille & Farchy 2015). The final investment decision for the project was made in December 2013, with the planned launch of LNG production in 2017 (Novatek 2014). Although the sectoral sanctions adopted by the USA and the EU do not concern the natural gas industry, the USA has imposed sanctions on Novatek and one of its owners, Gennady Timchenko, blocking Novatek's access to long-term financing from the USA.

As regards the industry-level sources of political risk and the concepts of domestic gas reserves and production, Russia's proved natural gas reserves are the second largest in the world after Iran, and Russia is the world's second largest producer of natural gas after the USA (BP 2015). In terms of the strength of the national gas company, the state-controlled Gazprom holds the dominant position in the gas production sector, which is further reinforced by its monopoly on pipeline gas exports and control over Russia's gas pipeline network. Novatek, in turn, is the largest privately owned gas company in Russia and the second largest gas company in Russia after Gazprom, producing some 10 percent of the Russian natural gas output. Novatek has managed to obtain licenses for some of Russia's most promising gas reserves in the Yamal Peninsula and its production has been growing in recent years (Gorst 2011; 'Novatek chief...' 2014; EIA 2015). In addition, Gorst (2011) argues that Novatek enjoys a high level of political support in Russia, having close relations with Gazprom, one of its shareholders, as well as strong political connections via the company's co-owner Timchenko. Consequently, the company has managed to emerge as a worthy player in the Russian gas sector (ibid.).

Currently, Russia is experiencing similar challenges in the natural gas industry as in the oil industry – old fields are depleting and production has to shift to more challenging conditions. In addition, Russia is facing increasing competition in the natural gas market. Unconventional gas production has increased significantly, particularly in the USA. Currently, Russia is dependent on the European demand for its gas and it has been aiming to diversify its gas trade by turning to Asian customers and developing LNG facilities ('State mulls...' 2012). Russia has only one functioning LNG plant in Sakhalin and the development of new LNG facilities is considered a political priority for Russia ('Novatek starts...' 2012; Panin 2014b). However, Russia needs foreign technology, funding, and, most particularly, expertise in order to develop LNG projects (Farchy 2014).

Regarding the firm-level sources of political risk and the concepts of bargaining advantages, the position of the firm in the world industry, and the dependence of the firm on the local market, Total is the world's fourth largest oil and gas company based on market capitalization and is present worldwide, having oil and gas production on six continents (Total 2015a). Consequently, the level of firm's operational diversification, in Total's case, is high, reducing its dependence on any single market. This can be considered to increase Total's bargaining power in Russia. However, the French energy major expects the largest share of its oil and gas output to come from Russia by 2020. Russia is important for Total's growth prospects, particularly because Total is experiencing difficulties in meeting its production targets due to delays and cost overruns in Kazakhstan ('Total sees...' 2014). Hence, in Total's case, the attractiveness of Russian energy resources may outweigh the potential risks.

In terms of the political and economic relationship between the host and the home government, relations between France and Russia have traditionally been good and, even after the crisis in Ukraine flared up, French politicians and businessmen have emphasized business over politics ('CEO of...' 2014; 'EU considers...' 2014). However, following the sanctions, France was forced to cancel a deal for the delivery of two Mistral-class helicopter carriers which the Russian Navy had ordered from France. Although Total has been able to remain in the Yamal LNG project as sanctions have only been imposed on the Russian oil industry, it had to suspend a JV with Lukoil for the exploration of shale oil in Western Siberia (Raval, Farchy & Stothard 2014). Hence, the Ukrainian crisis has also chilled Franco-Russian relations, constituting a clear firm-level source of political risk.

When it comes to the concept of company dealings with a host government, Total has 25 years of experience in working with the Russia Government (Total 2015b). The Russian Government approved the agreement between Novatek and Total for Total's purchase of a 20 percent stake in the Yamal LNG project, and Putin praised Total as Russia's long-time, reliable partner ('Total gets...' 2011). Total's CEO, Christophe de Margerie, who died in a plane crash in Russia in

October 2014, had good political connections with many world leaders, including President Putin. De Margerie was not afraid of expressing his opinion. For example, he has criticized the Western sanctions against Russia as harmful and emphasized the importance of maintaining close business relations with Russia despite political disagreements ('CEO of...' 2014). Total's new CEO, Patrick Poyanné, also seems committed to continue building good diplomatic relations with the leaders of oil-rich countries (Stothard 2014).

As regards the project-level sources of political risk, Russia is clearly in need of foreign technology, expertise, and capital in order to develop the LNG projects in the Yamal Peninsula. Besides the construction of the LNG facilities, the project also necessitates the development of LNG shipping infrastructure, such as the Sabetta port by Ob Bay and an ice-class LNG carrier fleet to ship the gas via the Northern Sea Route to Asia (Total 2015b). After the sanctions shut Novatek out of Western funding, the Yamal LNG project has been struggling to raise funds ('Russia–China joint...' 2015). Novatek, Total, and CNPC were planning to cover 30 percent of the project's funding themselves and borrow the remaining 70 percent, but now they may need to invest more of their own money in the project (Chazan & Farchy 2014). Other sources of financing have also been sought, talks have been held with Chinese investors, among others, and the Russian Government has also promised to support the project financially (Hille 2014b; Farchy 2015). However, by the end of 2015, the financing issue was as yet unsolved, according to media sources.

Yamal LNG is an economically strategic project for Russia. Russia aims to increase its LNG production from 10 million tons per year to 35–40 million tons by 2020, more than doubling its global market share to 10 percent (Chazan & Farchy 2014). The expected production capacity of the Yamal LNG plant is 16.5 million tons per year (Novatek 2014). All of the planned production volumes have already been sold to European and Asian customers with long-term contracts (Total 2015b); hence the implementation of the project is not likely to be interrupted due to lack of demand for its gas. Moreover, the uncertainty regarding the project's exports was reduced significantly when Novatek was granted a license to export LNG by the Energy Ministry in fall 2013, breaking Gazprom's monopoly on all Russian gas exports and reflecting the strategic importance of LNG projects in Russia (Panin 2014b). The exports generated by Yamal LNG are now less likely to be regulated from outside the project.

When it comes to the congruence of the project with governmental goals, Yamal LNG is currently the only LNG project under development in Russia and thus a political priority. While Russia aims to emerge as an important player in the LNG market, the project is not likely to be interrupted by political matters. However, regarding the extent of natural resource-seeking, the risk is high due to the strategic importance of the gas sector to Russia. Finally, in terms of the ownership or contractual relationship with the firm and the host, Novatek has retained a majority stake in Yamal LNG even after foreign partners have joined the project ('China signs...' 2013). As control over the project remains in Russia, the political risk for foreign investors is not that significant.

Conclusions

At the end of 2015, ExxonMobil's cooperation with Rosneft in the Kara Sea remains halted due to the sanctions, leaving the future of the ExxonMobil–Rosneft JV in doubt. The Yamal LNG project has been under increasing pressure after the sanctions shut Novatek out of Western funding, significantly limiting the project's financing options. The summary of the research findings is presented in Table 9.2.

Consequently, based on the media coverage of these projects in both the *Financial Times* and the *Moscow Times*, the Ukrainian crisis and ensuing

Table 9.2 A Summary of the Main Sources of Political Risk in the Kara Sea and Yamal LNG Projects Based on Media Coverage Review

	Micro sources of political risk	
	Exxon/Kara Sea	*Total/Yamal LNG*
Industry	• Political risk is increased by Russia's dependence on oil production • The economic viability of Arctic energy projects causes uncertainty among all stakeholders	• Political risk is increased by Russia's dependence on gas production • The economic viability of Arctic energy projects causes uncertainty among all stakeholders
Firm	• Political risk is reduced by Exxon's expertise, technology and capital, as well as lack of dependence on this particular project • Political risk is increased by the importance of the Russian Arctic for Exxon in terms of future growth prospects • The challenging host and home country relations (sanctions) constitute the main source of political risk	• Political risk is reduced by Total's expertise and technology, as well as lack of dependence on this particular project • Political risk is increased by the importance of Russia for Total in terms of future oil and gas output • The challenging host and home country relations (sanctions) constitute the main source of political risk
Project	• Political risk is reduced by Russia's dependence on foreign expertise and technology in the Kara Sea project • Accessing a new oil production field is in line with the government's goals, which reduces political risk • The firm–host contractual relationship does not constitute a serious source of political risk as the control of the project remains in Russia	• Political risk is reduced by Russia's dependence on foreign expertise and technology in the Yamal LNG project • The development of LNG facilities is a political priority for Russia, which reduces political risk • The firm–host contractual relationship does not constitute a serious source of political risk as the control of the project remains in Russia

challenging host- and home-country relations appear as the main sources of political risk, leading to indirect political risk exposure. This can particularly be seen in the case of ExxonMobil; although the Russian Government did not directly cause the stalling of operations in the Kara Sea project, it was Russia's actions in other parts of the world and the following international dispute that resulted in ExxonMobil's home government causing the suspending of operations through sanctions imposed on Russia. Such involvement of the host in international conflicts relates to governmental macro sources of political risk (which, as such, were left outside the scope of this study), but materializes at the level of specific industries due to their strategic importance to the host country. In fact, it can be stated that the Kara Sea project currently suffers from the materialization of political risk in the form of coerced stalling of the operations. The Yamal LNG project also faces political risk materialization, although, again, indirectly and more mildly through Novatek's problems in getting financing.

The analysis of the newspaper articles revealed that the content of reporting on these projects and the related political risk is rather similar in both newspapers. These two cases share, to some extent, the economic viability issue, which causes uncertainty among all stakeholders in terms of future development in the industries. Nevertheless, both the investor companies and the Russian Government have invested so much in these projects that there definitely is will from both sides to succeed in their materialization. Moreover, for the energy-dependent Russian economy, the only option is to proceed extracting the increasingly demanding and expensive fields. Both projects are also of great strategic importance to the involved Western investors, ExxonMobil and Total, striving to gain a foothold in exploiting the vast hydrocarbon resources of the Russian Arctic.

Furthermore, the review on media coverage indicated that the projects are quite similar in terms of Russia's dependence on foreign expertise and capital in implementing the projects, which was emphasized several times in both newspapers. However, the Yamal LNG project is considered even more important to Russia than the Kara Sea project, as the development of new LNG facilities is a political priority for Russia. Nevertheless, the Russian Government is likely to continue supporting the progress of both projects, although the importance of these sectors for the host also increases political risk for foreign investors. In both cases, however, the control of the project remains in Russia, which reduces political risk.

Besides these notions, this study suggests that the political risk construct, previously analyzed only in relation to the Shtokman gas field project, is applicable and representative of other energy projects. The chosen projects, within the same Russian context but at different times, allow the conclusion that the political risk construct illustrates the most relevant points also in these two empirical cases. Hence, the construct is also applicable for both the oil and gas industry. Nevertheless, the study proposes adding two concepts to the original framework. Referring to the political risk resulting from international sanctions, the level of the industry's strategic importance to the host country indicates whether foreign investments in a specific industry might become exposed to risks that are not directly created by the host country, but indirectly due to the host country's activities in other regions. Other countries (including the focal investor's home country) may try to pressurize the host country to engage in or cease certain activities by limiting international collaboration in its most strategic industries. In the case of the studied oil and gas projects, this issue appears, in fact, as one of the most relevant sources of political risk. This study also suggests adding the concept of coerced stalling of operations for an unknown period of time to the potential operational political risk effects. This issue was not discussed in the original framework, but constitutes a significant political risk for foreign investors in the studied cases.

Overall, this study suggests dividing political risk into direct and indirect risk. Direct political risk refers to the loss of return on investment due to the host government interrupting the project, whereas indirect political risk refers to the loss of return on investment due to the host government's actions outside the project that result in a third party interrupting the project. This illustrates the complexity of political risk, and indicates the need for further research.

Notes

1 The authors are grateful for the financial support of the Academy of Finland, grant no. 277961.
2 For more information on political risk, see e.g. Jones, Fallon, and Golov (2000), Aleshin (2001), Broadman and Recanatini (2001), Zarkada-Fraser and Fraser (2001), Fabry and Zeghni (2002), Click and Weiner (2007), Patton (2008), and Laaksonen (2010).
3 Here macro-level sources of political risk were excluded, as focusing on micro-level sources only enables a deep and rich analysis of the studied cases within their immediate contexts.
4 The *Financial Times* is an international newspaper, focusing particularly on business and economic news. It was owned by the British publishing and education company Pearson PLC until July 2015, when it was sold to the Japanese company Nikkei.
5 The *Moscow Times* is an English-language newspaper published in Moscow, Russia. It was owned by the Finnish media company Sanoma until April 2015, when it was sold to Demyan Kudryavtsev, a Russian entrepreneur.
6 The total circulation of the *Financial Times* was 780,000 in 2015 (*Financial Times* 2015).
7 For instance, prior to the 2015 UK General election, the *Financial Times* published an editorial advocating a Conservative-led coalition government with Liberal Democrats ('General election' 2015).
8 For more information on the perspective of the Financial Times, see e.g. Anderson and Weymouth (1999).
9 For more information on the criticism of the *Moscow Times*, see, e.g., 'Is western...' (2014) and 'Times of troubles' (2015).
10 Both the EU and the USA have prohibited the exports of products, services, and technology destined for oil exploration or production in deepwater, Arctic offshore, or shale projects in Russia.
11 For more information on the Subsoil Law, see e.g. Norton Rose Fulbright (2015).

Bibliography

Adams, C., Crooks, E. & Farchy, J. 2015, 'Shell's Arctic defeat ends dream of new frontier', *Financial Times*, 28 September, viewed 11 March 2016, http://www.ft.com

Aleshin, A. 2001, 'Risk management of international projects in Russia', *International Journal of Project Management*, vol. 19, no. 4, pp. 207–22.

Alon, I. & Herbert, T. 2009, 'A stranger in a strange land: micro political risk and the multinational firm', *Business Horizons*, vol. 52, no. 2, pp. 127–37.

Alon, I. & Martin, M. 1998, 'A normative model of macro political risk assessment', *Multinational Business Review*, vol. 6, no. 2, pp. 10–19.

Amos, H. 2014, 'Will Western sanctions stop Russia's Arctic oil expansion?', *Moscow Times*, 8 October, viewed 11 March 2016, http://www.themoscowtimes.com

Anderson, P.J. & Weymouth, T. 1999, *Insulting the Public? The British Press and the European Union*, Routledge, New York.

Aris, B. 2011, 'When global oil giants dance with the Kremlin', *Moscow Times*, 2 September, viewed 11 March 2016, http://www.themoscowtimes.com

Belton, C. 2011, 'Total to buy $4bn stake in Novatek', *Financial Times*, 3 March, viewed 11 March 2016, http://www.ft.com

Bowen, G.A. 2009, 'Document analysis as a qualitative research method', *Qualitative Research Journal*, vol. 9, no. 2, pp. 27–40.

BP 2015, *BP Statistical Review of World Energy*, viewed 3 March 2016, http://bp.com/statisticalreview

'BP defeat puts Arctic back on market' 2011, *Moscow Times*, 19 May, viewed 11 March 2016, http://www.themoscowtimes.com

Broadman, H.G. & Recanatini, F. 2001, *Where Has All the Foreign Investment Gone in Russia?*, The World Bank, Policy Research Working Paper 2640, Washington, DC.

'CEO of France's Total energy company killed in Moscow plane crash' 2014, *Moscow Times*, 21 October, viewed 11 March 2016, http://www.themoscowtimes.com

Chazan, G. & Farchy, J. 2014, 'Russia Arctic energy ambitions jeopardised by Western sanctions', *Financial Times*, 1 September, viewed 11 March 2016, http://www.ft.com

'China signs for 20% of Novatek's Yamal LNG project' 2013, *Moscow Times*, 6 September, viewed 11 March 2016, http://www.themoscowtimes.com

Click, R.W. & Weiner, R.J. 2007, *Does the Shadow of Political Risk Fall on Asset Prices?: Oily Evidence*, Center for International Business Education and Research, George Washington University, Washington, DC.

Crooks, E. 2011a, 'An embodiment of Exxon's no-nonsense culture', *Financial Times*, 2 September, viewed 11 March 2016, http://www.ft.com

Crooks, E. 2011b, 'Exxon shows surer tread in following BP's path', *Financial Times*, 30 August, viewed 11 March 2016, http://www.ft.com

EIA 2015, *Russia. International Energy Data and Analysis*, viewed 1 December 2015, http://www.eia.gov/beta/international/analysis.cfm?iso=RUS

Eisenhardt, K.M. 1989, 'Building theories from case study research', *Academy of Management Review*, vol. 14, no. 4, pp. 532–50.

'EU considers effect of more Russian sanctions' 2014, *Financial Times*, 19 March, viewed 11 March 2016, http://www.ft.com

ExxonMobil 2015, *Worldwide Operations*, viewed 1 December 2015, http://corporate.exxonmobil.com/en/company/worldwide-operations

'Exxon halts oil drilling in Russia's Arctic over US sanctions' 2014, *Moscow Times*, 19 September, viewed 11 March 2016, http://www.themoscowtimes.com

'Exxon–Rosneft deal signed in Putin's presence' 2012, *Moscow Times*, 17 April, viewed 11 March 2016, http://www.themoscowtimes.com

Fabry, N. & Zeghni, S. 2002, 'Foreign direct investment in Russia: how the investment climate matters', *Communist and Post-Communist Studies*, vol. 35, no. 3, pp. 289–303.

Farchy, J. 2014, 'Oil chiefs urge co-operation with Russia', *Financial Times*, 18 June, viewed 11 March 2016, http://www.ft.com

Farchy, J. 2015, 'Chinese invest in Norilsk Nickel's Russian copper project', *Financial Times*, 30 December, viewed 11 March 2016, http://www.ft.com

Farchy, J. & Crooks, E. 2014, 'Rosneft and ExxonMobil strike oil in Arctic well', *Financial Times*, 27 September, viewed 11 March 2016, http://www.ft.com

Financial Times 2015, *Financial Times: 2015 Results*, viewed 6 April 2016, http://aboutus.ft.com/2016/03/30/financial-times-2015-results/#axzz452UItMN0

'General election: the compelling case for continuity in Britain' 2015, *Financial Times*, 30 April, viewed 11 March 2016, http://www.ft.com

Gorst, I. 2011, 'Novatek: down but not out', *Financial Times*, 14 December, viewed 11 March 2016, http://www.ft.com

Gorst, I., Clover, C. & Crooks, E. 2011, 'Exxon and Rosneft sign Arctic deal', *Financial Times*, 30 August, viewed 11 March 2016, http://www.ft.com

Hille, K. 2014a, 'Fresh sanctions target groups with ties to the West', *Financial Times*, 17 July, viewed 11 March 2016, http://www.ft.com

Hille, K. 2014b, 'Russia takes steps to prop up struggling companies', *Financial Times*, 31 December, viewed 11 March 2016, http://www.ft.com

Hille, K. & Farchy, J. 2015, 'Russia courts Asian resource investors', *Financial Times*, 4 September, viewed 11 March 2016, http://www.ft.com

'Is western media coverage of the Ukraine crisis anti-Russian?' 2014, *Guardian*, 4 August, viewed 11 March 2016, http://www.theguardian.com

Jones, A., Fallon, G. & Golov, R. 2000, 'Obstacles to foreign direct investment in Russia', *European Business Review*, vol. 12, no. 4, pp. 187–97.

Laaksonen, E. 2010, *Political Risks of Foreign Direct Investment in the Russian Gas Industry: The Shtokman Gas Field Project in the Arctic Ocean*, Pan-European Institute, University of Turku, Turku.

Lax, H.L. 1983, *Political Risk in the International Oil and Gas Industry*, International Human Resources Development Corporation, Boston.

Milne, R., Adams, C. & Crooks, E. 2015, 'Oil companies put Arctic projects into deep freeze', *Financial Times*, 5 February, viewed 11 March 2016, http://www.ft.com

Norton Rose Fulbright 2015, *Russia: Shale Gas Handbook*, viewed 11 March 2016, http://www.nortonrosefulbright.com/knowledge/publications/129590/russia

Novatek 2014, *Yamal LNG*, viewed 1 December 2015, http://www.novatek.ru/en/business/yamal-lng/

'Novatek chief sees Russia matching Qatar in LNG' 2014, *Moscow Times*, 28 January, viewed 11 March 2016, http://www.themoscowtimes.com

'Novatek starts building northern port for LNG exports' 2012, *Moscow Times*, 23 July, viewed 11 March 2016, http://www.themoscowtimes.com

Panin, A. 2014a, 'Changes in regulations could help break the offshore ice', *Moscow Times*, 2 February, viewed 11 March 2016, http://www.themoscowtimes.com

Panin, A. 2014b, 'Gazprom's grip on Russian gas exports weakens as Novatek gets export license', *Moscow Times*, 7 September, viewed 11 March 2016, http://www.themoscowtimes.com

Political Risk of Western Oil and Gas Investments in Russia 153

Patton, J.R. 2008, 'Russian Federation energy policies and risks to international joint ventures in the oil and gas industry', *International Business: Research, Teaching and Practices*, vol. 2, no. 1, pp. 65–84.

Pfeifer, S. & Belton, C. 2011, 'Shell chief Voser in Russian talks', *Financial Times*, 25 May, viewed 11 March 2016, http://www.ft.com

Raval, A., Farchy, J. & Stothard, M. 2014, 'Sanctions scupper Total/Lukoil venture', *Financial Times*, 22 September, viewed 11 March 2016, http://www.ft.com

Robock, S.H. 1971, 'Political risk: identification and assessment', *Columbia Journal of World Business*, vol. 6, no. 4, pp. 6–20.

Root, F.R. 1987, *Entry Strategies for International Markets*, Lexington Books, Lexington.

Rosneft 2015, *Russia's Arctic Seas*, viewed 1 December 2015, http://www.rosneft.com/Upstream/Exploration/arctic_seas/

'Russia–China joint projects stonewalled by economic troubles' 2015, *Moscow Times*, 27 August, viewed 11 March 2016, http://www.themoscowtimes.com

'Russia turns to Arab states, others, to offset sanctions' 2015, *Moscow Times*, 28 September, viewed 11 March 2016, http://www.themoscowtimes.com

Salonen, J. 1987, *Poliittisen toimintaympäristön havainnointi ja muutoksiin varautuminen – käytäntö eurooppalaisissa suuryrityksissä*, Turku School of Economics, Series D –3: 1987, Turku.

'Sanctions or no, price of oil spells future of Russia's economy' 2014, *Moscow Times*, 1 August, viewed 11 March 2016, http://www.themoscowtimes.com

Schmidt, D.A. 2001, 'Analyzing political risk', *Business Horizons*, vol. 29, no. 4, pp. 43–50.

Simon, J.D. 1984, 'A theoretical perspective on political risk', *Journal of International Business Studies*, vol. 15, no. 3, pp. 123–43.

'State mulls exempting LNG from Gazprom export monopoly' 2012, *Moscow Times*, 21 November, viewed 11 March 2016, http://www.themoscowtimes.com

Stothard, M. 2014, 'Changing of the guard at the top of the French energy sector', *Financial Times*, 26 November, viewed 11 March 2016, http://www.ft.com

'Times of troubles: how anti-Russia "experts" change their tune to suit the market' 2015, *RT*, 20 October, viewed 11 March 2016, http://www.rt.com

Total 2015a, *Corporate Profile*, viewed 1 December 2015, http://www.total.com/en/total-global-energy-operator

Total 2015b, *Yamal LNG: The Gas That Came In From the Cold*, viewed 1 December 2015, http://www.total.com/en/energy-expertise/projects/oil-gas/lng/yamal-lng-cold-environment-gas

'Total gets Yamal buy approval' 2011, *Moscow Times*, 21 July, viewed 11 March 2016, http://www.themoscowtimes.com

'Total sees Russia as biggest source of its oil output by 2020' 2014, *Moscow Times*, 24 April, viewed 11 March 2016, http://www.themoscowtimes.com

Yin, R.K. 1994, *Case Study Research: Design and Methods*, 2nd edition, Sage, Newbury Park.

Zarkada-Fraser, A. & Fraser, C. 2001, 'Risk perception by UK firms towards the Russian market', *International Journal of Project Management*, vol. 20, no. 2, pp. 99–105.

10 Russian Foreign Direct Investments in the Eurasian Economic Union

Elena Efimova and Vladimir Sherov-Ignatev

Introduction

The Eurasian Economic Union (EAEU) began functioning in 2015; its current members are Armenia, Belarus, Kazakhstan, Kyrgyzstan, and Russia. The EAEU was arranged on the fundament of its precursor, the Customs Union of Belarus, Kazakhstan, and Russia. The EAEU countries play a minor role in Russian outward foreign direct investment (OFDI) stock (4 percent), but Russian investors hold an influential position in the respective economies. Russian FDI constitutes an important aspect of economic integration, especially for Armenia and Belarus.

There are several reasons to study Russia's FDI in the EAEU countries. First, Russia is a major investor with a natural resource-dependent economy: theories of FDI are not specified for such countries. Second, it might help other researchers, fighting with statistical discrepancies. Third, the study could be useful as a benchmarking case for similar studies of motives and reasons for OFDI of countries with somehow similar features. We concentrate not on the choice of location, but on the chronology of FDI.

The chapter is structured as follows. First, we consider the literature on FDI theories and discuss the peculiarities of OFDI from resource-exporting countries. Second, we describe methods and compare data on Russia's FDI and its reliability. Third, we try to explain formally and logically Russian OFDI, using statistical data and case studies of particular companies and their investments. Finally, conclusions are drawn.

OLI or Oil?: Theoretical Approaches for Explaining Russian FDI in the EAEU

This section combines a review of the theories, explaining the determinants of FDI, with theoretic considerations, concentrated on the specific features of Russia or other EAEU economies, helping to understand the peculiarities of Russian FDI in the region. We discuss whether the classic Ownership, Location, and Internationalization (OLI) paradigm of Dunning, as well as some other approaches, can be applied to the case of the EAEU. We also try to bring together the peculiarities of natural resource-rich countries and the trends and features of their OFDI.

Most FDI theories use either a macro- or microeconomic approach. Aliber (1970) explains multinational enterprises' (MNEs') investment activity by means of financial instruments, in particular "exchange rate", "interest rate", and "holding assets in selected currencies". In contrast to the Heckscher–Ohlin (H–O) theory, he considers MNEs' investment from strong currency countries to weak currency ones. His empirical studies are based on FDI flows of Japanese and European firms to the USA due to the decline of American firms' market values relative to the market value of home-headquartered firms. The theory has been criticized by many experts. Thus, Ragazzi (1973, p. 479) asserts that "net FDI of the UK grew quickly during the period when national currency was weak".

Kojima (1978) inquires into the nature of multinationals as a supplement to international trade. Based on the H–O model of international trade, he shows that a lack of technologies or financial capital prevents some countries well endowed with natural resources or labor to organize efficient production. Therefore, "FDI is required in order to make factor markets more competitive and efficient internationally and to improve production processes in the country which is well endowed with the given resource" (ibid., p. 22). Kojima distinguishes different strategies of MNEs depending on their primary goals. Trade-oriented MNEs increase production and sales, moving factors of production from the home country that has a comparative disadvantage compared to the host country. Efficiency-seeking and market-driven multinationals[1] transfer factors of production to a host country that has comparative disadvantage. The main idea of these MNEs is to capture the markets of the host country. Market expansion explains the investments of many Russian companies in the EAEU – at least, in some sectors, like telecoms. "Competition between telecom companies inside Russia gets stronger and they have to look for new growth opportunities. The outward internationalization strategy could be regarded as the best option for their development" (Lisitsyn *et al.* 2005, p. 41).

Regional integration is another factor relevant to the topic. Many authors share the opinion that the choice of locations for FDI is affected positively by common membership of the home and host countries in a regional trade agreement (RTA). Kindleberger (1966) introduced the concept of investment creation and investment diversion effects of regional integration. Blomström and Kokko (1997) show that intra-regional investments and FDI from outside would be affected in different ways by regional integration. Intra-regional FDI can decrease due to elimination of the need for tariff-jumping thanks to trade liberalization. However, trade creation stimulates the restructuring of integrating economies, providing opportunity for additional investments flows. Thus, trade creation stimulates intra-regional investment creation (as well as FDI inflows from the non-member countries). Baldwin, Forslid, and Haaland (1995) study geography of investments flows in Europe and discover investment creation and investment diversion effects in EFTA and partly in the EU. They link this phenomenon with various rules of origin within different RTAs. Shiff and Winters (2002) suggest that RTAs often stimulate inflows of investment from non-member countries but have ambiguous effects on intra-bloc FDI flows. They state, however, the impressing boom of intra-block FDI in NAFTA. Tariff-jumping FDI could decrease after RTA creation, but efficiency-driven and resource-driven investments must enjoy easy access to the market as well as cheaper transportation.

Most researchers study FDI issues on the microeconomic level. Kindleberger (1969) uses a corporate governance approach. He finds that rising multinational business is the result of two processes: reinvestments of the internally generated capital and growth of MNEs markets. He believes that "in a world of perfect competition in goods and markets, FDI cannot exist". He defines market imperfections as follows: "imperfections in goods market": ownership of trademarks and marketing instruments; and "imperfections in factor markets": lack of technology, capital, and labor, economies of scale, and legal restrictions on industrial output or market entry (ibid., pp. 14–16).[2]

Hymer (1979) investigates the industrial organization theory. He puts forward three key questions: "Why does enterprise enter foreign markets?", "How does it survive in host markets?", and "Why does it want to retain control and ownership?". The answers to the questions help to formulate the basic motives of foreign market entry: "monopolistic advantages" that the home-country firms enjoy over host-country firms and the "removal of competition" between firms in different countries (ibid., p. 3). Monopolistic advantage is reached by means of the economies of scale. Efficient functioning of firms' organization leads to removal of competition between companies at international level.

Vernon (1979), in the frame of the product cycle theory, uses technological innovations in producing industrial and consumer goods to explain FDI. Vernon analyzes multinationals through their oligopolistic behavior. Thus, multinational strategy can be focused on production factors: saving, capturing new markets and receiving locational advantages, creating new oligopolistic advantages, or looking for cheap spatial location in less developed countries. Hood and Young (1979) find that natural resource-oriented MNEs do not fit into this theory. Therefore, the theory cannot be used in the case of the most Russian MNEs.

Teece (1981) and Casson (1987) successfully apply transaction cost analysis to MNEs research. Firms create an internal market, or internalize an external market, in order to increase profits and avoid the costs. An internal market is formed in two ways: "First, internalization of a market refers to the replacement of an arm's length contractual relationship (i.e. external market), second, internalization of an externality refers to the creation of a market of any kind where non-existent before" (ibid., p. 46). Sullivan and Bauerschmidt (1990) consider MNEs as an internalization in the decision-making process. They believe the multinational is "a result of reduction of psychic distance through a manager's gradual accumulation of experiential knowledge for foreign markets" (ibid., p. 19).

The key theory that explains the phenomena of MNEs and FDI is the OLI paradigm. Based upon a revision of the previous theories, Dunning launched the eclectic approach in the mid-1970s. Subsequent investigations allowed him to summarize three basic motives of FDI. "The O-specific advantages are derived from the theories of industrial organization and the resource-based theory of the firm; the L-specific advantages from the theory of location and the I-specific advantages from the theory of the firm" (Dunning 2002, p. 104). Ownership advantages are "any kind of income generating assets which make it possible for firms to engage in foreign production" (Dunning 1991, p. 123). Locational advantages come from the firms which are involved in the international industrial process. To achieve the best results, multinationals combine spatially transferable intermediate goods, produced in the home country, with immobile factors or other intermediate products in host country. The internalization advantage refers to the advantages of controlling, coordinating ownership, and location specific advantages within the MNEs.

Country specific analysis, together with the key variable of OLI paradigm, results in the Investment Development Path (IDP) concept developed by Dunning. "The IDP suggests that countries tend to go through five main stages of development and these stages can be usefully classified according to the propensity of those countries to be outward and/or inward direct investors" (Dunning 2002, p. 138). Quantitative indicators, such as net outward investment flows, GDP, and qualitative OLI characteristics identify the stages. At present, the strategies of advanced industrial countries mean that the cross-border transactions are conducted "not through the market but internationalized by and within MNEs", and FDI positions "become more evenly balanced" (ibid., p. 144). Dunning believes that in the highest (fifth) stage, O-advantage is less dependent on national natural resources and more dependent upon an ability to acquire assets and to exploit the gains of cross-border governance.

Some researches apply macroeconomic findings into comparative economics. Liuhto (2015) adds to Dunning's traditional FDI factors three more home-country explanations of Russian OFDI: (1) risk aversion, (2) serving Russia's foreign policy objectives, (3) acquisition of real estate, or the establishment of a firm abroad in order to acquire a "Golden Visa".

Not many authors deal with OFDI from natural resource-rich countries. None of the experts (whom we could find) writing about FDI in general, concentrate on the specific problem, typical for this type of economy: volatility of commodity prices affecting macro- and microeconomic indicators of the natural resource-exporting country, such as the currency rate, budget revenues, incomes, business performance, and, among others, the ability to invest abroad. However, the problem itself is often discussed in other economic and political contexts.

Natural resource-exporting countries with weak institutions tend to be influenced by the Dutch disease (first described by Corden & Neary 1982). During periods of low prices for the exported commodity, when the country suffers from low incomes and low budget revenues, its trade balance deteriorates and national currency may depreciate. In the periods of high prices for the exported commodity, such countries enjoy growing incomes, high budget revenues, increasing company revenues, and increasing ability to invest. National currency in such a situation may appreciate, although relative price levels tend to increase. Imports grow, and national producers, competing with imports, find themselves in an unfavorable situation due to the over-valued national currency and the low interest of the government in improving the business climate in sectors of secondary importance.

Businesses in such economies can be divided into two or three groups, depending upon their size and competitiveness. Large companies grow in the most competitive sector – that is, the primary resources sector. Quite often a giant national company (most frequently in the fuel sector) becomes a cash cow of the national budget, and its top managers exert decisive influence over the government's decisions. Such companies possess the largest financial resources for investing abroad. Producers in the manufacturing sector are generally less competitive (it is reflected in the product structure of the exports) and more "introvert". Some may also try moving abroad, but the reasons for such decisions differ from those of large companies. Firms may do this after having been pushed out of the domestic market by high-quality imports from advanced economies. They can endeavor to win a market segment in smaller and poorer countries (exporting or investing there), where their product fits local demand by price/ quality ratio.[3] Other firms also seek better conditions for doing business, and we can consider such OFDI as efficiency-seeking. The size of capital invested abroad by less competitive businesses is hardly large, but the number of engaged firms is substantial (see the next section). The number of foreign firms and joint ventures (JVs) in the host country can be used as an alternative indicator of such activity. The third sector of business, engaged in OFDI in resource-rich economies, consists of service providers. This sector is less vulnerable to the Dutch disease (most services are non-tradable) and some of its companies also expand abroad.

Coming back to the features of the bull and bears[4] situation in commodity-exporting countries, let us discuss the probable behavior of their large multinationals. In the situation of high prices for the exported commodity, strong currency and abundant financial resources make OFDI feasible: the target asset appears cheap for the investor. In other words, the hypothesis that MNEs from resource-rich countries acquire foreign assets mostly during "fat cow" years sounds realistic. But even during the "lean cow" period, the situation can become FDI-supporting – for example, if the government, experiencing a lack of money, decides to tighten the tax burden for traditionally large taxpayers, such an MNE might prefer to move some of its business abroad. Besides this "push" factor, cheaper assets in a host country may become a "pull" factor.[5] Finally, FDI could also be seen by third world MNEs as an outlet for decreasing their exposure to political risk (Lecraw 1977; Nayak & Choudhury 2014).

In addition to what has been discussed above, politically driven investments are often met in transition economies. There can be some variations of them: (1) politicians help investors; (2) investors follow political trends expecting future political support or indirect advantages or preferences in a friendly country; and (3) investors are public companies, owned by the government and simply adhere to the choices of politicians, based on non-commercial reasons (e.g., the decisions of Russian companies RusHydro and Inter RAO to invest in hydroelectric projects in Kyrgyzstan was connected to that country's accession to the EAEU and supported with the Russia State credit).[6] In the EAEU countries FDI can be politically driven from both push and pull sides: investors' moves depend upon the support of their own government, but major deals such as the privatization of state-owned assets and selling them to a foreign company requires approval at the top political level. Strategic deals require approval in Western countries as well, but in post-Soviet countries the role of this factor is more prevalent due to the substantial set of public assets and due to a more authoritarian style of governance (Panibratov & Kalotay 2009; Heifets 2011).

Methodology and Data: Russia's FDI in the EAEU in the Mirror of Statistics

The key prerequisite to studying the FDI among post-Soviet countries is the compatibility of statistical data, obtained from different sources. The main body of this section is devoted to the analysis of these sources. FDI statistics are famous for their imprecision as a result of massive use of tax havens for the investments turnover. It does not mean that these statistics are totally senseless, but one must be cautious when receiving and interpreting FDI data. Post-Soviet countries, Cyprus, the British Virgin Islands (BVI), and Bermuda are among the most desirable places for registering firms. The Netherlands is also in this list due to the special features of their legal system.

Hereunder we consider the data sources and data availability in the following order: (1) FDI outflows from Russia and inflows to the EAEU countries; (2) Russian FDI stock in the EAEU countries by direct and company-based data; (3) data on the amount of the number of foreign (Russian)-owned enterprises in the EAEU countries.

FDI Flow Data

The longest timeline of OFDI data from Russia is available from the Russian official statistical agency (Rosstat 2014). The data spans from 1998 for FDI into Belarus and from 1999 into Armenia, Kazakhstan, and Kyrgyzstan. However, since 2014 Rosstat stopped collecting FDI data, and now only the Bank of Russia (the Central Bank of Russia/CBR) is responsible for this activity. CBR publishes FDI outflow data by recipient country only from 2007 onwards. But it is impossible to merge CBR and Rosstat datasets because the methods of the two organizations differ: Rosstat's figures do not include the investments of commercial banks – this fact explains the gap between figures from two official sources (Figure 10.1). The figures from CBR are also used by the Eurasian Economic Commission (EEC 2015b) and by UNCTAD (2015).[7] Unlike CBR, the central banks of other EAEU countries provided data on FDI inflows from Russia for the period from 2001 until 2012. The figures significantly differ from Russian outflow data, even being published in the same edition (EEC 2015b). Inflow figures of EAEU countries are usually higher than respective Russian outflow figures.

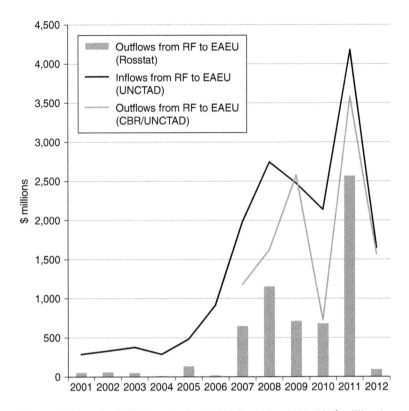

Figure 10.1 Russian FDI Flows to the EAEU Countries, 2001–12 ($ millions)

Sources: Based on data from Rosstat 2014; CBR 2015; EEC 2015a; UNCTAD 2015

Note: The data refers to Armenia, Belarus, Kazakhstan, and Kyrgyzstan even for the period before their EAEU accession

FDI Stock

In 2014, Russian OFDI to the EAEU was close to $15.4 billion, which is equivalent to 4.0 percent of the total Russian OFDI. Both figures nearly doubled in two years (2012–14) after the creation of the Customs Union between Russia, Belarus, and Kazakhstan. This modest share (Table 10.1) could be twice as high, after the subtraction of FDI turnover from the total figures (about half of the $388 billion Russian OFDI stock is located in Cyprus and the BVI). The role of Russian investments varies by country. For Belarus, Russia is the country of origin for 57 percent of FDI inward stock, while Cyprus and similar territories are responsible for less than 15 percent of that stock. For Armenia, Russian FDI are also significant (35 percent of the total inward stock). For Kazakhstan, the situation is opposite: Russia-originating FDI adds up to only 2.5 percent of total inward stock. However, the Netherlands' share is more than

Table 10.1 Russian FDI Stock in the EAEU Countries, 2014 ($ billions and percent)

Recipient	Russian OFDI stock, $ billions	Share of Russian FDI in recipient's inward stock, percent	Recipient's share of Russia's OFDI stock, percent
Armenia	1.7	35.2	0.4
Belarus	10.2	57.1	2.6
Kazakhstan	3.4	2.5	0.9
Kyrgyzstan	0.2	5.7	0.1
EAEU-4	15.4	9.7	4.0
World	388.4	1.6	100.0

Sources: Based on data from EEC 2015a; UNCTAD 2015

Note: Data for Kyrgyzstan is for 2012

40 percent. Many Russian companies are registered in the Netherlands, or arrange there their affiliates to conduct business abroad. Due to this, revealing the initial origin of Dutch FDI to Kazakhstan could increase the share of Russian FDI several fold. Russian investments in Kyrgyzstan are minor, both in absolute and relative terms. Substantial investments were promised for Kyrgyzstan, in order to make its EAEU accession more attractive, but the Russian economic problems of 2015–16 have put their implementation into question.

Russian OFDI and its dramatic fluctuations are primarily explained by large-scale deals of the giant state-owned or state-controlled companies, such as Gazprom, and large private MNEs, such as Lukoil. Some deals are conducted via foreign affiliates, and hence they are not captured by Russian statistics. Researchers from the Center for Integration Studies of the Eurasian Development Bank (EDB) carry out regular monitoring of Russian investments in the countries of the Commonwealth of Independent States (CIS), with special attention paid to the EAEU countries. They monitor company report data, which makes this data source very helpful for understanding the real picture of Russian FDI. A comparison of FDI stock data from two sources demonstrates that CBR figures reflect only about 40 percent of real Russian OFDI stock in the EAEU countries. Mineral extraction, refining, and transportation, accumulate nearly half of Russian FDI in the region, ICT represent high tech-related FDI, and their share can be approximated as 10 percent; ten to 15 companies dominate capital flows and FDI stock (EDB 2015).

The Number of Foreign Enterprises

Another source relevant for FDI analysis is the number of foreign enterprises (Figure 10.2), published in the annual reports of the EAEU. It helps to capture the relevant activity of small businesses. The share of firms with Russian ownership among all foreign-owned enterprises in the EAEU countries is 34 percent; it varies

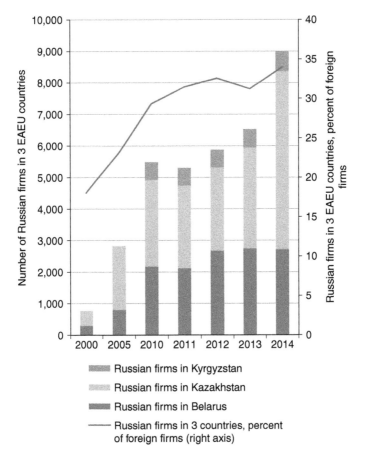

Figure 10.2 Number of Foreign-owned Enterprises (Full or Partial Ownership) in Three EAEU Countries, 2000, 2005, 2010–14

Note: Data on Kyrgyzstan starts from 2009, data on Armenia is not published

Source: Based on data from EEC 2015a

from 21 percent in Kyrgyzstan, which does not have a common border with Russia, to 35 percent in Kazakhstan, and 38 percent in Belarus (EEC 2015a). The most visible feature of the chart is the serious growth in the number of Russian-owned firms in Belarus and Kazakhstan in 2005–10 and again in Kazakhstan in 2014. The growth in 2014 resulted from the effect of the customs union arrange-ment, which led to the erasing of customs barriers on the Kazakhstan–Russian border and made business cooperation easier. Many Russian businesses moved to Kazakhstan in order to minimize their tax payments: the value added tax rate in Kazakhstan is only 12 percent, while in Russia it is 18 percent. In 2015, small firms constitute 99 percent of all Russian firms in Kazakhstan.

In the next section, we try to apply statistical methods to available data and then analyze the reasons for the investments. First, we test the influence of 15 potential FDI determinants with the help of Spearman rank correlation coefficients. The authors suppose these coefficients as an appropriate tool of respective quantitative analysis, since it can be used for short data sets as well, and because it operates with non-linear interdependences between variables. Second, we applied regression analysis to the FDI inflows data of UNCTAD. The short period of observation limits the use of econometric analysis: regression is possible only with one or two explaining variables. Due to the differences among countries, we construct separate regression equations for Belarus and Kazakhstan, as the key members of the EAEU besides Russia.

Research Findings: Analysis of FDI Factors, Explanation of Investment Peaks

In this section, we discuss the results of statistical analysis of the factors, explaining Russian FDI in the EAEU countries and their uneven chronology. The results of testing the influence of 15 potential FDI determinants with the aid of Spearman rank correlation coefficients are presented in Table 10.2.

The results achieved deviate from country to country, but some conclusions can be formulated. Time required starting a business in the EAEU member country is expectedly negatively correlated with Russian FDI flows, but the link is statistically insignificant. The bilateral exports and total exports of the EAEU members correlate with Russian FDI. Inflation rates in the EAEU members do not influence Russian FDI flows to the four countries, inflation is not an obstacle for Russian investors in Armenia, Kazakhstan, and Kyrgyzstan. The growth of GDP and GDP per capita in the EAEU members furthers Russian investment activity. We found that Russian FDI in Kazakhstan links with Russian merchandise imports from the country and average annual oil prices. Russian OFDI correlates with total inward direct investments in the EAEU countries, except Kyrgyzstan.

Now let us discuss the results of the regression analysis of FDI determinants. In the case of Kazakhstan, GDP proves to be the best determinant of Russian FDI inflow; oil price also strongly correlates with Russian FDI inflow to this country and can work as a sole explanatory variable. At the same time, combining GDP and oil price in one equation deteriorates t-statistics. This happens due to a very high mutual dependency upon these indicators in the case of an oil and gas exporting country (growth of oil prices increases GDP), bringing the situation close to multicollinearity.[8]

The statistical dependence of FDI flows from Russia upon oil prices is one of the peculiar features of Russian OFDI. From the push side, high oil prices generate financial resources to invest abroad, and induce the appreciation of national currency. From the pull side, it attracts capital to assets in the booming industry and underpins the growth of incomes, which attracts market-driven FDI. Facts also show that large inflows of Russian FDI to the EAEU happened mostly during the periods of booming commodity prices in 2002–7 and in 2011 (Figure

Table 10.2 Correlation Results for Russian FDI Flows to the EAEU Countries, 2001–14

Indicator	Armenia	Belarus	Kazakhstan	Kyrgyzstan
Population of the EAEU member[a,c]	−0.802[***]	−0.705[**]	0.745[***]	0.622[**]
GDP at market prices (constant 2005 $) of the EAEU member[a,c]	0.670[*]	0.714[**]	0.745[***]	0.569[**]
GDP per capita, PPP (constant 2011 international $) of the EAEU member[a,c]	0.670[*]	0.714[**]	0.745[***]	0.538[**]
Inflation, GDP deflator (annual %) of the EAEU member[a,c]	0.178	−0.347	0.059	0.165
Time required to start a business (days) in the EAEU member[a,c,e]	−0.143	−0.119	−0.250	−0.369
Energy use (kg of oil equivalent per capita) in the EAEU member[a,c]	0.797[***]	0.706[**]	0.902[***]	0.049
CO_2 emissions (metric tons per capita) in the EAEU member[a,c]	0.791[***]	0.836[***]	0.918[**]	0.045
Secondary school enrollment in the EAEU member[a,c,e]	n/a	0.486	n/a	0.512
Russian merchandise imports from the EAEU member[b,c,e]	0.506	0.262	0.833[**]	−0.405
Russian merchandise exports to the EAEU member[b,c,e]	0.851[***]	0.714[**]	0.738[**]	0.250
Exports of goods and services (current US$) of the EAEU member[a,c]	0.517[*]	0.732[***]	0.864[***]	0.429
Imports of goods and services (current US$) of the EAEU member[a,c]	0.631[**]	0.763[***]	0.811[***]	0.547[**]
High tech export of the EAEU member[a,b,c]	0.280	0.780[***]	0.884[***]	−0.111
Average annual oil prices[d,c]	0.596[**]	0.697[***]	0.873[***]	0.468[*]
FDI of the EAEU member, net inflows[a,c]	0.912[***]	0.912[***]	0.807[***]	0.437

Source: Calculations based on [a]World Bank 2015; [b]Trade Map 2015; [c]CBR 2015; [d]US Energy Information Administration 2015

Note: [e]2006–13; [*], [**], [***]significant at 10 percent, 5 percent, and 1 percent levels, respectively (three-tailed)

10.3). In contrast, in the situation of low and falling fuel prices in 2014–15, Lukoil sold its asset in Kazakhstan to Chinese Sinopec. Russian metal producer Mechel sold its Kazakhstan plant to Turkish Yildirim Group for one third of the original investment in 2008 (Alexeeva 2013). Falling oil prices, financial sanctions, and the devaluation of the Russian ruble have prompted Russian mobile provider VimpelCom to consider selling its business in Kazakhstan and other CIS countries (Bloomberg 2015). The waiver of the investments agreement on the construction of hydroelectric power stations in Kyrgyzstan fits the same trend.

Armenia and Belarus bear some common features: these two land-locked post-Soviet countries are poorly endowed with fuel resources and depend on Russian financial aid. GDP per capita in both countries shows higher interdependence with FDI inflow than overall GDP. For Armenia, GDP per capita explains Russian FDI inflow with R^2 = 0.63; adding other parameters (GDP, oil price, trade balance, lending rate, real interest rate) allows the rise of the determination coefficient to 0.88, although at the cost of statistical significance.

Russian outward investment to Belarus is a good example of the role of political factors as one more determinant of Russian FDI. Before passing on to the regression for Belarusian inflow of Russian FDI, let us discuss the reasons for the peaks of those FDI. The key fact about Russian acquisitions in Belarus is the overwhelming role of one company, namely Gazprom. Its main asset, Gazprom Transgaz Belarus (former name: Beltransgaz), in operating natural gas transit pipelines, connecting Russia with Poland/the EU, represents 49 percent of total Russian FDI stock in this country. Gazprom acquired key assets in Belarus as the result of a conflict over prices for oil and gas and tariffs for their transit, which occurred between 2006 and 2007. Russia was eager to increase prices for its fuel exports to Belarus in line with the global trend. At the end of 2005, Russia insisted on the dramatic increase of natural gas price for Ukraine, and then it was Belarus's turn. Belarus had neither the money to pay higher prices, nor enough instruments to resist Russian pressure. The result was the sale of 50 percent of the main transit pipe to Gazprom for $2.5 billion (Sherov 2007). One more reason for this deal was additional budget expenditures, in order to increase salaries on the eve of the 2006 presidential elections. The decision to sell the second half of the asset was taken during financial crisis, which Belarus experienced in 2011, as a result of one more populist increase in salaries, with the help of monetary emission before the next presidential elections of 2010. This huge purchase of the Beltransgaz pipeline is reflected in FDI inflow statistics for Belarus, by the outstanding peak of 2.5 billion in 2011 and four transfers of $625 million each in 2007–10 (Figure 10.3). From the push side, high prices for oil and natural gas in both 2007 and 2011 help to justify the readiness and willingness of Gazprom to invest in the acquisition of the pipeline.

Working on the regression equation for Belarus, we conducted additional manipulations to capture the repeated phenomenon of Belarusian presidential election consequences. Namely, we consider the first half of the price of the pipe to be paid not in four tranches, but simultaneously, in 2007. This somewhat artificial manipulation does not change the total sum of investment, but allows using a dummy variable to capture the effect of the presidential elections of the previous year – that is, an FDI deal is concluded the year following the presidential elections. The equation sufficiently explains Russian FDI inflows to Belarus in 2001–14 by Belarusian GDP per capita and the consequences of presidential elections in Belarus.[9]

Russian large private MNEs are deeply integrated into the global markets; they often arrange affiliates and are registered abroad, in order to conduct international activity and cooperate with Western and Chinese MNEs. Lukoil is the largest private company in the Russian oil and gas sector. Its foreign projects are operated via Lukoil Overseas, registered in the BVI in 1997; since 2013 its head office

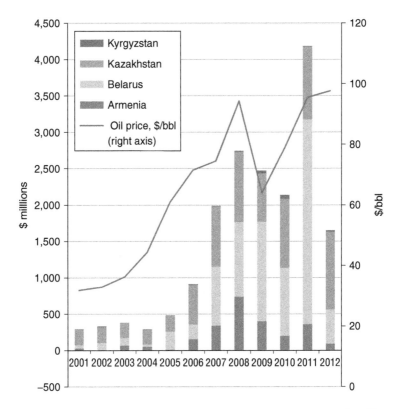

Figure 10.3 Russian FDI Flows to Other EAEU Countries, 2001–12 ($ millions)

Sources: Based on data from UNCTAD 2015; World Bank 2015

has resided in the United Arab Emirates. Its main assets in Kazakhstan are JVs with Western and local companies.[10] VimpelCom's foreign subsidiaries in the former USSR since 2009 have been controlled by an affiliate, registered in Bermuda, with a head office in the Netherlands. The company was a JV with Norwegian Telenor for a long time. Even the state-owned nuclear giant RosAtom behaves in a similar way. Russian firms have long experience of working in EAEU countries and cooperation with them in those territories is a beneficial idea for American and European investors.

RosAtom investments in Kazakhstan are one of the most interesting examples of a Russian MNE, expanding in the EAEU via its foreign affiliate. RosAtom's commercial activity in Kazakhstan began in 2001. RosAtom is a state corporation, one of the leaders in the world nuclear industry. In 2009 RosAtom (via its subsidiary, Atomredmetzoloto, ARMZ) started to gain control over assets of Canadian company Uranium One (UrAsia before 2007), possessing mines in Kazakhstan and other countries. Until 2013 RosAtom/ARMZ gained 100 percent of Uranium One.[11] Largely thanks to this acquisition, ARMZ extracts as much uranium in Kazakhstan as all other foreign companies taken together, or 1.5 times more than the company extracts in Russia (Tyurin 2014).

The political level of key decisions in the nuclear sector is inevitable and important – as well as in Kazakhstan–Russia relations. Bilateral programs of cooperation in the nuclear sector presume construction of the nuclear power station in Kazakhstan and the access of Kazatomprom to uranium refining facilities in Russia.[12] Thus, RosAtom combines a long-term resource-seeking strategy, based on respecting their partner's interest in the development of the higher stages of the nuclear cycle, and an efficiency-seeking strategy, built on common governance of interrelated activities in different locations.

The main research findings are summarized in Table 10.3.

Conclusions

Russian OFDI to the EAEU appear modest in comparison with overall Russian OFDI. Precise calculations are difficult, due to capital round-tripping. Real flows are much higher than officially reported by the CBR or UNCTAD, since large Russian companies frequently arrange their acquisitions via offshore countries. Company data more adequately reflects the real presence and influence of Russian business in the EAEU countries.

FDI in the sectors of mineral extraction, refining, and transportation adds up to a half of Russian FDI in the region, of which the share of ICT is about 10 percent. Investments of ten to 15 large companies prevail in capital flows and FDI stock; their motives include strategic asset-seeking (pipeline in Belarus), or resource-seeking (acquisitions of natural resource fields in Kazakhstan). At the same time,

Table 10.3 Main Research Findings: Explanations of Russian OFDI to the EAEU Countries

Factors of OFDI	*Conclusions and comments*
Macroeconomic	GDP and oil prices sufficiently explain the variation of Russian OFDI to Kazakhstan over time, while GDP per capita and the effects of presidential elections explain the time variation of Russian OFDI to Belarus. Dunning's investment development path theory does not fit to the Russian case
Political	Political level of decision-making, bargaining and problem fixing is important for state-controlled companies. Large-scale FDI, induced by state authorities, explain some FDI peaks
Institutional	Tax avoidance explains statistical missing of part of real investments and statistical discrepancies; easier tax regime explains the transfer of thousands of businesses from Russia to Kazakhstan. FDI round tripping affects both Russian OFDI and the EAEU countries FDI inflow statistics
Regional integration	The creation of the Customs Union contributed to the growth of Russian FDI to Belarus and Kazakhstan

up to 98 percent of firms with Russian ownership or participation are small firms, and their investments are efficiency-seeking and market-seeking. Part of efficiency growth happens thanks to institutional advantages of the host countries (lower taxes in Kazakhstan). Political factors influence the major deals from both the home-country and host-country sides.

Belarus and Kazakhstan, as the main FDI-receiving countries in the EAEU (besides Russia) should be treated individually due to different endowment with natural resources, and greater role of state-owned companies in the case of Belarus. The importance of Russian FDI is much higher for Belarus; the Belarusian example demonstrates the role of Russian investments in the sustaining of the political regime. The significance of Russian FDI for Kazakhstan is smaller, but higher than statistics suggest due to extensive use of FDI round-tripping. Russian companies in the EAEU often rely on support from the Russian authorities. At the same time, they actively cooperate with Western companies, where they find it profitable, and such cooperation can be fruitful thanks to special competitive advantages of Russian firms in the former Soviet countries.

Russian FDI in the EAEU are uneven and their fluctuation depends upon GDP, oil prices, and political factors. Russian FDI in the EAEU grew rapidly in 2001–8, which correlates with increasing commodity prices and affordability of borrowing cheap money to finance OFDI. Some large deals occurred after the crisis of 2008–9 as well: the stock of Russian OFDI in the EAEU doubled in 2012–14 thanks to the start of the integration project. Later on, the trend reversed: falling oil prices, financial sanctions, and devaluation of the Russian ruble prompted some MNEs (Lukoil, Mechel, and VimpelCom) to consider selling some of their assets in Kazakhstan. One can expect a slowdown in investment activity of large Russian companies in the EAEU in the short-term, but small and medium-sized enterprises can continue their expansion (or exodus from Russia – for some). Continuing sanctions against a number of Russian companies will hardly push them to invest in the EAEU, due to their limited access to the global financial market, which provides necessary financial resources. All in all, the investment component of the Eurasian integration project has encountered problems, and its intensive expansion in the near future is doubtful. The withdrawal of investments from partner countries may become a threat to political stability or, at least, lead to the substitution of Russian influence to a competitor's one: the case of Kyrgyzstan will be interesting in this context.

After summarizing the empirical results of the study, let us formulate conclusions, applicable not just to the case of Russian OFDI in the EAEU, but in a broader context.

Studying the FDI from natural resource(commodities)-exporting countries deserves a special approach. FDI theories usually do not take into account variations in FDI over time. However, in the case of commodity exporters, financial abilities to invest abroad depend highly upon volatile global commodity markets. This link is both direct – via commodity prices, and indirect – via exchange rates. Due to this, the time dimension of OFDI must become a separate subject of research.

Motivation of investors from countries – exporters of natural resources – also has its peculiarities and depends upon the sector and the size of the company. Successful firms – commodity exporters – tend to expand their grip over resources. They can also work on vertical integration and try to invest in transportation facilities, processing, and distribution. In such cases, resource-seeking behavior is combined with strategic asset-seeking and market-seeking.

Companies from natural resource-exporting countries, which are producing manufactured goods and services, usually have limited financial resources to invest abroad. They can minimize FDI costs by directing investments to neighboring countries with cultural and/or linguistic proximities, belonging to the same regional integration project, but possessing some institutional attractiveness, such as low tax rates. Thus, regional integration allows the combination of advantages of both institutional proximity and institutional diversity of the home and host countries. It offers an additional explanation to the existence of Kindleberger's (1966) and Baldwin, Forslid, and Haaland's (1995) investment creation and investment diversion effects within the trade blocs.

Notes

1   Dunning (2002) determines four groups of motives for foreign production: resource-seeking, market-seeking, efficiency-seeking, and strategic asset-seeking.
2   The struggle of Gazprom against attempts by host governments to limit its role is a good illustration of the statement of Kindleberger (1969).
3   One can hold a remote parallel with the approach of Kojima (1985) and Nayak and Choudhury (2014), who argued that the inability of firms to compete domestically in Japan had stimulated them to seek investment opportunities abroad. The example of Japan, of course, is far from our topic, but the very idea that not only most successful firms, but also less lucky ones can consider OFDI as an option looks promising. One more parallel – with labor mobility: workforce flow consists of skilled, educated people, on the one hand, and of unskilled people, on the other hand.
4   A bull market is when the economy is growing and stocks are rising. A bear market is when the economy is declining and stock prices are falling.
5   The RosAtom example illustrates this statement: this public company took advantage of the temporary downturn in the uranium market after the Fukushima accident for the acquisition of additional assets in Kazakhstan at a lower price.
6   The relevant agreement was waived in January 2016 due to financial problems in Russia.
7   Eurasian Economic Commission (EEC) is the supranational governing body of the EAEU.
8   The regression equation, describing the dependence of FDI flows from Russia to Kazakhstan on GDP of the host country looks as following:

FDI Inflows from RF to Kaz $= -36.5 + 5.9$ *GDP*
   t-stat.   *(0.52)*   *(11.4)*
   $n - 14;$ $R^2 = 0.92;$ $F = 131$

Another option is to regress FDI inflows on oil prices:

FDI Inflows from RF to Kaz $= -317.9 + 13.9$ *Oil price*
   t-stat.   *(-2.7)*   *(8.3)*
   $n - 14;$ $R^2 = 0.87;$ $F = 69$

9   The equation looks as follows:

$$FDI\ Inflows\ from\ RF\ to\ Bel = -505.6 + 0.18\ GDPperCap + 1512.9\ PrevPresEl$$

t-stat.   (−1.5)   (2.8)   (4.6)

n − 14;   R2 = 0.71;   F = 13

where

PrevPresEl is a dummy variable for presidential elections of the previous year;
PrevPresEl = 1 for 2002, 2007 and 2011;
PrevPresEl = 0 for the other years of the time set.

10 Lukoil is the largest Russian investor in Kazakhstan: the company's cumulative investment in this economy is $7 billion and its share in hydrocarbon production is 10 percent.

11 According to the *New York Times* investigation (Andrews 2015), "September 2005: Frank Giustra, a Canadian mining financier, wins a major uranium deal in Kazakhstan for his company, UrAsia, days after visiting the country with former President Bill Clinton. 2006: Mr. Giustra donates $31.3 million to the Clinton Foundation." Later on: "October 2010: Rosatom's majority ownership approved by Committee on Foreign Investment in the United States. January 2013: Rosatom takes full control of Uranium One and takes it private."

12 The last program of this kind, a Comprehensive Development Program for Russia–Kazakhstan Cooperation in the Peaceful Uses of Atomic Energy, was signed in 2014.

Bibliography

Alexeeva, O. 2013, 'Mechel prodolzhaet rasprodazhu', 1 August, *Gazeta.ru*, viewed 11 January 2016, http://www.gazeta.ru/business/2013/08/01/5537309.shtml

Aliber, R.Z. 1970, 'A theory of direct foreign investment', in C.P. Kindleberger (ed.), *The International Firm*, MIT Press, Cambridge, MA.

Andrews, W. 2015, 'Donations to the Clinton Foundation, and a Russian uranium takeover', *The New York Times*, 22 April, viewed 22 December 2015, http://www.nytimes.com/interactive/2015/04/23/us/clinton-foundation-donations-uranium-investors.html

Baldwin, R.E., Forslid, R. & Haaland, J. 1995, *Investment Creation and Investment Diversion: Simulation Analysis of the Single Market Programme*, NBER Working Paper, no. 5364, National Bureau of Economic Research, Cambridge, MA.

Blomström, M. & Kokko, A. 1997, *Regional Integration and Foreign Direct Investment*, Working Paper Series in Economics and Finance no. 172, Stockholm School of Economics, Stockholm.

Bloomberg 2015, '*VimpelCom Said to Hire UBS, TAP for $5 Billion Mobile-Tower Sale*', 21 October, viewed 9 December 2015, http://www.bloomberg.com/news/articles/2015-10-21/vimpelcom-said-to-hire-ubs-tap-on-5-billion-mobile-towers-sale

Casson, M. 1987, 'Multinational firm', in R. Clarke & T. McGuiness (eds.), *The Economics of the Firm*, Blackwell, Oxford.

CBR 2015, *Russian Direct Investment Abroad: Stocks Broken Down by Instrument and Country (Asset/Liabilities Principle)*, Central Bank of Russia, viewed 19 December 2015, http://www.cbr.ru/eng/statistics/?PrtId=svs

Corden, W.M. & Neary, J.P. 1982, 'Booming sector and de-industrialisation in a small open economy', *The Economic Journal*, vol. 92, no. 368, pp. 825–48.

Dunning, J.H. 1988, 'The eclectic paradigm of international production: a restatement and some possible extensions', *Journal of International Business Studies*, vol. 19, no. 1, pp. 1–31.

Dunning, J.H. 1991, 'The eclectic paradigm of international production: a personal perspective', in C.N. Pitelis & R. Sugden (eds.), *The Nature of Transnational Firm*, Routledge, London.

Dunning, J.H. 2002, *Theories and Paradigms of International Business Activity: The Selected Essays of John H. Dunning*, vol. I, Edward Elgar, Northampton, MA.

EDB 2015, *Monitoring of Mutual Investments in CIS Countries 2015*, Eurasian Development Bank Center of Integration Studies Report, no. 32, Saint Petersburg.

EEC 2015a, *Gosudarstva – Chleny Evraziyskogo Economicheskogo Soyuza v Tsyfrah*, Eurasian Economic Commission, Moscow.

EEC 2015b, *Pryamye Investitsii – Export I Import Uslug 2014*, Eurasian Economic Commission, Moscow.

Heifets, B. 2011, 'Rossiyskiy Capital: Belorusskiy Vektor', *Pryamye investitsii*, no. 7 (111), pp. 12–16

Hood, N. & Young, S. 1979, *The Economics of Multinational Enterprise*, Longman, London.

Hymer, S. 1979, *The Multinational Corporation: A Radical Approach*, Cambridge University Press, Cambridge.

Kindleberger, C.P. 1966, 'European integration and the international corporation', *Columbia Journal of World Business*, vol. 1, no. 1, pp. 65–73.

Kindleberger, C.P. 1969, *American Business Abroad*, Yale University Press, New Haven.

Knickerbocker, F.T. 1973, *Oligopolistic Reaction and Multinational Enterprise*, Division of Research, Graduate School of Business Administration, Harvard University, Boston, MA.

Kojima, K. 1978, *Direct Foreign Investment: A Japanese Model of Multinational Business Operations*, Croom Helm, London.

Kojima, K. & Ozawa, T. 1985, 'Toward a theory of industrial restructuring and dynamic comparative advantage', *Hitotsubashi Journal of Economics*, vol.26, no. 2, pp. 135–45.

Lecraw, D. 1977, 'Direct investment by firms from less developed countries', *Oxford Economic Papers*, vol. 29, no. 3, pp. 442–57.

Lisitsyn, N., Sutyrin, S., Trofimenko, O. & Vorobieva, I. 2005, *Outward Internationalisation of Russian Leading Telecom Companies*, Pan-European Institute, University of Turku, Turku.

Liuhto, K. 2015, 'Motivations of Russian firms to invest abroad: how sanctions affect the Russian outward foreign direct investment?', *Baltic Region*, no. 4(26), pp. 4–19.

Liuhto, K. & Majuri, S. 2014, 'Outward foreign direct investment from Russia: a literature review', *Journal of East–West Business*, vol. 20, no. 4, pp. 198–224.

Nayak, D.R. & Choudhury, A. 2014, *Selective Review of Foreign Direct Investment Theories*, Asia-Pacific Research and Training Network on Trade Working Paper, no. 143, ESCAP, Bangkok.

Panibratov, A. & Kalotay, K. 2009, 'Russian outward FDI and its policy context', *Vale Columbia Center on Sustainable International Investment*, no. 1, viewed 19 January 2016, http://ccsi.columbia.edu/files/2014/03/FDI_Profile-_Russia.pdf

Ragazzi, G. 1973, 'Theories of the determinants of direct foreign investment', *IMF Staff Papers,* vol. 20, no. 2, pp. 471–98.

Rosstat 2014, *Finansy Rossii*, viewed 21 December 2015, http://www.gks.ru/bgd/regl/b02_51/IssWWW.exe/Stg/d010/i011650r.htm

Sherov, V. 2007, 'Lights and shades of Russia–Belarus economic relations', in K. Liuhto (ed.), *External Economic Relations of Belarus*, Pan-European Institute, University of Turku, Turku.

Shiff, M. & Winters, A. 2002, *Regional Integration and Development*, World Bank, Washington, DC.

Sullivan, D. & Bauerschmidt, A. 1990, 'Incremental internalisation: a test of Johnson and Vahlne's thesis', *Management International Review*, vol. 30, no. 1, pp. 19–30.

Teece, D.J. 1981, 'The multinational enterprise: market failure and market power considerations', *Sloan Management Review*, vol. 22, no. 3, pp. 3–17.

Trade Map 2015, *Trade Statistics for International Business Development*, viewed 14 November 2015, http://trademap.org/Index.aspx

Tyurin, A. 2014, *Bolshoy uran Kazahstana, Chast' 2*, viewed 17 December 2015, http://www.centrasia.ru/newsA.php?st=1407203280

UNCTAD 2015, *Bilateral FDI Statistics*, viewed 11 December 2015, http://unctad.org/en/Pages/DIAE/FDI%20Statistics/FDI-Statistics-Bilateral.aspx

US Energy Information Administration 2015, viewed 5 December 2015, https://www.eia.gov/

Vernon, R. 1979, 'The product cycle hypothesis in a new international environment', *Oxford Bulletin of Economics and Statistics*, vol. 41, no. 4, pp. 255–67.

World Bank 2015, viewed 14 December 2015, http://data.worldbank.org/

11 Outward Investments from China and Russia

The Case of the Sino-Russian Investment Relationship

Andrei Panibratov and Liubov Ermolaeva[1]

Introduction

Over the past two decades, international business (IB) researchers have shown an increased interest in FDI from emerging economies generally, and in the BRICS (Brazil, Russia, India, China, and South Africa) as major players among developing economies specifically. Interest in how these countries invest internationally, with a substantial focus on outward foreign direct investment (OFDI) from China (Buckley *et al.* 2007; Morck, Yeung & Zhao 2008; Deng 2009; Kotabe, Jiang & Murray 2010), has led to an attempt to understand the comparative features of OFDI from various emerging markets (Del Sol & Kogan 2007; Tolentino 2010). The research questions we aim to answer in this study are:

- Does Chinese and Russian OFDI differ from the OFDI of other counties?
- What are the main special features of Chinese and Russian OFDI? and
- What are the key determinants of Russian and Chinese FDI exchange?

Over the last 13 years, annual FDI inflows to the Russian Federation grew almost 23 times from $2.7 billion in 2000 to $69 billion in 2013, though they fell drastically in 2014 to $21 billion. In 2014, China, excluding Hong Kong, received FDI worth $129 billion, making it the world's largest FDI recipient (UNCTAD 2015).

In 2014, the OFDI stock from China and Russia reached $730 billion and $432 billion respectively. Although Russian OFDI flows decreased significantly in 2014–15, it still represented 4 percent of total world OFDI flows, down from 6.6 percent in 2013. Chinese OFDI flows in 2014 constituted 8.5 percent of the world total (ibid.).

The year 2005 was the first time that Russia became a net capital exporter, indicating a notably large amount of capital flow for Russian commercial entities and residents (Vahtra 2009). While Chinese OFDI started to grow significantly in 2007, inflows remained relatively high for a longer period (Cheng & Ma 2010). Every year since 2009, Russian OFDI has exceeded its FDI inflows. China still remains a major recipient of FDI, though the gap between FDI inflows and FDI outflows is decreasing. Due to the preceding situation, little attention was given to the dynamics of capital exchange between the two investing countries.

State of Research and Literature Review on Chinese and Russian OFDI

Most of the literature about FDI from emerging economies focuses on China, India, and Brazil and neglects Russia. However, there is some research that emphasizes Russian OFDI. For example, different strains of FDI theory and its relevance for illuminating the Russian context have been discussed by Vahtra and Liuhto (2006), Panibratov and Kalotay (2009), Kalotay and Sulstarova (2010), and Panibratov and Latukha (2014). Vahtra and Liuhto (2006) have examined Russian FDI activities with a focus on companies in the oil and gas industries and the motives for Russian international investment. Panibratov and Kalotay (2009) have investigated political interference in Russia's OFDI. They argue Russia shows significant differences in FDI patterns from other countries, including countries in transition, since Russian companies seek to decrease the possible negative effects of domestic risks by means of establishing an immediate international presence. In other words, Russian OFDI can be only partly described and explained by the existing FDI literature and, hence, additional theoretical frameworks are needed to explain it (Mihailova & Panibratov 2012).

In contrast to the relatively minor focus on Russia's OFDI among the BRICs, many studies have been conducted in order to assess whether existing FDI frameworks can adequately explain Chinese OFDI (Child & Rodrigues 2005; Buckley et al. 2007). Child and Rodrigues (2005) state that studying Chinese OFDI provides an opportunity to extend existing FDI theory to four primary areas: (1) the latecomer perspective; (2) catch-up strategies; (3) institutional analysis with reference to the role of government; and (4) the relations between entrepreneurs and institutions. Buckley *et al.* (2007) suggest that while Western theories have some relevance for explaining developed country OFDI, there is a need to undertake modifications to account properly for the case of China. Namely, researchers need to incorporate special ownership advantages and institutional factors into general FDI theories to explain China's OFDI. In sum, past theoretical investigations suggest that traditional FDI theory can explain Chinese OFDI to a certain degree. However, additional amendments, supplements, and explanations are needed to capture fully the case of China.

Although both Chinese and Russian OFDI have generated considerable interest in recent years, few empirical studies have been conducted to investigate the determinants behind and consequences of the presence of Chinese and Russian multinational enterprises (MNEs) in other countries. To the best of our knowledge, the motives and determinants for Russia and China to invest in each other have not received much attention by scholars, though there were a few studies in the 1990s examining Sino-Russian economic relations such as work by Kerr (1998) and Rozman (1998). Dixon (2010) published an article on the case of a Chinese-financed residential mega project, namely the Baltic Pearl, located in Saint Petersburg, where she analyzes the origin and development of the project in the context of state-level Sino-Russian relations. There is a large scope of literature on the host-country determinants of FDI, which suggests that investment is attracted to countries with good institutions (Globerman & Shapiro 2006). However this statement is applicable only for FDI outflow from developed countries, since the empirical research conducted by Cheng and Ma (2010) exposed the inverse situation, whereby Chinese OFDI is attracted by countries with weaker institutions.

Sino-Russian FDI Relations

OFDI from China

Although China's OFDI is still less than its massive volumes of inward foreign direct investment (IFDI), it has been picking up in recent years as Chinese companies seek momentum by moving internationally, acquiring capital abroad in a broad range of sectors from natural resources to manufacturing and telecoms (Salidjanova 2011). With respect to natural resources, the Chinese economy is growing at a high speed and integrating into the global economy, fulfilling the role of a global production facility. As a consequence, China faces a severe shortage of resources in almost all types of raw materials including oil, uranium, iron ore, and aluminum. It therefore is actively either building trade relations with natural resource-endowed countries, such as Australia, Brazil, Russia, and Central Asian countries, or acquiring needed resources through FDI.

During the period between 1990 and 2000, Chinese OFDI did not show any extraordinary growth. Between 2001 and 2005 Chinese firms started to turn their interest towards sending their capital abroad. By 2014, China's FDI outflows had increased dramatically. Compared with the beginning of the 2000s, FDI outflow from China, excluding Hong Kong, went up more than tenfold, from $6.8 billion in 2001 to $116 billion in 2014. In 2006, FDI outflows almost doubled to $21 billion from $12 billion in 2005. The second doubling of Chinese OFDI happened in 2008, when it hit $52 billion versus $22 billion in 2007. Even the outbreak of the global financial crisis (GFC) did not affect much the growth of Chinese investment activity, which slowed down, but continued expanding.

It is important to mention one of the Chinese Government's major initiatives to stimulate OFDI. In 2006, China began to explore the ideas of setting up "overseas China economic and trade cooperation zones" in host countries. These zones were supposed to fulfill the following purposes: expanding exports through the host economies in order to decrease bilateral trade frictions caused by the rapid increase in Chinese exports; developing Chinese firms and building Chinese brands in the global marketplace; reducing excess foreign reserves; and creating clusters of Chinese companies abroad, which would be easier to support.

The target countries for these zones were those, who, first, maintained good political bilateral relationships with China and, second, could bring trade and FDI benefits to China by means of economy specialization (mainly natural resources, which are lacking in China). Based on these criteria, relevant target countries include Cambodia, Kazakhstan, Nigeria, North Korea, Pakistan, and Russia (Cheng & Ma 2010).

According to studies (Luo, Xue & Han 2010; Wang *et al.* 2012), substantial state ownership increases the likelihood of Chinese OFDI. Indeed, the major sources of Chinese OFDI are profitable and listed state-owned companies. Cheng and Ma (2010) specifically report that the share of Chinese OFDI made by state-owned enterprises (SOEs) in the first decade of the twenty-first century was approximately 83 percent. It is hard to uncover the political motives and factors influencing the decision-making processes of these large enterprises and it may vary across sectors and regions. Nevertheless, there apparently are clear political motives and effects in the natural resources sector, while, in other sectors, investment decisions appear to be on a commercial basis and only limited political involvement can been observed.

Chinese OFDI goes to more than 165 countries across all regions of the world. In 2013, the Asian region took the major share of Chinese OFDI, receiving 68 percent of China's total OFDI stock (World Resource Institute 2015). The dominant destination in the Asia region was Hong Kong, an administrative unit of China with a high degree of autonomy, including FDI policy. Hong Kong has been a top destination for Chinese OFDI since the very beginning of China's overseas expansion and it remains the absolute leader among recipients of mainland China's total OFDI, absorbing 83 percent of the regional share and making an outstanding 58 percent of total outward investment (China Statistical Yearbook 2014). Other newly industrialized Asian countries (Indonesia and Singapore) also represent a target of China's investment, though they are in the shadow of Hong Kong's giant share, altogether receiving only 3 percent.

Latin America accounts for 13 percent of Chinese OFDI stock, Europe 8 percent, and North America 4 percent. Although Africa constitutes just 4 percent of Chinese OFDI stock, Chinese OFDI in Africa has grown rapidly from $1 billion in 2004 to $24.5 billion in 2013 (Ministry of Commerce of the People's Republic of China 2014). Today, China is one of the largest investors in Africa.

There are three major, distinct factors driving Chinese OFDI: proximity (both territorial and cultural), market size and growth, and natural resource endowment (Buckley *et al.* 2007). All investment activities and the spread of Chinese investment are predetermined by one or a combination of these factors. Australia and Central Asia appeal for natural resource investment. The European Union (EU) and the United States (USA) are attractive for their market size and opportunities. Hong Kong and Singapore are close in terms of their culture and business environment. As for Russia, it is attractive in regards to all three factors and hence is an "ideal" target for Chinese investors, which explains booming OFDI from China to Russia in 2013 (Table 11.1).

OFDI from Russia

OFDI from Russia has significantly increased over the past few years (Panibratov 2012a). With more than $95 billion of FDI outflow in 2013, the Russian Federation appears to be one of the leading countries in terms of annual FDI outflow after the USA, Japan, and mainland China. In 2014, however, Russia

Table 11.1 Largest Chinese Investment Projects in Russia, 2013 ($ millions)

Project	Year of Establishment	Chinese parent company	Investments, $ millions	Industry
12.5 percent stake in OAO Uralkali, Perm Krai	2013	Chengdong Investment Corporation	2,000	Potash
20 percent stake in Novatek's project Yamal LNG, Yamalo-Nenets Autonomous Okrug	2013	CNPC (China National Petroleum Corporation)	810	Natural gas
JV with East Siberian Metals Corporation (MBC), Republic of Buryatia	2013	China Nonferrous Metal Industry's Foreign Engineering and Construction Co. Ltd (NFC)	750	Metals

Source: Ministry of Economic Development of the Russian Federation 2014

slipped to sixth position behind Germany and Hong Kong. Nevertheless, the rate of growth of Russian OFDI was one of the highest in the world.

Russian companies tend to focus on simple import–export activities and use a broad variety of more sophisticated investment tools in cross-country value exchange. This tendency was noticed in Russian oil and gas sector almost two decades ago (Liuhto 2001). Russia's OFDI stock has risen dramatically from $20 billion in 2000 to more than $370 billion in 2007 to $501 billion in 2013 (UNCTAD 2014). There was a significant drop in Russian OFDI growth in 2008, which clearly was the result of the onset of the world financial crisis, when the investment climate throughout the world became very unpredictable. By 2009, however, Russian OFDI returned to growth. The next crisis point for Russian OFDI was 2014, when annual flows plummeted by almost 35 percent and OFDI stock decreased to $432 billion (UNCTAD 2015). The drop was caused by low commodity prices, the depreciation of Russian ruble, and the difficult geopolitical situation, which included the imposition of sanctions against Russia by the EU, Japan, and the USA.

FDI flows from Russia indicate a growing interest by Russian companies in seeking newer and better opportunities for business expansion outside the borders of their home country, a readiness to increase their international competitiveness, and a desire to strengthen their international position in the global market by means of gaining access to resources, strategic assets, and new markets worldwide. The outstanding growth of Russian OFDI indicates, in some cases, that companies find the overseas investment contexts more attractive than domestic ones because of drawbacks in the domestic business environment, underdeveloped policies and regulations, and pitfalls with governmental practices (Vahtra & Liuhto 2006). In other words, companies seek to escape the unfavorable system of the home country environment and safeguard their business from domestic risks by establishing an immediate international presence (Settles 2008).

The key features of the recent trends in OFDI from Russia are that companies start to expand from both the traditional investment direction of the neighborhood (the Commonwealth of Independent States [CIS] and Eastern Europe) and developed countries (Western Europe and the USA) towards very new regions with vast opportunities – that is, Latin America and the Asia-Pacific.

Another distinctive characteristic of Russian OFDI is so-called round-tripping, which entails investment into Russia through foreign investment in companies located in third countries. This explains why Cyprus always has been traditionally the leading destination of Russian OFDI flows – it provides an offshore platform for further investment activities or trans-shipping of investment. Some Western organizations estimate that up to 50 percent of IFDI into Russia consists of capital that has been already transferred out of the country in order to get tax reductions and other benefits provided to external investors (Kalotay 2010), which is confirmed by the statistics of the Central Bank of Russia (CBR), which found that almost 50 percent of Russia's IFDI in 2013 came from offshore countries (Central Bank of Russia 2015).

The third major feature of Russian OFDI is its unequal distribution between huge industrial companies and smaller firms, including small and medium-sized enterprises (SMEs). Large enterprises exercise control over the OFDI flows and make up the absolute majority of investment activities. Nevertheless, recent trends show growth in SMEs' interest in investing abroad (e.g., Latukha, Panibratov & Safonova-Salvadori 2011; Panibratov 2012b), which is, nevertheless, an exception in the overall investment activity of MNEs. Principally, this gap in the volumes of FDI by large firms and SMEs links to their different investment financing capabilities and objectives. SMEs are limited in resources. Therefore, their OFDI activities mostly pertain to seeking market niches and technologies and rarely to acquiring assets (Vahtra & Liuhto 2006).

EU countries are still the main recipients of Russian investment. The share of the EU, excluding Cyprus, was about 35 percent in 2014. CIS countries have always been an important destination for Russian OFDI. However, in 2014 OFDI in CIS fell to $1 billion versus $4.4 billion in 2011. The major reasons for the decline were the general unfavorable macroeconomic situation and geopolitical conflict between Russia and Ukraine. Whereas Russian OFDI to Ukraine constituted on average 20 percent of total Russian OFDI to CIS countries between 2007 and 2013, by 2014 we witness divestment flows with OFDI to Ukraine plummeting to $493 million (Central Bank of Russia 2015).

The new destinations of Latin America and the Asia-Pacific region mainly comprise developing countries, which have become increasingly attractive for Russian companies. In terms of developing countries, there is a better understanding of the opportunities Brazil, Chile, China, and India can provide in terms of new markets, greater efficiency, or natural resources. For their part, Asia-Pacific countries like Australia, Hong Kong, and Singapore, being developed countries, provide many opportunities in terms of strategic assets and technologies. Despite the above, the share of Latin America and Asia-Pacific in Russian OFDI flows is insignificant.

Sino-Russian Investment Relations

China is one of the Russian Federation's main trade partners. In 2012, the volume of Russia's trade with China was the largest ($87.5 billion), ahead of the Netherlands ($82.7 billion) and Germany ($73.9 billion). In 2014, foreign trade with China fell by 0.8 percent from 2013 to $88.1 billion. In 2015, the exchange of goods between two countries dropped by 29.3 percent to $50 billion (Ministry of Economic Development of the Russian Federation 2014). The slowdown in trade relations results from several factors: (1) the general geopolitical situation (Russia–Ukraine conflict, Western sanctions against Russia, the drop in oil prices); (2) slowing economic growth in both countries; (3) declining oil and gas prices (oil and gas constitute almost 70 percent of Russian exports to China); and (4) the erosion of purchasing power in Russia, which has lowered demand for Chinese goods. Nevertheless, China remains a major trade partner of Russia.

In 2015, Russia ranked as China's 15th largest trade partner. Regardless, according to the China Statistical Yearbook 2014, Russia's share in China's foreign trade is rather small: 2.15 percent of the total, 2.24 percent of exports, and 2.03 percent of imports. Thus, trade with Russia has much less input for China than the latter's trade with the USA, Japan, and South Korea, which are China's major trade partners.

Despite the significance of China as a trade partner for Russia, both countries' attractiveness as a platform for FDI leaves a lot to be desired. While China takes about 20 percent of Russian imports, it had only 0.8 percent of Russia's IFDI stock as of the end of 2014 (Central Bank of Russia 2015). Russian investments in China are very modest, too. The first Russian OFDI targeted at China took place only in 2005; by 2007 the total OFDI forwarded to China had only risen to approximately $54 million, which accounted for about 1.2 percent of the value of total Russian OFDI stock. Seven years later, Russian OFDI stock in China was only $195 million which represented only 0.05 percent of its total OFDI stock (China Statistical Yearbook 2013, 2014; Central Bank of Russia 2015).

Nevertheless, there is a political will to improve the situation. Despite the low level of bilateral investment exchange, both countries expect the level of FDI from China to Russia to rise significantly, hitting $12 billion by 2020 (Ministry of Economic Development of the Russian Federation 2014). By June 2015, Chinese OFDI flows in Russia already had exceeded the 2014 level, reaching $3.1 billion (Central Bank of Russia 2015). The main targets for Chinese investments, on a sectoral basis, in Russia are natural resources, forestry, energy, retail, and construction (Table 11.2 and Table 11.3).

Yet, according to the Ministry of Economic Development of the Russian Federation (2014), the number of Russian investment projects in China in 2013

Table 11.2 Largest Russian Investment Projects in China, 2008–12 ($ millions)

Project	Year of establishment	Russian parent company	Investment, $ millions	Industry
Oil refinery (joint venture Rosneft–CNPC), Tiānjīn	2010	Rosneft	2,000	Oil
Production of titanium (joint project with China Aluminum Corp.)	2008	GK Petropavlovsk	319.1	Metal
Monocrystal PV Technology (Changzhou) Co., Ltd, ChangZhou City, JiangSu	2012	The Concern "Energomera" JSC	15.0	Electronic materials and components
JV KuibyshevAzot Engineering Plastics (Shanghai) Company, Shanghai	2005	KuibyshevAzot	8.1	Chemical

Source: Ministry of Economic Development of the Russian Federation 2014

reached 2,500, indicating the very active presence of Russian SMEs in China. Moreover, there is likely some undercounting of Russian investment in China because it enters China through Hong Kong or other offshore zones. Put differently, the use of offshore vehicles based in the British Virgin Islands (BVI), Hong Kong, and elsewhere obfuscate the true origin of investments. Second, Chinese companies prefer establishing wholly owned companies with the minimum statutory capital of around $400, which are likely to require significantly higher financing (Krkoska & Korniyenko 2008). These projects, while nominally small, are likely worth far more in reality.

Chinese investments in Russia are concentrated in Siberia, the Russian Far East, Moscow, and Saint Petersburg, with the vast majority located close to the

Table 11.3 The Development of Sino-Russian Investment Relations, 2010–14 ($ millions and percent)

	Russia's FDI stock in China, $ millions	China's share in Russian OFDI stock, %	Russia's share in Chinese IFDI stock, %	China's FDI stock in Russia, $ millions	Russia's share in Chinese OFDI stock, %	China's share in Russian IFDI stock, %
2010	108	0.03	0.03	–	–	–
2011	114	0.03	0.03	1,385	0.9	0.3
2012	249	0.06	0.03	1,987	0.9	0.4
2013	186	0.03	0.02	4,547	1.2	0.8
2014	195	0.05	–	2,811	–	0.8

Sources: China Statistical Yearbook 2013, 2014; Central Bank of Russia 2015

Chinese border (Xu 2011). Consistent with their overall internationalization motives, the primary driver for Chinese OFDI in Russia is resource-seeking. Generally speaking, prominent industries include energy (natural gas and oil), forestry, and retail trade.

The recent crisis in Russia has spurred a new wave of Chinese investment in the energy sector. In 2014, China struck two large energy deals with Russian enterprises: the first was $400 billion deal between Gazprom and China National Petroleum Corporation (CNPC) while the second was the sale of 10 percent stake in the Siberian unit of Rosneft to CNPC in order to finance the company's debts, which Rosneft was unable to pay due to depressed oil prices (Hirst 2014).

Determinants of Chinese and Russian OFDI: A Comparative Analysis

Hypotheses Development

Returning to the research question posed at the beginning of this chapter, we compare the macroeconomic and institutional determinants of Chinese and Russian OFDI in order to isolate their specific features and uncover differences between these two large emerging markets.

Host-country natural resource endowments: Previous research has extensively considered the issue of resource-seeking investment (Buckley 2007; Cheung & Qian 2008). Recent analyses of Chinese OFDI demonstrate Chinese investors are strongly motivated by the need to satisfy their growing demand for primary resources and this is especially the case with respect to Chinese OFDI in developing countries (Buckley 2007). For Russia, resource-seeking investment motives are strong in the metal mining and metallurgical industries, which face ongoing trade barriers imposed by other countries and growing production costs in their home country and, at the same time, are eager to diversify their resource base (Kalotay & Sulstarova 2010). Still, Chinese OFDI is expected to have a positive correlation with the resource endowment of the host country whereas Russia's OFDI is not expected to do so. In order to test these hypotheses, we introduce natural resource endowments as an explanatory variable.

Hypothesis 1: When investing abroad, China chooses countries rich with natural resources whereas Russia does not.

Technology-seeking motive: Technology is an important resource for modern MNEs. There is some evidence Chinese MNEs are becoming less interested in market information and more interested in knowledge of technology intensive production and local markets. Thus, Chinese enterprises establish research-oriented affiliates in developed countries to assist in acquiring state of the art technology and knowledge intensive products (Buckley *et al.* 2008). Although Russia needs to modernize its production, a good scientific tradition has persisted since the fall of the Soviet Union, when technology development in manufacturing industries was at higher level. Thus, we assume that technology-seeking motive is not as significant for Russia as it is for China.

Hypothesis 2: When investing abroad, China seeks technologies whereas Russia does not.

Institutional factors and institutional distance: Apart from macroeconomic variables, our study also incorporates the investigation of institutional variables (e.g., institutional development and governance factors) that might shape Russian and Chinese OFDI.

It is likely that institutions and governance are important determinants of FDI, especially in case of less-developed countries (Blonigen 2005). Poor legal protection leads to increasing costs of business operations, decreasing the appeal of FDI, while poor institutions result in underdevelopment of infrastructure, which, in turn, negatively influence FDI. Beyond this, there is empirical evidence that corruption strongly and negatively influences FDI (Wei 2000).

This said, a number of studies on Chinese OFDI have come to the conclusion that Chinese companies have competitive advantage in countries with poor institutions. The level of corruption in China is much higher than in developed countries so Chinese multinational companies are much more experienced in operating in an opaque business environment, possibly including bribery (Kolstad & Wiig 2012). Despite the lack of empirical studies, the same situation can be observed in the case of Russia's institutions and Russian companies, so we assume that there is basic similarity between two countries. By institutional distance, we understand here the difference in formal institutional environment between home and host countries. We calculated it as absolute difference of square sum of four institutional indicators introduced by World Governance Index (rule of law, government effectiveness, political instability, and control of corruption). We derive following hypothesis:

Hypothesis 3: Institutional distance between Russia and host country/China and host country negatively affects the volume of OFDI.

Rule of law: Regulatory quality captures perceptions of the ability of the government to formulate and implement sound policies and regulations that permit and promote private sector development. It encapsulates such aspects as price control, tax policy, antimonopoly policy, protectionism, competition, subsidies, and many others. Based on common sense, the quality of governmental regulations should have a positive impact on OFDI; however, taking into consideration the above-mentioned relationship between institutional underdevelopment in host and home countries and investment performance of Chinese firms, we suppose a negative correlation between regulatory quality in the host country and OFDI specifically for Russian and Chinese companies. We use rule of law index as indicator of regulatory quality in host country.

Hypothesis 4: Chinese and Russian OFDI negatively associate with host government regulatory quality.

Cultural distance: According to North (1990), informal institutions as well as formal define the rules of the game in the society. Many scholars argue that in emerging markets informal institutions often substitute for formal because of the latter's underdevelopment (Peng 2012). Therefore, we suggest that for Russian and Chinese firms a similar cultural environment plays an important role when choosing where to allocate OFDI. We measured cultural distance using the Kogut and Singh (1988) formula based on the Hofstede index.

Hypothesis 5: Russian and Chinese OFDI are positively associated with smaller cultural distance.

State policy support for FDI: Both China and Russia are the most frequent cases where researchers study the informal role of the state and politics in the process of international investments of domestic firms, with the Russian case, it can be argued, being the most controversial (Panibratov 2013, 2014). This informal role of the government affects OFDI from China and Russia at least to the same extent as more formal instruments.

Nevertheless, formal state engagement in overseas investments of Russian and Chinese companies should not be overlooked. Recently, bilateral investment treaties (BITs) have received significant attention from scholars. BITs legitimize the host market in the eyes of foreign investors; reduce the ambiguity of the host government's obligations; and offer the prospect of international arbitration (Trevino, Thomas & Culle 2008). Therefore, we assume that there is a direct effect between BITs the two governments have signed and the volume of OFDI between the two countries (a BIT between China and the Russian Federation was ratified in 2009).

Hypothesis 6: OFDI from China and Russia is largely driven and supported by state initiatives and political mechanisms, which may promote OFDI.

Control variables – home-country GDP: The home-country environment, including GDP growth, can be perceived as a macro-level extension of the ownership advantage of local MNEs and, therefore, is expected to play an important role in determining OFDI flows from a particular country (Kalotay & Sulstarova 2010). It is expected to be of particularly high importance in the case of Russian and Chinese OFDI since the largest share of total OFDI is perceived to be carried out by large multinational companies that contribute the most to GDP growth.

Host-country GDP: As a proxy for market-seeking motivation for the internationalization of the companies, and therefore determinants for market-seeking investments, we use host-country GDP and GDP per capita indicators as a measure of the absolute market size and market attractiveness of the host country (Dunning 1979; Chakraborty & Basu 2002). Host-country market size is expected to be a significant determinant and have a positive impact on FDI flows. As the market grows, so do the opportunities for investors for achieving better results in profit generation. Market size is estimated to be one of the major determinants for Russian OFDI, whereas for Chinese firms it is not the major driver.

Geographic distance: Market-seeking companies are more likely to serve geographically proximate locations through export and more distant markets through FDI (Buckley & Casson 1981). This would suggest a substitution of FDI for other modes of serving markets as distance increases. However, the correlation between FDI and distance could be negative since, according to the gravity model, the increase in distance could result in growth in transaction costs (Kolstad & Wiig 2012). However, an overview of recent trends in Russian and

Chinese OFDI (Blomkvist & Drogendijk 2013) shows an inverse correlation, meaning that the majority of FDI flows into nearby countries. We take the geographical proximity variable as a control for China whereas for Russia the proxy variable is membership of the CIS. Despite much more than just geographical proximity linking Russia to CIS countries, we assume that this control variable will positively affect OFDI from Russia.

Research Method

We collected data on Chinese OFDI from the Chinese Statistical Yearbook, which is published annually by the National Bureau of Statistics of China. Data on Russian OFDI we derived from the website of the CBR, where this data has been published since 2007. We limit our timeframe under study to 2007–13. All macro data were collected from secondary sources such as the Thomson Reuters database, World Bank database, and UNCTAD. In order to avoid biased results, we eliminated tax havens from the sample.[2] Including these countries in the sample would not add value to the research. Consequently, we obtained 411 observations for Russia and 154 observations for China. The variables description is presented in Table 11.4.

We conduct panel data regression analysis using following model:

$$FDI_{it} = \alpha + \beta_1 BIT_i + \beta_2 HGDP_{it} + \beta_3 HmGDP_{it} + \beta_4 RULE_{it} + \beta_5 NATRES_{it} + \beta_6 RD_{it} + \beta_7 CDIST_i + \beta_8 DIST_{it} + \beta_9 GEOi + \varepsilon_{it}$$

where dependent variable FDIit, represents Russia/China OFDI in country i in year t and is a function of the following explanatory variables: BITi – dummy variable reflecting whether there is bilateral investment contract with host country

Table 11.4 Variables Description

Variable	Name	Description
Dependent	FDI	OFDI flows from China and Russia at certain year
Macroeconomic factors	HGDP	GDP host country ($)
	HmGDP	GDP per capita host country ($)
	NATRES	Total natural resource rents, % of GDP
	RD	R&D expenditure, % of GDP host country
Formal institutions	WGI	World Government Indicators Rule of low host
	RULE	country
Informal institutions	CDIST	Cultural distance calculated by Hofstede indices
Regions	GEO	Commonwealth of Independent States (CIS) or Asian region
Institutional distance	DIST	Coefficient calculated as a root of squared sum of four world governance indicators: rule of law, political instability, control of corruption, and government effectiveness (absolute value)
Role of the state	BIT	Bilateral investment treaties

or not; HGDPit, HmGDPit – GDP of host and home country at certain year respectively; RULEit– rule of law indicator in host country; NATRES – natural resource endowment in certain country at certain year; RDit – RD expenditure as percentage of GDP in certain country at certain year; CDISTi – cultural distance between home and host country; DISTit – institutional distance between home and host country; GEOi – geographical proximity to host country.

Discussion of Results

We conducted random effects panel regression analysis for four models (Chinese and Russian) using Stata 13 software. In Russia Model 1 and China Model 1, we tested separately rule of law variable. In order to avoid multicollinearity, we tested two other models – China Model 2 and Russia Model 2 with institutional distance variable. The results of the four regression models are presented in Table 11.5.

As shown in Table 11.6, our hypotheses are just partly supported. Among the control variables, host-country GDP (market size) positively correlates with volume of Chinese OFDI, but does not have the same impact for Russia. At the same time, home-country GDP turns significant in each model for both countries, confirming that economic growth at home positively affects OFDI. Contrary to our hypothesis, geographical proximity is not significant in both Chinese models while CIS is positively significant in both models for Russia.

Neither R&D expenditure nor natural resources endowment showed significant results in China Model 1 and Russia Model 1. However, in China Model 2 and Russia Model 2, R&D variable reveals a positive, significant coefficient for both countries, confirming the technology-seeking motive.

The guiding role of the government was confirmed for Russia in both models. Signed BIT with host country stimulates OFDI to this country. However, for China we obtained a negative result in the second model including institutional distance, while in the first model this factor was insignificant. The reasons for this might be that the study covers a seven-year period, while companies need time to react to government actions. In the short run, signed BITs might not have imme-diate positive effect on OFDI. Moreover, companies may wait for further explicit signals, especially if the host market is unfamiliar.

Regarding institutional factors, the rule of the law in host country is signifi-cant. Better rule of law leads to more investment from Russia and China. Therefore, our hypothesis that Chinese and Russian OFDI are attracted by weak institutional environment is not supported. Moreover, institutional distance, in the case of Russia, positively associates with volume of outward investment. This means that Russian firms prefer to invest into markets either with strong formal institutions or very weak institutions (the variable has an absolute value). Taking into consideration the positive association of rule of law with OFDI volume, we can assume that Russian firms tend to invest in more mature countries in terms of institutions. In the Chinese model, the institutional distance variable was not significant.

Table 11.5 Regression Results

Independent variables	Russia Model 1	China Model 1	Russia Model 2	Chinese Model 2
GDP host country	.0500125(1.63)	.0788838**(2.08)	.062221(1.44)	.1095287***(4.75)
GDP home country	.0414795**(2.25)	1.663826***(5.03)	.0434737**(2.36)	1.792456***(5.66)
Cultural distance	.0062214(0.64)	.0716407**(2.09)	.0014188(0.07)	.057845*(1.77)
BITs	.681624**(2.26)	.076487(0.19)	.7661529**(2.32)	.8989313*(1.79)
Rule of law host country	.0532424***(4.30)	.0249457*(1.69)		
Institutional distance	.0132972(1.23)		.0159974**(2.04)	.0108633(1.20)
Natural resources endowments	.0386058(0.25)	.0266659(1.18)	.0050194(0.35)	.0182382(0.80)
R&D expenditure, % of GDP host country	2.87536***(3.77)	.2725065(1.14)	.5180091**(2.06)	.5056399**(2.11)
CIS			1.707314**(2.37)	
GEO		.3452722(0.62)		.5037419(0.97)
cons	.3231701(0.23)	39.6377**(4.43)	1.642821(1.30)	45.5605***(4.87)
Rsq overall:	0.2492	0.3535	0.1848	0.3553
Prob>chi	0.0000	0.0000	0.0000	0.0000
Sample size	411	154	411	154

Table 11.6 Hypotheses Testing

Hypotheses	China	Russia
Macroeconomic factors		
1 When investing abroad, China chooses countries rich with natural resources, whereas Russia does not	Not supported	Not supported
2 When investing abroad, China seeks technologies, whereas Russia does not	Supported in Model 2	Supported in Model 1
Institutional factors		
3 Institutional distance between Russia, China, and host country negatively affects the volume of OFDI	Not supported	Not supported, contrary results; institutional distance positively associates with OFDI
4 Chinese and Russian OFDI negatively associate with host-government regulatory quality	Not supported, rule of law has positive correlation with OFDI	Not supported, rule of law has positive correlation with OFDI
5 Russian and Chinese OFDI are positively associated with smaller cultural distance	Supported in both models	Not supported
6 OFDI from China and Russia is largely driven and supported by state initiatives and political mechanisms	Not supported, contrary results; there is negative correlation between BIT and OFDI	Supported in both models

In regards to informal institutions, we observe a difference between the two countries. Cultural distance negatively affects OFDI from China, showing significant results in both models, whereas for Russia this variable is insignificant. Nevertheless, regional variable, such as membership in the CIS, positively associates with the volume of OFDI from Russia. Countries belonging to the CIS might be very distant from Russia culturally, but a common past provides firms with some understanding of economic, institutional, and political environment. Furthermore, in a majority of those countries, people still speak Russian, which facilitates cooperation.

Conclusions

The study shows differences and similarities between Chinese and Russian OFDI. First, both countries demonstrate the intention to develop technologically by means of foreign technology acquisitions. Some scholars argue that access to technologies and new knowledge may not be critical for China as Chinese OFDI by value was invested primarily for natural resource-seeking reasons, especially in the early 1990s (Buckley *et al.* 2008). Our study does not support this assumption, which shows a change in China's OFDI patterns. Put differently, in the 2007–13 period probed for this chapter, natural resources-seeking motives became less important for China in comparison to technology-seeking motives. The focus on this time period also can explain significance of R&D for Russia's OFDI. Since the disintegration of the Soviet Union, the technological base in the country has been getting outdated and there is a need, especially in some industries, for companies to acquire new modern technologies. Summing up, macroeconomic factors similarly shape OFDI from both countries today.

Formal and informal institutions affect outward investment from Russia and China a bit differently. In case of formal institutions, we observe a similar trend. Better regulatory quality of host country encourages OFDI from both countries. Contrary to our hypothesis, neither China nor Russia chooses countries with weak regulations – they aim to invest safely, relying on formal rules and regulations as it fosters long-term business development. Moreover, in case of Russia we observe institutional distance does not impede, but actually has the opposite effect of attracting more outward investment. The explanation for this is that, over time, Russian MNEs learn about their different institutional environments and thus their international environment is not unfamiliar anymore.

Governmental support still plays a crucial role for Russian MNEs. The state specifies the direction of OFDI by making an agreement on a governmental level. A signed BIT is an important "signal" for Russian MNEs that their operations in particular host country will be most probably protected by the state. We do not observe the same dependence in the Chinese case, which might be explained by time lag between an agreement being signed and when the agreement comes into force, which provides Chinese MNEs with additional time to reconsider BIT opportunities and optimize FDI flows.

For Chinese firms, informal institutions are more important than for their Russian counterparts. Informal institutions are embedded deeper in Chinese society, therefore it requires much time for change. Hence, Chinese companies rely on informal institutions, networks, and personal relations, which is why they tend to invest in culturally close countries.

Russian companies are much more dependent on formal institutions. They traditionally rely on state support (or try to prevent state intervention), and follow (or carefully avoid) official policies.

Notes

1 The authors in part based this chapter on their working paper "Outward investments from China and Russia: macroeconomic and institutional perspective", WP#25(E)–2015, Graduate School of Management, Saint Petersburg State University, Saint Petersburg, 2015. Research has been conducted within the Center for the Study of Emerging Market and Russian Multinational Enterprises with financial support from SPbSU grant (project No. 15.61.172.2015).
2 Tax haven countries excluded from the sample are Bermuda, the British Virgin Islands, Curacao, Cyprus, and the Marshall Islands.

Bibliography

Blomkvist, K. & Drogendijk, R. 2013, 'The impact of psychic distance on Chinese outward foreign direct investments', *Management International Review*, vol. 53, no. 6, pp. 659–86.

Blonigen, A.B. 2005, 'A review of the empirical literature on FDI determinants', *Atlantic Economic Journal*, vol. 33, no. 4, pp. 383–403.

Buckley, P.J. 2007, 'The strategy of multinational enterprises in the light of the rise of China', *Scandinavian Journal of Management*, vol. 23, no. 2, pp. 107–26.

Buckley, P.J. & Casson, M. 1981, 'The optimal timing of a foreign direct investment', *Economic Journal*, vol. 91, no. 361, pp. 75–87.

Buckley, P.J., Clegg L.J., Cross, A.R., Liu, X. Voss, H. & Zheng, P. 2007, 'The determinants of Chinese outward foreign direct investment', *Journal of International Business Studies*, vol. 38, no. 4, pp. 499–518.

Buckley, P.J., Cross, A. Tan, H. Xin, L. & Voss, H. 2008, 'Historic and emergent trends in Chinese outward direct investment', *Management International Review*, vol. 48, no. 6, pp. 715–48.

Central Bank of Russia 2015, *External Sector Statistics, Flows Broken Down by Instrument and Country*, viewed 13 May 2015, http://www.cbr.ru/eng/statistics/?PrtId=svs

Chakraborty, C. & Basu, P. 2002, 'Foreign direct investment and growth in India: a cointegration approach', *Applied Economics*, vol.34, no. 90, pp. 1061–73.

Cheng, L.K. & Ma, Z. 2010, 'China's outward foreign direct investment', in R.C. Feenstra & S.J. Wei (eds.), *China's Growing Role in World Trade*, University of Chicago Press, Chicago.

Cheung, Y.W. & Qian, X.W. 2008, *The Empirics of China's Outward Direct Investment*, CESifo GmbH, Munich.

Child, J. & Rodrigues, S.B. 2005, 'The internationalization of Chinese firms: a case for theoretical extension?', *Management and Organization Review*, vol.1, no 3, pp. 381–410.

China Statistical Yearbook 2013, *17–20 Overseas Direct Investment by Countries or Regions*, viewed 11 May 2015, http://www.stats.gov.cn/tjsj/ndsj/2014/indexeh.htm

China Statistical Yearbook 2014, *17–20 Overseas Direct Investment by Countries or Regions*, viewed 11 May 2015, http://www.stats.gov.cn/tjsj/ndsj/2014/indexeh.htm

Del Sol, P. & Kogan, J. 2007, 'Regional competitive advantage based on pioneering economic reforms: the case of Chilean FDI', *Journal of International Business Studies*, vol. 38, no. 6, pp. 901–27.

Deng, P. 2009, 'Why do Chinese firms tend to acquire strategic assets in international expansion?', *Journal of World Business*, vol. 44, no 1, pp. 74–84.

Dixon, M. 2010, 'Emerging Chinese role in shaping St Petersburg's urban landscape: interscalar investment strategies in the development of a residential megaproject', *Eurasian Geography and Economics*, vol. 51, no. 6, pp. 803–19.

Dunning, J.H. 1979, 'Explaining changing patterns of international production: in defense of the eclectic theory', *Oxford Bulletin of Economics and Statistics*, vol. 41, no. 2, pp. 269–95.

Globerman, S. & Shapiro, D. 2008, 'Outward FDI and the economic performance of emerging markets', in K. Sauvant, K. Mendoza & I. Ince (eds.), *The Rise of Transnational Corporations from Emerging Markets: Threat or Opportunity?*, Edward Elgar, Cheltenham.

Hirst, T. 2014, 'The Russians have persuaded the Chinese to bail out their oil industry', *Business Insider*, 12 November, viewed 25 April 2015, http://www.businessinsider.com/russia-china-oil-and-debt-deal-2014-11

Kalotay, K. 2010, 'Patterns of inward FDI in economies in transition', *Eastern Journal of European Studies,* vol. 1, no. 2, pp. 55–76.

Kalotay, K. & Sulstarova, A. 2010, 'Modelling Russian outward FDI', *Journal of International Management*, vol. 16, no. 2, pp. 131–42.

Kerr, D. 1998, 'Problem in Sino-Russian economic relations', *Europe–Asia Studies*, vol. 50, no. 7, pp. 1133–56.

Kogut, B. & Singh, H. 1988, 'The effect of national culture on the choice of entry mode', *Journal of International Business Studies*, vol. 19, no. 3, pp. 411–32.

Kolstad, I. & Wiig, A. 2012, 'What determines Chinese outward FDI?', *Journal of World Business*, vol. 47, no. 1, pp. 26–34.

Kotabe, M. Jiang, C.X. & Murray, J.Y. 2010, 'Managerial ties, knowledge acquisition, realized absorptive capacity and new product market performance of emerging multinational companies: a case of China', *Journal of World Business*, vol. 46, no. 2, pp. 166–76.

Krkoska, L. & Korniyenko, E. 2008, 'China's investments in Russia: where do they go and how important are they?', *China and Eurasia Forum Quarterly*, vol. 6, no.1, pp. 39–49.

Latukha, M. Panibratov, A. & Safonova-Salvadori, E. 2011, 'Entrepreneurial FDI in emerging economies: Russian SME strategy for Brazil', *International Journal of Entrepreneurship and Innovation*, vol. 12, no. 3, pp. 201–12.

Liuhto, K. 2001, 'A Russian oil and gas giants conquer markets in the West: evidence on the internationalization of Gazprom and Lukoil', *Journal of East–West Business*, vol. 7, no. 3, pp. 31–72.

Luo, Y. Xue, Q. & Han, B. 2010, 'How emerging market governments promote outward FDI: experience from China', *Journal of World Business*, vol. 45, no.1, pp. 68–79.

Mihailova, I. & Panibratov, A. 2012, 'Determinants of internationalization strategies of emerging market firms: a multilevel approach', *Journal of East–West Business*, vol. 18, no. 2, pp. 157–84.

Ministry of Commerce of the People's Republic of China 2014, *Joint Report on Statistics of China's Outbound FDI 2013 Released,* viewed 20 February 2015, http://english.mofcom.gov.cn/article/newsrelease/significantnews/201409/20140900727958.shtml

Ministry of Economic Development of the Russian Federation 2014, *Osnovnye itogi investitsionnogo sotrudnichestva Rossii i Kitaya*, viewed 12 January 2016, http://www.ved.gov.ru/exportcountries/cn/cn_ru_relations/cn_rus_projects/

Morck, R. Yeung, B. & Zhao, M.Y. 2008, 'Perspectives on China's outward foreign direct investment', *Journal of International Business Studies*, vol. 39, no. 3, pp. 337–51.

North, D. 1990, *Institutions, Institutional Change and Economic Performance*, Cambridge University Press, New York.

Panibratov, A. 2012a, *Russian Multinationals: From Regional Supremacy to Global Lead*, Routledge, London & New York.

Panibratov, A. 2012b, 'Russian restaurant with Japanese cuisine makes foreign markets' selection: the case of two sticks', *Asian Case Research Journal*, vol. 16, no 2, pp. 335–46.

Panibratov, A. 2013, *The Influence of the State on Expanding Russian MNEs: Advantage or Handicap? (L'influence de l'Etat sur l'expansion des multinationales russes: atout ou handicap?), Online collection Russie.Nei.Visions*, no. 73, viewed 18 March 2014, https://www.ifri.org/en/publications/enotes/russieneivisions/influence-state-expanding-russian-mnes-advantage-or-handicap

Panibratov, A. 2014, 'Classifying the roles of government in the expansion of Russian MNEs', *The European Financial Review*, June–July, pp. 70–2.

Panibratov, A. & Ermolaeva, L. 2015, *Outward Investments from China and Russia: Macroeconomic and Institutional Perspective*, WP # 25 (E) – 2015, Graduate School of Management, Saint Petersburg State University, Saint Petersburg.

Panibratov, A. & Kalotay, K. 2009, *Russian Outward FDI and its Policy Context*, Columbia FDI Profiles, Vale Columbia Centre on Sustainable International Investment, Columbia University, New York.

Panibratov, A. & Latukha, M. 2014, 'Obtaining international results through partnerships: evidence from Russian MNEs in the IT sector', *Journal for East European Management Studies*, vol. 19, no. 1, pp. 31–57.

Peng, M.W. 2012, 'The global strategy of emerging multinationals from China', *Global Strategy Journal*, vol. 2, no. 2, pp. 97–107.

Rosstat 2015, viewed 20 March 2015, http://www.gks.ru

Rozman, G. 1998, 'Sino-Russian relations in the 1990s: a balance sheet', *Post-Soviet Affairs*, vol. 14, no. 2, pp. 93–113.

Salidjanova, N. 2011, *Going Out: An Overview of China's Outward Foreign Direct Investment*, USCC Staff Research Report, US–China Economic & Security Review Commission, Washington, DC.

Settles, A. 2008, 'International investment activities of Russian corporations', *The 1st Copenhagen Conference: Emerging Multinationals: Outward Investment From Emerging and Developing Economies*, 9–10 October, Copenhagen Business School, Copenhagen.

Thomson Reuters Database 2015, *Macroexplorer*, viewed 20 March 2015, http://thomson-reuters.com

Tolentino, P.E. 2010, 'Home country macroeconomic factors and outward FDI of China and India', *Journal of International Management*, vol. 16, no. 2, pp. 102–20.

Trevino, L. Thomas, D. & Culle, N. 2008, 'The three pillars of institutional theory and FDI in Latin America: an institutionalization process', *International Business Review*, vol. 17, no. 1, pp. 118–33.

UNCTAD 2014, *World Investment Report (WIR) 2014: Investing in the SDGs: An Action Plan*, United Nations, New York & Geneva.

UNCTAD 2015, *World Investment Report (WIR) 2015: Reforming International Investment Governance*, United Nations, New York & Geneva.

Vahtra, P. 2009, *Expansion or Exodus?: Russian TNCs Amidst the Global Economic Crisis*, Pan-European Institute, Turku School of Economics, Turku.

Vahtra, P. & Liuhto, K. 2006, *International Expansion of Russia's Largest Industrial Corporations: Investment Patterns and Strategies*, INDEUNIS Papers, The Vienna Institute for International Economic Studies, Vienna.

Wang, C. Hong, J. Kafouros, M. & Wright, M. 2012, 'Exploring the role of government involvement in outward FDI from emerging economies', *Journal of International Business Studies*, vol. 43, no. 7, pp. 655–76.

Wei, S. 2000, 'How taxing is corruption on international investors?', *Review of Economics and Statistics*, vol. 82, no. 1, pp. 1–11.

World Bank Database 2015, viewed 3 April 2015, http://data.worldbank.org

World Resource Institute 2015, *Insights: WRI's Blog*, viewed 20 January 2016, http://www.wri.org/blog/2015/01/china's-overseas-investments-explained-10-graphics#fn:7

Xu, L. (ed.) 2011, *China's Economy in the Post-WTO Environment: Stock Markets, FDI and Challenges of Sustainability*, Advances in Chinese Economic Studies series, RMIT University, Melbourne.

12 Investment Cooperation between Russia and the Republic of Korea during 1999–2009

Major Trends and Main Lessons

Irina A. Korgun

Introduction

The investment cooperation between Russia and the Republic of Korea[1] increased significantly during 1999–2009, which led these two countries to sign an agreement for strategic partnership in 2009. Recognizing the importance of this growth, the given study re-examines factors of growth by comparing Russia to other countries that experienced an increased inflow of Korean outward foreign direct investment (OFDI) during the same period. Those countries include some Commonwealth of Independent States (CIS), Central Eastern European countries, plus Turkey[2] and Asian economies. Some economies that should automatically be part of the analysis were excluded due to unstable nature of Korean investment. As shown in Annex 12.1, South Korean companies did not invest into Bulgaria, Kyrgyzstan and Ukraine until 1996–7; Bulgaria and Slovakia stopped receiving Korean FDI after 2008. A lack of data limited the timeframe of analysis to years when data was available for the largest number of countries. For the same reason, Armenia, Azerbaijan, Belarus, Estonia, Georgia, Latvia, Lithuania, Moldova, and Tajikistan were left out of the scope.

On the whole, Korean OFDI during 1999–2009 increased steadily. Growth occurred in all geographic destinations but investments into East Asia, the CIS, and Central Eastern Europe economies were the most prominent. Expansion into these markets was dictated by an array of factors among which were the needs of a Korean export-oriented economy, domestic market conditions as well as attention directed to emerging markets internationally. Weak and saturated demand at home combined with competitive environment in developed countries pushed Korean firms to look for new frontiers elsewhere. Emerging and transition economies, including Russia, provided opportunities to increase sales volume.

In this context, it is important to understand how market factors influenced levels of Korean OFDI into Russia during 1999–2009 and whether their impact was similar to what could be observed in other countries. Therefore, this research aims to investigate this issue by seeking answers to the following three questions: (1) what were the main trends of Korean OFDI in Russia and how do they compare with trends in other markets?; (2) what place Russia occupied in Korea's general overseas investment strategy?; and, finally, (3) do factors of growth in

Korean OFDI to Russia in 1999–2009 differ from determinants of Korean investment to other countries?

The results of an empirical analysis contribute to a discussion on the problems of FDI in several ways. First, they show the evolution of Korean OFDI in Russia and place it in the general context of Korean OFDI growth. Second, they reveal dissimilarities in Korean businesses' approach to different countries. Third, results reconfirm the importance of basic market indicators and particularly the level of income as determinants of FDI flows. The number of studies exploring Korean OFDI in Russia remains very limited, with most of them published in the Korean language. Thus, materials and findings of this given research can serve as a base for further studies on Korean–Russian economic cooperation.

Trends in Korea's Outward Foreign Direct Investments

General Trends in Korean Outward Foreign Direct Investment

Korea started to invest abroad at the beginning of the 1990s. By that time, the country had already developed a strong industrial sector that could compete in global markets and support globalization of its economy. In addition, during rapid industrialization between the 1960s and the 1980s, Korean corporations accumulated capital, which they were able to use for international expansion in the 1990s. The deregulation of foreign exchange control and overseas activity, carried out by the Korean Government in preparation for OECD membership, further incentivized outward investment (Kim, YH 2007; Kim & Rhe 2009).[3] Already in 1996, annual flows of Korean OFDI were five times larger than in 1990. Further liberalization of capital movement under the IMF reform package after the Asian financial crisis (Harvie & Lee 2003) promoted more OFDI. By the mid-2000s, Korean firms initiated overseas projects worth $13 billion; by 2009 their total value exceeded $17 billion (Figure 12.1).

However, more liberal regulation can only partially explain the growing trend. Technological upgrading and internationalization of the Korean corporate sector was another reason. With their overseas investments, firms sought to enhance efficiency and avoid pressures of domestic competition. They quickly gained a large majority in the country's investments abroad (Kwak & Mortimore 2007, p. 96). According to Korea Export–Import Bank (2016), today a share of large firms in country's OFDI exceeds 70 percent.

In 1990, Korean OFDI concentrated mainly in North America (43 percent) and Asia (34 percent) (Figure 12.2). But in the 2000s emerging East Asian countries became the main recipients of South Korean investments because lower labor costs created opportunities for projects in manufacturing (Kwak & Mortimore 2007). By 2005 Asia started to account for more than a half of Korea's annual OFDI flows (Figure 12.3). Such a shift in geography of investment also meant an important change in tactics of Korean firms. At the start of international expansion, they put efforts into building global distribution networks and, thus, directed investment flows into wholesale and retail sectors. Also, to achieve a

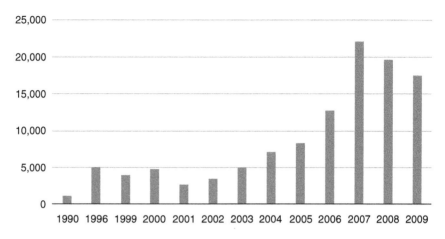

Figure 12.1 Annual Flows of Korean OFDI, 1990, 1996, 1999, 2000–9 ($ millions)
Source: UNCTAD 2015

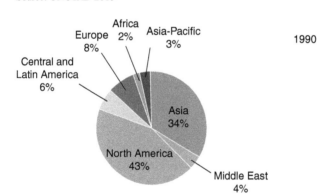

Figure 12.2 Geographic Distribution of Korean OFDI Flow, 1990 (percent)
Source: Korea Export–Import Bank 2016

better representation and more effective distribution globally Korean businesses targeted such logistic hubs as Germany, Hong Kong (China), and the Netherlands (Korgun & Popova 2011, pp. 139–41). Over time, however, as the network was building and needed less additional investment, Korean business decreased OFDI flows into the distribution sector and focused more on production. In the mid-2000s, 50–60 percent of Korean OFDI flows went to manufacturing industries, particularly in East Asia (Korea Export–Import Bank 2016). In these countries, Korean companies also found unsaturated and growing consumer markets (Kwak & Mortimore 2007; Kim & Rhe 2009; Kwon, Kim & Ko 2009) that helped large corporations, such as Samsung, Hyundai, and LG, to increase their international sales.

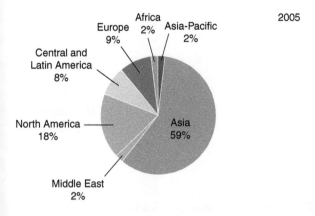

Figure 12.3 Geographic Distribution of Korean OFDI Flow, 2005 (percent)

Source: Korea Export–Import Bank 2016

Asian consumerism produced a strong impact on the corporate sector's motiva-tion for OFDI. Before 2002, almost 60 percent of Korean corporate investments, excluding investments of state companies that were mainly engaged in resource-seeking projects, were explained by export promotion (Table 12.1). But accord-ing to a survey by Korea Industrial Complex Corporation (2013), after 2002 the share of companies that reported such a motive fell to 27 percent. Instead, a more complex goal of gaining access to new growing markets started to prevail. According to the same study, more than 40 percent of Korean companies was entering local markets in order to be able to respond to consumer needs, a marked increase from 6 percent a decade earlier.

Korean Outward Foreign Direct Investment in Russia, the CIS, and Central Eastern Europe

After diplomatic relations between the Russian Federation and the Republic of Korea were established in 1990, Russia came into the focus of Korean business

Table 12.1 Motivations for Korean OFDI, 1993–2012 (percent)

	1993–2002	*2003–12*
Access to local markets	6.3	44.8
Low labor costs	12.7	15.2
Avoiding trade barriers	2.5	2.3
Participation in resource projects	5.4	4.8
Export promotion	59.7	27.0
Acquiring advanced technology or management know-how	3.0	2.7
Overcoming trade barriers	1.5	1.7

Source: Korea Industrial Complex Corporation 2013, p. 14

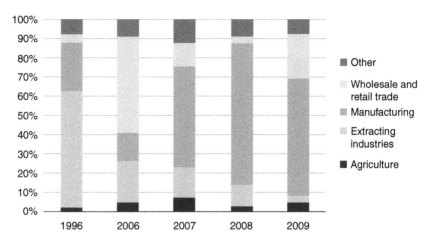

Figure 12.4 Annual Outflow of Korean FDI to Russia by Sector, 1996, 2006–9 (percent)
Source: Korea Export–Import Bank 2016

primarily as a promising source of natural resources (MOFE 2005; Lee *et al.* 2008). In 1996, around 60 percent of investments by Korean companies went to extracting industries, predominantly to coal mining (Figure 12.4). Apart from the natural resource sector, Russia was not regarded as a priority market for the Korean investment. At that time Korean firms preferred such countries as Hungary, Slovakia, and, especially, Poland due to more favorable investment environments and lower business risks. In addition, these countries served as a base to explore markets of former Soviet republics, including Russia, within their strategies for Central Eastern Europe. Due to these factors, Korea–Russia investment cooperation remained rather modest during the first decade of cooperation.

Korean investment flows to Russia started to pick up slowly in the 2000s. For several years, annual OFDI into Russia stayed at $30–40 million; in 2009 it reached a record $430 million. In 2006–9, Russia was among the top 20 destinations for Korea's OFDIs (Korea Export–Import Bank 2016). This tendency coincided with the rapid growth of Korean–Russian bilateral trade. Over the period of 1999–2008 until the global financial crisis (GFC), the total trade turnover between countries increased from $2 billion to $18 billion (KITA 2016).

During years of growth, the Russian industrial sector was of particular interest for Korean corporations. Almost 80 percent of Korea's investments in the 2000s went to four manufacturing sectors: automobile, electronics, machinery, and food and tobacco. Central Federal District[4] of Russia hosted the majority of Korean firms in 2007 this region received 21 percent of Korean FDI (Moscow's share was 26 percent), and in 2008–13 its share fluctuated between 54 percent and 72 percent (Rosstat 2016). Only later in the decade Korean firms started to enter other regions, for example Korean automaker Hyundai set up a manufacturing plant near Saint Petersburg, which became the largest investment project by a Korean firm in Russia. Some other projects included the construction of Lotte Hotel in Moscow by Lotte Company and the reconstruction of shipyards in the Russian Far East by shipbuilding company STX.

Korean Scholars explained the growing trend into Russia's manufacturing sector by the market-seeking motives of Korean business. According to a survey conducted by Lee *et al.* (2008), 73 percent of investments made before 2008 fell into the market-seeking category. In Moscow, this figure was as high as 91 percent while in Vladivostok it was around 70 percent. So, it seems that in Russia, like in East Asia, rising consumer income attracted Korean firms. The next section investigates whether it was indeed the case.

Empirical Analysis

Previous Studies on Motivation for Foreign Direct Investment

Ownership, Location, and Internationalization (OLI) paradigm (Dunning 1980, 1981, 1988, 1993) was used to establish causal relations between market factors and flow of Korean OFDI to Russia in 1999–2009. This paradigm explains FDI flows by factors of ownership, location, and internationalization (Dunning 1980, 1981, 1988, 1993; Dunning & Narula 1996; Dunning & Lundan 2009; Rugman 2010). Despite the critique of Kojima (1978), OLI remains widely used to study investment flows because it allows us to include a variety of factors into analysis (Dunning 1988). Also, the paradigm framework allows to treat the data with panel or time series statistical techniques when conducting an empirical investigation.

Based on Dunning's work, UNCTAD developed a list of factors that could affect FDI flows. They are generally divided into five groups: policy, business, market, resource, and efficiency variables (Table 12.2). The division depends on whether factors represent a market size, economic stability and growth prospects, labor or infrastructure. Our choice of variable for the market size was guided by this classification.

A number of studies that adhered to OLI considered Russia and Eastern Europe. Bevan and Estrin (2000) analyzed FDI flows to Central and Eastern

Table 12.2 UNCTAD's Classification of Host-country FDI Determinants

Determining variables	Examples
Policy variables	Tax policy, trade policy, privatization policy, macroeconomic policy
Business variables	Investment incentives
Market-related economic determinants	Market size, market growth, market structure
Resource-related economic determinants	Raw materials, labor costs, labor productivity
Efficiency-related economic determinants	Transport and communication costs, labor

Sources: Adopted from UNCTAD 1998, p. 91; Ranjan and Agrawal 2011, pp. 255–63

Europe during 1994–8, whereas Garibaldi *et al.* (2002) focused on FDI into Eastern Europe and the former USSR in 1990–9. Most recently, Ranjan and Agrawal (2011) applied panel analysis for BRIC using UNCTAD (2015) data from 1975–2009. Similar studies exist for Asian economies; for example, Wadhwa and Sudhakara (2011), Yoshitomi and Montgomery (1996), Zhu, Liang, and Ren (2011) and Petri (2012) contributed to the discussion on FDI patterns in Asia. The mentioned works found both positive and statistically significant effects of economic fundamentals on the level of FDI flows into a country. Specifically, such factors as market size, growth potential, trade openness, labor costs, infrastructure facilities, and macroeconomic stability influenced inflow of FDIs into economies for which analysis was done.

Building on the results from these studies, we could make an assumption that improvement of economic fundamentals stimulated Korean OFDI into Russia, the CIS, Central Eastern Europe, and developing East Asian countries. If this assumption proves to be correct, market size, taken in this study as GDP per capita, should be a particularly important determinant of Korean investments during the period under investigation.

Choice of Variables

GDP per capita (*gdppc*) in current prices in US dollars was chosen as a determinant for a market size. This indicator is often used in an empirical analysis. Higher levels of GDP per capita are generally associated with higher purchasing power of consumers in an economy.

Consumer price index (CPI) stands for economic stability and is an important determinant of FDI inflow (Vijayakumar, Sridharan & Rao 2010; Ranjan & Agrawal 2011; Petri 2012; Garibaldi *et al.* 2002). A country with a stable and more predictable environment and lower CPI levels will receive more FDI than a volatile economy. Coefficient on CPI is expected to get a negative sign.

Total exports and import share of GDP, or trade openness, are used to show intensity of a country's foreign trade. Following findings by Markusen (2002) and Neary (2007) that investment tends to follow trade, *tradeop* was introduced into analysis assuming that a country with higher coefficient for the trade openness will attract more Korean OFDI. The coefficient for *tradeop* is expected to be positive.

Size of the labor market is another important determinant of FDI (Yeaple 2003). In this study it is taken as a number of persons engaged (*eng*).[5] Analysis also employs human capital (*hc*) as an indicator of the quality of the labor because a better-educated labor force can potentially attract more investment.

Fixed capital formation (*fcf*) stands for the growth potential of an economy. It can also give foreign firms information about regulatory risks. If economic environment in a country improves and risks decrease, confidence of local business will tend to grow as firms will engage in various projects. Such activity of local businesses will send strong positive signals to foreign firms, who can decide to increase investments into a country.

Finally, a variable for the R&D spending by Korean firms (*rdbizsp*) is introduced. Here it represents ownership advantage as proposed by OLI. In introducing R&D spending, we follow Hennart (1982) because easier access to technology may enable businesses to internalize cross-border markets of intermediate product and increase outward investment. It is assumed that larger R&D spending is associated with improving technological capabilities which Korean firms use for outward expansion.

Data for trade, GDP per capita, CPI, and fixed capital formation were taken from UNCTAD, whereas a number of persons engaged and human development are from World Penn tables (Feenstra, Inklaar & Timmer 2015); statistics on R&D spending by Korean business sector is from OECD statistical department (OECD 2015). The period of data is from 1999–2009.

Methods and Results

This section presents results of empirical testing for 25 countries.[6] The analyzed countries were divided into two groups: Group 0 includes Central Eastern European and the CIS countries, plus Turkey, and Group 1 consists of East Asian countries, plus India. The descriptive statistics is given in Annex 12.2. With exception of *cpi* and human capital other indicators are in natural logarithms; *gdppc*, *eng*, *cpi*, and *fcf* are also lagged by one year meaning that previous levels of these variables can influence future values of the dependent variable – level of Korean OFDI. The model we estimate looks in the following way (1.1):

$$\text{Logofdi} = \text{Loggdppc} + \text{Logtradeop} + \text{Logeng} + \text{cpi} + \text{Logfcf} + \text{hc} + \text{Logrdbizsp} \qquad (1.1)$$

The estimation was performed with panel fixed and random effect. These two methods require a different set of assumptions. The country fixed effect allows us to control for time-invariant unobserved heterogeneity that is specific to individual countries – that is, country specific characteristics are correlated with explanatory variables. The fixed effect allows us to remove such specific characteristics and estimate the net effect of variables considered in the analysis. Estimates with fixed effects relate specifically to the set of countries in the sample and cannot be generalized outside the data set. The random effect, on the contrary, assumes that time-invariant characteristics of entities are not correlated with the predictor or independent variables (Greene 2008, p. 183).

The results of estimations with fixed and random effects are given in Annex 12.3. The aforementioned annex also includes results of the Hausman test with "sigmamor" option that is preferred when a standard version of the test does not give clear results which of the two should be preferred. Test outcome confirms presence of a fixed effect but still there are other considerations in favor of the random effect results. According to Clarke *et al.* (2015), the Hausman test may not be an effective tool for the ultimate choice of the estimation technique. Besides, there are conditions when a random effect can produce better results. Such conditions include a relatively small data set and modest level of correlations. Our case does not have exceptionally high (0.8–0.9) correlation levels, a fact that would rule out the random effect model. Additional consideration for the use of random effect include the presence of variables like trade openness, which changes over time rather slowly, and business R&D spending, which varies over time but is constant across observations. One more strength of the random effect is that it allows dummy variables. This feature is critical for our analysis in order to check whether Russia differs from other countries in the sample.

Considering all the arguments above, the random effect model is preferred. Table 12.3 summarizes estimations it produced for three specifications: Specification 1 for the whole set of study, Specification 2 for Group 0, and Specification 3 for Group 1. Estimation for Group 0 employs dummy for Russia. The results obtained by the empirical testing are conclusive of the following. When all countries are considered, trade openness, amount of labor engaged, and fixed capital formation have strong positive effects on the level of Korean OFDI, while the variable of inflation has a moderate negative impact. All these variables have expected signs but the coefficient for the market size is not statistically significant when all countries are considered. The level of business R&D spending seems to have a larger effect than other variables. This may be due to the fact that firms that spend more on research have higher technological capabilities and are more likely to look for business opportunities in overseas markets (Hennart

Table 12.3 Estimation Results with Random Effects

Variables	(1) logofdi	(2) logofdi	(3) logofdi
L.loggdppc	0.364	1.274***	0.844***
	(0.242)	(0.278)	(0.327)
logtrop	1.678***	1.155	1.343***
	(0.470)	(1.248)	(0.417)
L.logeng	0.826***	0.00953	0.862***
	(0.186)	(0.370)	(0.205)
L.cpi	−0.0202**	−0.0308*	−0.0316***
	(0.00849)	(0.0163)	(0.00669)
L.logfcf	2.777***	3.837***	1.581***
	(0.672)	(1.194)	(0.574)
hc	−1.034	−3.494***	−2.131*
	(0.663)	(1.257)	(1.095)
logrdbizsp	1.086***	−1.607**	2.193***
	(0.402)	(0.763)	(0.298)
rus		4.308***	
		(1.086)	
Constant	−18.89***	8.156	−25.77***
	(4.109)	(7.478)	(2.965)
Observations	237	119	118
Number of id	24	12	12
R-sq	52	40	73

Note: Standard errors in parentheses; ***p < 0.01, **p < 0.05, *p < 0.1

1982). The variable for human capital is not statistically significant either. So, in general Korea's OFDI in developing markets is influenced by the economic fundamentals of the host countries and technological capabilities of its firms.

Re-estimation for two separate groups reveals differences in patterns of Korean investment flows. In Group 0 (Table 12.3: Specification 2), that relates to Russia, the CIS, and Central Eastern European economies, market size and fixed capital formation seem to be the most important determinants of the level of Korean OFDI. At the same time, trade openness has lost its significance compared with the estimation for all 25 countries. The coefficient for human capital is statistically significant at the 1 percent level and has a negative sign. This is an unexpected outcome because quality of the labor force is regarded as a positive factor for FDI. Perhaps, this outcome is due to the fact that a higher level of human capital is associated with higher labor costs, which can have a negative impact on investments. Dummy variables for Russia are both positive and statistically significant. This particular outcome implies that flow of Korean OFDI to Russia was higher than to other countries in this group.

In estimation for Group 0, a variable of business R&D spending has changed its sign from positive to negative, meaning that R&D had a downward effect on Korean OFDI. But in Group 1 (Table 12.3: Specification 3), in contrast, the coefficient for business R&D spending has a positive, both statistically and economically significant effect on the level of Korean OFDI flows. It can be suggested that the level of technology development in Korean firms led to higher OFDI flows to countries of East Asia (included into Group 1). This effect can be explained by earlier findings obtained by Petri (2012), who argued that FDI between Asian countries flows from high tech economies, including Korea, to medium tech economies. High connectivity of East Asian economies through value chains also facilitates such flows. Trade openness has an even higher coefficient here than in Specification 2 for Group 0. In Group 1, GDP per capita proves to be an important determinant albeit its effect is lower than in Group 0. Human capital and inflation seem to affect investment in the same direction as in the previous case.

Lower R-sq for the second specification (40 for Group 0 versus 73 for Group 1) implies that variables used in the analysis explain a smaller share of variation in comparison to Group 1. We would suggest that unaccounted factors could have influenced investment decisions of Korean companies in Russia, the CIS, and Central Eastern Europe – although, to say it with the certainty, more research is needed.

As a robustness check, we re-estimate the model by a pooled ordinary least squares (pooled OLS) with Driscoll–Kraay standard errors, as recommended by Hoechle (2007) and Woolridge (2009). The overall results are in line with the random effect estimation.

Discussion

Statistical analysis helped us to confirm the importance of macroeconomic fundamentals for decisions regarding FDI into the CIS, Central Eastern Europe, and

East Asia by Korean companies. The effect seems to be uneven between countries, and patterns of Korean OFDI vary depending on the regions where countries are located. In Asia, trade, labor, and market size, as well as technological capabilities of Korean firms were major determinants of OFDI flows during 1999–2009. For Russia, the CIS, and Central Eastern Europe, market size and fixed capital formation seem to be the most critical factors. Because low levels of fixed capital formation are prone to regulatory risks and sometimes linked to capital flight from the country, it reflects businesses' perception about overall country risks. A high and positive coefficient that this variable obtained for Russia, the CIS, and Central Eastern Europe can imply that considerable reduction in risks associated with operating a business has contributed to the growth of the Korean OFDI in 1999–2009. Coupled with increasing income levels, the more stable environment attracted Korean capital.

In the case of Russia, factors used in the analysis explain a smaller share of variation than in the case of East Asia. This can imply that other factors may influence business decisions. Among factors that could be considered are access to resources and exchange rate fluctuations, as well as other non-economic factors. Sutyrin, Popova, and Korgun (2014) point out that elites in both countries are more concerned about relations with traditional economic partners – that is, the USA in Korea's case and the EU in Russia's case – and this too could have a downward effect on Korean–Russian economic cooperation.

Low availability of financing and risk guaranteeing programs to support Korea's investments in Russia and a lack of information could also have an influence on decisions of Korean business. It is worth mentioning that the Korean Government provides special programs that subsidize transportation of energy resources from the Middle East and investment projects in Southeast Asian countries. Such schemes in the past prompted Korean firms to explore those markets even in the presence of relatively high risks. Similar programs could be run by Russia and Korea. One more area that requires more attention seems to be information provision and dissemination. Korean firms continue to point out that the availability of general information on the Russian market in Korea remains very limited.

Case of Hyundai Motors Manufacturing Rus

The construction of the Hyundai automobile plant (Hyundai Motors Manufacturing Rus) near Saint Petersburg became the largest investment project carried out by a Korean firm in Russia in 25 years after establishing diplomatic relations in 1990. Before the plant went into operation, Hyundai exported cars. Until 2003, the annual exports to Russia by two Korean brands – Hyundai and Kia – did not exceed $200 million (KITA 2016). In 2004, the exports went up to $566 million and were growing rapidly until reaching a peak in 2008 at $3.8 billion. Rapidly increasing income level at an annual rate of 5.7 percent during 2000–10 and 7.9 percent during 2004–7 (UNCTAD 2015) prompted Hyundai to build a manufacturing plant. With an average GDP per capita of $9,048 in 2007, a larger part of the Russian population could afford to own a car than in 2000, when GDP per capita was $1,770. Thus, the company had a quite clear economic rationale to enter the local market. It also benefited from the advantages of Saint Petersburg being the second largest city in Russia with a sizable consumer market. In addition, the city's positioning as a major Baltic Sea port with easy access to major highways and railroads opened opportunities for exports to other CIS and overseas markets. The presence of other car producers, namely Ford and Nissan, created an agglomeration effect supplemented by strong support from the federal and regional governments. All these factors enhanced the attractiveness of Saint Petersburg as investment destination.

Construction of the Hyundai plant was completed in three years; investments totaled $600 million of which $500 million were realized during first three years (2008–10) when construction was in progress (Figure 12.5). Initially, manufacturing capacity of the plant was set at 100,000 vehicles per year but in later years was raised to 150,000 and then to 200,000 cars per year. Hyundai Motors Manufacturing Rus became one of the largest foreign investment projects in Russia's automobile industry. Only Volkswagen in the Kaluga region produced more – 225,000 vehicles; Ford in Alabuga (Yelabuga) produces 200,000 vehicles (Liuima 2015).

The fact that the Korean company carried out the project in the atmosphere of the GFC demonstrated that it sought long-term strategic opportunities in Russia and intended to integrate this manufacturing plant into its global production-distribution network. Indeed, today Hyundai Motors Manufacturing Rus is one of seven overseas plants built by Hyundai abroad. Others are located in Brazil, China, the Czech Republic, India, Turkey, and the United States. Cars produced for the Russian market were also exported to Armenia, Azerbaijan, Belarus,

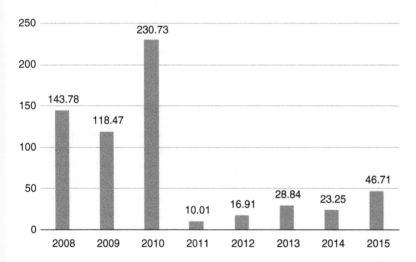

Figure 12.5 Korean FDIs into Russian Automobile Industry, 2008–15 ($ millions)
Source: Korea Export–Import Bank 2016

Kazakhstan, Kyrgyzstan, Moldova, Ukraine, and Uzbekistan. So far, Kazakhstan is the main export market. In 2015, the number of vehicles sold in Kazakhstan equaled 10,300, which was more than 80 percent of the total number of exported cars by Hyundai Motors Manufacturing Rus. Cars produced in Saint Petersburg were also sold in Egypt and Lebanon. In 2015, 2,500 vehicles were shipped to these two aforementioned countries (Autostat 2016a).

Hyundai's project in Russia did not face major difficulties until 2014, when a decline in the Russian auto industry started to affect it. However, the fact that the total amount of cars sold in Russia contracted by 13 percent in 2014 and 15 percent in 2015 and the company's own sales dropped by more than 10.3 percent in 2015 (Autostat 2016b) did not force the company to leave the market. The Korean media claimed that the company strongly believed in the economic recovery of Russia (Park 2015). To cope with unfavorable conditions, management applied tactics that allowed the company to improve its position.

Hyundai's anti-crisis strategy included several elements: delayed price increases to allow consumers to adjust to ruble–dollar exchange rate fluctuations, investment in advertising, the expansion of the distribution networks through wider representation of Hyundai products in local car dealer chains, and launch of new cheaper models that could appeal to tastes of the Russian consumers. Finally, it introduced new models that fall under the state program of preferential consumer credits (Hyundai Motors Manufacturing Rus 2016). This flexible marketing mix that took into account changing conditions of the local and global economy moved the company to first place in Russia with the total market share going up by 3 percent and exceeding 19 percent.

Currently, the management of Hyundai Motors Manufacturing Rus is looking for new possibilities to keep plant operation in full capacity and rebalance negative conditions of the Russian market. One of the possible solutions could become sales to new markets – Iran and Iraq in particular. If these plans are realized, export shipments could strengthen Russia's position in the global network of the Korean automaker. In this network, Russia could evolve as a key production and distribution center in Eurasia.

Korean Foreign Direct Investment in Russia after 2010

After period of growth in 1999–2009, Korean OFDI to Russia showed a declining trend staring from 2010. During 2010–15, the annual flow went from $334 million down to $71 million (Korea Export–Import Bank 2016). However, the reported OFDI varied significantly depending on the source of statistical data (Table 12.4). For example, the Central Bank of Russia (CBR 2016) reports a withdrawal of Korean investment worth $270 million in 2011 while Rosstat (2016) shows an inflow of $281 million. We do not have information that would offer an explanation for the results in this particular year. The discussion below adheres to the Korean statistical sources.

The completion of the Hyundai project in Saint Petersburg in 2010 explains a large part of the declining trend in Korean investment after 2010. In 2011–14, the

Table 12.4 Korean OFDI to Russia by Statistical Source, 2010–15 ($ millions)

	2010	*2011*	*2012*	*2013*	*2014*	*2015*
Rosstat	519.7	281.3	311.9	168.8	n.a.	n.a.
Central Bank of Russia	318	−270	119	71	130	50*
Korea Export–Import Bank	334	99.6	107.2	122.1	113.5	71.3

Sources: Central Bank of Russia 2016; Korea Export–Import Bank 2016; Rosstat 2016

Note: *Total for January–June 2015

annual inflows fluctuated around $100–120 million, which was close to the 2006 level. Despite the GFC, Korean firms continued to see opportunities in the Russian market. This was partially due to the integration process of the CIS space which opened access to markets of Central Asia through Russia.[7]

Active investment by Korean manufacturing companies into Russia at the end of the first decade of this century generally improved their position in the host market. If the sectoral distribution of Korean FDI stock in the Russian economy is compared with the distribution of Russia's inward foreign direct investment (IFDI) stock and the structure of Korea's OFDI stock in other countries, one can see that the share of investments in production in Russia was rather high. As of 2011, almost 60 percent of Korean FDI stock in Russia went into manufacturing, while the share of manufacturing in the total stock of FDI accumulated by Russia was just 32 percent. Correspondingly, manufacturing industries made up 39 percent in the overall stock of the Korean OFDI (Figure 12.6). The share of investments into extracting industries and wholesale and retail, on the contrary, was lower than corresponding shares in the Korean OFDI and the total FDI in Russia.

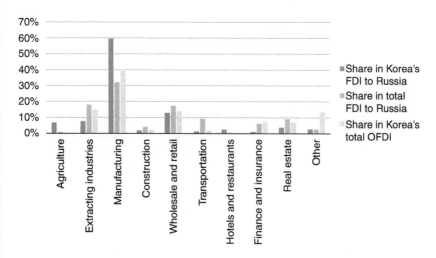

Figure 12.6 Stock of Korean FDI in Russia and in the World by Sector, as of 2011 (percent)

Source: Korea Export–Import Bank 2016

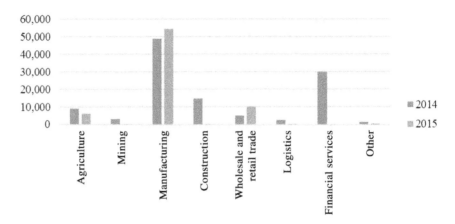

Figure 12.7 Distribution of Korean FDI in Russia by Sector, 2014–15 ($ thousands)
Source: Korea Export–Import Bank 2016

The immediate effect of Western sanctions on the Korean investment to Russia was limited, as results for 2014 were only slightly lower than in 2013 – $113 million and $122 million respectively. But in 2015 Korean OFDI to Russia contracted to $71 million.[8] The decrease came primarily at the expense of construction, financial services, logistics, and the mining industry (Figure 12.7). Manufacturing, in contrast, reported slightly higher figures – $56 million in 2015 against $40 million in 2014. Of those $56 million, more than 80 percent, or $46 million, came from the automobile sector; the other major contributor was steel industry with $6 million. Inflow into sectors, such as electronics, machinery, food, and beverages, which used to be major recipients of Korean OFDI in previous years, remained very low (under $1 million).

Conclusion

This research analyzed Korean OFDI in Russia. The main focus was the period from 1999–2009, when Korean companies were increasing the overall volume of their outward direct investment, including investment to Russia. Findings confirm that the motives of Korean OFDI were market-seeking by nature.

   The statistical analysis, however, revealed different aspects in patterns of Korean OFDI in Russia and East Asia. The first major difference lies in the greater importance of income for Korean OFDI in Russia than for Korean OFDI in East Asia. Another dissimilarity relates to the role of trade openness of host countries and technological capabilities of Korean firms. These two factors were the key determinants of Korean OFDI to East Asia while in Russia their role was smaller. This result seems to be natural considering Asia's interconnectedness through global value chains.

The case study of the project by Korean automaker Hyundai Motors Manufacturing Rus further demonstrated importance of income levels for decisions regarding investment to Russia. The Hyundai project started as a response to improving living standards of the Russian population. When entering the market, the Korean automaker tried to come closer to Russian consumers and offer customized products. From the beginning, Hyundai took into account opportunities to export products manufactured in Russia to other CIS countries. As a result, the company enjoys popularity among Russian consumers even during the current economic downturn. Favorable geographic positioning of its plant opened prospects of access to markets in Central Asia and the Middle East.

The example set by the Hyundai company in Russia can help to improve the perceptions of Korean companies about the Russian market in future, when the current economic downturn is over. Still there is a possibility that unfavorable thinking will persist unless it is addressed with adequate measures. Such measures could include information services in the Korean language provided by Russian agencies in cooperation with Korea Export–Import Bank and the Korea Institute for International Economic Policy. Training programs between related institutions in order to improve dissemination of information among end users could also be considered. Specific measures to advance cooperation in strategic sectors might also be helpful. Without such efforts, the Korean–Russian investment cooperation will need a long time to grow.

Appendix

Table 12.A1 Korean FDI into Russia, the CIS, Central and Eastern Europe, and Turkey, 1991–2015 ($ millions)

	1991	1992	1993	1994	1995	1996	1997	1998	1999	2000	2001	2002	2003
Azerbaijan	-	-	-	-	-	-	0.01	-	-	-	-	-	-
Bulgaria	-	-	-	-	-	-	25.16	2.04	2.81	27.55	0.30	2.18	0.04
Czech	-	-	1.00	3.04	0.30	5.60	28.50	5.47	10.10	111.75	535.73	230.50	93.93
Georgia	-	-	-	-	-	-	-	-	-	-	-	-	-
Hungary	2.75	4.22	6.78	4.84	35.21	0.94	9.02	27.70	4.75	9.66	32.99	89.20	13.27
Kazakhstan	0.51	0.99	0.11	4.51	0.86	1.03	102.80	0.06	1.83	0.35	1.82	0.50	13.82
Kyrgyzstan	-	-	-	-	-	-	0.15	5.80	2.65	0.35	0.18	0.04	0.36
Lithuania	-	-	-	-	-	-	-	1.53	0.02	-	-	0.01	-
Mongolia	-	-	-	0.24	4.81	0.57	1.40	0.13	1.85	2.58	2.63	2.88	1.34
Poland	0.53	0.03	0.95	5.10	38.07	123.14	49.77	268.64	40.08	48.56	13.59	37.82	16.92
Romania	0.18	0.32	-	50.99	106.27	-	53.00	25.00	1.00	0.29	6.35	2.42	18.26
Russia	17.24	3.25	3.04	11.98	30.96	41.36	8.42	35.37	0.83	4.00	6.89	24.00	24.36
Slovakia	0.00	6.08	4.70	0.20	1.80	2.00	0.00	83.62	227.82	291.07	134.15	117.97	53.06
Tajikistan	-	-	-	-	29.00	-	-	-	-	-	29.00	0.10	-
Turkey	0.80	1.30	-	0.05	0.26	22.50	3.00	0.00	15.50	12.31	22.60	0.35	3.89
Ukraine	-	-	-	-	-	4.08	4.20	190.47	1.50	37.48	0.40	0.18	0.14
Uzbekistan	-	-	15.00	66.30	28.55	78.14	16.03	11.27	0.33	17.77	60.18	0.46	5.25

(Continued)

Table 12.A1 Continued

	2004	2005	2006	2007	2008	2009	2010	2011	2012	2013	2014	2015
Azerbaijan	-	-	-	0.08	2.37	-	-	0.16	0.04	-	0.19	-
Bulgaria	-	36.12	56.02	44.18	4.11	-	-	-	-	-	-	-
Czech	13.48	12.33	2.65	118.37	4.50	4.00	-	-	-	-	-	-
Georgia	-	-	-	-	-	-	-	336.03	766.23	51.57	24.42	-
Hungary	3.66	12.57	70.55	15.37	2.80	7.74	13.77	1.28	0.49	37.92	0.74	8.43
Kazakhstan	22.53	25.56	249.29	286.62	822.62	152.63	131.18	101.69	193.00	174.06	158.83	56.24
Kyrgyzstan	0.73	12.78	33.04	9.57	12.22	3.32	1.92	3.63	2.53	0.49	-	-
Lithuania	0.18	-	-	-	-	0.24	0.00	0.28	-	-	-	-
Mongolia	3.48	6.70	19.70	44.43	58.31	25.51	26.34	44.12	55.91	49.21	32.04	9.50
Poland	36.07	78.13	226.91	118.51	93.53	28.94	29.43	55.55	22.42	21.62	54.42	5.65
Romania	3.96	130.24	0.74	30.16	5.29	51.30	-	54.31	0.08	-	-	-
Russia	25.34	34.72	113.64	237.89	358.43	427.87	334.02	99.63	107.22	122.14	113.54	16.97
Slovakia	22.32	31.42	211.78	15.90	14.58	2.93	-	-	-	-	-	-
Tajikistan	-	-	-	0.12	0.86	0.56	0.01	0.09	0.03	0.04	-	-
Turkey	4.14	43.34	15.90	112.95	67.18	192.42	63.64	72.41	221.87	115.27	121.61	69.66
Ukraine	0.27	0.07	6.14	0.08	0.07	0.06	0.64	0.24	0.02	0.01	-	-
Uzbekistan	0.56	8.69	22.40	69.46	65.15	32.34	40.64	54.90	18.87	13.02	11.58	0.19

Source: Korea Export–Import Bank 2016

Table 12.A2 Descriptive Statistics

Variable	Number of observations	Mean	Standard deviation	Minimum	Maximum
logofdi	273	10.16987	2.491255	1.386294	15.50919
loggdppc	275	7.896665	1.338426	5.541264	10.57776
logtrop	275	4.418325	0.580315	2.900437	5.85218
logeng	275	2.498923	1.615336	−0.23055	6.655923
hc	264	2.633913	0.49058	1.687006	3.535638
cpi	274	8.45804	12.83226	−3.95316	128.7414
logrdbizsp	275	9.927344	0.35213	9.310002	10.39482
logfcf	275	3.174931	0.232276	2.626897	3.85343

Table 12.A3 Results of Estimation with Fixed and Random Effects

Variables	Fixed effect logofdi	Random effect logofdi
L.loggdppc	−0.738	0.364
	(0.611)	(0.242)
logtrop	1.036	1.678***
	(0.789)	(0.470)
L.logeng	6.292***	0.826***
	(2.285)	(0.186)
L.cpi	−0.0269***	−0.0202**
	(0.00943)	(0.00849)
hc	−3.065	−1.034
	(3.734)	(0.663)
L.logfcf	3.356***	2.777***
	(0.830)	(0.672)
logrdbizsp	1.946	1.086***
	(1.200)	(0.402)
Constant	−25.99***	−18.89***
	(6.251)	(4.109)
Observations	237	237
R-squared	0.348	
Number of id	24	24
Hausman test	Prob>chi2 =	0.0412

Note: Standard errors in parentheses; ***$p < 0.01$, **$p < 0.05$, *$p < 0.1$

Notes

1 In this chapter, the Republic of Korea, South Korea, and Korea are used interchangeably.
2 Turkey was added to the analysis because in the official Korean sources Turkey is regarded in the nexus Turkey–Eastern Europe (KIEP 2016).
3 See more on the issue: Kim (2000), Shik, Seok, and Baker (2009), and Lim and Jang (2012).
4 The territory of the Russian Federation consists of 85 administrative regions grouped into nine Federal Districts. Central Federal District has the largest number of administrative regions and includes the capital city, Moscow.
5 For this indicator, we used Penn World Tables (Feenstra, Inklaar & Timmer 2015), where indicator "persons engaged" includes all persons aged 15 years and over, who during the reference week performed work, even just for one hour a week, or were not at work but had a job or business from which they were temporarily absent.
6 These countries are Bulgaria, Cambodia, China, the Czech Republic, Hong Kong (China), Hungary, India, Indonesia, Kazakhstan, Kyrgyzstan, Laos, Malaysia, Mongolia, Philippines, Poland, Romania, Russia, Singapore, Slovakia, Taiwan, Thailand, Turkey, Ukraine, Uzbekistan, and Vietnam.
7 Importance of integration processes on the post-Soviet space is often linked to the "Eurasian Initiative" program announced by the Korean President Park Geun-hye (Han *et al.* 2014).
8 Korean–Russian bilateral trade showed a very similar trend – i.e., the volume of Korean exports to Russia contracted by 9 percent in 2014 while the Korean imports from Russia increased by 36 percent compared to their 2013 level. The negative effect on trade was more pronounced in 2015, when Korean exports to Russia fell by more than 50 percent to $4.7 billion and the imports from Russia by 27 percent to $11.3 billion (KITA 2016).

Bibliography

Autostat 2016a, 'Russian Hyundai plant starts the export of Solaris cars to Egypt and Lebanon', *Autostat Analytic Agency*, viewed 27 January 2016, http://eng.autostat.ru/news/view/11352/

Autostat 2016b, 'Hyundai decreased sales by 10% in Russia in 2015', *Autostat Analytic Agency*, viewed 27 January 2016, http://eng.autostat.ru/news/view/11925/

Bevan, A.A. & Estrin, S. 2000, *The Determinants of Foreign Direct Investment in Transition Economies*, William Davidson Institute Working Paper 342, viewed 12 November 2015, http://citeseerx.ist.psu.edu/viewdoc/download?doi=10.1.1.124.8766&rep=rep1&type=pdf

CBR 2016, *Central Bank of Russia*, viewed 26 January 2016, www.cbr.ru

Clarke, P., Crawford, C., Steele, F. & Vignoles, A. 2015, 'Revisiting fixed- and random-effects models: some considerations for policy-relevant education research', *Education Economics* vol. 23, no 3, pp. 259–77.

Dunning, J.H. 1980, 'Toward an eclectic theory of international production: some empirical tests', *Journal of International Business Studies*, vol. 11, no.1, pp. 9–31.

Dunning, J.H. 1981, *International Production and the Multinational Enterprise*, Allen and Unwin, London.

Dunning, J.H. 1988, *Explaining International Production*, Unwin Hyman, London.

Dunning, J.H. 1992, *Multinational Enterprises and the Global Economy*, Addison-Wesley, Wokingham, UK, and Reading, MA.

Dunning, J.H. 1993, *The Globalization of Business*, Routledge, London & New York.

Dunning, J.H. 1997, *Alliance Capitalism and Global Business*, Routledge, London.
Dunning, J.H. & Lundan, S. 2009, *Multinational Enterprises and the Global Economy*, 2nd edition, Edward Elgar, Cheltenham.
Dunning, J.H. & Narula, R. 1996, 'The investment development path revisited', in J.H. Dunning & R. Narula (eds.), *Foreign Direct Investment and Governments*, Routledge, London & New York.
Feenstra, R.C., Inklaar, R. & Timmer, M.P. 2015, *The Next Generation of the Penn World Table*, viewed 12 September 2015, www.ggdc.net/pwt
Garibaldi, P., Mora, N., Sahay, R. & Zettelmeyer, J. 2002, *What Moves Capital to Transition Economies?*, IMF working paper, WP/02/64, Washington, DC.
Greene, W.H. 2008, *Econometric Analysis*, 6th edition, Prentice Hall, New Jersey.
Han, H., Park, J.H., Yoon, S. & Cho, H. 2014, *The Establishment of the EEU and Changes in International Relations in Eurasia*, KIEP Strategic research 14-09 (in Korean), viewed 1 March 2016, http://www.kiep.go.kr/sub/view.do?bbsId=search_report&nttId=186010
Harvie, C. & Lee, H. 2003, *Korea's Economic Miracle Fading or Reviving?*, Palgrave Macmillan, New York.
Hennart, J.F. 1982, *A Theory of Multinational Enterprise*, University of Michigan Press, Ann Arbor.
Hoechle, D. 2007, 'Robust standard errors for panel regressions with cross-sectional dependence', *The Stata Journal*, vol. 7, no. 3, pp. 281–312.
Hyundai Group 2013, 'Hyundai expands successful made-for-you strategy with two new small cars', *Hyundai blog*, viewed 2 February 2016, https://globalpr.hyundai.com/prCenter/blog/blogView.do?bID=96
Hyundai Motors Manufacturing Rus 2016, viewed 25 January 2016, http://www.hyundai.ru
KIEP 2016, *Korea Institute for International Economic Policy*, viewed 26 January 2016, www.kiep.go.kr
Kim, D.K. 2007, *Investment Environment in Russia and Opportunities for Inter-Firm Cooperation* (in Korean), Samsung Economic Institute (SERI) seminar materials, Seoul.
Kim, J.M. & Rhe, D.K. 2009, 'Trends and determinants of South Korean outward foreign direct investment', *The Copenhagen Journal of Asian Studies*, vol. 27, no.1, pp. 126–54.
Kim, S.S. (ed.) 2000, *Korea's Globalization*, Cambridge University Press, Cambridge, UK.
Kim, Y.H. 2007, *Government Support for OFDI in Korea* (in Korean), unpublished presentation at the Korean Ministry of Industry and Resource, Seoul.
KITA 2016, *Korea International Trade Association*, viewed 27 January 2016, www.kita.net
Kojima, K. 1978, *Direct Foreign Investment*, Croom Helm, London.
Korea Export–Import Bank 2016, viewed 26 January 2016, http://www.koreaexim.go.kr
Korea Industrial Complex Corporation 2013, *Trends in Korea's Manufacturing OFDI and Proposals for Improvement of the Investment Regime in Korea* (in Korean), Planning research-2013, Seoul.
Korgun, I. & Popova, L. 2011, *Foreign Economic Factors in Development of the Republic of Korea in 1950–2011* (in Russian), Saint Petersburg State University Press, Saint Petersburg.
Kwak, J.S. & Mortimore, M. 2007, 'Republic of Korea: investment and corporate strategies in Latin America and the Caribbean', in *ECLAC 2007*, Foreign Direct Investment in Latin America 2006, UN, Santiago.
Kwon, K.S., Kim, J.O. & Ko, H.C. 2009, *Korea's Overseas Direct Investment in Latin America: Its Performance and Challenges*, Policy Analysis 09-20, Korea Institute for International Economic Policy, Seoul.

Lee, J.Y., Lee, S.C., Hwan, J.Y. & Lee, J.M. 2008, *Korean Firms' Investment and Future Agenda in Russia* (in Korean), No. 08–15, Korea Institute for International Economic Policy, Seoul.

Lee, S.B. 2007, *Korea's New Trade and Outward FDI Policies: Facilitating the Presence of Korean SMEs in Regional and Global Markets*, Seoul, Korea Institute for International Economic Policy, Presentation UN ESCAP, KIEP, Seoul.

Lim, H.C. & Jang, J.H. 2012, 'Whither democracy?: South Korea under globalization revisited', in P.J. Nederveen & JT Kim (eds.), *Globalization and Development*, Routledge, New York.

Liuima, J. 2015, *Overview of Russian New Car Market Part 1: Insights and Forecasts for Russian Car Industry*, Euromonitor International, viewed 2 February 2016, http://blog. euromonitor.com/2015/07/overview-of-russian-new-car-market-part-1-insights-and-forecasts-for-russian-car-industry.html

Markusen, J.R. 2002, *Multinational Firms and the Theory of International Trade*, MIT Press, Cambridge, MA.

MOFE 2005, *OFDI Promotion Plan* (in Korean), Ministry of Finance and Economy, Seoul.

Neary, J.P. 2007, *Trade Costs and Foreign Direct Investment*, viewed 20 August 2015, http://ssrn.com/abstract=1262212

OECD 2015, *Organisation for Economic Co-operation and Development*, viewed 29 November 2015, http://stats.oecd.org/

Park, J.H. 2015, 'Hyundai, Kia models top in July sales in Russia', *The Korea Times*, 12 August, viewed 2 February 2016, http://www.koreatimes.co.kr/www/news/biz/2015/08/388_184736.html

Petri, P.A. 2012, 'The determinants of bilateral FDI: is Asia different?', *Journal of Asian Economics*, vol. 23, no. 3, pp. 201–9.

Ranjan, V. & Agrawal, G. 2011, 'FDI inflow determinants in BRIC countries: a panel data analysis', *International Business Research*, vol. 4, no. 4, pp. 255–63.

Rugman, A.M. 2010, 'Reconciling internalization theory and the eclectic paradigm', *Multinational Business Review*, vol. 18, no. 2, pp, 1–12, viewed 3 July 2015, http:// centaur.reading.ac.uk/6112/

Rosstat 2016, *Russian Statistical Service*, viewed 26 January 2016, http://www.gks.ru

Shik, C.Y., Seok, H.H. & Baker, D.L. (eds.) 2009, *Korea Confronts Globalization*, Routledge, Oxford & New York.

Sutyrin, S., Popova, L. & Korgun, I. 2014, 'Russia–South Korea economic cooperation: current state and prospects', *Journal of Saint-Petersburg State University*, Series 5: Economics, no. 3, pp. 27–51.

UNCTAD 1998, *World Investment Report (WIR) 1998: Trends and Determinants*, United Nations Conference on Trade and Development, New York & Geneva.

UNCTAD 2015, *United Nations Conference on Trade and Development*, viewed 30 November 2015, http://unctad.org/en/Pages/Statistics.aspx

Vijayakumar, N., Sridharan, P. & Rao, K.C.S. 2010, 'Determinants of FDI in BRICS countries: a panel analysis', *International Journal of Business Science and Applied Management*, vol. 5, no. 3, pp. 1–13.

Wadhwa, K. & Sudhakara, R.S. 2011 'Foreign direct investment into developing Asian countries: the role of market seeking, resource seeking and efficiency seeking factors', *International Journal of Business and Management*, vol. 6, no. 11, pp. 219–26.

Woolridge, J. 2009, *Introductory Econometrics: A Modern Approach*, 4th edition, South Western, Mason.

Yeaple, S. 2003, 'The role of skill endowments in the structure of US outward foreign direct investment', *Review of Economics and Statistics*, vol. 85, no. 3, pp. 726–34.

Yoshitomi, M. & Montgomery, E.M. 1996, *Foreign Direct Investment in Japan*, Edward Elgar, Cheltenham.

Zhu, H., Liang, H. & Ren, B. 2011, *Revisiting the OLI Paradigm: The Institutions, the State, and China's OFDI,* CESifo Working Paper: Fiscal Policy, Macroeconomics and Growth, No. 3642, presented at CESIFO Venice Summer Institute, Workshop on "China and the Global Economy Post Crisis", July, Venice.

13 Turkish Multinationals in Russia

Caner Bakır and Nuran Acur[1]

Introduction

The accelerated internationalization of Turkish multinational companies (MNCs) over the last few years has been phenomenal. Turkish MNCs' foreign direct investment (FDI) outflows increased over threefold from $840 million in 2000 to $3.1 billion in 2013 (UNCTADSTAT 2014). During the same period, the volume of Turkish MNCs' outbound acquisitions increased over 17 times from $108 million to $1.8 billion (Thomson Reuters Mergers and Acquisitions Database 2016; Deloitte 2014). Over the ten-year period from 2004–13, their greenfield investments increased over threefold from $2.2 billion to $6.9 billion (fDi Intelligence Database 2016).[2] Clearly, Turkish MNCs are increasingly integrating with the global economy.

An analysis based on private databases shows that Turkish MNCs make one of their largest greenfield investments and undertake one of their largest mergers and acquisitions (M&As) in the Russian Federation (hereafter Russia), the world's sixth largest economy measured by gross domestic product (GDP) at purchasing power parity. However, it is surprising that we do not know much about recent trends in these investments or key corporate investors, their motivations and strategies.

This chapter aims to fill this gap in the literature. It aims to identify key Turkish MNCs investing in Russia and map their greenfield and acquisition investments, with particular emphasis on their value, geographic, and sectoral distribution, as well as their internationalization motivations and strategies. It also offers a detailed account of the internationalization of Enka and Anadolu Efes (AE), the largest two Turkish MNCs in Russia.

The rest of this chapter is organized as follows. Section 2 offers a brief overview of the literature, with special attention to the theoretical framework favored in this chapter. Section 3 describes the data sources used for our analysis. Section 4 focuses on Turkish MNCs' greenfield investment trends in Russia, with special reference to their value and sectors. It also offers a comparative analysis of the share of Russia in overall Turkish MNCs' investments. Section 5 does something similar for outbound acquisitions. Section 6 discusses the internationalization strategies and motivations of the aforementioned two largest Turkish MNCs. The conclusion summarizes the main findings.

Literature Review

In the international business (IB) literature, the country specific advantages (CSAs) and firm specific advantages (FSAs) framework is widely used to explain internationalization of MNCs (Dunning 1980; Rugman 2009). FSAs refer to the competitive advantages of firms such as brands and technology. CSAs relate to comparative advantages of countries such as skilled labor and natural resources. Recent research on MNCs from developing countries has been able to exploit these conceptual frameworks to generate new insights (Ramamurti & Singh 2009; Ramamurti 2012). It has been widely noted that developing country MNCs have some FSAs or ownership advantages that are different from developed country MNCs. As Ramamurti notes, this includes:

> their deep understanding of customer needs in emerging markets, the abil-
> ity to function in difficult business environments, their ability to make
> products and services at ultra-low costs, their ability to develop "good
> enough" products with the right feature–price mix for local customers.
> (Ramamurti 2012, p. 42)

It also has been pointed out that developing country MNCs internationalize to acquire dynamic capabilities and FSAs like global brands, technology, market knowledge, managerial experience, and know-how (Williamson *et al.* 2013). This chapter benefits from these theoretical and empirical insights.

There are four main internationalization motivations identified in the IB literature: market-seeking, resource-seeking, efficiency-seeking, and strategic asset-seeking (Dunning 1993). Market-seeking FDI aims to secure access to host-country markets. Resource-seeking FDI aims to access to natural resources and skilled human capital in foreign markets. Efficiency-seeking FDI seeks lower costs by accessing cheap labor. Strategic asset-seeking FDI aims to acquire strategic assets such as brands, technology, and distribution networks. This chapter adopts this scheme as a basis for analyzing Turkish MNCs' expansion in Russia.

Previous research on Turkish MNCs found that Turkish firms mostly invested in neighboring countries, relying on comparative advantages of Turkey such as geographical and cultural proximity (see, for example, Erdilek 2003, 2007; Kayam & Hisarcıklılar 2009). It has been noted that the outward foreign direct investment (OFDI) of Turkish MNCs was driven by a mix of the four motivations noted above.

Data Sources

In terms of the general analysis, this study uses greenfield investment data from the *Financial Times*'s fDi Intelligence Database (2003–13), with data available from 2003. Data for M&As comes from the Thomson Reuters Mergers and Acquisitions Database (from 1 January 2000 to 30 January 2011), and Deloitte (2014), whose data set includes some of the deals that were not covered by Thomson Reuters. The analyses based on these data focus on the 62 largest

Turkish MNCs' acquisitions, over $10 million, which constituted 72 percent of total Turkish MNCs' acquisitions worldwide.[3]

This chapter also exploits secondary sources such as company reports and newspaper articles. Written information was compiled from the EMIS database, which enabled a search of news and company reports published in English and Turkish. The search covered the period from January 2000–January 2016 and used the broad keywords "Turkey, Russia, investment". For company-based information, relevant keywords included "Enka and Russia" and "Anadolu Efes and Russia". We also searched Turkish newspapers not covered by the EMIS database as well as scholarly articles for relevant information. Other research sources included company webpages and reports of international organizations, governmental agencies, and private firms.

This chapter specifically examines the strategies and motivations of two Turkish MNCs, Enka and AE. We selected Enka because it is one of the largest greenfield investors in the real estate sector, which has the largest amount of Turkish MNC greenfield investment in Russia. We chose AE because it is one of the top Turkish acquirers in the food and beverages sector, which delivers the largest Turkish MNCs' acquisitions in this sector in Russia.

Greenfield Investments by Turkish MNCs

An analysis of the fDi database shows that transition economies and developing countries together received the highest amount of Turkish MNCs' greenfield investments, with over a 75 percent share in the total value of their greenfield investments worldwide (Bakır & Acur 2016). The Commonwealth of Independent States (CIS), with about $18 billion (or 39 percent of the total greenfield investments), is the top region for Turkish MNCs' greenfield investments. There have been 215 Turkish MNCs' greenfield investments in CIS countries, which employ about 95,000 people. The CIS has about a 60 percent share in the Turkish MNCs' total investments and total employment.

Table 13.1 shows Turkish MNCs' greenfield investments in Russia between 2003 and 2013. During this period, Turkish multinationals made 105 investments (13 percent of their total worldwide greenfield investments), invested about $10 billion (22 percent of the total), and created jobs for over 55,000 people (29 percent of the total) in Russia. On average, each Turkish MNC invested about $104 million and created employment for 523 people.

Figure 13.1 shows the top five Russian cities that attracted Turkish MNCs' greenfield investments. Saint Petersburg (28 percent) and Moscow (22 percent) are the top two destinations, receiving over $5 billion or about half of the total Turkish MNCs' investments in Russia. Russia's two largest cities offer relatively strong markets for Turkish MNCs' goods as well as services with physical infrastructure. It is surprising that Saint Petersburg, the second largest city in Russia, attracts more Turkish MNCs' investments than Moscow. This is because Saint Petersburg hosts some of the largest car manufacturers in the world and Turkish MNCs have undertaken construction of factories for some of these manufacturers. For example, Renaissance Construction built Ford's factory; Enka did the same job for Toyota

Table 13.1 Turkish MNCs' Greenfield Investments in Russia, 2003–13 ($ millions, number, and percent)

Year	Number of investments	Total investment value ($ millions)	Average investment ($ millions)	Total employment created (number of persons)	Average employment created (number of persons)
2003	21	1,759.70	83.80	6,499.00	309.48
2004	11	273.20	24.84	2, 110.00	191.82
2005	24	2,238.50	93.27	17,928.00	747.00
2006	8	399.70	49.96	3,335.00	416.88
2007	6	680.50	113.42	1,462.00	243.67
2008	10	1, 195.07	119.51	3,742.00	374.20
2009	4	1,025.60	256.40	5,084.00	1,271.00
2010	13	1,507.50	115.96	11,471.00	882.38
2011	3	41.70	13.90	171.00	57.00
2012	3	361.00	120.33	780.00	260.00
2013	3	450.60	150.20	3,003.00	1,001.00
Total	105	9,933.07	103.78	55,585.00	523.13
Share in total greenfield investments in CIS	50%	60%		61%	
Share in worldwide greenfield investments	13%	22%		29%	

Source: Authors' calculations based on fDi Intelligence Database 2016
Note: Database starts from 2003

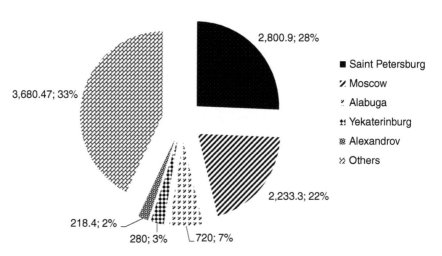

Figure 13.1 Turkish MNCs' Greenfield Investments in Russia by Region, 2000–13 ($ millions and percent)

Source: Authors' calculations based on fDi Intelligence Database 2016

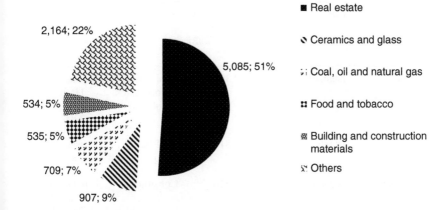

2,164; 22%

5,085; 51%

534; 5%

535; 5%

709; 7%

907; 9%

■ Real estate

❖ Ceramics and glass

⁖ Coal, oil and natural gas

⁘ Food and tobacco

▦ Building and construction
materials

⁙ Others

Figure 13.2 Turkish MNCs' Greenfield Investments in Russia by Industry, 2000–13
($ millions and percent)

Source: fDi Intelligence Database 2016

and General Motors; and Beta Tek constructed the Nissan factory (Deik 2015). Saint Petersburg and Moscow are followed by the Alabuga (Yelabuga) Special Economic Zone in the Republic of Tatarstan in Russia (6 percent), Yekaterinburg (3 percent), and Alexandrov, the Vladimir region (2 percent).

Figure 13.2 shows that real estate is the sector that attracted the largest amount of Turkish MNC greenfield investments in Russia between 2003 and 2013. The largest Turkish construction companies are active in three construction sectors: building, infrastructure, and industrial construction. In particular, most of them are investment builders who build, for example, shopping malls or hotels on their own account. These construction activities are classified in the real estate sector rather than construction. The real estate sector is followed by ceramics and glass, coal, oil and gas, food and tobacco, and building and construction materials.

Table 13.2 shows the top ten Turkish MNCs having the highest value of capital investments (i.e., greenfield investments) in Russia between 2003 and 2013. They mostly originate from İstanbul and have created over 48,000 jobs with about $8 billion worth of investment. There has been a heavy concentration of Turkish MNCs' investment and employment creation in a small number of corporations. For example, the share of the top ten Turkish MNCs in total employment and investment in Russia is 87 percent and 81 percent, respectively. These corporations also have a considerable share in overall Turkish MNCs' greenfield investments, a 25 percent share in total jobs created, and an 18 percent share in total capital investments (i.e., greenfield investments) made.

The top three Turkish MNCs include Ramenka, a subsidiary of Enka which operates the Ramstore hypermarkets, Enka, and Renaissance Construction. They have been very active in the retail, real estate, construction, and energy sectors. Enka and Renaissance participated in high-profile projects such as the reconstruction of the State Duma building and the Moscow City business center,

Table 13.2 Top Ten Turkish MNCs in Russia, 2003–13 ($ millions, number, and percent)

Investor company	City	Jobs created (number of persons)	Investment amount ($ millions)	Sectors	Investment year and number of investments
Ramenka*	İstanbul	21,245	2,396	Real estate; food and tobacco	Russia (2003, 11; 2004, 3; 2005, 18; 2006, 4; 2013, 1)
Enka*	İstanbul	4,590	1,814	Real estate; coal, oil and natural gas	Russia (2003, 1; 2008, 2)
Renaissance Construction	İstanbul	11,761	1,548	Construction	Russia (2005, 1; 2008, 1; 2010, 4)
Trakya Cam	İstanbul	859	525	Ceramics and glass	Russia (2008, 1; 2009, 1)
Kastamonu Entegre	İstanbul	1,294	385	Wood products	Russia (2009, 1)
Anadolu Cam	İstanbul	661	345	Building and construction materials; ceramics and glass	Russia (2004, 3; 2005, 1; 2006, 1; 2007, 1)
Efes Beverage Group	İstanbul	1,283	288	Beverages	Russia (2003, 2; 2005, 1)
Yenigun Insaat Sanayi Ve Ticaret	Ankara	3,000	280	Construction	Russia (2009, 1)
Ado Cimento (As Cement)	Antalya	676	250	Building and construction materials	Russia (2007, 1)
Vestel	İstanbul	2,724	218.4	Consumer electronics	Russia (2003, 1; 2004, 2; 2006, 1)
Total of top 10		48,093	8,049		
Share of top 10 in Turkish MNCs' greenfield investments in Russia		87%	81%		
Share of top 10 in total Turkish MNCs' international investments		25%	18%		

Source: Authors' calculations based on fDi Intelligence Database 2016

Note: *Koc Holding, which then owned Migros supermarket chain, and Enka launched a Russian retailer, Ramenka, as a JV in 1997, with equal stakes to operate shopping malls and Ramstore hyper-markets in Russia. Koc Holding sold its 50 percent stake in Ramenka to Enka Construction, for $542.5 million in 2007 respectively. Russian commercial building developers also work with Turkish MNCs: "In particular, Renaissance Construction participated in the construction of the first tower in Moscow-City, the Federation Tower, and is continuing to build skyscrapers on this platform" (Mashinistova 2015).

Acquisitions by Turkish MNCs

In regard to acquisitions, Bakır and Acur (2016) show that, between 2000 and 2013, Turkish MNCs had $11.2 billion of outbound acquisitions worldwide. The 62 largest Turkish MNCs' acquisitions, over $10 million, totaled about $9.9 billion, or 72 percent of the total value of acquisitions, during this period (ibid.). The CIS (at $3.1 billion, or 32 percent) is the second largest destination for Turkish MNCs' acquisitions after the EU ($3.6 billion or 37 percent). Turkish MNCs' acquisitions increased 44 times from about $41 million in 2003 to $1.8 billion in 2013. The years 2001, 2003, and 2008 were those during which no acquisitions were made. The 2001 Turkish economic crisis and the effects of the 2008 global financial crisis (GFC) were the main reasons for this. The year 2011 marked the highest investments in value terms, with $2.6 billion invested (ibid.).

Most of these private firms are family-owned diversified companies. Turkish MNCs, in general, prefer 100 percent ownership or majority ownership. Some of them initially acquire 100 percent ownership of their investees, while others make subsequent investments to increase their shares to 100 percent or a majority position. However, some of the Turkish MNCs are cautious when they enter the emerging markets for the first time (Bakır 2016). They generally prefer partnerships with local firms. This is because they aim to overcome liability of foreignness and a partnership option is less costly in case the company needs to exit the market. Those Turkish MNCs such as AE, which have already entered the Russian market, also prefer strategic alliances with foreign MNCs. In doing so, they explore FSAs, such as access to new international brands, distribution networks, and production facilities, in order to increase their existing market share in Russia and neighboring countries.

Figure 13.3 shows the distribution of the top 62 Turkish MNCs' acquisitions whose value exceeded $10 million, with special reference to target countries. Russia attracts the highest value of foreign acquisitions by these top Turkish multinationals ($2.6 billion, or 26 percent of the total value of acquisitions), followed by the Netherlands and the USA (each with $1.3 billion, or 13 percent).

As Figure 13.4 shows, 75 percent of Turkish MNCs' acquisitions in Russia are in the food and beverages sector, followed by mining, real estate, manufacturing, and banking and finance (25 percent). Like greenfield investments, Turkish MNCs' acquisitions in Russia show a pronounced sectoral concentration.

In addition to the sectoral concentration in the value of Turkish MNCs' acquisitions in the beverages sector, there is also market concentration of such investments at MNC level. There were nine Turkish MNCs' acquisitions in Russia, which were among the top 62 acquisitions (Table 13.3). These firms' M&As totaled about $2.6 billion. This figure corresponded to a 26 percent share in the total value of the top 62 worldwide Turkish MNC acquisitions.

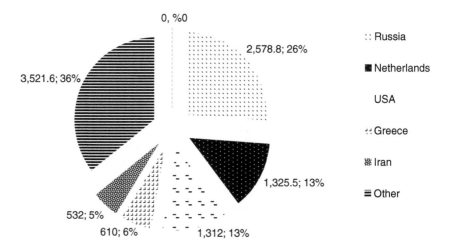

Figure 13.3 Distribution of the Top 62 Turkish MNCs' Acquisitions by Country, 2000–13 ($ millions and percent)

Sources: Deloitte 2014; Thomson Reuters Mergers and Acquisitions Database 2016

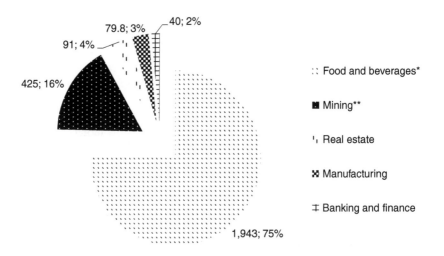

Figure 13.4 Distribution of Turkish MNCs' Acquisitions in Russia by Sector, 2000–13 ($ millions and percent)

Sources: Deloitte 2014; Thomson Reuters Mergers and Acquisitions Database 2016

Note: *Part of this M&A is in Ukraine; **Part of this M&A is in Kazakhstan

Table 13.3 Top Nine Turkish MNCs' Acquisitions in Russia, 2000–13 ($ millions and percent)

Value of M&As, $ millions	Agreement year	Target firm	Industry	Target country	Turkish MNCs	Acquired share, %
1,900.0	2011	Russia and Ukraine businesses of SABMiller	Beverages	Russia, Ukraine	Anadolu Efes	100
425.0	2013	Chrome Division of Mechel	Mining	Russia, Kazakhstan	Yıldırım Holding	100
91.0	2012	Moskva-Krasnye Kholmy	Real estate	Russia	Enka İnşaat	20
43.0	2013	CJSC Efes Brewery	Beverages	Russia	Anadolu Efes	9
40.0	2010	AKB Sofiya	Banking, finance	Russia	Türkiye İş Bankası	100
29.3	2008	OAO Kirishsky Stekolny Zavod	Manufacturing	Russia	Anadolu Cam Sanayii	100
18.5	2011	Forte Rus; Forte Ukraina	Manufacturing	Russia	Boydak Foreign Trade Company	100
18.0	2012	Automotive Glass Alliance Rus Trading ZAO	Manufacturing	Russia	Trakya Cam Sanayii	70
14.0	2013	LLC Ruscam Kuban	Production	Russia	Anadolu Cam Sanayii	40

Sources: Authors' calculations based on Deloitte 2014; Thomson Reuters Mergers and Acquisitions Database 2016

Note: Table excludes Credit Europe Bank, a bank registered in the Netherlands and owned by the Turkish financial holding company FIBA group (for a detailed discussion on internationalization of the Turkish banks, see Bakır 2016, Chapter 9)

Motivations and Strategies of Turkish MNCs' Investments

The previous section noted that the real estate sector receives the largest amount of Turkish MNCs' greenfield investments and that Enka is one of the largest investors in this sector. It has also been shown that the food and beverages sector receives the largest amount of Turkish MNCs' M&As and that AE is the top Turkish MNC in this sector in Russia. Thus, it is reasonable to focus on the internationalization motivations and strategies of Enka and AE.

Enka

Enka is the largest Turkish construction conglomerate. It has completed over 479 projects in 45 countries in the energy delivery, oil, gas, and petrochemicals, and infrastructure and transportation industries (Enka 2015). Besides Turkey and Russia, Enka has large investments in Algeria, Azerbaijan, Croatia, Germany, Kazakhstan, Libya, and the Netherlands. It is ranked 52nd on the "Top 250 International Contractors" list (Engineering News-Record Magazine 2014) and is ranked first among the 42 Turkish contractors on the list. It concentrates on "engineering and project management activities, comprising general contracting, civil works, power plants, industrial plants, infrastructural projects, real estate investment, manufacturing and trading" (Enka n.a.). It specializes in "power plants, motorways, bridges and tunnels, petrochemicals, urban development, business centers and high rises, public buildings, malls and shopping centers, industrial plants, offshore construction, manufacturing, airports and harbors, offshore construction, and real estate" (Enka n.a.). For example,

> [Enka] built hypermarkets of IKEA in St Petersburg and Kazan, the contractor selected to build the plants of Toyota and General Motors in St Petersburg. Enka owns about 135 thousand sqm of office space in Moscow, constructed several towers in the complex "Moscow City". Retail business of Enka in Russia is operated by the LLC "Enka TC". In 2008 the majority of supermarkets "Ramstore", which are managed by the company. (Vestnikkavkaza 2016)

In the early 1990s, Enka founded two joint stock companies, Mosenka and Moskva Krasnye Holmy, to develop and manage office and residential buildings in Moscow. As of 2014, it "owned and managed 318,500 sqm of office space providing local headquarters and facilities to a variety of global firms and 230,000 sqm of shopping malls in Russia". By 2015, Enka had completed over 130 projects in Russia and the CIS, ranging from buildings, hospitals, and industrial plants, to oil and gas projects. It has constructed a new terminal at Moscow's Sheremetyevo Airport, a Toyota car factory in Saint Petersburg, and oil field infrastructure on Sakhalin Island in Russia (Enka 2015).

Enka is also active in the retail business. Its first shopping mall and supermarket were opened in Moscow in 1997 under the Ramstore brand (ibid.).

The company became the largest operator in Moscow's retail market. It entered the promising Moscow city market where "Moscow's food retail sector lags behind all major European cities with comparable populations, and Ramenka was eager to tap into the growing buying power of Muscovites" (Shanetskaya 2001).

Access to a growing Russian market and CIS countries such as Azerbaijan and Kazakhstan has been the key motivation behind such investments. The level of economic activity has a strong impact on Turkish MNCs' business performance. In the words of Mustafa Saglam, General Manager of Ramenka, "Thanks to a stronger economy, consumer spending is up, and Muscovites are loading their shopping cart" (ibid.). In order to deal with strong local competitors, which controlled more than 50 percent of the retail food sector, Ramenka established strong relationships with roughly 2,000 local distributors (ibid.). Ramenka was rebranded as Enka TC Company in 2010, and currently owns and operates 63 supermarkets, hypermarkets, and shopping malls in Russia. In doing so, it serves over 135,000 customers a day (Enka 2015).

The key FSA that Turkish construction companies have is the know-how that they gained in their operations in Turkey and its neighboring regions (Bakır 2016). These firms also exploit home CSAs such as geographical and cultural proximity and access to cheap and skilled labor force.

Anadolu Efes

AE, with investments of $1.9 billion in the beverages sector, generates over 70 percent of total Turkish MNCs' acquisitions in Russia. It is the largest producer and marketer of beer, malt, and non-alcoholic beverages in Turkey. AE has a strong position in the oligopolistic Turkish market: it has an 89 percent share in the beer market and a 69 percent share in the carbonated soft drinks market via its 50 percent share in Coca-Cola Icecek ('Russia/Ukraine' 2011). It is the 11th largest beverage company in the world, and the sixth largest in Europe, in terms of sales volume, serving over 300 million customers with over 40 brands (Anadolu Efes 2015a). It has beer production facilities in six countries and employs over 8,000 people in its 15 breweries distributed as follows: Russia (six), Turkey (four), Kazakhstan (two), Georgia, Moldova, and Ukraine (one in each country), six malt-houses: Russia (four) and Turkey (two), and one hops processing facility (Turkey). It has operated in Russia since 1997, with six breweries and four malt-houses. In Russia, the company is ranked second with a 14 percent market share (Anadolu Efes 2015b).

AE generated $4.1 billion in revenue and 24.5 million hectoliters sales volume in 2014. Sixty percent of its sales revenues and 71 percent of its sales volume are generated internationally. AE's "Russian sales account for about half of its sales revenues from beer and almost 20 percent of total sales revenues" (CEEMarketWatch Daily News 2015). Efes's subsidiary in Russia, Moskva-Efes Pivovarnya ZAO, has nine brands including Bely Medved (Anadolu Group), Efes (Anadolu Group), Gold Mine Beer (Anadolu Group), Miller Genuine Draft (SABMiller Plc), Redd's (SABMiller Plc), Sokol (Anadolu Group), Stary Melnik

(Anadolu Group), Velkopopovicky Kozel (SABMiller Plc), and Zolotaya Bochka (Anadolu Group) (Euromonitor International 2015, p. 3).

AE has adopted various internationalization strategies over the years. It exploited FSAs such as market knowledge in Russia and its neighbors in the late 1990s. It also has profited from FSAs obtained from its subsidiaries and alliances in foreign markets, such as a portfolio of high-quality international and regional brands and distribution networks. It further exploited FSAs (dynamic capabilities) obtained in Turkey such as scale advantages arising from oligopolistic home market as well as experience garnered from working in an environment with weak institutions and economic uncertainty. Finally, it exploited home-country CSAs such as geographical proximity to Russia and the CIS in general.

One of the major internationalization strategies of AE was observed in 2011, when it formed a strategic alliance with SABMiller, the world's second largest beer producer, "through either brewing, soft drinks or export operations" (SABMiller 2012, p. 4). It took over SABMiller's three breweries in Russia and one brewery in Ukraine while giving SABMiller a 24 percent equity stake in AE. Why would AE, which already was established in the Russian market, need this strategic alliance?

This deal was mainly motivated by the market-seeking motive of expanding AE's market share in Turkey, Russia, and Ukraine, and effectively penetrating market segments in CIS countries. This strategic alliance was formed not only to target Russia, but also the CIS, Central Asia, and the Middle East. Following the deal, the company became the second largest beer producer in Russia. In the words of the Chairman of AE, Tuncay Özilhan, the strategic alliance will grow AE's Russian business:

> We are delighted to join forces with such a strong business partner as SABMiller and to enlarge the Anadolu Efes business in Russia and Ukraine... this will enable us to better capitalize on the potential growth opportunities in our operating region in line with our long term growth plans. ('Russian SABMiller...' 2011)

In its search for exploration of FSAs, the strategic alliance with SABMiller will also enable AE to access new international brands, business practices, and distribution networks. "The deal also gave Anadolu Efes entrée into the Russian market's premium and superpremium sectors, which are expected to grow rapidly as the country's middle class grows and its tastes become more sophisticated" (Kengelbach, Klemmer & Roos 2013).

A strategic alliance with AE, which has strong market knowledge and experience, regional brands, production facilities, and distribution and marketing networks, would facilitate SABMiller's growth and penetration to CIS and the Middle East. In the words of the Chief Executive of SABMiller at the time, Graham Mackay, "Both SABMiller and Anadolu Efes have proved to be successful operators in diverse and challenging emerging beer markets and this strategic alliance will allow both our groups to benefit from each other's expertise, and the combination of our resources" (ibid.). SABMiller also noted that:

> in Russia, the combined business has a strong number two position and is benefiting from greater scale, an attractive portfolio of brands and cost synergy opportunities amounting to at least $120 million. The two partners will share best practice and Anadolu Efes will develop SABMiller's international brands across the territory. (SABMiller 2012, p. 9)

In sum, AE's internationalization strategy aims to expand in host markets where it has operations and enter new market segments via strategic alliances and acquisitions. In doing so, it responds to changing consumer demand for premium products via diversification of its brands and production. Apparently, AE has acquired FSAs over the years in Russia such as managerial experience and market knowledge *vis-à-vis* its foreign competitors.

A Crisis between Russia and Turkey: A Misfortune for Turkish MNCs?

When Turkish fighter jets shot down a Russian fighter-bomber near the Turkish–Syrian border on 24 November 2015, Turkish–Russian relations entered into a crisis period. Following this incident, Russia introduced a package of sanctions against Turkey, which affected Turkish trade and investment links with Russia (BBC 2016).

> The expanded sanctions included limitation on operations in Russia by firms under the jurisdiction of Turkey or firms controlled by Turkish citizens… as well as prohibition of Turkish companies from construction, tourism, hotel businesses and services for state and municipal needs as of January 1 [2016]. (CEEMarketWatch Daily News 2016)

The Turkish tourism sector and some of the exporting sectors, especially agriculture, which have exposure to the Russian market, experienced losses in 2016. Enka could have been one of the most affected Turkish MNCs if it were targeted directly by the sanctions. This is because Russia is one of Enka's first foreign markets, where its investment over 30 years has exceeded $4 billion. The share of Russia in Enka's total revenues is about 14 percent "while the weight of Russia is significantly higher for Enka in terms of its ongoing investments" (CEEMarketWatch Daily News 2015).

However, the Russian Government excluded large Turkish construction firms, including Enka and Renaissance Construction, from sanctions. Furthermore, these firms along with 51 construction companies, automobile manufacturers, and firms operating in installation and installation equipment were allowed to continue employing Turkish citizens (CEEMarketWatch Daily News 2016). In a similar vein, AE, which employs over 5,000 people, was excluded from the sanctions list ('Russia excludes…' 2015). Apparently, those Turkish MNCs, which are embedded in the Russian economy contributing to investment, production, and employment are less likely to be affected by such policy reversals. This also shows increased structural dependence of the Russian Government on the activities of such MNCs.

Nevertheless, Turkish MNCs already faced further economic challenges in Russia. The decline in oil prices and Western sanctions following the Ukraine crisis led to Russia's economic contraction. This has negatively affected the sales and profits of Turkish MNCs. For example, Enka had "a 25 percent YoY [year on year] contraction at the top line in US dollar terms (mainly due to the 25 percent contraction in construction revenues and problems in Russia). Backlog retreated to $2.2bn, down 6 percent QoQ [quarter on quarter]" (Garanti Securities 2015a, p. 1). In a similar vein, AE's "international beer sales volumes declined by 17.9 percent YoY in Q2 mainly attributable to the challenging environment in Russia, Kazakhstan and Ukraine" (Garanti Securities 2015b, p. 1).

Conclusion

Although Russia has been the one of the main destinations for Turkish MNCs' outward investments, the literature on Turkish MNCs is silent on the recent internationalization of Turkish MNCs in Russia. Based on the data supplied by private databases, this chapter offered an analysis of the current trends of Turkish MNCs' investments, their FSAs obtained from home- and host-country CSAs, and their motivations, with special reference to their major greenfield investments, strategic alliances, and acquisitions in Russia.

There are four main findings of this study. First, there has been market concentration (i.e., a relatively small number of Turkish MNCs generate a majority of the total Turkish MNCs' investments in Russia) and sectoral concentration in greenfield investments in the real estate sector, and acquisitions in the beverages sector. Second, some of the largest Turkish MNCs in Russia exploit and explore FSAs. For example, they exploit FSAs (dynamic capabilities) obtained in Russia such as market and managerial knowledge and expertise, as well as FSAs obtained in Turkey such as technology, local/regional brands, and distribution channels. Further, they explore FSAs through strategic alliances and acquisitions. For example, they aim to have new and competitive production facilities, distribution and marketing networks, and access to international brands. Third, they also exploit home and host CSAs. CSAs obtained from Turkey include economies of scale, experience operating in volatile economic and institutional environments, which also translated into FSAs, leadership in their home market, and geographical proximity. Host CSAs include growing markets and emerging premium market segments. Finally, market-seeking FDI is the key motivation forTurkish MNCs to respond to profitable business opportunities arising in the real estate, retail, and beverage sectors, and increased demand for infrastructure investments especially in the energy sector. By focusing on Russia, these findings also complement recent research on Turkish MNCs (Bakır 2016; Bakır & Acur 2016).

Notes

1 Bakır gratefully acknowledges the support of the Scientific and Technological Research Council of Turkey TÜBİTAK, 110K346, and Postdoctoral Fellowship for Research Abroad, TÜBİTAK 2219. This chapter is also related to COST Action IS0905 "The Emergence of Southern Multinationals and their Impact on Europe". The authors thank Sergei Sutyrin, Kari Liuhto, Peter Williamson, Louis Brennan, and Hafız Mirza for their insightful comments Authors also thank Pınar Dönmez, Mustafa Yağcı, Sinan Akgunay, and Mina Kozluca for their assistance.
2 2004–13 rather than 2003–12 is preferred in a ten-year comparison. This is because 2001 was an economic crisis year in Turkey and the significantly high 2003 figure reflects delayed Turkish MNCs' investments, making a ten-year comparison less accurate.
3 It should be noted that there are differences between the figures cited here and those released by the Central Bank of Turkey and the Central Bank of Russia. It is widely accepted that these differences arise from differences in data collection method. For example, fDi Intelligence Database includes announced projects planned as well as actual investments. Database also includes estimated figures for some of the actual investments. However, the key advantage of this private database is that it enables one to identify corporate investors and investment details such as value and destination. Thomson Reuters Mergers and Acquisitions database includes actual investments.

Bibliography

Anadolu Efes 2015a, *About Anadolu Efes*, Anadolu Efes, viewed 22 November 2015, http://www.anadoluefes.com/index.php?gdil=in&gsayfa=hk&galtsayfa=anadoluefeshakkind a&gicsayfa=&gislem=&gbilgi=

Anadolu Efes 2015b, *Operation Countries*, Anadolu Efes, viewed 22 November 2015, http://www.anadoluefes.com/index.php?gdil=inandgsayfa=asandgaltsayfa=andgicsayfa= andgislem=andgbilgi=

Bakır, C. 2016, *Küreselleşme sürecinde Turk cok uluslulari: Eğilimler, Motivasyonlar ve Stratejiler [Turkish Multinationals in the Globalisation Process: Trends, Motivations and Strategies]*, Koc University Press, İstanbul.

Bakır, C. & Acur, N. 2016, 'Greenfield investments and acquisitions of Turkish multinationals: trends, motivations and strategies', in L. Brennan & C. Bakır (eds.), *Emerging Market Multinationals in Europe* (pp. 129–159), Routledge, London.

BBC 2016, 'Turkey faces big losses as Russia sanctions bite', viewed 8 April 2016, http://www.bbc.com/news/world-europe-35209987

CEEMarketWatch Daily News 2015, 'Turkey: Putin signs decree on economic sanctions against Turkey', viewed 30 November 2015, CEEMarketWatch database.

CEEMarketWatch Daily News 2016, 'Turkey: Russia expands economic sanctions against Turkey', viewed 4 January 2016, CEEMarketWatch database.

Deik 2015, *St.Petersburg'da Hızla Gelişen Otomotiv Sektörü*, Deik, viewed 25 October 2015, https://www.deik.org.tr/1515/St_Petersburg_da_H percentC4 percentB1zla_Geli percentC5 percent9Fen_Otomotiv_Sekt percentC3 percentB6r percentC3 percentBC. html

Deloitte 2014, *Deloitte Turkish Outbound M&A Review 2012–2013*, viewed 25 October 2015, http://www2.deloitte.com/tr/en/pages/mergers-and-acquisitions/articles/turkish-outbound-ma-review-2012-2013.html

Dunning, J.H. 1980, 'Towards an eclectic theory of international production: some empirical tests', *Journal of International Business Studies*, vol. 11, no. 1, pp. 9–31.

Dunning, J.H. 1993, *Multinational Enterprises and the Global Economy*, Addison Wesley, New York.

Engineering News-Record Magazine 2014, 'Top 250 International contractors', viewed 26 August 2015, http://www.enr.com/toplists/2015_Top_250_International_Contractors1

Enka n.a., *Enka*, LinkedIn Profile, viewed 17 September 2015, https://www.linkedin.com/company/enka

Enka 2015, viewed 15 September 2015, http://www.enka.com/Enka.aspx?MainID=65and ContentID=74

Erdilek, A. 2003, 'A comparative analysis of inward and outward FDI in Turkey', *Transnational Corporations*, vol. 12, no. 3, pp. 79–105.

Erdilek, A. 2007, 'Outward foreign direct investment by enterprises from Turkey', in *Global Players from Emerging Markets: Strengthening Enterprise Competitiveness through Outward Investment*, UNCTAD, New York & Geneva.

Euromonitor International 2015, 'Sector Capsule in Russia', viewed 10 November 2015, http://www.euromonitor.com/

fDi Intelligence Database 2016, Financial Times Ltd, http://www.fdiintelligence.com/

Garanti Securities 2015a, *Enka Insaat*, viewed 6 November 2015, http://www.garantisecurities.com/DefaultEn.aspx

Garanti Securities 2015b, *Anadolu Efes*, viewed 6 November 2015, http://www.garantisecurities.com/DefaultEn.aspx

Kayam, S. & Hisarcıklılar, M. 2009, 'Türkiye'den çıkan doğrudan yatırımları belirleyen etmenler: 1992–2005', *İşletme, İktisat ve Finans*, vol. 24, no. 280, pp. 47–70.

Kengelbach, J., Klemmer, D. & Roos, A. 2013, 'The Global M&A Market Remains in a Deep Freeze', *Boston Consulting Group blog*, web log post, 29 August, viewed 13 September 2015, https://www.bcgperspectives.com/content/articles/mergers_acquisitions_alliances_joint_ventures_global_m_and_a_market_remains_deep_freeze/

Mashinistova, N. 2015, 'Press digest: Moscow may exclude Turkish construction firms from Russia', *Russia Beyond the Headlines*, 27 November, viewed 12 December 2015, http://rbth.com/international/2015/11/27/pres-digest-moscow-may-exclude-turkish-construction-firms-from-rusia_545325

Ramamurti, R. 2012, 'What is really different about emerging market multinationals?', *Global Strategy Journal*, vol. 2, no 1, pp. 41–7.

Ramamurti, R. & Singh, J.V. 2009, *Emerging Multinationals in Emerging Markets*, Cambridge University Press, Cambridge.

Rugman, A.M. 2009, 'Theoretical aspects of MNEs from emerging economies', in R. Ramamurti & J.V. Singh (eds.) *Emerging Multinationals in Emerging Markets*, Cambridge University Press, Cambridge.

'Russia excludes 10 Turkish brands from sanctions list' 2015, *Hurriyet Daily News*, 29 December, viewed 10 January 2016, http://www.hurriyetdailynews.com/russia-excludes-10-turkish-brands-from-sanctions-list-report.aspx?PageID=238&NID=93167&NewsCatID=345

'Russia/Ukraine: Anadolu Efes and SABMiller to form strategic alliance' 2011, *GlobalMalt*, 19 October, viewed 22 November 2015, http://www.globalmalt.de/russiaukraine-anadolu-efes-and-sabmiller-to-form-strategic-alliance/?lang=pl

'Russian SABMiller brewing assets to go to Efes in Strategic Alliance deal' 2011, *Russian Times*, 19 October, viewed 12 November 2015, https://www.rt.com/business/russian-brewing-assets-strategic-165/

SABMiller 2012, *Annual Report*, viewed 16 November 2015, http://www.sabmiller.com/docs/default-source/investor-documents/reports/2012/financial-reports/annual-report-2012.pdf?sfvrsn=2

Shanetskaya, N. 2001, 'Ramenka launches 3rd mall', *Moscow Times*, 19 January, viewed 22 September 2015, http://www.themoscowtimes.com/business/article/ramenka-launches-3rd-mall/255978.html

Thomson Reuters Mergers and Acquisitions Database 2016, http://thomsonreuters.com/en.html

UNCTAD 2015, *World Investment Report (WIR) 2015: Reforming International Investment Governance*, United Nations, New York & Geneva.

UNCTADSTAT 2014, http://unctadstat.unctad.org/wds/ReportFolders/reportFolders.aspx?sRF_ActivePath=P,5,27andsRF_Expanded=,P,5,27

Vestnikkavkaza 2016, 'Sharyk Tara: "I consider the high degree of tension between Russia and Turkey to be a misfortune"', viewed 8 April 2016, http://vestnikkavkaza.net/articles/Sharyk-Tara-I-consider-the-high-degree-of-tension-between-Russia-and-Turkey-to-be-a-misfortune.html

Williamson, P., Ramamurti, R., Fleury, A. & Fleury, M.T.L. 2013, *The Competitive Advantage of Emerging Market Multinationals,* Cambridge University Press, Cambridge.

14 Russian Outward Foreign Direct Investments in Latin America

Contemporary Challenges and Prospects

Alexandra Koval

Introduction

Russia recently has intensified its relations with Latin American countries, with more Russian companies investing in the region. In 2008, after the visit of former President Dmitry Medvedev to Peru, Brazil, Venezuela, and Cuba, many experts argued that Russia had returned to Latin America and would compete in this market (Koval 2009). The financial crisis of 2008–9 limited the growth of ties. Nevertheless, the visit of incumbent President Vladimir Putin to Cuba, Nicaragua, Argentina, and Brazil in 2014 re-confirmed Russia's strategic interest in expanding its presence in Latin America (Davydov 2014). Moreover, the Ukrainian crisis has strengthened the necessity for both the Russian Government and Russian businesses to broaden cooperation with non-traditional partners. The recognition of this was reflected in the official visit of former Argentine President Cristina Kirchner to Russia in April 2015, when a number of notable agreements establishing a strategic partnership between the countries were signed.

Russia's newfound focus on the region links, on the one hand, to the recovery of Russian–Latin American economic relations after the collapse of almost all business ties during the period of Russia's transformation in the 1990s. On the other hand, it reflects Russia's foreign policy goals of building a multipolar order and re-emerging on the global scene. The geopolitical perspective prevails in most research on Russian–Latin American relations while relatively modest attention has been paid to economic cooperation (Sánchez Ramírez 2010; Blank & Kim 2015).

The *Concept of the Russian Federation Foreign Policy* 2013 (Ministry of Foreign Affairs of Russia 2013) highlights that Russia will strengthen its economic relations with Latin America "securing the position of Russian companies in dynamically developing industrial, energy, communications and transport sectors of the region's economies". In other words, Russia intends to increase its exports and investments in Latin America in the specified areas. Such a strategy corresponds to the geopolitical perception of Russia as a re-emerging power.

Growing foreign direct investments (FDIs) from Russia to Latin America could be one of the instruments for increasing Russia's position in the global governance generally and in the region specifically. However, the amount of these investments remains an insignificant part of overall Russian outward foreign direct investment (OFDI). When capital flows to Caribbean and Central American tax havens are excluded, Russian FDI stock in Latin America accounts for a meagre 0.1 percent of Russia's total overseas FDI as of the end of December 2014 (Central Bank of Russia 2016). Moreover, current Russian–Latin American investment relations could hardly be defined as wide ranging.

This chapter identifies goals behind, barriers to, and determinants of Russian OFDI in Latin America. It first reveals the motives of Russian investments in the region. Second, it contemplates if the political factor plays any role in Russian–Latin American investment cooperation. Finally, it examines the major threats facing and opportunities for contemporary Russian TNCs in the region.

Theoretical Foundation

Studying Russian transnational corporations' (TNCs') internationalization enhances our discussion about the unique features of OFDI from emerging markets. To date, scholars specifically have analyzed the motives of emerging market firms to go abroad, the factors enhancing their internationalization process, and the determinants of their expansion (Goldstein 2007; Mihailova & Panibratov 2012; Cuervo-Cazurra & Ramamurti 2014).

Dunning (1993) explains OFDI with the Ownership, Location, and Internationalization (OLI) paradigm: why (Ownership advantage), where (Localization advantage), and how (Internalization advantage) the company invests abroad. The O-advantage is based on firm specific assets that can be exploited internationally. The L-advantage specifies the characteristics of host country attracting overseas investments. The I-advantage looks at managerial capabilities to internationalize, among other things. However, some researchers (Rugman 2008) argue that, in the case of emerging market firms, home-country specific advantages also affect investment decisions. Regarding Russian OFDI, Kalotay and Sulstarova (2010) indicate that home-country factors such as a market size, natural resource endowment, state policy, and domestic business conditions can influence TNCs' activities.

Dunning (2000) also introduces four main motivations for TNCs' outbound investments: resource-seeking, market-seeking, efficiency-seeking, and strategic asset-seeking. Resource-seeking investments aim to access resources like minerals, agricultural products, and labor. Market-seeking investments intend to satisfy the demand for foreign markets with TNCs either aspiring to find new buyers or move closer to consumers. Efficiency-seeking investments promote a more efficient division of labor or the specialization of a TNC's existing portfolio of foreign and domestic assets. Strategic asset-seeking investments refer to the acquisition of latest technologies in order to protect the existing ownership advantages of the company and reduce those of its competitors.

Scholars indicate that emerging market firms usually invest in developing countries to acquire resources (resource-seeking), to expand market (market-seeking), or to take advantage of economies of scale and scope (efficiency-seeking).

However, OFDI from emerging economies to developed countries often has something to do with strategic asset-seeking motives; that is, emerging market firms invest in Europe or the United States (USA) by acquiring local companies so they can use their technologies and reduce the technological gap with Western TNCs (Sauvant 2008). Russian investments reflect all four types of motivations (Liuhto 2015). Still, the majority relate to resource-seeking in energy and mining (Dunning, Kim & Park 2008). Kalotay (2008) argues that one difference between Russian OFDI and OFDI from other emerging markets is that Russian investors are less motivated by strategic asset- or knowledge-seeking as most Russian TNCs are natural resource-based and focus on upstream and downstream FDI. In contrast, Filippov (2011) observes some high tech Russian companies indeed act on the basis of strategic asset-seeking motivations.

Dunning and Lundan (2008) incorporate an institutional dimension into the study of emerging TNCs' internationalization. Currently, the institutional approach is widespread in the literature on OFDI from emerging economies (Stoian 2013; Hitt, Li &Xu 2015). Institutional factors can be divided into two groups: national and supranational. The national ones include governmental policy and FDI regulation in the home country. Supranational factors can be characterized by "soft" and "hard" power. "Soft" power refers to state visits while "hard" power refers to formal bilateral investment treaties (BITs) or other international investment agreements (Buckley *et al.* 2008). For TNCs from emerging economies, where there might be greater state involvement, institutional factors could play more significant role than for Western companies. From an institutional perspective, the most discussed issue in studies on Russia OFDI is whether political leverage affects TNCs' activities. Here the arguments relate not only to "soft" power, but also to the performance of state-owned companies (Liuhto & Vahtra 2007).

The governments of developing countries often support their TNCs in strengthening their presence in different foreign markets. For instance, China's "Go Global" and Brazil's "National Champions" (Kroger 2012) strategies aim to turn their national corporations into leading players in the global arena. In comparison to other BRIC (Brazil, Russia, India, and China) countries, Russia has not developed a special strategy for TNCs. Nevertheless, the general concept of Russian foreign economic policy includes incentives to support Russian companies abroad.

Kalotay (2006) argues that the state has played a significant role in Russian OFDI. Vahtra (2007), however, counters that while political factors might affect Russian OFDI in the energy sector, there is not enough evidence to claim such a linkage generally. Fortescue and Hanson's (2015) study of the steel industry also suggests that a political explanation of Russian TNCs' internationalization is unconvincing.

Recent changes in Latin America may have reinforced the significance of governmental support for Russian investors. In the beginning of the twenty-first century, Latin America experienced a "left turn" phenomenon where left-wing parties came to power in several countries (Luna & Filgueira 2009). This meant greater state involvement in economic policies varying from the nationalization of strategic industries to price controls. On the basis of the extent of government intervention in business, Latin American countries can be divided into two groups (Pezoldt & Koval 2012). The first group includes Argentina, Brazil, Paraguay, Peru, and Uruguay. In these countries, only few key industries have been nationalized or only few industries are dominated by state-owned companies. Bolivia, Ecuador, Nicaragua, and Venezuela represent the second group because they have embraced more radical economic policies entailing more comprehensive nationalization, authoritarianism based on a leading role of the state in the majority of sectors, monetary and financial control, and the expansion of bureaucratic procedures.

This "left turn" increased the level of political risk for business and, in turn, decreased investors' interest in the region. Still, Latin America continued attracting foreign companies that could adjust to the changing rules and procedures (Winter & Scharmanski 2009). Indeed, the increase in corruption and bureaucracy that followed the "left turn" might have created an advantageous situation for TNCs from emerging economies, including Russian ones, because they would be doing business in "familiar" circumstances (Gymez-Mera *et al.* 2015). Still, high political risks in Latin American left-oriented states may overwhelm such an advantage, which makes the establishment of strong state-to-state relations that support the development of bilateral business ties even more crucial.

The aforementioned changes in Latin American countries not only affected their domestic environment, but also their respective foreign policies. One key goal of many countries was to decrease US influence and strengthen their relations with partners in the region and beyond. China took advantage from the emergence of such attitudes in left-wing party-driven countries: Chinese OFDI to the region has been jumping and reached more than $8 billion in 2014 (UNCTAD 2015). To some extent, Russian companies have utilized the new political atmosphere in Latin America and created business networks with the support of the Russian Government in order to decrease their political risks. However, in the past couple of years, the popularity of many Latin American leftist governments has evaporated as the recent parliamentary election in Venezuela and the presidential election in Argentina demonstrate.

Beyond these political challenges, emerging market firms as latecomers may need additional support to enlarge their activities (Matthews 2002). While some researchers (Lebedev *et al.* 2015) indicate a latecomer advantage for emerging market firms, especially in case of mergers and acquisitions (M&As), other studies stress that in order to catch up Western companies, emerging market firms face difficulties investing abroad to become global players and increase competitiveness on international markets (Sauvant 2008). As far as Russia is concerned, its firms are still gaining experience in internationalization and their foreign acquisitions have not always been success stories (Bertrand & Betschinger 2012). Thus, one important barrier for Russian investors could be the latecomer effect.

Another challenge for TNCs can be the existence of a long geographical distance between home and host countries because remoteness from the market means a lack of information, fewer partners, and higher transaction costs. In fact, Tolentino (2000) argues that companies invest in far-away countries only at the final stage of their internationalization, which may partly explain why it took so much time for Russian companies to begin investing in Latin America. Nevertheless, in order to be "truly" global, large TNCs need to invest in far-away regions.

The majority of earlier studies examine Russian FDI in European countries and the CIS (Lisitsyn *et al.* 2005; Liuhto & Majuri 2014), largely neglecting the developing world. Collins (2013) indicates that OFDI from Russia to developing countries, especially in Africa and Asia, is a relatively recent phenomenon. Only a few contributions focus on Russian OFDI in Latin America. A case study of Russian technology intensive small and medium-sized enterprises (SMEs) in Brazil (Latukha, Panibratov & Safonova-Salvadori 2011), an analysis of Russian–Brazilian investment cooperation in the framework of the BRICS (Koval 2011; Kheyfets 2014), and Kuznetsov's overview of Russian–Latin American investment relations (2014) are rare examples. This chapter aims to plug this lacuna by investigating Russian OFDI in Latin America.

Methodology

There are several reasons why the case study method is the most appropriate way to investigate the motives and determinants of contemporary Russian OFDI in Latin America. First, Russian–Latin American investment relations have just begun to develop and the number of investment projects is relatively limited. The case study method allows one to probe the distinguishing features of these projects. Second, the insufficiency and inconsistency of statistical data does not allow one to use quantitative methods. Third, a comparative case analysis of Russian TNCs in various sectors can reveal the peculiarities of Russian OFDI in this region and illuminate the political framework shaping investment cooperation. Finally, case studies take into account the "real-life" context characterizing the motives and determinants of contemporary Russia investors in Latin America.

According to the Central Bank of Russia (CBR) (2016), Russian FDI flows to Latin America in 2014 equaled $4.65 billion. However, if we exclude tax havens such as the Bahamas, Bermuda, the British Virginia Islands (BVI) from the list of recipients, the sum drops to just $45.2 million. This is not surprising as capital outflows to tax havens represent one of the key features of Russian OFDI (Liuhto & Majuri 2014). For Russian investors, the Caribbean islands are among the most popular offshore destinations.[1] To truly delve into "real" Russian TNCs' investments in Latin America, this chapter excludes tax havens from the analysis.

The statistical data very often do not show the "real" situation with respect to Russian–Latin American investment cooperation. Figure 14.1 provides the estimates of Russian FDI flows to Latin America given by the CBR. According to its data, Russian OFDI fluctuated considerably over the 2007–14 period, with extraordinary peaks in 2008 and 2013. The analysis shows that these peaks relate to a huge jump in Russian OFDI in Argentina ($218.5 million) in 2008 and a large surge in Russian OFDI in Cuba ($115.6 million) in 2013. Of note, corporate

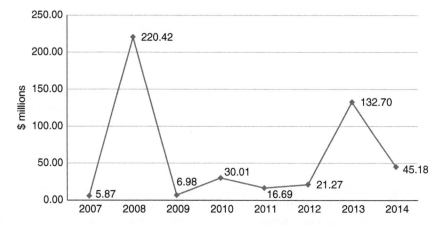

Figure 14.1 Russia's Annual FDI Flows to Latin America, Excluding Tax Havens, 2007–14 ($ millions)

Source: Central Bank of Russia 2016

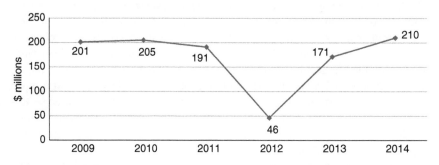

Figure 14.2 Russia's FDI Stock in Latin America, Excluding Tax Havens, 2009–14 ($ millions)

Source: Central Bank of Russia 2016

reports or governmental sources do not indicate any such development. For instance, according to the Ministry of Economic Development of Russia (2014), FDI flows from Russia to Cuba were less than $1 million in 2013. The comparison of Russian data with Latin American national statistics reveals a number of statistical disparities. For instance, the UN Economic Commission for Latin America and the Caribbean (CEPAL 2015), which relies on the data from Latin American countries, indicated a fall of 51 percent in OFDI to the region from transition economies, especially Russia, in 2014. Moreover, the CBR (2016) does not show any Russian OFDI in Venezuela even though Rosneft (2015)'s financial statements show investments in various energy projects in the country (see Figure 14.2).

A comparison of national statistics with corporate reports not only indicates statistical imperfection, but also hints at a prevailing feature of Russian OFDI;

that is, part of Russian OFDI to Latin America is conducted either via intermediaries or subsidiaries of Russian TNCs located in tax havens. For instance, the CBR reports there was no FDI from Russia to Guatemala in 2014. In contrast, CEPAL (2015) points out that Russia was one of the main investors in the country in 2014, with investments of approximately $86 million! Moreover, Solway Investment Group Ltd, a firm with Russian capital registered in Cyprus (which the statistical agency of Guatemala still considers as Russian investments), has poured more than $300 million into developing ferronickel mining in Guatemala. So, discrepancies in data provided by central banks of Russia and Latin American countries impede the analysis of Russian FDI in this region.

Due to these statistical deficiencies, this chapter uses the case study method and information compiled from secondary sources. One is corporate website. A second is analytical articles in business newspapers and magazines. The author has compared data from different sources in order to verify its accuracy.

The cases provide a new perspective on a relatively underexplored subject and can be considered as the initial steps in a new research area. The cross-sectoral approach to case studies offers a comprehensive view on the framework of Russian–Latin American investment cooperation. This study specifically analyzes Russian OFDI in the energy, manufacturing, and information technology sectors, which were named in the *Concept of the Russian Federation Foreign Policy* 2013 (Ministry of Foreign Affairs of Russia 2013). It does not analyze transport[2] and telecommunications,[3] as up to now there are almost no significant projects in these sectors. This research does not focus on the mining industry either since Russian FDI in this sector has not been included in the priority list of the *Concept of the Russian Federation Foreign Policy* or it has been developing at a much slower space compared with energy cooperation.[4] From each of the three sectors mentioned above, the author has chosen one Russian TNC, which either has developed the most diversified strategy on the Latin American market or has implemented the most significant project.

Among energy companies, Rosneft was the first Russian investor in the region, and, moreover, is involved in an impressive set of FDI projects.[5] In the manufacturing sector, Russian–Latin American investment cooperation has been developing very slowly. The most prominent seems to be the electric power industry, and, therefore, this chapter focuses on the operations of Power Machines.[6] In the IT sector, Softline[7] was selected as it is Russia's leading IT investor in Latin American countries.

Research Findings

Rosneft

In 2001, Rosneft, a state-owned company, made its first OFDI in Latin America in Colombian oil extraction. It acquired 45 percent of the "Colombia energy" consortium, with two Colombian companies each holding a 27.5 percent share. In December 2002, the company started to develop the Surroriente oil field

(Rosneft 2016). However, two years later Rosneft quit the project due to security concerns flowing from the conflict between the Colombian Government and insurgents (Vedomosti 2004).

Despite its difficulties in the Colombian market, Rosneft's attempt to operate in Latin American market fueled interest by other Russian TNCs in the region. This is seen in Lukoil, a privately owned company, investing in Colombia in 2002. However, due to unsuccessful exploration results, an inability to find partners for further investments, and the remoteness of its Colombian investment from other projects, it sold its stake in 2012 (Lukoil 2016). The examples of Rosneft and Lukoil demonstrate how long distances impact their project developments. They also illustrate how the "Go Global" strategy of Russian TNCs led to geographical expansion, though it resulted in low benefits.

Rosneft's subsequent Latin American projects appeared to be more successful. In 2008, during the official visit of former President Dmitry Medvedev to Venezuela, Gazpromneft, Lukoil, Rosneft, Surgutneftegaz, and TNK-BP established the National Oil Consortium (NOC), with each founder possessing a 20 percent ownership. In 2009, NOC launched a joint venture (JV) called Petromiranda with a Venezuelan state-owned company, PdVSA, with PdVSA owning 60 percent of the JV and the rest belonging to NOC. The JV's purpose was to produce oil in the Junin-6 block in Orinoco, which has estimated reserves of 50 billion barrels. The planned investments for this project amounted to $25 billion.

Even though production at Junin-6 started in 2012, Surgutneftegaz sold its share to Rosneft. The profitability of the project was a controversial issue. In 2014, Lukoil decided to withdraw from NOC as well. Rosneft bought its share and thus became the major owner of NOC with 80 percent ownership (separately Rosneft earlier had purchased all of TNK-BP). According to non-official information, this deal was for less $200 million, the sum of Lukoil's initial investments in NOC (Interfax 2014). With this deal, all private Russian companies have quit the project.

The reasons for their withdrawal could be the following. First, they were disappointed with the project's revenues. Second, Petromiranda did not present core assets for the JV. Third, some of the private companies separately had begun to reduce their presence in Latin America. For example, Lukoil minimized its presence in Latin America in order to consolidate assets and focus on activities in Africa and Asia. We see another example of Lukoil's divestment strategy in the case of Mexico, where the company had established a representative office in 2015 and subsequently left the Mexican market (Lukoil 2016). All in all, it seems the creation of NOC is attributable primarily to geopolitical decisions. Moreover, the business risks were relatively high, as the Venezuelan partner was not ready for sophisticated technological development (Aalto 2012).

In addition to Petromiranda, Rosneft began to participate in four other JVs linked with oil extraction in Venezuela. Moreover, it bought assets of Precision Drilling Venezuela CA in order to increase the quality of drilling and thus decrease expenditures in its projects. Rosneft and PdVSA also signed two long-term oil delivery contracts. Furthermore, the two firms are developing JVs in oilfield services. According to Rosneft (2016), its investments in Venezuela between 2010 and 2014 reached $1.8 billion. It seems that the company is using its Latin American projects in order to diversify its business. Moreover, several experts argue that some of Rosneft's offshore oil fields in Russia are not so profitable in modern conditions and that Venezuela, with its huge oil reserves, is attractive for the company in the long term (Vzglyad 2015). Thus, it is trying to diversify its portfolio by buying assets in Latin America. The motivation seems to be efficiency-seeking. However, the profitability of projects in Venezuela is very uncertain in terms of contemporary oil price trends.

As a result of the aforementioned investments, Venezuela has become the main recipient of Rosneft FDI in Latin America. The company also is expanding its activities in Cuba. In 2014, Rosneft signed an exploration agreement with Cuba Petroleo and a year later it discussed the possibility of expanding their cooperation. Rosneft apparently is strengthening its presence elsewhere in Latin America, as it has purchased 100 percent in the Brazilian oil and gas field Solimoes, and has investment plans for Ecuador.

The "left turn" in Latin American states, especially where it was more radical, opened extra opportunities for state-owned Rosneft. Therefore, the rise of Russian OFDI in the region should not be explained by more favorable macroeconomic environment alone, but also by the change in the political climate of host countries as well. Support from the Russian Government allowed Russian companies to avoid political risks and concurrently linked investment projects closely to the development of state-to-state relations. Recent changes in the Venezuelan Parliament, where the opposition won a majority in December 2015, suggest future challenges for Russian business in the country. The contemporary political situation in the region as a whole seems to be unstable and that illustrates the negative effect of political factors on investment cooperation rather than the positive one which Russian companies were able to enjoy earlier. This is why one can hardly expect major expansion of Russian TNCs in the Latin American energy sector in the foreseeable future.

Power Machines

Power Machines is a privately owned power engineering company and one of the world's top ten industry leaders in terms of installed-equipment volume. It operates in 57 countries all around the world. Since the end of the 2000s, it has actively participated in governmental tenders related to the construction of hydropower and thermal power plants in Latin America, carrying out projects in Argentina, Brazil, Chile, Colombia, Cuba, Mexico, and Uruguay. The company has avoided the radical left-wing party-driven states because of their high political risks. Illustrating its risk aversion, the company operates in the Venezuelan market via its Argentinian partner IMPSA (Polpred 2009).

The majority of Power Machines' projects are related to trade – the exports of turbines and other equipment and the subsequent supply of construction and engineering services. The company's representatives in the Latin American market used to be responsible for supplying these services. However, the growth of its service exports pushed the firm to establish a permanent presence in Latin America in the form of representative offices in Argentina, Brazil, Chile, Colombia, and Mexico. Thus, the long distance between Russia and the Latin American market could partly be interpreted as a factor that encourages investments when the demand for services grows. To put it differently, in order to be closer to the client, the company decided to open representative offices as a first step in its internationalization process. The available evidence indicates that market-seeking motive was the driving force in the investment expansion of Power Machines in Latin America.

Russian–Latin American trade growth could be an essential factor enhancing Russian OFDI in the industrial sector of Latin America. However, the small share of industrial goods and high tech products in Russian exports to Latin America could be considered as a barrier to further investment growth (Kokorev 2013). A lack of market information because of long distance and fewer trade contacts also could be regarded as an obstacle. In this context, it is worth mentioning that tough competition between American, Chinese, and European TNCs in Latin America serves as another hindrance to Russian OFDI there.

Latin American countries opened their markets in the 1990s as a result of the prescriptions of the Washington Consensus and many foreign companies exploited the opportunity. At that time, due to its internal political and socioeconomic turmoil, Russia lost all its commercial ties with Latin America and began to re-establish links only in the 2000s. Given this, Russian TNCs could be perceived as latecomers, facing difficulties in these competitive Latin American markets.

Despite market challenges, Power Machines continued its expansion and launched a JV with Brazilian Fezer S.A. in 2015, taking a 51 percent in the JV called Power Machines Fezer S.A. (its Brazilian partner took 49 percent). The amount of the investment has not been disclosed. Power Machines considers Brazil as a promising market and a platform for developing its ties with other Latin American states. In addition to the Brazilian foothold, this firm has expanded its product mix and localized its production of hydropower equipment, which meets Brazilian requirements. Local operations allow the company to decrease its transportation costs and to shorten its delivery times. Finally, Power Machines could enhance its supply of service. Overall, the author concludes that both market-seeking and efficiency-seeking motives were behind the Power Machines' expansion in Latin America.

The political factor seems irrelevant in the case of Power Machines, though the company frequently participated in the activities of intergovernmental commissions as well as the Russian National Committee for Economic Cooperation with Latin American countries (CN CEPLA), a non-commercial partnership supported by the Russian Ministry of Foreign Affairs and the Chamber of Commerce and Industry of the Russian Federation (CN CEPLA 2016). The number of meetings at these institutions has been increasing lately, resulting in better dissemination of information on Latin American market potential to the Russian firms. However, these meetings primarily target large companies rather than SMEs. To conclude, one may argue that a certain level of indirect state support could have enhanced the investment initiatives of Russian industrial companies in Latin America. However, state visits seem to have a more substantial impact on Russia's state-owned TNCs than on private companies. Furthermore, the influence of state visits is more relevant in the left-wing driven countries of Latin America.

Softline

Softline, founded in 1993, is the fifth largest software provider in Russia (Softline 2016). The company's internationalization process started in 2001, when it established its first foreign unit in Belarus. As the company had already utilized the business opportunities in Russia and the neighboring states, Softline decided to go truly overseas and thus opened its first Latin American office in Venezuela in 2009. The political factor had some impact on its choice of host country. As Venezuela was a close ally of Russia, Softline received a favorable reception in Venezuela, with, it should be noted, 80 percent of the company's Venezuelan clients being governmental agencies and companies (CNews 2009), a clear indication that political support played a significant role. Moreover, in order to decrease expenditures, Venezuelan clients searched for new software providers such as Softline, which delivered cheaper services in comparison with Western companies.

Success in Venezuela resulted in Softline's further expansion in Latin America: Argentina (2010), Peru and Colombia (2011), Costa Rica (2012), Chile (2013), and Brazil (2014). The internationalization to these countries was determined by the relatively fast growth of their IT markets and the market-seeking motivation of the company.

It is noteworthy that in 2014 the company participated in business meetings organized during the visit of the Russian president Vladimir Putin to Argentina as well as Brazil in the framework of the BRICS summit. The participation in these meetings strengthened the presence of the company in the region. Therefore, the BRICS meetings, having a geopolitical context, encouraged the development of economic ties that resulted in rising attention towards the Russian companies. In addition, Softline also actively participates in the CN CEPLA meetings. As a whole, one may argue that soft power has played a certain role in Softline's development in the region.

Being challenged by the contemporary economic crisis in Russia, Softline emphasizes the importance of far-away foreign markets such as Latin America (Softline 2016). The purchase of Brazilian Compusoftware in January 2016 confirms the aforementioned conclusion. In fact, this acquisition took place within the framework of Softline's preparation for its initial public offering (IPO) (Vedomosti 2016). The company plans to use the same strategy in Mexico, but so far the harsh competition on the Mexican market has prevented Softline's expansion there.

Conclusions

Russian TNCs have relatively recently expanded their activities in Latin America. Traditional ties with Russia and the Latin American countries seriously declined during the period of the transformation in Russia in the 1990s, which is why Russian companies need to re-launch their activities in the region from scratch.

Russian–Latin American investment cooperation has developed only in few sectors. The energy sector dominates OFDI from Russia to this region, though there are several FDI projects in the mining, machinery, transport, and IT industries. The sectoral structure clearly demonstrates the influence of the home-country factor. More specifically, natural resource abundance, state intervention in the energy sector, and the dominance of oil and gas TNCs in Russia could explain the prevalence of energy projects as far as Russian–Latin American investment cooperation is concerned.

Case analysis reveals that Russian OFDI in Latin America can be explained by market- and efficiency-seeking motives. Russian TNCs also have expanded their businesses in Latin America to diversify, increase the scope of their activities, enhance their links with clients, and get a better access to growing markets. The acquisition of strategic knowledge or technologies has not been a critical driver of Russian TNCs in Latin America (Table 14.1).

Russian OFDI in the Latin American energy sector has been motivated, on the one hand, by the efficiency-seeking goals in order to benefit from geographically diversified activities. Russian companies, as latecomers, were faced with certain losses due to the lack of market information and ambitious goals to be global players. On the other hand, the political factor has a substantial impact on the operations of Russian energy TNCs in Latin America. As the majority of the energy-related projects did not appear to be economically viable, private companies withdrew their participation, and thus the author concludes that the presence of Rosneft in Latin American has a clear geopolitical foundation.

The political factor has been present in the internationalization process of state-owned Rosneft as well as in the international expansion of the studied private firms as investment in some Latin American countries would have been an almost impossible task without a political foundation. In some cases, FDI expansion is connected with host-country specific political factors. For example, the "left turn" in Latin America necessitated state support, especially in strongly leftist countries like Venezuela. A close relationship between Russia and these states provided unique opportunities for companies to cooperate, a fact evident beyond the energy sector alone. However, the "left turn" implied higher business risks, which, in many cases, constituted a substantial barrier to the internationalization for private companies. Nevertheless, an improvement of cooperation at the governmental level could strengthen business links via a dissemination of information about investment opportunities. Thus, the development of intergovernmental BRICS meetings caused the rising interest of Russian companies in the Brazilian market.

Table 14.1 The Motives and Determinants of Russian FDI in Latin America: Case Studies of Rosneft, Power Machines, and Softline

Company	Sector	Ownership	Internationalization mode	Political system of host countries	Motivation	Political factor	Long-distance effect	Latecomer effect
Rosneft	Energy	State-owned	Acquisition and JVs	Mostly left-wing party-driven	Efficiency-seeking	Significant	Negative	Negative
Power Machines	Manufacturing	Privately owned	Representative offices and later acquisition	Very few left-wing party-driven	Mostly market-seeking/ efficiency-seeking	Almost none	Both negative and positive	Negative
Softline	Information technology	Privately owned	Regional offices and later acquisition	Partly left-wing party-driven	Mostly market-seeking/ efficiency-seeking	Minor	Positive	None

We may assume that state visits have positively affected the operations of all the studied firms. However, this institutional aspect associated with Russian OFDI in Latin America requires further study. In-depth interviews as a research method might be used for this type of analysis in future investigations.

On the one hand, long distances were one of the reasons for relatively late investments by Russian TNCs in Latin America. The geographical distance between Russia and Latin America remains a barrier to Russian OFDI, especially for SMEs that lack market information and are largely left outside Russia's institutional framework supporting the internationalization of its larger firms. On the other hand, long distance may encourage FDI as well. Softline and Power Machines illustrate the positive impact of geographical distance, as these companies were forced to move closer to their clients, and thus they searched for opportunities to open representative offices as a precondition for their further expansion in Latin America.

The interest of Russian investors towards Latin America has been growing lately, albeit quite gradually. Russian TNCs have already accumulated valuable business experience. However, Russia's current economic crisis as well as the political turbulence in some Latin American countries restrains further expansion plans. More than that, taking into consideration that trade links stimulate investments, a decrease in Russian–Latin American trade relations in 2015 could be accompanied by the reduction of the Russian OFDI in Latin America in the foreseeable future.

Notes

1 One could make an assumption that a part of these Russian offshore investments to the Caribbean could be reinvested to other Latin American states, but there is no clear evidence or data available.
2 Several declarations concerning the prospects of Russian Railways company (RZD) in Argentina, Brazil, Ecuador etc., can be found. However, these declarations have not been realized yet (RZD 2015). One of the rare examples in the transportation is the acquisition of Peruvian Helisur, a helicopter transport company, by Russian UTair Aviation in 2009 (Delovoy Peterburg 2009).
3 In the telecommunications sector, there was only one rather unsuccessful story of Yota, which began operating in Peru and Nicaragua in 2009, but was forced to withdraw from these markets due to harsh competition and the redirection of its strategy in 2011 (Kuznetsov 2014). In 2015, Yota Devices announced the sale of YotaPhone2 in North America and South America (El Ruso Latino 2016).
4 Rusal, Severstal, and Mechel have been the main investors in Latin America. In 2004, Rusal founded a company in Guyana and later purchased a bauxite and aluminum plant, Alpart, in Jamaica (Rusal 2016). In 2010, Severstal bought 25 percent of the Brazilian iron ore company, SPG Mineracao, but had sold it by 2013 (Severstal 2016). In 2011, Mechel created a JV with Brazilian Cosipar. However, this investment was not carried out by Mechel itself but by its core owner Igor Zyuzin (Forbes 2010).
5 Gazprom has also actively expanded in Latin America. The company has participated in several projects in Bolivia, Cuba, and Venezuela. However, it has already quit some of these projects. Gazprom has also signed memorandums of understanding with Brazil, the Dominican Republic, and Ecuador. At the moment, the company does not intend to internationalize further in the region (Gazprom 2016).

6   Russian FDI to other industries was hard to find. However, one example can be given –
    i.e., Kamaz Latinoamerica, which conducted a project related to production of buses in
    Peru in 2014 (Kamaz 2016).
7   One can name the opening of a representative office of Omnicomm in Mexico in
    2015 (CNews 2015), as well as the internationalization of KGK-global in Brazil as
    examples of Russian investments in the information and communications technology
    in Latin America (Latukha, Panibratov & Safonova-Salvadori 2011). All in all, only
    few Russian IT companies have opened representative offices in Latin America; they
    usually operate in the region via their branches in the USA or employ a regional
    manager developing business from Russia. Such strategies are used, for example, by
    Kaspersky Lab (Kaspersky Lab 2016) and ABBYY (ABBYY 2016).

Bibliography

Aalto, P. 2012, *Russia's Energy Policies: National, Interregional and Global Levels*,
    Edward Elgar, Northampton, MA.
ABBYY 2016, viewed 15 March 2016, http://latam.abbyy.com/?noRedirect=1
Bertrand, O. & Betschinger, M. 2012, 'Performance of domestic and cross-border acquisi-
    tions: empirical evidence from Russian acquirers', *Journal of Comparative Economics*,
    vol. 40, no. 3, pp. 413–37.
Blank, S. & Kim, Y. 2015, 'Russia and Latin America: the new frontier for geopolitics,
    arms sales and energy', *Problems of Post-Communism*, vol. 62, no. 3, pp. 159–73.
Buckley, P.J., Clegg, J.L., Cross, A.R., Voss, H., Rhodes, M. & Zheng, P. 2008, 'Explaining
    China's outward FDI: an institutional perspective', in K.P. Sauvant (ed.), *The Rise of
    Transnational Corporations from Emerging Markets: Threat or Opportunity?*, Edward
    Elgar, Cheltenham, UK, and Northampton, MA.
Central Bank of Russia 2016, *Russian Direct Investment Abroad*, viewed 15 February
    2016, http://www.cbr.ru/statistics
CEPAL 2015, *La Inversión Extranjera Directa en América Latina y el Caribe*, CEPAL
    Report, United Nations, Santiago de Chile.
CN CEPLA 2016, viewed 15 March 2016, http://cncepla.ru/
CNews 2009, *Softline vyhodit na latinoamerikanskij rinok: ofic v Venezuele*, viewed 15
    March 2016, http://www.cnews.ru/news/line/softline_vyhodit_na_latinoamerikanskij
CNews 2015, *Omnicomm_otkryla predstavitelstvo v Meksike*, viewed 15 March 2016,
    http://www.cnews.ru/news/line/2015-09-24_omnicomm_otkryla_predstavitelstvo_v_
    meksike
Collins, D. 2013, *The BRIC States and Outward Foreign Direct Investment*, Oxford
    University Press, Oxford.
Cuervo-Cazurra, A. & Ramamurti, R. 2014, *Understanding Multinationals from Emerging
    Markets*, Cambridge University Press, Cambridge.
Davydov, V. 2014, 'Missiya, vipolnennaya s maksimalnim rezultatom', *Latinskaya
    Amerika*, no. 8, pp. 14–15.
Delovoy Petersburg 2009, *UTair priobrela vertoletnuyu kompaniyu v Peru*, viewed 15
    March 2016, http://www.dp.ru/a/2009/08/25/UTair_priobrela_vertoletn/
Dunning, J.H. 1993, *Multinational Enterprises and the Global Economy*, Addison-Wesley,
    Wokingham, Berkshire.
Dunning, J.H. 2000, 'The eclectic paradigm as an envelope for economic and
    business theories of MNE activity', *International Business Review*, vol. 9, no. 2,
    pp. 163–90.

Dunning, J.H. & Lundan, S.M. 2008, 'Institutions and the OLI paradigm of the multinational enterprise', *Asia Pacific Journal of Management*, vol. 25, no. 4, pp. 573–93.

Dunning, J.H., Kim, C. & Park, D. 2008, 'Old wine in new bottles: a comparison of emerging market TNCs today and developed country TNCs thirty years ago', in KP Sauvant (ed.), *The Rise of Transnational Corporations from Emerging Markets: Threat or Opportunity?*, Edward Elgar, Cheltenham, UK, and Northampton, MA.

El Ruso Latino 2016, viewed 15 March 2016, http://cncepla.ru/press-center/rusolatino/index.php

Filippov, S. 2011, 'Emerging Russian multinationals: innovation, technology, and internationalization', *Journal of East–West Business*, vol. 17, no. 2–3, pp. 184–94.

Forbes 2010, *Vladelets Mechela Zyuzin zakryl sdelku po priobreteniyu aktivov v Brazilii*, viewed 15 March 2016, http://www.forbes.ru/news/59451-vladelets-mechela-zyuzin-zakryl-sdelku-po-priobreteniyu-aktivov-v-brazilii

Fortescue, S. & Hanson, P. 2015, 'What drives Russian outward foreign direct investment?: Some observations on the steel industry', *Post-Communist Economies*, vol. 27, no. 3, pp. 283–305.

Gazprom 2016, viewed 15 March 2016, http://www.gazprom.ru/

Goldstein, A. 2007, *Multinational Companies from Emerging Economies: Composition, Conceptualization and Direction in the Global Economy*, Palgrave Macmillan, London.

Gymez-Mera, L., Kenyon, T., Margalit, Y. Reis, J.G. & Varela, G. 2015, *New Voices in Investment: A Survey of Investors from Emerging Countries*, World Bank, Washington, DC.

Hitt, M.A., Li, D. & Xu, K. 2015, 'International strategy: from local to global and beyond', *Journal of World Business*, vol. 51, no. 1, pp. 1–16.

Interfax 2014, '*LUKOIL' has Agreed the Sale of 20% for Rosneft in the Consortium in Venezuela*, viewed 15 March 2016, http://www.interfax.ru/business/399996

Kalotay, K. 2006, 'Outward foreign direct investment from Russia in a global context', *Journal of East–West Business*, vol. 11, no. 3–4, pp. 9–22.

Kalotay, K. 2008, 'Russian transnationals and international investment paradigms', *Research in International Business and Finance*, vol. 22, no. 2, pp. 85–107.

Kalotay, K. & Sulstarova, A. 2010, 'Modelling Russian outward FDI', *Journal of International Management*, vol. 16, no. 2, pp.131–42.

Kamaz 2016, viewed 15 March 2016, http://www.kamaz.ru/

Kaspersky Lab 2016, viewed 15 March 2016, http://www.kaspersky.ru/

Kheyfets, B.A. 2014, *Rossiya y BRICS: Noviye vozmojnosti dlya vzaimnih investiziy*, Publishing and trading Corporation «Dashkov and K°», Moscow.

Kokorev, V.M. 2013, 'Pryamii inostrannie investizii v Argentine', *Latinskaya Amerika*, no. 3, pp. 49–70.

Koval, A. 2009, 'Perspektivi razvitiya torgovo-ekonomicheskih otnosheniy Rossii so stranami Latinskoy Ameriki v usloviyah finansovogo krizisa', *Vestnik Sankt-Peterburgskogo universiteta*, Seriya 5: Ekonomika, no. 3, pp. 94–104.

Koval, A. 2011, 'Contemporary perspectives and trends in Russian–Brazilian relations', *Russian Analytical Digest*, no. 91, pp. 8–10, viewed 15 February 2016, http://www.css.ethz.ch/content/dam/ethz/special-interest/gess/cis/center-for-securities-studies/pdfs/RAD-91.pdf

Kroger, M. 2012, 'Neo-mercantilist capitalism and post-2008 cleavages in economic decision-making power in Brazil', *Third World Quarterly*, vol. 33, no. 5, pp. 887–901.

Kuznetsov, A.V. 2014, 'Geographia rossiyskih pryamih investiziy v Latinskoy Amerike', *Regionalniye issledovania*, no. 3(45), pp. 65–71.

Latukha, M., Panibratov, A. & Safonova-Salvadori, E. 2011, 'Entrepreneurial FDI in emerging economies: Russian SME strategy for Brazil', *Entrepreneurship and Innovation*, vol. 12, no. 3, pp. 201–12.

Lebedev, S., Peng, M.W., Xie, E. & Stevens, C.E. 2015, 'Mergers and acquisitions in and out of emerging economies', *Journal of World Business*, vol. 50, no. 4, pp. 651–62.

Lisitsyn, N.E., Sutyrin, S.F., Trofimenko, O.Y. & Vorobieva, I.V. 2005, 'Russian telecommunication company MTS goes to the CIS: an overview of Russia's largest corporations abroad', *Journal of East–West Business*, vol. 11, no. 3–4, pp. 129–47.

Liuhto, K. 2015, 'Motivations of Russian firms to invest abroad: how do sanctions affect Russia's outward foreign direct investment?', *Baltic Region*, vol. 4, no. 26, pp. 4–19.

Liuhto, K. & Majuri, S. 2014, 'Outward foreign direct investment from Russia: A Literature Review', *Journal of East–West Business*, vol. 20, no. 4, pp. 198–224.

Liuhto, K. & Vahtra, P. 2007, 'Foreign operations of Russia's largest industrial corporations: building a typology', *Transnational Corporations*, vol. 16, no. 1, pp. 117–44.

Lukoil 2016, viewed 15 March 2016, http://lukoil-overseas.ru/

Luna, J.P. & Filgueira, F. 2009, 'The left turns as multiple paradigmatic crises', *Third World Quarterly*, vol. 30, no. 2, pp. 371–95.

Matthews, J.A. 2002, 'Competitive advantages of the latecomer firm: a resource based account of industrial catch-up strategies', *Asia Pacific Journal of Management*, vol. 19, no. 4, pp. 467–88.

Mihailova, I. & Panibratov, A. 2012, 'Determinants of internationalization strategies of emerging market firms: a multilevel approach', *Journal of East–West Business*, vol. 18, no. 2, pp. 157–84.

Ministry of Foreign Affairs of Russia 2013, *Concept of the Foreign Policy of the Russian Federation*, viewed 15 March 2016, http://archive.mid.ru/brp_4.nsf/0/76389fec168189 ed44257b2e0039b16d

Ministry of Economic Development of Russia 2014, *Nakoplennie rossiyskie investizii na Kube sostavili poryadka 370 mln. dollarov*, viewed 15 March 2016, http://economy.gov. ru/minec/activity/sections/foreignEconomicActivity/201407104

Pezoldt, K. & Koval, A. 2012, 'Transformatsionnie prozessi v Latinskoy Amerike: prichini i tendenzii', *Latinskaya Amerika*, no. 9, pp. 4–18.

Polpred 2009, viewed 15 March 2016, http://polpred.com/?ns=1&ns_id=189499

Power Machines 2016, viewed 15 March 2016, http://www.power-m.ru/

Rosneft 2015, *Consolidated Financial Statements of Rosneft Oil Company for the Year Ended December 31, 2015 with Independent Auditor's Report*, viewed 15 March 2016, http://www.rosneft.com/attach/0/23/02/2015_Rosneft_FS_IFRS_ENG_SIGNED.pdf

Rosneft 2016, viewed 15 March 2016, www.rosneft.ru

Rugman, A. 2008, 'How global are TNCs from emerging markets?', in K.P. Sauvant (ed.), *The Rise of Transnational Corporations from Emerging Markets: Threat or Opportunity?*, Edward Elgar, Cheltenham, UK, and Northampton, MA.

Rusal 2016, viewed 15 March 2016, http://www.rusal.ru/

RZD 2015, viewed 15 March 2016, http://press.rzd.ru/smi/public/ru?STRUCTURE_ID=2

Sauvant, K.P. (ed.) 2008, *The Rise of Transnational Corporations from Emerging Markets: Threat or Opportunity?*, Edward Elgar, Cheltenham, UK, and Northampton, MA.

Sánchez Ramírez, P.T. 2010, 'Is a new climate of confrontation between Russia and the United States possible in Latin America?', *Latin American Policy*, vol. 1, no. 2, pp. 230–43.

Severstal 2016, viewed 15 March 2016, http://www.severstal.com/rus/index.phtml

Softline 2016, viewed 15 March 2016, http://www.softlinegroup.com/en/index.php

Stoian, C. 2013, 'Extending Dunning's Investment Development Path: the role of home country institutional determinants in explaining outward foreign direct investment', *International Business Review*, vol. 22, no. 3, pp. 615–37.

Tolentino, P.E. 2000, *Multinational Corporations: Emergence and Evolution*, Routledge, London.

UNCTAD 2015, *World Investment Report (WIR) 2015: Reforming International Investment Governance*, United Nations, New York & Geneva.

Vahtra, P. 2007, *Expansion or Exodus?: The New Leaders Among the Russian TNCs*, Pan-European Institute, University of Turku, Turku.

Vedomosti 2004, *Rosneft pokinula kolumbiyu*, viewed 15 March 2016, https://www.vedomosti.ru/newspaper/articles/2004/07/05/rosneft-pokinula-kolumbiyu

Vedomosti 2016, *Softline kupila brazilskuyu IT kompaniyu compusoftware*, viewed 15 March 2016, https://www.vedomosti.ru/technology/articles/2016/01/18/624326-softline-kupila-brazilskuyu-it-kompaniyu-compusoftware

Vzglyad 2015, *Rossiyskaya neftyanka prirastaet neftyu Latinskoy Ameriki*, viewed 15 March 2016, http://www.vz.ru/economy/2015/5/28/747830.html

Winter, J. & Scharmanski, A. 2009, '"Swing to the Left" and its impact on investment decisions in Latin America: the example of the energy sector in Bolivia and the commercial real estate market in Brazil', in T.N. Caldeira (ed.), *Economics of Developing Countries*, Nova Science, New York.

15 Does Ownership Matter in an OFDI Decision of a Russian Firm?

The Case of Russia's Ten Largest Investors Abroad

Kari Liuhto

Introduction

UNCTAD indicates that Russia's outward foreign direct investment (OFDI) stock[1] was non-existent, below $1 billion, when the USSR collapsed at the end of 1991. However, a unique growth has taken place, after the disintegration of the Soviet Union. Russian OFDI stock multiplied by 20-fold, both in the 1990s and the 2000s. As a result, the Russian OFDI stock exceeded $400 billion in the year 2010, and peaked in 2013, when the accumulated value of Russian investments abroad exceeded $500 billion; but, in 2014, a decline was experienced. Due to the drop of 2014, Russia's OFDI stock was on the level of 2010 at the end of 2014 (Table 15.1).

Due to such a rapid FDI expansion, Russia's share in the global OFDI stock jumped from a mere 0.10 percent in 1995, to 1.67 percent in 2014. Russia's annual FDI outflow figures lead us to assume that the aforementioned share is set to continue increasing since Russia's proportion of the global FDI outflows *per annum* has, on average, been 4.53 percent during this decade.

According to the Central Bank of Russia (CBR) (2015a), as of the end of 2014, two-thirds of Russian OFDI stock has landed in the EU, including Cyprus. However, the geographical distribution of the Russian OFDI stock should not be taken too literally, as a great part of the Russian OFDI does not stay in the first foreign country it has been invested in. It is impossible to state precisely how much Russian capital has stayed abroad, and how much has returned to Russia.

However, an analysis of six possible capital round-tripping countries, namely the Bahamas, Bermuda, the British Virgin Islands (BVI), the Cayman Islands, Cyprus, and Jersey sheds some light to this mystery. The share of the aforementioned six island states, in the Russian OFDI stock, was 40 percent at the end of 2014. Correspondingly, the share of these countries in the Russian inward foreign direct investment (IFDI) stock was practically the same (Central Bank of Russia 2015b). Due to such "islandization", the true amount of Russian FDI abroad at the end of 2014, was probably closer to $250 billion rather than $432 billion, a figure reported by UNCTAD. This "offshorization" of the Russian FDI also leads the author to conclude that one could probably

Table 15.1 Development of Russia's Annual FDI Outflow, OFDI Stock and Share of Possible Capital Round-tripping via Six Island States, 1995, 2000, 2005, 2010–14 ($ millions and percent)

	1995	2000	2005	2010	2011	2012	2013	2014
Russia's annual FDI outflow, $ millions*	358	3,050	12,767	52,616	66,851	48,822	86,507	56,438
Russia's share in the world's annual FDI outflow, percent*	0.10	0.27	1.45	3.85	4.21	3.80	6.62	4.17
Russia's OFDI stock, $ millions*	3,015	20,141	120,417	433,655	362,101	413,159	501,202	431,865
Russia's share in the world's OFDI stock, percent*	0.10	0.28	1.13	2.12	1.71	1.75	1.90	1.67
Share of six island states in Russia's OFDI stock, percent**	n.a.	n.a.	n.a.	57.08	51.83	52.48	54.11	42.34
Share of six island states in Russia's IFDI stock, percent**	n.a.	n.a.	n.a.	n.a.	57.90	57.58	50.71	42.90

Sources: *UNCTAD 2001, 2006, 2011, 2012, 2013, 2014, 2015; **Central Bank of Russia 2015a, 2015b

Note: The FDI figures are not constant in all the UNCTAD reports. The author has used the newest data provide by UNCTAD. The author has included six island states, namely the Bahamas, Bermuda, the British Virgin Islands, the Cayman Islands, Cyprus, and Jersey, to measure the share of possible capital round-tripping to and from Russia

reduce Russia's official IFDI stock by 40–50 percent, to discover the true size of Russia's IFDI stock.

The ten most outward-oriented investors account for one third of Russia's total OFDI stock (Kuznetsov 2015). Among them, one may find state-owned enterprises (SOEs), privately owned firms and several companies with substantial foreign ownership. Inspired by Kuznetsov's research, the author started to wonder to what extent ownership matters in the outward internationalization of Russian firms. In order to decipher this enigma, the author defines the research question as follows: What is the link between the ownership structure and the OFDI in Russia's ten leading non-financial investors abroad?

Review of Earlier Literature

Relationship between Ownership and an Investment Decision in the Russian Context

Filatotchev *et al.* (2001b) concluded that a large-block shareholding is negatively associated with a firm's investment activity and that this relationship does not depend on the identity of controlling shareholders. This finding was linked to investment activity in general, not investment activity towards foreign countries, in particular. In another study, Filatotchev *et al.* (2001a) found that managerial ownership is positively associated with external acquisitions. In this research, an external acquisition was not synonymous with a foreign acquisition. Although Filatotchev *et al.* (2001a, 2001b) investigated the relationship between ownership and an investment decision of a Russian enterprise, they did not address the ownership impact on the investment outside Russia, and thus these findings do not directly support the implementation of this research.

Liuhto and Majuri (2014) have identified approximately 100 studies that deal with Russian OFDI. Their literature review reveals that earlier studies have not specifically focused on the impact of ownership on a firm's OFDI decision. After the aforementioned literature review was published, one relevant study was found.

Tepavcevic (2015) analyzed OFDI motives of three Russian state-owned energy corporations, namely, Atomstroyexport, Gazprom, and Zarubezhneft. The author argues that the motives of the Russian state-controlled companies vary, depending on the location of OFDI. In developed countries, market- and technology-seeking motives dominate, whereas in less developed countries, they attempt to take advantage of inexpensive labor and the absence of foreign competitors. In addition, she claims that these Russian state-owned energy firms predominantly act in accordance with their business interests, rather than official Russian foreign policy. The article ends as follows: "Russian state interests may well be fulfilled in the long run, but largely as an unintentional outcome" (ibid., p. 54).

As the author of this research was unable to find any other relevant study – that is, empirically based firm-level research – concentrating on the impact of ownership on a Russian firm's OFDI decision, the researcher decided to review earlier findings related to the relationship of the ownership and an FDI decision of a firm, in a non-Russian context.

Relationship between Ownership and a Firm's OFDI Decision in a Non-Russian Context

Tihanyi *et al.* (2003) used several data sets to study approximately 200 US firms. Their study suggests that professional investment funds are interested in a firm's international strategy owing to the short-term performance, whereas pension funds are interested in a firm's internationalization, due to its long-term performance orientation. These scholars expect a stronger interest in exporting, licensing, and international joint ventures (JVs) on the part of professional investment funds, as these entry modes return their investment faster and their performance is easier to evaluate by an outside board of directors. Pension funds, however, may be supportive of acquisitions and greenfield ventures, which are longer-term efforts.

Zahra (2003) conducted two surveys among US manufacturing firms in 1997 and 2000. Over 400 firms were covered in these surveys. Zahra concluded that ownership is a significant variable that determines the degree and geographical scope of internationalization. Owner-managers are likely to proceed with internationalization if it improves their family's employment and involvement, despite the potential reduction in short-term payoffs as resources are shifted to support internationalization. The author continues that with high ownership comes the motivation to enhance the firm's long-term performance through internationalization.

The survey data from nearly 900 Swedish small and medium-sized enterprises (SMEs) reveals that internal owners, such as the CEO and other senior executives, tend to be risk averse and have a lower proclivity to increase scale and the scope of internationalization than do external owners, such as venture capitalists and institutional investors (George, Wiklund & Zahra 2005).

Fernandez and Nieto (2006) used large, firm-level panel data on Spanish SMEs collected by a Spanish ministry. They concluded that ownership type influences the decision to internationalize. They observed a negative relationship between family ownership and export intensity. However, a positive correlation was found between corporate block-holders and internationalization as a whole.

Lien *et al.* (2005) utilized a data set of over 200 publicly listed firms in Taiwan to investigate the impact of ownership on the OFDI decision. Their findings indicate that family control is positively associated with decisions to invest in China, whereas state and institutional ownership is positively associated with FDI in the rest of the world. They also reported that family-controlled firms[2] are significantly more likely to undertake FDI than foreign-controlled firms. They particularize that foreign-controlled firms are significantly less likely to undertake FDI in China than are family-controlled firms.

Filatotchev *et al.* (2007) studied Taiwanese firms investing in China as well. This research team found that share ownership by a foreign financial institution is associated with a high-commitment FDI strategy. Furthermore, they suggest that high levels of share ownership, by the family and domestic institutional investors, are associated with low levels of equity commitment abroad. The Sino-Taiwanese research context – that is, a cultural proximity between home and host country and the historical background – should be kept in mind before taking the findings of Lien *et al.* (2005) and Filatotchev *et al.* (2007) out of their research context.

Filatotchev, Stephan and Jindra (2008) hand-collected a data set of over 400 foreign-invested firms in Estonia, Hungary, Poland, Slovakia, and Slovenia. Their study suggests that the larger size of the foreign investors' equity stakes in local firms is positively associated with export intensity.

Bhaumik, Driffield, and Pal (2010) utilized a firm-level data set of almost 200 automotive firms and nearly 600 pharmaceutical firms under Indian ownership. Their results suggest that family firms and firms with concentrated ownerships are less likely to invest abroad. Moreover, Bhaumik, Driffield, and Pal concluded that the strategic equity holding of foreign investors facilitates OFDI.

Majocchi and Strange (2012) used a panel data of some 80 Italian firms over the period 2005–7. Their study shows that a high level of family ownership has a negative effect on international diversification. Furthermore, they found that a high level of state ownership results in less international diversification. The authors also report that financial institutional shareholdings do not have a significant effect upon international diversification.

Wang *et al.* (2012) employed two firm-level data sets when they studied the involvement of the Chinese Government in the OFDI of Chinese firms. Their research sample consisted of over 1,200 Chinese manufacturing enterprises that have invested in nearly 1,400 projects abroad. Their results partially support the assumption that government involvement through state ownership and government affiliation positively interacts with the OFDI. They suggest that state ownership plays a more important role in Chinese resource-seeking OFDI than in market-seeking OFDI. Another interesting finding is that type of government affiliation could be a more significant explanatory factor for determining OFDI than state ownership *per se.*

Ramasamy, Yeung, and Laforet (2012) analyzed approximately 60 Chinese firms. They found that SOEs are attracted to invest in countries with large natural resources and risky political environments, whereas private Chinese firms are more market-seekers. They conclude that existing theories can sufficiently explain actions of private Chinese enterprises, but adjustment is required to comprehend the behavior of state-controlled multinationals.

Cui and Jiang (2012) investigated the effect of state ownership on Chinese firms' FDI ownership decisions. They used primary date for over 130 FDI entries made by Chinese enterprises. They found that the firms with a high state ownership share prefer joint ownership structures when investing abroad.

Majocchi, Odorici, and Presutti (2013) exploited the data based on nearly 900 firms from Germany, France, Italy, Poland, and Spain. Their findings suggest that firms with a bank as first shareholder have a lower level of overall internationalization, compared to other firms. However, bank ownership has a positive effect on the scope of FDI – that is, it increases the number of foreign countries invested in. In their research context, institutional investors promote internationalization, even if mainly through FDI. In other words, their results suggest a positive link between an institutional investor and the FDI decision of a firm.

Using panel data for over 100 of the largest German manufacturing firms, Oesterle, Richta, and Fisch (2013) suggest a u-shaped relationship between the stake of the largest shareholder and a firm's internationalization. The authors conclude that the relationship between ownership concentration and the degree of internationalization is non-linear. The degree of internationalization is considered to be high when ownership concentration is either low or high. In the case of medium ownership concentration, the degree of internationalization is low. Such a u-shaped relationship is due to the different risk behavior of owners and managers in relation to internationalization, different preferences related to the degree of internationalization and a weaker possibility for owners to control managers' opportunistic behavior in firms with highly dispersed ownership.

Sheng and Pereira (2014) investigated the relationship between internationalization and ownership in over 400 Latin American multinationals. They found that greater internationalization via the equity entry mode is associated with lower levels of ownership concentration. In a pulverized ownership structure, shareholders do not have incentives to influence management; hence executives have greater freedom to pursue their own interests in moving towards internationalization. Their findings suggest that more dispersed ownership tends to promote internationalization via the equity entry mode.

On the basis of the literature review above, one may conclude that the research findings dealing with companies from the advanced economies seem to indicate a negative relationship between state ownership and a firm's OFDI decision, whereas the Chinese experience indicates a positive correlation. Second, the earlier literature suggests that external ownership tends to increase the likelihood of OFDI, while internal ownership, family ownership in particular, decreases it. Third, firms with concentrated ownership are less likely to undertake FDI than firms with a dispersed ownership structure. And, finally, foreign ownership seems to support the OFDI decision. Here, it should be noted that some researchers have recently suggested that there is non-linear correlation between ownership concentration and internationalization.

Accomplishment of Research

As a large survey of Russian firms was beyond the scope of this study and the appropriate data sets were not available to the researcher, this study focuses on Russia's largest investors abroad. Thus, the ranking created by Kuznetsov (2015) was chosen, as it presents ten non-financial Russian corporations with the largest assets abroad at the end of 2013, which is the newest list publicly available. Although two of the listed companies had their headquarters abroad, and hence do not meet the strictest definition[3] of a Russian firm, it was decided not to exclude them from the analysis, since these enterprises are controlled by Russians.

A selection of the ten largest non-financial corporations with the largest assets abroad does not offer a representative sample, and hence does not allow us to generalize the findings. From the perspective of a probability sampling, this research has limitations (Honigmann 1982). Even if the selected companies do not form a representative sample, they form an economically purposeful sample (Merriam 2009), as the studied companies account for a third of Russia's OFDI stock.

Data was collected from the case companies' websites. Annual reports were not used because the newest annual reports available describe the situation in

2014. At this point, it should be acknowledged that the ownership structures of companies evolve over time, and therefore it needs to be stressed that this section presents the most recent ownership structure publicly available. The data collection took place in the beginning of March 2016.

In reporting the research findings, this chapter refers to ownership by some of Russia's major capitalists – so-called oligarchs. Even if Forbes (2016) has listed the wealth of the world's billionaires for 30 years, the Forbes billionaire list[4] should be regarded as an approximate comparison rather than a scientifically precise measure of wealth. The Forbes figures should be treated as referential information.

Despite the limitations of the used methodology, this research nevertheless provides a fresh angle in the study of Russian OFDI, and hence may provide some insight for better comprehending the relationship between ownership and outbound investments by Russian firms.

Research Findings: Ownership History, Recent Ownership Structure, and International Activities of Case Companies

Nine out of Russia's ten largest outward investors can be found among the country's 25 largest corporations in terms of their 2014 turnover. Only one of these companies, namely Sovcomflot, was not included in Russia's 25 largest corporations. It ranked number 199 (Expert 2015). Russia's ten largest outward investors cover a third of Russia's total OFDI stock. Taking into account the extensive capital round-tripping back to Russia, one may assume that the share of these ten companies in Russia's genuine investments overseas is considerably larger than one third. Oil, gas, and metallurgy dominate the foreign assets of Russian firms. Telecommunications and transport have started to play an increasingly visible role in the outward capital expansion of Russian corporations, though the active international expansion of Russian telecommunications companies was observed by Lisitsyn *et al.* (2005) more than ten years ago. A short description of Russia's ten largest outbound investors and their ownership history, recent ownership structure, and international activities is given below.

Gazprom: In 1989, the Soviet Ministry of Gas Industry was converted into a corporation called Gazprom. The privatization of Gazprom started in 1994, but, in spite of this privatization, the Russian state still owns a bit more than a half of all Gazprom shares. The remaining shares are on free float (Gazprom 2016).

The corporation is the globe's leading natural gas producer. Gazprom is responsible for over a tenth of global gas production and nearly 70 percent of Russia's gas production. In 2014, Gazprom produced almost 450 billion cubic meters (bcm) of gas. Over 200 bcm of Gazprom's gas was exported, the main destination being the EU. Gazprom exports almost half of its gas production; however, nearly three-quarters of the corporation's gas sales revenues came from its exports, meaning that export prices are still higher than domestic gas prices within Russia. Gazprom has a presence in most European countries. In addition to Europe, Gazprom has established its presence in Africa, the Americas, and

Asia (Gazprom, 2016). In 2013, the total value of Gazprom's foreign assets exceeded $40 billion (Kuznetsov 2015).

VimpelCom: The company was founded by a Russian scientist and an American entrepreneur in 1992. In November 1996, VimpelCom became the first Russian firm, since 1903, to list its shares on the New York Stock Exchange. In December 1998, Telenor, a Norwegian state-controlled corporation, signed an agreement to acquire a 25 percent stake in VimpelCom, which at the time was close to bankruptcy. The Russian Alfa Group became a major owner in 2001. In October 2009, Altimo, a part of the Russian Alfa Group, and Telenor combined their holdings in VimpelCom and Kyivstar into a new jointly owned mobile telecoms operator, VimpelCom Ltd. This is resulted in Altimo owning 43.9 percent of the voting rights, Telenor 35.4 percent, and 20.7 percent was left on free float. In March 2016, LetterOne, the Luxembourg-based holding company of Altimo, possessed 47.9 percent and Telenor 43.0 percent of the voting rights, the remaining 9.1 percent being on free float.[5]

In 2010, VimpelCom moved its headquarters to Amsterdam, the Netherlands, and thus, following the strictest definition of nationality of a corporation, VimpelCom has since ceased to be a Russian firm. Even if the company headquarters are currently located in the Netherlands and the principal owner is officially from Luxembourg (VimpelCom 2016), the company can still be regarded as Russian, since it is controlled by Russia's second wealthiest billionaire, Mikhail Fridman (Forbes 2016).

The company is the world's seventh largest mobile service provider, in terms of customer base. The corporation has over 200 million customers in 14 countries. Russia is the main clientele base, with nearly 60 million customers. Russia is followed by Pakistan (39 million consumers), Bangladesh (31 million), the Ukraine (26 million), Italy (22 million), and Algeria (18 million). In 2013, VimpelCom's assets abroad were valued at nearly $40 billion (Kuznetsov 2015). It should be noted that the company's foreign expansion only began in 2004, when VimpelCom entered the Kazakh market (VimpelCom 2016).

Lukoil: In 1991, a governmental decree to establish the petroleum corporation LangepasUrayKogalymneft was issued. Two years later, the open Joint Stock Company Lukoil was founded, and in the same year, the company's privatization started. In 1995, Lukoil's charter capital was extended and an American company became an owner, with an 8 percent stake. A year later, Lukoil became one of the first Russian companies to issue American depositary receipts (ADRs). Currently, Lukoil is Russia's largest non-governmental company, in terms of turnover. The company's President Vagit Alekperov and Executive Director Leonid Fedun, together, hold a third of the company's shares (Lukoil 2016). US Conoco used to be a major owner in Lukoil with an ownership share up to 20 percent until rather recently (Farchy 2015b).

The corporation is one of the world's largest oil companies, accounting for around 1 percent of the proven hydrocarbon reserves and over 2 percent of the crude oil production globally. Lukoil's international projects cover 10 percent of the company's hydrocarbon reserves, 13 percent of production,

24 percent of staff, 32 percent of oil refining, and 82 percent of crude oil sales. The corporation's first international operation took place in Azerbaijan in 1994. Now, the company is present in over 30 countries (Lukoil 2016). The total value of Lukoil's foreign assets exceeded $30 billion in 2013 (Kuznetsov 2015).

Evraz: The company's history began with the establishment of a relatively small private company called Evrazmetall in 1992, which specialized in selling steel products. Alexander Abramov is considered to be the founder of Evraz. In 2005, the company's global depositary receipts (GDRs) started to be traded on the London Stock Exchange. A year later, Roman Abramovich became the major owner of the corporation (Ostrovsky 2006b), which he still is, with a 31 percent stake. Abramovich, together with five other Russian businessmen, own three-quarters of the company. In 2005, Evraz moved its headquarters to Luxembourg, and then to London six years later. Should the location of the company headquarters define the nationality of a firm, Evraz has not been a Russian enterprise for a decade now (Evraz 2016).

The company operates in the steel industry. Out of the enterprise's nearly 100,000 employees, a fifth work outside Russian borders. However, the share of foreign markets in Evraz's revenues exceeds one half. The Americas alone account for over a quarter of the company's revenues. The company started its expansion outside the former USSR in 2005, and is now present in eight foreign countries, namely Canada, the Czech Republic, Italy, Kazakhstan, South Africa, Switzerland, Ukraine, and the USA (Evraz 2016). At the end of 2013, Evraz's foreign assets totaled nearly $9 billion and, with that sum, the enterprise ranked fourth on the list of Russia's most active overseas investors (Kuznetsov 2015).

Rosneft: The State enterprise Rosneft was founded in 1993. Two years later, it was transformed into an open joint stock company. In the aftermath of the 1998 financial crisis, Rosneft was the first Russian company to place an issue of Eurobonds. In 2006, the firm conducted its initial public offering (IPO) on the London Stock Exchange. The offering raised over $10 billion – the largest IPO completed to date in Russia's oil and gas industry. Despite this IPO, Rosneft has remained an SOE, with nearly 70 percent still in the hands of the Russian Government. In spite of state control, British Petroleum (BP) possesses a large share of the company, around a fifth of the charter capital. The representatives of the board of directors and the members of the management committee hold a minor stake in the company (around 0.2 percent). Igor Sechin,[6] the corporation's president, owns a bit more than 0.1 percent of the company shares. In contrast to Lukoil, the ownership stake of the management in Rosneft is marginal (Rosneft 2016).

The corporation is Russia's largest oil producer, accounting for nearly 40 percent of the country's oil production and 6 percent of global oil production (ibid.). The group was domestic market-oriented until the early years of the millennium (Vahtra & Liuhto 2004), but its international expansion has since sped up.[7] By now, the company has established its presence in approximately

15 countries. Taking into consideration the company's substantial size, Rosneft has only lightly invested outside Russian borders. According to Kuznetsov (2015), the group's foreign assets were valued at $8.4 billion in 2013.

Sovcomflot (SCF): The organization was formed in 1973 to give the Soviet Ministry of the Maritime Fleet an opportunity to rent foreign vessels on long-term leases. In 1988, the joint stock commercial enterprise Sovcomflot was registered. SCF's founders were the Ministry of the Marine Fleet of the USSR and the country's leading shipping companies. After the disintegration of the USSR, the Russian Government became the sole owner of the company, and SCF has remained as a fully state-owned enterprise ever since (Sovcomflot 2016).

The enterprise is Russia's largest shipping company and one of the world's largest firms in the shipment of hydrocarbons. SCF has approximately 150 vessels, with a total deadweight of nearly 13 million tons. Oil tankers cover close to 95 percent of the company's deadweight tonnage. SCF owns 11 fully owned subsidiaries abroad, four of them being registered in Liberia, another four in Cyprus, and one in Spain, Switzerland, and the United Kingdom respectively (ibid.). The firm's foreign assets exceed $5 billion (Kuznetsov 2015). Flagging ships overseas (i.e. tax planning) seems to play a leading role in the overall internationalization of Sovcomflot.

Severstal: 1955 is considered to be the founding year of Cherepovets Steel Mill. In 1993, State Enterprise Cherepovets Steel Mill was registered as the Joint Stock Company Severstal and, a little later, the company's privatization phase began. Severstal's privatization process during the mid-1990s has not been made entirely clear to the public (Ostrovsky 2006a). It is apparent that Alexey Mordashov bought shares in the company from the workers and benefited from the support of the previous director of the plant. As a result, Mordashov controls around 80 percent of the firm's share capital (Severstal 2016).

The corporation is one of the world's leading steel companies. Severstal has assets in Belarus, Italy, Kazakhstan, Latvia, Liberia, Poland, Russia, and Ukraine. Russia accounts for two-thirds of the company's sales, while the remaining third of the revenues comes from exports. Europe, excluding Russia, represented a fifth of the enterprise's total sales, in 2014 (ibid.). According to Kuznetsov (2015), Severstal's foreign assets amounted to approximately $4.8 billion at the end of 2013.

Rusal: The Russian aluminum industry was in disorder in the 1990s. After a turbulent decade the assets of Sibirsky Aluminium, owned by Oleg Deripaska, and Millhouse Capital, controlled by Roman Abramovich, were combined to form a new company, Rusal, in 2000. Seven years later the company went through a major reorganization. Currently, four major owners are En+ (Oleg Deripaska), Onexim (Mikhail Prokhorov), SUAL (a part of the Rusal Group), and Amokenga Holdings (controlled by foreign-owned Glencore). Despite 8.8 percent of the ownership of belonging to Glencore, Rusal is, without any doubt, a Russian-controlled corporation, as more than three-quarters of the company's shareholding belong to Russian billionaires (Rusal 2016).

The corporation is the world's largest producer of aluminum. It accounted for nearly 7 percent of the global aluminum output, in 2014. Rusal's internationalization began in 2002, when the company acquired a foil mill in Armenia and a mining complex in Guinea. To date, the company has established its business presence in a dozen foreign countries, namely Armenia, Australia, China, Guinea, Guyana, Ireland, Italy, Jamaica, Kazakhstan, Nigeria, Sweden, and Ukraine (ibid.). The value of Rusal's foreign assets was around $3.7 billion, as of 2013 (Kuznetsov 2015).

Russian Railways (RZD): Russia's first railway line was erected between Saint Petersburg and Tsarskoye Selo, the Czar's summer residence, in 1837. Five years later, Russia's Czar held a meeting, which is regarded as the first initiative to develop the railway system in Russia. However, due to the Russian state's inability to finance a comprehensive railroad network, all railroads in Russia were owned by private companies by the early 1880s. After the socialist revolution in 1917, all railroads became government-owned by the USSR. Russian Railways was formally established in 2003, when a decree was passed to remove the railways from the Russian Ministry of the Means of Communication. Nowadays, RZD is fully owned by the Russian state (Russian Railways 2016).

The corporation, with over 800,000 employees, is one of the core companies of Russian society. It is responsible for a quarter of the country's total passenger turnover and nearly 90 percent of Russia's total freight turnover, excluding pipeline transport. Russian Railways currently carries passengers to 20 countries in Europe and Asia (ibid.). According to Kuznetsov (2015), the foreign assets of RZD totaled approximately $3.2 billion, as of the end of 2013.

Sistema: The firm was founded as a private investment company, in 1993. In 2005, Vladimir Evtushenkov became the company's president. Now, he owns over 60 percent of Sistema, while the remainder of the shares are on free float in both Russia and abroad. Sistema can be characterized as a family-owned business. Felix Evtushenkov, the son of the main owner, is also involved in the company's management (Sistema 2016).

This conglomerate is involved in telecommunications and more than ten other industry fields. MTS, Russia's leading mobile operator, is the most distinguished company controlled by Sistema. Over 60 percent of Sistema's revenues came from the telecommunications business in 2014 (ibid.). According to Kuznetsov (2015), the value of Sistema's foreign assets was almost $3.0 billion.

To summarize, SOEs play a visible role among Russia's ten leading corporations with foreign assets. Four out of these ten corporations can be regarded as SOEs. One of them is Russia's leading gas producer; another is Russia's leading oil producer; and two others operate in transportation (maritime and rail transport). The remaining six companies are privately owned. Three of them, namely Evraz, Severstal, and Sistema, can be classified as family businesses. Even if a few of the studied companies possess a notable foreign ownership, none of them is under foreign control; even VimpelCom is, in reality, in Russian hands. Several Russian billionaires are involved in the majority of the private firms described above (see Table 15.2).

Table 15.2 Russia's Ten Leading Non-financial Investors Abroad and Their Ownership Structure, 2013 ($ millions)

Company, founding year; industry, location of headquarters	Foreign assets 2013, $ millions*	Ownership structure (based on data available on the company website in March 2016)**
Gazprom, 1989/1993, oil and gas, Moscow	40,128	State-owned: Russian Government 50.2 percent, the rest being on free float. Apart from the Russian Government and companies controlled by it, no one has registered an ownership exceeding 5 percent at the end of 2014
VimpelCom, 1992, telecom, Amsterdam	36,948	Foreign-owned: LetterOne (a Luxembourg-based holding company of Russian Altimo) 47.9 percent; Telenor (a Norwegian state-controlled company) 43.0 percent; free float 9.1 percent of voting rights in March 2016
Lukoil, 1991/1993, oil and gas, Moscow	32,640	Privately owned: the Lukoil management 34 percent (Vagit Alekperov 22.67 percent and Leonid Fedun 9.78 percent), treasury shares 11 percent, others 55 percent at the end of 2014
Evraz, 1992, ferrous metallurgy, London	8,715	Privately owned: ultimate beneficial owners are Roman Abramovich 31.28 percent, Alexander Abramov 21.79 percent, Alexander Frolov 10.88 percent, Gennady Kozovoy 5.95 percent, Alexander Vagin 5.89 percent, Eugene Shvidler 3.11 percent, on free float 21.0 percent in October 2015
Rosneft, 1993, oil and gas, Moscow	8,399	State-owned: fully state-owned Rosneftegaz 69.50 percent, National Settlement Depository 30.10 percent (BP 19.75 percent), individuals 0.40 percent in February 2016
Sovcomflot (SFC), 1973/1988, maritime transport, St Petersburg	5,293	State-owned: Russian Government 100 percent in March 2016
Severstal, 1955/1993, metallurgy, Cherepovets/Moscow	4,784	Privately owned: Alexey Mordashov holds 79.2 percent, on free float 20.8 percent in March 2016
Rusal, 2000, metallurgy, Moscow	3,655	Privately owned: En+ 48.13 percent, Onexim 17.02 percent, SUAL Partners 15.80 percent, Amokenga Holdings (Glencore) 8.75 percent, management 0.26 percent, free float 10.04 percent in March 2016
Russian Railways (RZD), 1837/ 2003, rail transport, Moscow	3,222	State-owned: Russian Government 100 percent in March 2016
Sistema, 1993, conglomerate, Moscow	2,966	Privately owned: Vladimir Evtushenkov 64.2 percent, Deutsche Bank (GDR Program) 17.6 percent, Moscow Exchange 9.5 percent, Sistema Finance Investments 0.8 percent, Sistema Holding Ltd. 1.4 percent and others 6.5 percent at the end of 2014
Total 10	**146,750**	

Sources: *Kuznetsov 2015, p. 29; **websites of each company

Note: Even if the table above does not show any foreign ownership in Gazprom and Lukoil, notable foreign ownership participation is present. In addition, one should not forget that some of the companies listed in the table have taken a substantial amount of loans from foreign banks, creating some uncertainty about the future ownership structure

Conclusions

Russia's leading outbound investors bring new information to the discussion on the relationship between ownership structure and OFDI decision of a firm. First, the findings of this study do not unanimously support the earlier conclusions that state ownership results in lesser investment abroad, as four out of ten of the most OFDI-oriented Russian corporations are under state control. These four SOEs represent nearly 40 percent of the total value of foreign assets of the studied firms, or more than 10 percent of the total value of Russia's OFDI stock at the end of 2013. Taking these figures into consideration, it would be incorrect to argue that state ownership would be a barrier to investment abroad. However, we should acknowledge here that industry membership may possess stronger explanatory power than the ownership structure of the company. In other words, it well may be that Russian oil and gas companies would have more actively invested abroad without their state ownership.

Privately owned companies dominate the studied firms as they own about 60 percent of the foreign assets of the studied companies. When one compares the role of private and state ownership, attention should be paid to the fact that state ownership becomes overemphasized when dealing with the internationalization of Russia's largest corporations. Taking into account that thousands of private Russian SMEs have invested abroad, one should not exaggerate the role of the Russian Government in the overall phenomenon. However, if it is assumed that private corporations are behind the majority of the capital round-tripping, which accounts for roughly 40 percent of Russia's OFDI stock, this may lead to a situation where up to a quarter of Russia's "real" foreign assets could be in the hands of Russian SOEs. This would, nevertheless, mean that three-quarters of Russia's OFDI stock would still be in private hands, and thus the author argues that Russian OFDI continues to be dominated by private corporations with versatile relations to government policies (e.g., Liuhto & Vahtra 2007).

Three of the studied corporations can be characterized as family-owned firms despite their enormous size. Perhaps, the giant company size and the fast and relatively easy generation of massive wealth over the past 25 years have made it psychologically easier for their owners to expand abroad. The situation would probably be different if all Russian firms that have invested abroad were analyzed; a large survey among the Russian firms would be needed to shed more light on the impact of ownership on Russian outbound investments.

The observations made in this study challenge the earlier findings that firms with concentrated ownership are less likely to undertake outbound FDI. Practically all of Russia's leading outward investors have a concentrated ownership structure, reflecting either government supremacy or oligarchic dominance over key Russian corporations. It could further be argued that the accumulated wealth and concentrated ownership has made it easier for Russia's largest corporations to expand abroad as the decision-making process is faster, they possess sufficient capital, and the major private owners of contemporary Russian companies cannot be viewed as risk averse. On the contrary, the contemporary oligarchs would probably not be in their current positions if they had been overly sensitive to risk taking, particularly in the 1990s.

The findings of this study tentatively support earlier conclusions that foreign ownership may support the FDI decision. In light of the findings of this research, it may be presumed that American ownership in Lukoil, British ownership in Rosneft, Norwegian ownership in VimpelCom, and Swiss ownership in Rusal may have enhanced the outbound investments of these companies. It is worth noting that foreigners occupy more than one third of the board seats in all of the aforementioned corporations, indicating that foreign management participation may have played a role in the strategic OFDI decisions of these firms.

The review of earlier literature on the relationship between ownership and a firm's OFDI offered ambiguous research evidence. Moreover, some of the earlier studies emphasized the non-linear association between the ownership structure and FDI behavior of a firm (Oesterle, Richta & Fisch 2013). Some researchers have even questioned the causality between corporate characteristics and a firm's internationalization (e.g. Buckley, Devinney & Louviere 2007; Oxelheim *et al.* 2013). In other words, it is not completely clear whether a certain ownership type enhances a firm's FDI decision, or *vice versa*, whether a firm's investment abroad affects its ownership structure.

The author of this study considers the FDI behavior of a firm to be so dynamic and complex a phenomenon that conclusions should not be derived from the analysis of some corporate features, such as the ownership structure, alone. In other words, it is recommended that research should focus more on studying organizational behavior instead of organizational genetics – and that, in the future, more attention should be paid to studying the execution of internationalization strategies rather than analyzing corporate characteristics, which can be either a cause or a consequence of an FDI decision.

Notes

1 FDI is defined as investment by a resident entity in one economy that reflects the objective of obtaining a lasting interest in an enterprise resident in another economy. The lasting interest implies the existence of a long-term relationship between the direct investor and the enterprise and a significant degree of influence by the direct investor on the management of the enterprise. The ownership of at least 10 percent of the voting power, representing the influence by the investor, is the basic criterion used. Hence, control by the foreign investor (ownership of more than 50 percent of the voting power) is not required. In turn, an OFDI stock is the accumulated total FDI of the reporting economy held abroad (OECD 2010).

2 According to the European Commission (2016), the definition of family business is as follows: "The majority of decision-making rights are in the possession of the natural person(s) who established the firm, or in the possession of the natural person(s) who has/have acquired the share capital of the firm, or in the possession of their spouses, parents, child, or children's direct heirs.... Listed companies meet the definition of family enterprise if the person who established or acquired the firm (share capital) or their families or descendants possess 25 per cent of the decision-making rights mandated by their share capital.... At least one representative of the family or kin is formally involved in the governance of the firm."

3 No commonly accepted definition of a corporate nationality exists. Muth (2014) lists a few corporate characteristics, such as place of incorporation, place of headquarters, place of maximum workers employed, place of maximum net revenue earned, place of maximum gross revenue earned, place of maximum shareholder presence, and place of regulatory authority over securities transactions, which can be used to determine the nationality of a firm.

4 The majority of the Russians mentioned in this article can be found in the Forbes list of billionaires. All in all, Forbes named, in the beginning of 2016, approximately 1,800 billionaires in the world, out which 77 were Russians. The real number of billionaires in Russia could be higher, as some Russians do not want to end up on the Forbes list for political reasons.

5 In October 2015, Telenor published a plan concerning selling its stake in Vimpelcom (Thomas 2015). The sale has so far been postponed due to the ongoing legal process involving VimpelCom (Chopping & Malkenes 2016).

6 Forbes (2016) does not list Igor Sechin among Russia's 77 billionaires. Despite his absence in the list, Sechin probably exercises more economic decision-making power than the majority of the billionaires ranked in the list.

7 Rosneft's acquisition of the Yukos assets in 2007 has probably increased Rosneft's internationalization (Farchy 2015a), since, prior to the arrest of Mikhail Khodorkovsky in October 2003, Yukos used to be one of the most international Russian enterprises (Vahtra & Liuhto 2004).

Bibliography

Bhaumik, S.K., Driffield, N. & Pal S. 2010, 'Does ownership structure of emerging-market firms affect their outward FDI?: The case of the Indian automotive and pharmaceutical sectors', *Journal of International Business* Studies, vol. 41, no. 3, pp. 437–50.

Buckley, P.J., Devinney, T.M. & Louviere, J.J. 2007, 'Do managers behave the way theory suggests?: A choice-theoretic examination of foreign direct investment location decision-making', *Journal of International Business Studies*, vol. 38, no. 7, pp. 1069–94.

Central Bank of Russia 2015a, *Russian Direct Investment Abroad: Stocks Broken Down by Instrument and Country (Asset/Liabilities Principle)*, viewed 5 March 2016, http://www.cbr.ru/Eng/statistics/?PrtId=svs

Central Bank of Russia 2015b, *Foreign Direct Investment in the Russian Federation: Stocks Broken Down by Instrument and Country (Asset/Liabilities Principle)*, viewed 5 March 2016, http://www.cbr.ru/Eng/statistics/?PrtId=svs

Chopping, D. & Malkenes, K. 2016, 'Telenor awaits VimpelCom settlements', *The Wall Street Journal*, 17 February, viewed 5 March 2016, http://www.wsj.com/articles/telenor-awaits-vimpelcom-settlements-1455747141

Cui, L. & Jiang, F. 2012, 'State ownership effect on firms' FDI ownership decisions under institutional pressure: a study of Chinese outward-investing firms', *Journal of International Business Studies*, vol. 43, no. 3, pp. 264–84.

European Commission 2016, *Family Business*, European Commission, viewed 5 March 2016, http://ec.europa.eu/growth/smes/promoting-entrepreneurship/we-work-for/family-business/index_en.htm

Evraz 2016, viewed 5 March 2016, https://www.evraz.com/

Expert 2015, *Эксперт 400 – рейтинг ведущих российских компаний*, viewed 10 October 2015, http://expert.ru/ratings/rejting-krupnejshih-kompanij-rossii-2014-po-ob_emu-realizatsii-produktsii/

Farchy, J. 2015a, 'Rosneft settles legal dispute with Yukos shareholders', *Financial Times*, 1 April, viewed 7 March 2016, http://www.ft.com/intl/cms/s/0/e95c3cd4-d87b-11e4-ba53-00144feab7de.html#axzz42E0XftJi

Farchy, J. 2015b, 'Conoco quits Russia after 25 years', *Financial Times*, 22 December, viewed 24 March 2016, http://www.ft.com/intl/cms/s/0/01a4e6d2-a811-11e5-955c-1e1d6de94879.html

Fernandez, Z. & Nieto, M.J. 2006, 'Impact of ownership on the international involvement of SMEs', *Journal of International Business Studies*, vol. 37, no. 3, pp. 340–51.

Filatotchev, I., Stephan, J. & Jindra, B. 2008, 'Ownership structure, strategic controls and export intensity of foreign-invested firms in transition economies', *Journal of International Business Studies*, vol. 39, no. 7, pp. 1133–48.

Filatotchev, I., Dyomina, N., Wright, M. & Buck, T. 2001a, 'Effects of post-privatization governance and strategies on export intensity in the former Soviet Union', *Journal of International Business Studies*, vol. 32, no. 4, pp. 853–71.

Filatotchev, I., Kapelyushnikov, R., Dyomina, N. & Aukutsionek, S. 2001b, 'The effects of ownership concentration on investment and performance in privatized firms in Russia', *Managerial and Decision Economics*, vol. 22, no. 6, pp. 299–313.

Filatotchev, I., Strange, R., Piesse, J. & Lien, Y-C. 2007, 'FDI by firms from newly industrialized economies in emerging markets: corporate governance, entry mode and location', *Journal of International Business Studies*, vol. 38, no. 4, pp. 556–72.

Forbes 2016, *The World's Billionaires*, viewed 5 March 2016, http://www.forbes.com/billionaires/list/#version:static_country:Russia

Gazprom 2016, viewed 5 March 2016, http://www.gazprom.com/

George, G., Wiklund, J. & Zahra, S.A. 2005, 'Ownership and the internationalization of small firms', *Journal of Management*, vol. 31, no. 2, pp. 210–33.

Honigmann, J.J. 1982, 'Sampling in ethnographic fieldwork', in RG Burgess (ed.), *Field Research: A Sourcebook and Field Manual*, Allen and Unwin, London.

Kuznetsov, A. 2015, 'The Baltics in the geography of the largest transnational corporations of Europe', *The Baltic Region*, vol. 1, no. 23, pp. 25–35.

Lien, Y-C., Piesse, J., Strange, R. & Filatotchev, I. 2005, 'The role of corporate governance in FDI decisions: evidence from Taiwan', *International Business Review*, vol. 14, no. 6, pp. 739–63.

Lisitsyn, N.E., Sutyrin, S.F., Trofimenko, O.Y. & Vorobieva, I.V. 2005, *Outward Internationalisation of Russian Leading Telecom Companies*, Pan-European Institute, University of Turku, Turku.

Liuhto, K.T. & Majuri, S.S. 2014, 'Outward foreign direct investment from Russia: a literature review', *Journal of East–West Business*, vol. 20, no. 4, pp. 198–224.

Liuhto, K. & Vahtra, P. 2007, 'Foreign operations of Russia's largest industrial corporations: building a typology', *Transnational Corporations*, vol. 16, no. 1, pp. 117–44.

Lukoil 2016, viewed 5 March 2016, http://www.lukoil.com/

Majocchi, A., Odorici, V. & Presutti, M. 2013, 'Corporate ownership and internationalization: the effects of family, bank and institutional investor ownership in the UK and in continental Europe', *Corporate Ownership & Control*, vol. 10, no. 2, pp. 721–32.

Majocchi, A. & Strange, R. 2012, 'International diversification: the impact of ownership structure, the market for corporate control and board independence', *Management International Review*, vol. 52, no. 6, pp. 879–900.

Merriam, S. 2009, *Qualitative Research: A Guide to Design and Implementation (Revised and Expanded from 'Qualitative Research and Case Study Applications in Education')*, Jossey-Bass (Wiley), Hoboken, NJ.

Muth, K.A. 2014, 'The puzzle of corporate nationality', *Global Policy*, 29 April, viewed 3 March 2016, http://www.globalpolicyjournal.com/blog/29/04/2014/puzzle-corporate-nationality

OECD 2010, *FDI Flows and Stocks, OECD Factbook 2010: Economic Environmental and Social Statistics*, viewed 10 October 2015, http://www.oecd-ilibrary.org/sites/factbook-2010-en/03/02/01/index.html?itemId=/content/chapter/factbook-2010-28-en

Oesterle, M-J., Richta, H.N. & Fisch, J.H. 2013, 'The influence of ownership structure on internationalization', *International Business Review*, vol. 22, no. 1, pp. 187–201.

Ostrovsky, A. 2006a, 'Severstal chief makes his mark with share deal', *Financial Times*, 27 May, viewed 10 October 2015, http://www.ft.com/intl/cms/s/0/d0040c84-ed1c-11da-a307-0000779e2340.html#axzz3obXpqa6m

Ostrovsky, A. 2006b, 'Abramovich takes 41% of Evraz and looks abroad', *Financial Times*, 20 June, viewed 10 October 2015, http://www.ft.com/intl/cms/s/0/b8efd2be-fff8-11da-93a0-0000779e2340.html#axzz3ok5G7ck7

Oxelheim, L., Gregoric, A., Randoy, T. & Thomsen, S. 2013, 'On the internationalization of corporate boards: the case of Nordic firms', *Journal of International Business Studies*, vol. 44, no. 3, 173–94.

Ramasamy, B., Yeung, M. & Laforet, S. 2012, 'China's outward foreign direct investment: location choice and firm ownership', *Journal of World Business*, vol. 47, no. 1, pp. 17–25.

Rosneft 2015, viewed 5 March 2016, http://www.rosneft.com/

Rusal 2016, viewed 5 March 2016, http://www.rusal.ru/en/

Russian Railways 2016, viewed 5 March 2016, http://eng.rzd.ru/

Severstal 2016, viewed 5 March 2016, http://www.severstal.com/eng/

Sheng, H.H. & Pereira, V.S. 2014, 'Effects of internationalization on ownership structure: evidence from Latin American firms', *BAR Brazilian Administration Review*, vol. 11, no. 3, pp. 323–39.

Sistema 2016, viewed 5 March 2016, http://www.sistema.com/domashnjaja-stranica/

Sovcomflot 2016, viewed 5 March 2016, http://www.scf-group.com/en/

Tepavcevic, S. 2015, 'The motives of Russian state-owned companies for outward foreign direct investment and its impact on state-company cooperation: observations concerning the energy sector', *Transnational Corporations*, vol. 23, no. 1, pp. 29–58.

Thomas, D. 2015, 'Telenor to sell USD 2.3bn VimpelCom stake', *Financial Times*, 5 October, viewed 10 October 2015, http://www.ft.com/intl/cms/s/0/d8b85b90-6b4e-11e5-8171-ba1968cf791a.html

Tihanyi, L., Johnson, R.A., Hoskisson, R.E. & Hitt, M.A. 2003, 'Institutional ownership differences and international diversification: the effects of boards of directors and technological opportunity', *Academy of Management Journal*, vol. 46, no. 2, pp. 195–211.

UNCTAD 2001, *World Investment Report (WIR) 2001: Promoting Linkages*, United Nations, New York & Geneva.

UNCTAD 2006, *World Investment Report (WIR) 2006: FDI from Developing and Transition Economies*, United Nations, New York & Geneva.

UNCTAD 2011, *World Investment Report (WIR) 2011: Non-Equity Modes of International Production and Development*, United Nations, New York & Geneva.

UNCTAD 2012, *World Investment Report (WIR) 2012: Towards a New Generation of Investment Policies*, United Nations, New York & Geneva.

UNCTAD 2013, *World Investment Report (WIR) 2013: Global Value Chains: Investment and Trade for Development*, United Nations, New York & Geneva.

UNCTAD 2014, *World Investment Report (WIR) 2014: Investing in the SDGs: An Action Plan*, United Nations, New York & Geneva.

UNCTAD 2015, *World Investment Report (WIR) 2015: Reforming International Investment Governance*, United Nations, New York & Geneva.

Vahtra, P. & Liuhto, K. 2004, *Expansion or Exodus?: Foreign Operations of Russia's Largest Corporations*, Pan-European Institute, University of Turku, Turku.

VimpelCom 2016, viewed 5 March 2016, http://www.vimpelcom.com/

Wang, C., Hong, J., Kafouros, M. & Wright, M. 2012, 'Exploring the role of government involvement in outward FDI from emerging economies', *Journal of International Business Studies*, vol. 43, no. 7, pp. 655–76.

Zahra, S.A. 2003, 'International expansion of US manufacturing family businesses: the effect of ownership and involvement', *Journal of Business Venturing*, vol. 18, no. 4, pp. 495–512.

16 Conclusion

Sergei Sutyrin

An international team of social scientists contributing to this book investigated Russian participation in an extremely dynamic process of the international investment cooperation. In the majority of chapters, the authors used a geographical perspective with a special focus on Russia's investment to individual countries, such as China, Estonia, Finland, the Republic of Korea, Sweden, and the USA, or regions, such as the EU, the EAEU, and Latin America. In addition to the regional focus, the chapters vary in their selection of theoretical framework (OLI paradigm, institutionalism, network industry concept, and others), the methodology (qualitative versus quantitative research approach), direction of FDI flows (inbound versus outbound, or sometimes both), more or less distinctive emphasis on particular MNEs, individual industries, etc.

Such a diversity of approaches results in a rather comprehensive picture of the Russian role in the global FDI arena, though the authors are fully aware that a number of research lacunas remain. For example, the book does not deal with Russian OFDI in Africa or the Middle East and it does not cover some industries, such as agriculture. The main reason for their exclusion is their minor role in both Russia's inbound and outbound FDI flows.

With good reason, one may argue that the detailed discussion on different experiences and practices recounted in the chapters could provide a reader a meaningful payoff. The chapters of the book clearly demonstrate how the specificities of the context truly matter. This largely relates to gradually growing complexity of the process as well as the expanding diversity of interests among stakeholders, frequently reaching the level of an open rivalry. Under the circumstances, one should definitely take into consideration the risk that a certain number of generalizations could become excessively simplified. At the same time, despite the miscellany of particular experiences, certain similarities are discernible among the issues arising in each of the chapters. They could be summarized as follows.

During the past 15 years, the Russian Federation has experienced substantial ups and downs in its IFDI and OFDI. Regardless of various obstacles, Russia gradually became a notable FDI actor in the world, and as a consequence the country, for most of the period, has solidified its place among the world's ten leading recipients and senders of FDI. Table 16.1 depicts the rise of Russia among the world's FDI elite.

Table 16.1 Global Rank of Russia Among Top FDI Host/Home Countries, 2004–14

	2004	*2005*	*2006*	*2007*	*2008*	*2009*	*2010*	*2011*	*2012*	*2013*	*2014*
Host (recipient)	14	15	11	9	5	7	8	9	9	5	16
Home (sender)	15	15	17	13	12	8	8	7	8	4	6

Source: Author's compilation using UNCTAD *WIR* Annex Tables downloaded at http://unctad.org/en/Pages/DIAE/World%20Investment%20Report/Annex-Tables.aspx

However, after reaching a peak in 2013, Russia faced a dramatic downturn in its international investment cooperation in 2014. Negative impact of the declining economic growth was intensified by economic sanctions and counter-sanctions resulting from political tension between the Russian Federation and Western powers over the Ukrainian crisis. During the last quarter of 2014, excessive volatility of the Russian ruble exchange rate contributed to further decay in FDI. The year 2015 appeared to be even worse. Against the background of 3.7 percent reduction of Russian GDP and almost twofold contraction of the world oil prices, net FDI inflows to the Russian Federation fell to $4.8 billion in 2015 – the lowest level since 2003. As for outward Russian FDI, it dropped to $21.6 billion – the lowest level since 2005 (CBR 2016). The majority of the authors of this book do not expect, over the coming several years, any sustainable recommencement of an upward trend, as typical of the 2000s. On the one hand, it goes without saying that, in the case of the substantial increase in world oil prices, Russian FDI flows could jump rapidly. On the other hand, the probability of such a scenario is quite low.

One of the most typical concerns of researchers dealing with FDIs, including all contributors to the present book, relates to the reliability of statistics. Data on total inbound and outbound FDI flows provided by UNCTAD vividly illustrate these concerns. In principle, the amount of all outward investments summed up globally should equal to that of inward investments. However, *World Investment Reports* (*WIRs*) refute the assumption clearly (see Table 16.2). An average annual gap between the inward and outward flows for the period 2006–14 equaled $96 billion with no systematic positive balance in favor of either IFDI or OFDI. Moreover, revisions introduced for the particular years in subsequent editions of *WIRs* do not tend to reduce the gap. On contrary, the gap has grown larger, being in the range of $180–$190 billion in 2010 and 2011. Data for individual countries also exhibit such discrepancy. Thus, the authors have put a lot of emphasis in collecting statistics from several sources and comparing them.

Several chapters of the book provide rather convincing evidence to support the claim that no single theory has a monopoly on explaining global FDI development. Even in the case of John Dunning – who, with his OLI paradigm and IDP model, has inspired the majority of the authors herein – a number of instances require alternative interpretations, at least to some extent. In particular, Dunning's OLI paradigm fails to take into consideration specific features of OFDI from

Table 16.2 Discrepancy in Global Outward and Inward FDI Flows, 2006–14 ($ billions)

	2006	*2007*	*2008*	*2009*	*2010*	*2011*	*2012*	*2013*	*2014*
WIR 2011	–56	204	166	–15	80				
WIR 2012	–48	222	178	–22	142	170			
WIR 2013		269	189	–66	96	26	40		
WIR 2014			180	51	–46	–12	–17	41	
WIR 2015				85	–38	–23	119	161	–126

Source: Author's compilation using UNCTAD 2011, p. 6; UNCTAD 2012, p. 169; UNCTAD 2013, p. 213; UNCTAD 2014, p. 205; UNCTAD 2015, p. A4

Note: Negative values indicate excess of OFDI over IFDI

natural resource-rich countries, such as Russia. Moreover, the OLI paradigm does not take into account OFDI related to risk aversion, foreign policy objectives, or the establishment of a firm abroad in order to acquire a permanent residence permit in a country, where the investment takes place. Adequate explanation of these peculiarities should be sought in other theoretical avenues. All in all, the theoretical diversity on the top of aforementioned statistical discrepancies causes us to agree with Thomas Piketty (2014, p. 571) who claimed: "It is not the purpose of social science research to produce mathematical certainties that can substitute for open, democratic debate in which all shades of opinion are represented."

Russia as a relative newcomer in the field of international investment cooperation (from the point of view of global developments as well as practices) should primarily be perceived as a trend-taker and a pattern-taker. Besides, the recent expansion of the studies dealing with FDI activities of developing economies, large emerging markets in particular, ultimately results in widening of a general theoretical framework. As in the case in other subject areas – be it international trade, labor migration or foreign exchange policy – something that might be called the mainstream paradigm frequently tends to absorb the ideas that initially have been perceived as challenging, alternative, or even revolutionary. They become progressively incorporated in the "general theory". The latter, in its turn, merges reflections on a much broader variety of the diverse experiences or "particular cases". The findings of this book suggest that Russian FDI performance does not ultimately look as exotic and unique as many observers have previously tended to think. In other words, the internationalization of Russian corporations is gradually losing its peculiar characteristics.

Nevertheless, the authors of this book were still able to find some peculiarities typical for the Russian Federation as an actor in international investment cooperation. In case of IFDI, these special features relate to the fact that Russian capital, previously withdrawn from Russia, mimics foreign capital when it returns home. Another special FDI characteristic is related to the use of Russia as a gateway to other post-Soviet markets – that is, first a foreign firm invests in Russia to start production there, and thereafter exports its goods, manufactured in Russia, to other CIS countries. In case of OFDI, a multidimensional set of peculiarities exist as well. These peculiarities include, for example, dominance of tactical considerations over long-term strategic goals. In addition, a notable difference in OFDI strategies could be detected between companies exploiting natural resources and companies in processing industries.

The role of political factors deserves special attention here as well. Some of the authors justifiably argue that Russian MNEs tend to rely on support from the Russian authorities. It seems that the intergovernmental agreements frequently predefine the direction of Russian OFDI, as these agreements send clear messages to Russian MNEs demonstrating that their operations in a particular host economy will most probably be protected. In some cases, Russian OFDI results primarily from geopolitical interests of the Russian Government – that is, little, if any, attention is paid to the economic feasibility of the investment. Under these circumstances, Russian state-owned enterprises are better suited to accomplish this type of investment project than private companies. At the same time, political factors should not be narrowed only to the performance of the SOEs, especially taking into consideration the fact that private corporations appear to be the major carriers of Russian capital abroad.

With respect to the current political situation, political factors include another extremely relevant dimension – that is, sanctions imposed on the Russian Federation by the EU, the USA, and some other countries in connection with the Ukrainian crisis in 2014, as well as a retaliatory ban on imports of certain categories of foodstuffs introduced by the Russian Federation. Several experts rightfully argue that the financial component of Western sanctions has the most significant negative impact on Russian FDI flows. In terms of direct impact, the EU outlawed investments in real estate and businesses in Crimea. In addition, trading with new bonds, equity or similar financial instruments issued by five major Russian banks, namely Gazprombank, Rosselkozbank, Sberbank, VTB Bank, and Vnesheconombank, has been prohibited (EU 2014). In any case, the possibility of investment cooperation with Russia's three major energy companies – Gazprom Neft, Rosneft, and Transneft – has substantially been reduced. In terms of indirect impact, the sanctions and counter-sanctions, according to some estimates, accounted for 1.0–1.5 percent of the Russian GDP drop in 2015 (IMF 2015). From this perspective, the sanctions and counter-sanctions contributed to the deterioration of Russian investment climate, and hence the contraction of FDI flows.

However, sanctions might sometimes stimulate foreign investments; the Russian food embargo provides an illustration of this point. It is a well-known fact that the interrelation between foreign trade and FDI is of dual nature; sometimes they complement each other, whereas sometimes FDI substitutes the trade. In the latter case, the companies that want either to retain the market share being threatened by extra trade barriers or to get initial access to the Russian market could achieve their goal by relocating their production to Russia.

To conclude, the book demonstrates that Russia's involvement in international investment cooperation has, in principle, the potential to generate substantial gains for all the participants involved. However, a large number of various obstacles prevents these potential gains becoming tangible results, fairly distributed between the partners. Therefore, the variety of issues covered in this book deserves further attention from the academic community.

Bibliography

CBR 2016, *External Sector Statistics*, Central Bank of Russia, viewed 7 May 2016, http://www.cbr.ru/eng/statistics/?PrtId=svs

EU 2014, *COUNCIL DECISION 2014/512/CFSP of 31 July 2014 Concerning Restrictive Measures in View of Russia's Actions Destabilising the Situation in Ukraine*, viewed 8 May 2016, http://eur-lex.europa.eu/legal-content/EN/TXT/?uri=CELEX:32014D0512

IMF 2015, *Russian Federation*, IMF Country Report No. 15/211, viewed 8 May 2016, http://www.imf.org/external/pubs/ft/scr/2015/cr15211.pdf

Piketty, T. 2014, *Capital in the Twenty-First Century*, Belknap Press, Harvard University Press, London & Cambridge, MA.

UNCTAD 2011, *World Investment Report (WIR) 2011: Non-Equity Modes of International Production and Development* (full), United Nations, New York & Geneva.

UNCTAD 2012, *World Investment Report (WIR) 2012: Towards a New Generation of Investment Policies* (full), United Nations, New York & Geneva.

UNCTAD 2013, *World Investment Report (WIR) 2013: Global Value Chains: Investment and Trade for Development* (full), United Nations, New York & Geneva.

UNCTAD 2014, *World Investment Report (WIR) 2014: Investing in the SDGs: An Action Plan* (full), United Nations, New York & Geneva.

UNCTAD 2015, *World Investment Report (WIR) 2015: Reforming International Investment Governance* (full), United Nations, New York & Geneva.

Index

For Product Safety Concerns and Information please contact our EU
representative GPSR@taylorandfrancis.com
Taylor & Francis Verlag GmbH, Kaufingerstraße 24, 80331 München, Germany

www.ingramcontent.com/pod-product-compliance
Ingram Content Group UK Ltd.
Pitfield, Milton Keynes, MK11 3LW, UK
UKHW021012180425
457613UK00020B/918